The Power of Sovereignty

The Power of Sovereignty attempts to understand the ideas and thoughts of Sayyid Qutb whose corpus of work and, in particular, his theory of *hakimiyyah* (sovereignty) is viewed as a threat to nationalistic government and peace worldwide.

This book provides a detailed perspective of Sayyid Qutb's writings and examines:

- The relation between the specifics of the concept of *hakimiyyah* and that of *jahiliyyah*
- The force and intent of these two concepts
- How Qutb employs their specifics to critically assess the political establishments like nationalism and capitalism
- The influence of the two concepts on Egypt's radical Islamic movements, where many of al'Qa'ida's lieutenants, officers, ideologues and conspirators were fomented

This book provides a timely and topical understanding of the intellectual origins and conceptual and methodological thinking of radical Islamist movement in the modern world. *The Power of Sovereignty* is essential reading for those with interests in political Islam and religious politics.

Dr Sayed Khatab is a researcher in the School of Political and Social Inquiry, Monash University. His research interests focus on politics in the Middle East, Islamic political thought and movements in the modern world. His publications include *The Political Thought of Sayyid Qutb: The Theory of* Jahiliyyah (Routledge, 2006) and 'Arabism and Islamism in Sayyid Qutb's Thought on Nationalism', *The Muslim World*, 94, 2 (2004), 217–44.

Routledge Studies in Political Islam

1. **The Flourishing of Islamic Reformism in Iran**
   Political Islamic groups in Iran (1941–61)
   Seyed Mohammad Ali Taghavi

2. **The Political Thought of Sayyid Qutb**
   The theory of *Jahiliyyah*
   Sayed Khatab

3. **The Power of Sovereignty**
   The political and ideological philosophy of Sayyid Qutb
   Sayed Khatab

The Power of Sovereignty

The political and ideological philosophy of Sayyid Qutb

Sayed Khatab

LONDON AND NEW YORK

First published 2006
by Routledge
2 Park Square, Milton Park, Abingdon, Oxon OX14 4RN

Simultaneously published in the USA and Canada
by Routledge
270 Madison Ave, New York, NY 10016

Routledge is an imprint of the Taylor & Francis Group

Transferred to Digital Printing 2009

Typeset in Garamond by
Newgen Imaging Systems (P) Ltd, Chennai, India

British Library Cataloguing in Publication Data
A catalogue record for this book is available
from the British Library

Library of Congress Cataloging in Publication Data
A catalog record for this book has been requested

ISBN10: 0–415–37250–X (hbk)
ISBN10: 0–415–55384–9 (pbk)

ISBN13: 978–0–415–37250–3 (hbk)
ISBN13: 978–0–415–55384–1 (pbk)

Sayyid Qutb in the Colorado State Teachers College in 1949.

Source: University Archives, University of Northern Colorado.

Note

This photo shows Sayyid Qutb on the right and Dr William R. Ross on the left examining Qutb's *Social Justice in Islam*, published in Cairo in 1949. This photo appeared in the College's 17 October 1949 Bulletin.

The world is an undutiful boy!

Sayed Kotb

History, the wayward child, has forgotten the examples of mother Egypt.

There was an ancient legend in Egypt. When the god of wisdom and Knowledge created History, he gave him a great writing book and a big pen, and said to him: 'Go walking on this earth, and write notes about everything you see or hear.'

History went down and did as his god had told him, but sometimes he did not understand some subjects or did not know some things because he was yet young. Then he asked his god who answered every question.

Once History was walking and writing in his great book when, surprised, he saw a beautiful young woman who was a wise woman, too; she had a little boy whom she was teaching in a gentle manner.

History looked at her with the great astonishment and cried, 'Who is it?', raising his face to the sky.

'She is Egypt', his god answered. 'She is Egypt and that little boy is the world who is studying' – the god answered again.

'When was she born?' History asked.

'I don't know' – the god of wisdom and knowledge said – 'I should ask the headgod.'

'Oh, sacred chief, when was Egypt born?'

'I don't remember' – replied the chief god – 'my grandfather told me a long story about this matter but I don't remember now. You may ask her about it. She knows that. She knows everything. She drank from the sacred Nile and learnt all.'

The god of wisdom and knowledge said to History: 'You are allowed to ask her about her birth and about any other matter you have no knowledge of. Don't ask me anything else. Sit down now to study this lesson, and I will listen.'

Why did those ancient Egyptians hold this belief? Because they were very advanced and possessed a great civilization before any other country. Egypt was a civilized country when other peoples were living in forests. Egypt taught Greece, and Greece taught Europe.

What happened when that little boy grew up?

When he grew up, he had thrown out his nurse, his kind nurse! He struck her, trying to kill her. I am sorry. This is not a figure of speech. This is a fact. This is what has actually happened.

When we came here to appeal to England for our rights, the world helped England against justice. When we came here to appeal against Jews, the World helped the Jews against justice. During the war between Arabs and Jews, the world helped the Jews, too.

Oh! What an undutiful world! What an undutiful boy!

To the memory and the souls of my parents

Sayed Khatab

Contents

Acknowledgements

During my work on this book I have received great help and support from friends and colleagues and now it is time to acknowledge my debt to all of them. Some of this debt is clearly visible in the notes accompanying each chapter; it is, in fact, not possible to mention by name all those, whether colleagues or fellow scholars, library or secretarial staff or other interested individuals, who have helped me over the years to locate the materials required for this work. I do, however, wish to mention a few people and certainly a number of institutions. The Australian Academy of the Humanities' generous grant has made possible some portion of this volume. I have also received considerable support and facilities from the Melbourne Institute of Asian Languages and Societies, the University of Melbourne and the School of Political and Social Inquiry, Monash University. I wish to extend my deepest gratitude to those, who supported me and placed their trust in me, in the Academy Council, especially Graeme Turner, Stuart Cunningham and Iain MacCalman, as well as to Abdullah Saeed, Director of the Melbourne Institute of Asian Languages and Societies, the University of Melbourne, and Gary Bouma, the UNESCO Chair of Interreligious & Intercultural Relations Asia-Pacific, Head of the School of Political and Social Inquiry, Monash University, with whom I have recently completed *Governance in Islam: Structures and Functions of Muslim Organizations in Asia-Pacific*, for his trust in me and for his invaluable support and advice.

A number of scholars have read the manuscript at various stages. Their criticisms and our exchange of views have always stimulated my thinking and encouraged me to complete this book. I am also grateful to William E. Shepard, John L. Esposito, Yvonne Haddad, Ibrahim Abu Rabi', John Voll and John Calvert. I have benefited enormously from their writings, which are frequently referred to in the chapters of this book.

I wish to extend my deepest gratitude to Ibrahim M. Abu Rabi' and Joe Whiting who have both read the entire manuscript for Routledge and supplied valuable criticisms and identified areas requiring special attention.

I am most grateful to William E. Shepard of the University of Canterbury, for reading the entire manuscript and for his invaluable criticisms which have helped me to appreciate some important matters. Shepard has also provided me with some materials, including some of his own writings, that I found useful for this research. His works, and in particular *Sayyid Qutb and Islamic Activism: A Translation and Critical Analysis of Social Justice in Islam*, Leiden: Brill (1996), provided me with the earliest and unavailable editions of Qutb's main text, *Social Justice in Islam* (1949).

I do owe a special debt of gratitude to Abdullah Saeed and Abdul Khaliq Kazi, both at the University of Melbourne, for reading the entire manuscript, at its early stage, and for their critical comments, which stimulated and clarified my thinking on the topic.

I have been fortunate in my colleagues at Monash University, Melbourne, Australia. They are of course in no way responsible for this book, but I have received from them invaluable support and encouragement to complete this work. Special thanks are due to Peter Lentini, Shahram Akbarzadeh, David Wright-Neville, Marika Vicziany, Andrew Newman, Millicent Vladiv-Glover and Constant Mews, for their support.

My great thanks are due to Janet Waters, Head of Archival Services at the University of Northern Colorado, for providing me with some materials, especially the article which was written by Qutb during his visit to Colorado State College of Education in 1949. She also has provided me with Qutb's photograph with Dr William R. Ross, President of the College at the time of his visit. Both the article and the photograph are made available in this volume with permission from the University of Northern Colorado.

I am deeply grateful to Routledge and every staff member who was involved in the preparation of this book and making it available to the readers in this present form. I would like to acknowledge my great debt to all of them, especially James (Joe) Whiting and Nadia Seemungal for their patience and for the quality of their work and their meticulousness.

Various members of my family have read large parts of the manuscript at various stages. I want to make special mention here of my daughters Randah and Sara, as well as Nevien Elfeil from whose help I have benefited in the library area.

I do express my deepest gratitude to Mr Clement and the staff. I wish to extend my profound gratitude to the editorial team including Mr Clement for their excellent professionalism and the English eye which searched for any small flaw or error which often found its way undetected. I was personally pleased and benefited from their reading of these chapters.

All these people have done their best for me and none of them is responsible for whatever errors and omissions that still remain.

Finally, I would like to express my debt, appreciation and gratitude to my wife for her energetic encouragement, and to my son Mustafa without whose patience and whose sacrifice of part of his parental rights this book would not have been completed.

Introduction

The development of Islamic revivalism, as a political movement, is closely associated with particular individuals and their intellectual contributions of formative ideas. These ideas have reshaped public debate and the political experience of many in the Muslim world and have made a permanent contribution to eternal questions about freedom, justice and equality. In this respect, the Egyptian Sayyid Qutb (1906–1966) occupies a unique position in contemporary Muslim thought and in the current Islamic revivalism in Egypt and abroad. Qutb emerged as a pre-eminent figure in the articulation of a coherent Islamic ideology mainly centred on his concept of Sovereignty (*hakimiyyah*), a political concept that has been puzzled over at times and alarmed and often frustrated the media and political establishments at other times. This book was set out to explore its force and intent and the challenge to the ideological and political establishments.

Appreciation of Qutb's ideology is not only essential for a study of contemporary Islamic political thought but also critical to its understanding. Qutb's political and ideological legacy located the roots of Islamic revivalism in the contemporary political processes with its associated events. He provided a systematically focused and balanced explanation of political, economic and social issues with a variety of complex events such as industrialization, urbanization, imperialism and the world's uneven development in these areas.

Qutb's works are highly significant for a number of reasons. He was one of the prominent Muslim thinkers to develop a systematic political, economic, social, intellectual and moral reading of Islam. He was personally involved in the debate and the plan for sociopolitical reform in Egypt. His life represents a sacrifice in the systematic removal of what he considers obstacles to reform. His works demonstrate his legacy as signposts along the way to replace the obstacles and reinstate the Sovereignty of Islamic Law. To him Islam is the end of history. He saw Islam as a perfectly balanced and harmonious system based on sound universal principles of social cohesion and as an ideology that was inherently protective of both society and state.

His prolific writings played a significant role in modernizing Islamic thought in Egypt and elsewhere. As a result of Qutb's contribution, the idealized lives of the early Muslims and, in particular, the first four Caliphs were reaffirmed in a modern context. They became role models for today's Muslims seeking a revitalized Islam. As Cantwell Smith suggested, Qutb transformed the Islamic conception from an irrelevant, purely transcendental static ideal, to an operative force actively at work on modern problems.[1]

Qutb's concept of Sovereignty (*hakimiyyah*) can certainly not be independent of his concept of *jahiliyyah*. It is through the prism of these two ideas that the Islamic political movements divide the world into two camps of potential clash. The camp of *hakimiyyah* and that of *jahiliyyah* are the real binary opposites and the clash, in the future, will be between them. These two concepts, therefore, have been considered as a threat to the political establishments and the nationalistic regimes in the Muslim world and are now viewed as a threat to the West and America.

Subsequently, the question of what is *hakimiyyah* and what is *jahiliyyah* is not as simple as it should be. The potential of Islamic radicalism to draw strength from Qutb's writings and influence international relations as well as domestic politics is also critical. This theme has occupied me for the past few years and provided the conceptual framework for a few scholarly works among which is a volume on *The Theory of Jahiliyyah*, London and New York: Routledge (2006). It explores the seeds of this theory in Qutb's early writings and traces the growth and proliferations of the key ideas, within their timeframe and sociopolitical context, until they have attained their conceptual and intellectual maturity as a full-fledged confrontational theory in his later writings.

This confrontational theory that revealed the concept of Sovereignty was critical. Apart from a few studies touching briefly on the concept of Sovereignty (*hakimiyyah*), no systematic in-depth study has so far been done on this important theory, which influenced all shades of Muslim thought since the second half of the twentieth century; and it is not likely to go away soon. It is for this that the present volume *The Power of Sovereignty* examines the relation between these important concepts (*hakimiyyah* and *Jahiliyyah*) in Qutb's thought. It investigates the force and intent of the relationship between these two concepts and how Qutb employs their specifics to critically assess the political establishments (i.e. nationalism, capitalism, socialism, communism and secular democracy) and demonstrates the influence of the two concepts on Egypt's radical Islamic groups with whom Bin Laden's right-hand man Ayman al-Zawahiri and his conspirators of what has later come to be called al-Qa'idah were fomented.

The book is divided into four interrelated parts each of which consists of a number of chapters as follows:

Part I consists of three chapters exploring the power of Sovereignty (*hakimiyyah*) in Qutb's religio-political discourse. Investigation provides a considerable detail on the place of Islam in the polity, the force and intent of the concept of Sovereignty, the political theory and its relevant issues and how Qutb employs Sovereignty to empower his theory of society, on the one hand, and the confrontational theory of jahiliyyah on the other.

Part II Consists of three chapters exploring the power of Sovereignty (*hakimiyyah*) in Qutb's philosophical discourse with special attention being paid to many contentious issues which reflect basic values such as free will, individual liberty, the relation between intellect and Text, the role of human intellect in this life, rationalism and the liberal discourse in matters of faith and the affairs of human life.

Part III Consists of one long chapter of five sections investigating the impact of Sovereignty (*hakimiyyah*) on the political establishments. It brings the concept of Sovereignty face to face with nationalism, capitalism, socialism, communism and secular democracy and examines their political, economic, social, intellectual and moral specifics and implications.

Part IV Consists of one long chapter of three sections investigating the influence of Sovereignty and its relevant constructs on the development of Egypt's Islamic movement with special focus on the Post-Qutbian Islamic groups. These groups are The Military Technical Academy, The Society of Muslims (also Jama'ah Islamiyyah),[2] and The Society of Jihad. Special attention is also given to the ideological differences between these groups and Qutb's ideas, theories that have been more recently claimed since Qutb's death, and why these groups have resorted to violence.

The primary sources of this book are Sayyid Qutb's own Arabic writings, from the early to the last *Milestones* (1964). The large number of essays and articles that form the balance of his corpus in his extensive writing career of more than 40 years are considered as one entity and an important primary source of this study. The significance of Qutb's works is interpreted in the light of his experience, taking the political, economic, social and intellectual development in Egypt into consideration and relating his concept of Sovereignty (*hakimiyyah*) to the environment within which he was functioning and to which he was responding.

A certain number of Qutb's words are not easily translated into English without the risk of their being seriously misconstrued or losing their force and intent. In some cases it has seemed appropriate either to use the Arabic word in place of an English word or put it in parentheses following the English word or phrase chosen as a translation.

In conclusion, the book explains the many complexities of political Islam and provides the conceptual and intellectual framework for further conversation on the place of Islam in the polity and talks of the relation between *al-hakimiyyah* 'Sovereignty' and the notion implied by the 'end of history and the last man'. To Qutb, the end of history is the democracy of *al-hakimiyyah*.

Part I

Religio-political discourse

1 Sovereignty (*al-Hakimiyyah*)

The ultimate goal of Sayyid Qutb is to establish an Islamic state. In his analysis, Qutb uses a number of comprehensive ideas to foster his ideological discourse. The first three chapters (Part I) of this book examine a number of religio-political concepts (Sovereignty, Servitude, and Universality of Islam) that Qutb uses, conceptually and intellectually, to promote his ideological goal. He also uses this *trio* as religio-political foundations of his confrontational theory of *Jahiliyyah*, which divides the world into two large camps of potential clash. To Qutb, *jahiliyyah* is a condition of any place or society where Allah is not held to be the ultimate sovereign. He says that Islam and *Jahiliyyah* are the real opposite and that the clash in the future will be between them and not between civilizations as such.[1] Consequently, the *theory of jahiliyyah* encompasses the '*clash of civilizations*'. Therefore, these concepts (Sovereignty, Servitude and Universality of Islam) are fundamental in Qutb's political and ideological discourse and have in common their timelessness.

Focusing on Sovereignty (*hakimiyyah*), the present chapter examines the lexical and cultural origins of *hakimiyyah*, the meaning of the Qur'anic term *hukm* (rule) and its socio-political implication; the influence of *hakimiyyah* on governance in Islam; the difference between the concept of *hakimiyyah* and that of the modern political term 'sovereignty'; and the difference between the source of authority in Islamic and non-Islamic states. Examination will take into account the confrontational theory of *Jahiliyyah* and the question of whether Islam is only a religion or a religion and state in one. It will elucidate that the government in Islam is a limited and constitutional government and that the Islamic State is not theocratic or autocratic or anything but 'Islamic'.

The place of Islam in the polity

The role of Islam in the state has become one of the most contentious issues in the Muslim countries. It holds a central position in every public debate over constitution, law and civil rights and the very essence of cultural identity as well. In Qutb's view, Islam, by its very nature, is a 'political religion'.[2] The unity between religion and politics is a great principle in Islam. To him, the link between religion and politics is a very important and critical matter.

Qutb drew heavily from the Qur'an to support his view. For example, in his *In the Shade of the Qur'an* (1952–1959),[3] Qutb states that

> this group of verses [5: 41–50] deals with the most important and serious (*akhtar*) issue (*qadiyya*) in Islamic creed. This is because this group of verses in its positive terms sharply defines governance in Islam. This matter concerns government, the Islamic law (*shari'ah*) and legitimization.[4]

In short, Qutb means that Islam is a religion and State in one. To him, the State is not a vague concept but clearly defined and characterized by Sovereignty (*hakimiyyah*).

In the Islamic State, God is the supreme legislator and the ultimate source of governmental and legal authority. Government in Islam is thus specifically designed to implement Islamic law, that is, to administer justice in accordance with its decrees. Enforcing the law and facilitating its application requires Islam to function as a religion and state. Although there is no place in the Islamic system for arbitrary rule by a single individual or group, there is always room for consultation (*shurah*) within the boundary of law.[5]

Arguments that oppose this view tend to be of two types: The first claims that *hakimiyyah* is not a Qur'anic term but derived from the Arabic verb 'to judge'.[6] The second considers that the term *hukm* has no political connotation. This view asserts that 'the word *hakam*, as a noun, is still used in Arabic for referee'.[7] These views seek to separate the term *hakimiyyah* (sovereignty) from the Qur'anic terms *hukm* (to rule and to judge). They thus exclude the Qur'anic word group of *hukm* from any political connotation. Such arguments view Islam as simply a religion without the right to govern and order human life or to organize the daily affairs of the Muslims. Lexical origins of the term *hukm*, which constitute one aspect of this controversy, are detailed in the following pages. What should be noted here is that much of the support for these arguments, in modern times, derives from the thinking of 'Ali 'Abd al-ziq's *Islam and the Foundations of Government*, which was published in Egypt in 1925.[8] This book, as asserted by Shepard, emphasizes that 'religion and government should be separate in Islam'.[9] According to Shepard, this book, 'to this day . . . is one of the major points of reference in the debate'.[10] The other point of reference is *Preachers, not Judges* a book attributed to Hasan al-Hudaybi in 1969.[11] These two books have continued to be seen as a major point of reference as to whether Religion and State should be separate in Islam.

However, this major point of reference has been challenged by 'Ali 'Abd al-Raziq himself and by 'Abd al-Aziz Fahmi, the Minister of Justice in 1925.[12] In addition, the newly released information also doubted the authenticity of the book *Preachers, not Judges* (*Du'ah la Qudah*) which is commonly attributed to al-Hudaybi the judge at the Supreme Court in the 1940s and the Supreme Guide of the Muslim Brotherhood from 1949 until his death in 1973.

'Ali 'Abd al-Raziq's text was published in 1925, a year after the collapse of Islamic Caliphate in Turkey in 1924. According to the Egyptian Muhammad 'Umarah,[13] it was written in opposition to King Fu'ad's claim to the Caliphate.[14] Consequently, under the instruction of King Fu'ad, the Supreme Council of al-Azhar 'banned the text and excluded 'Ali from the Council of the *'Ulama* on 12 August 1925'.[15] These political circumstances are familiar ground in the literature and there is no need for repetition.[16] The question here is that does 'Ali 'Abd al-Raziq suggest, in his book, that Islam is only a religion, not a religion and State?

'Abd al-Raziq's book, from its title *al-Islam wa Usul al-Hum* (*Islam and the Foundations of Government*) indicates its content. The title explicitly suggested the link between religion and government in Islam. The title expresses that there is rule or 'government' in Islam and that the government has 'foundations'. In other words, Islam is Religion and State in one.

'Abd al-Raziq (1888–1966) never confined Islam to ritual duties or claimed that 'Islam is only spiritual' as claimed by Kepel (1985),[17] Haddad (1983),[18] and Abukhalil (1994),[19] or Mortimer (1982).[20] On the contrary, 'Abd al-Raziq states that

> I do not believe that the Islamic law (*shari'iah*) is merely spiritual and I have not said this in the book or in [writings] other than the book. I have not said anything similar to this opinion or closer to it . . .[21]
>
> Islam is a legislative religion. The application of Islamic law is obligatory on Muslims. This is the command of Allah to them all . . . The Muslims must establish a government to carry on this burden. Allah does not impose upon Muslims a specific type or form of government, but they are free to choose what is better for the welfare of their society at any time.[22]

In response to his critics, 'Ali 'Abd al-Raziq replied,

> They say that in my book I have suggested that Islam is only spiritual and has nothing to do with the affairs of life . . . Some people still believe that I have said that religion [Islam] is only spiritual and has nothing to do with material [things] or the affairs of life. They also think that this is the prime aim of this book. This view in fact has no trace in my book and it never was my opinion. What I do believe is that Islam is a legislative religion (*din tashri'i*), and its law impacts on most spheres of life . . . They also say that I have proclaimed that the Caliphate is not and never was a valid Islamic system at any time. And [they say that] I have changed my mind in the later report[23] to suggest that if the Muslims agreed that their government should be a Caliphate and viewed the Caliphate as the foremost system for their common welfare, then the Caliphate was a lawful Islamic government and the people should be loyal to whatever in it was not in conflict with religion. My view in the book and what I believe is that the application of Islamic law for the welfare

> of the people depends on the Caliphate which means government (*hukumah*) of any form and of any type, limited or unlimited, autocratic or republican, tyrannical or constitutional, consultative or democratic, socialistic or Bolshevik. Religion [Islam] does not impose upon Muslims a certain type or form of those governments, but allows us to choose the best form that appeared to have the best foundation of government.[24]

Echoes of these words, are the words of ‘Abd al-‘Aziz Fahmi the Minister of Justice in 1925. About ‘Ali ‘Abd al-Raziq's matter, Fahmi says,

> As for the second matter which increased my abhorrence of the Ministry, its account is as follows. I know Hasan ‘Abd al-Raziq Basha and his older children; Hasan, Husayn, Mahmud, and Mustafa,[25] as I met them on my frequent visits to their father's home which was usually open for his friends. I was not so well acquainted, however, with his younger sons ‘Ali and Isma‘il, who were often occupied with their studies. When I was the Minister of Justice, in 1925, I received information about the allegations of al-Azhar against ‘Ali ‘Abd al-Raziq; the son of Hasan ‘Abd al-Raziq Basha. At that time, ‘Ali was a Judge at the Juridical Courts, but I had not seen him before. Al-Azhar requested that ‘Ali be divested of his degree, which he earned at al-Azhar, on the pretext that he violated the image of the Degree. He wrote a book titled *‘al-Islam wa Usul al-Hukm’* [*Islam and the Foundations of Government*] and suggested that there is no caliphate in Islam; and that the present leaders of Muslims are kings, not caliphs. I acquired the book, I have read it once, twice, and I have not found a slightest idea for which the author could be accused. On the contrary, I have found him [‘Ali] praises Islam; and the Prophet of Islam; and perfectly glorifies the Prophet. He emphasizes that the prophethood in Islam is revelation (*wahy*) from Allah, and there is no *khilafah* (succession)[26] in the revelation. The revelation comes to specific individuals who have been chosen by Allah . . .[27]

This leaves no doubt that ‘Ali ‘Abd al-Raziq sees Islam as a Religion and State and that the Qur'anic term *hukm*, has connotation of governance. The logical implication of this is that *hakimiyyah* (sovereignty) has political signification. ‘Ali ‘Abd al-Raziq's position is no different to that of Qutb concerning the concept of the Qur'anic term *hukm*.

The Egyptian Hasan al-Hudaybi was a judge at the Supreme Court. After the death of al-Banna in 1949, al-Hudaybi became the Supreme Guide of the Muslim Brotherhood (Ikhwan). He remained in this position until his death in 1973. Al-Hudaybi also considered that Islam is a Religion and State, and that the Qur'anic term *hukm* means ‘to govern’. Al-Hudaybi's book (*Preachers, not Judges*) *Du'ah la Qudah* was written at the time when al-Hudaybi and his fellow brethren (Ikhwan) were in prison in 1965. Consulting the book, in its original Arabic, it seemed to me that the style and argumentation do look rather Azharitis. What is interesting is that this book is not al-Hudaybi's book and he did not write a single word of it. According to Brigadier General Fu'ad 'Allam (1995), an official of the Egyptian Ministry of Interior at the time, al-Hudaybi's book was written by a group of al-Azhar scholars in conjunction with a group from the Security Apparatus of the Ministry of Interior. 'Allam brought to light this claim in an article (among the series of his memoirs) published in *Rose el-Youssef* in August 1995 under the title 'The most dangerous (*akhtar*) book of al-Hudaybi's works is written by the investigators of the Security Apparatus of the State'.[28] Under this title 'Allam outlined the background to the incident, as follows:

> In the aftermath of 1967,[29] 'Abd al-Nasser made a decision to leave the Ikhwan in prison indefinitely, and not to release them. However, the security authorities opposed the decision due to the previously approved plan that the Brothers who would change their ideas on extremism would be released in groups, one after the other. We wrote a memorandum, presented to 'Abd al-Nasser in hand writing, and he approved it. Within 72 hours a group of the detainees was released...
>
> Around this time, we obtained information about the thinking of takfir[30] in Liman Turah prison. These ideas were spread among the youth Brothers, who were arrested in 1965, and who believed that the book '*Ma'alim fi al-Tariq*' (Milestones), by Sayyid Qutb, was their strategy. Thus, on the map of the Brothers in Liman Tura prison there were three groups, comprising followers of al-Banna... followers of al-Hudaybi... and followers of Sayyid Qutb... There was no disagreement among them; they all were agreed that contemporary society was in the condition of *kufr* [i.e. *jahiliyyah*], which must be changed and the Islamic State established. Exactly when the Islamic State should be established was debated among the three groups... The followers of al-Hudaybi and al-Banna preferred to delay the establishing of the Islamic State, since delay was in the interest of the survival of the organization...
>
> Given these circumstances, we have received important information about extreme Islamic ideas among the Brothers in Turah prison. Investigations revealed sufficient evidence to result in 37 potential charges. Important were those who branded the society with *kufr* (unbelief), and those that called the society *jahili*...
>
> The memorandum suggested moving quickly to face this kind of thinking and treat it in a proper way, particularly, because those youths have no knowledge of legal opinion (*fataw*), and interpret Islam according to their desires...
>
> It was natural that we should seriously deal with this way of thinking in a scientific style (i.e. intelligently). We needed to ask the grand *'ulama* and the men of al-Azhar. This was because the ideas were spreading from prison and gaining public support due to current socioeconomic discontent in the wider society...

> We have planned that we should take advantage of the differences about *takfir* that we found among the extreme groups... The security [authority] successfully induced Hasan al-Hudaybi to issue, unknowingly, the book *'Du'ah la Qudah'* to emphasize his view about these ideas...
>
> The truth of this matter is that Hasan al-Hudaybi did not cooperate by an opinion, or legal opinion (*fatwa*) in this book. The book was not written by al-Hudaybi, but by select members at al-Azhar... We managed to get the prepared chapters into the Liman Tura prison and circulate them among the Brothers and let them meet with Ma'mun al-Hudaybi to discuss and pass him the chapters. Ma'mun [the son of al-Hudaybi] pretended that the chapters were his own and passed them to his father. The fact is that he [Hasan al-Hudaybi] had nothing to do with this book at all...
>
> Among the Brothers who were in the prison and cooperated with us in preparing this book were 'Abd al-Mut'al al-Jabri and Sa'd al-Din Mutwally Ibrahim. We then turned a blind eye to Hasan al-Hudaybi passing, secretly, the book out of the prison. We then collected the chapters and facilitated the book's publication and rapid distribution...
>
> The book made a significant impact on the Brothers and presented their extreme thinking, particularly inside prison. Muhammad Qutb and some of his supporters separated themselves from the extreme group. Although with Muhammad Qutb were Shukri Ahmad Mustafa,[31] Sayyid 'Id Yusuf, and 'Ali 'Abd al-Fattah 'Abduh Isma'il.[32] These three Brothers were, however, the first to spread the militant extremism after they were released...[33]

With regard to the reliability of Brigadier General 'Allam's claims, neither al-Hudaybi nor his son, or al-Azhar, has decided to challenge 'Allam's account. We may thus presume it to be accurate. Ma'mun the son of al-Hudaybi was born in 1920 and graduated from the School of Law at Cairo University (Fu'ad I) in 1942. He worked as a prosecutor and then judge and president of Cairo's appellate court and retired in 1981.[34] Ma'mun was 45 by 1965 when his father was in prison. At that time Ma'mun had a professional background of 23 years experience at Law. There has been no reply from Ma'mun or from al-Azhar concerning this matter.

On the other hand, one could interpret the long silence in the following way. Al-Hudaybi was not the author of *Preachers not Judges* (*Du'ah la Qudah*). This book was written by his critics. Like other Ikhwan in prison, al-Hudaybi considers Islam a Religion and State. He, like others, described contemporary Egyptian society as 'a *jahili* society that should be changed to establish an Islamic state'.[35] Extracts from the book *Preachers not Judges*, circulated in the literature, about al-Hudaybi's position with regard to this particular matter of whether Islam is both Religion and State, are doubtful. Similarly, apart from the original text of 'Ali 'Abd al-Raziq, the data found in the literature[36] concerning his position on this particular issue are doubtful and should be viewed with caution.

In the book *Preachers not Judges*, the author says: 'There is no doubt that the *hakim* (ruler) is Allah and to Him alone is the command. The *shari'ah* of Allah is the law which should be implemented whether the ruler accepts or rejects it.'[37] Elsewhere, the author of the book *Preachers not Judges* expressed his agreement with those who say

> The *hakimiyyah* is the meaning of the testimony that Allah is One, and that the lordship (*rububiyyah*) is to Allah only ... If you meant by sovereignty (*hakimiyyah*) the absolute authority (*sultan*) and command of Allah and He judges and legislates as He wills and when He wills ... So, we are with you one on the straight path.[38]

The position of 'Ali 'Abd al-Raziq and al-Hudaybi, on this matter under discussion, is similar to the position of a considerable number of Muslim scholars. For example, in his commentary on the Qur'anic verse 4: 59, Ibn Kathir (d. 774/1383) points out 'The *hakim* is Allah. He alone is the legislator and His law represents the boundary between Islam and *kufr* (unbelief).'[39] Al-Jassas (d. 370/ 987) referred to the Qur'anic verse 4: 65 and stated that 'the role of *shari'ah* is strongly bound with the Islamic creed and there is no Islam without the rule of *shari'ah*'.[40] According to the contemporary scholar of al-Azhar Muhammad al-Ghazali (b. 1917)[41] the head of the regime's appointed committee which examined and approved Qutb's *In the Shade of the Qur'an*, 'Allah is the legislator and the nation (*ummah*) must establish a government of *shurah* (consultation).'[42] In an article written by Shaykh Muhammad al-Nawawi of al-Azhar in 1952 and republished in al-Azhar Magazine in 1993,

> Yes, Islam is a State and has an unambiguous political theory. Muslims know that the *hukm* (rule) belongs to Allah. His law has been the constitution of the Islamic polity since the time of the Prophet. This is the consensus of the Muslim *ummah*. Even those who refer to the role of human intellect in this particular matter, confine their theory to the cases and affairs upon which the Revelation does not offer specific regulation or necessary guidance.[43]

Judge 'Abd al-Aziz al-Maraghi, a justice and Professor of Islamic Law, and Rizq al-Zalabani, Professor of Law and politics, were at Al-Azhar University during the time of Qutb. In 1947, both al-Maraghi and al-Zalabani pointed out the highest governmental and legal authority as in the following: Al-Zalabani stated that 'the *hukm* belongs to none but Allah. He is the Creator and He alone is the legislator. All affairs are in His hands ... Every member of the *ummah* falls within the boundary of His law'.[44] Both al-Maraghi and al-Zalabani base their argument on a number of Qur'anic verses, of which *surah* 5 is of central importance: 'Those who do not judge in accordance with Allah's revelation, are indeed unbelievers.'[45]

'Those who do not judge in accordance with Allah's Revelation, are indeed the transgressors',[46] and 'Those who do not judge in accordance with Allah's Revelation, are indeed the evil-doers',[47] and finally, 'Is it the *jahili* laws that they like to be judged by?'[48]

Al-Qurtubi (d. 671/1285) referred to earlier sources and stated that 'there is no difference between the opinion of Muslim *ummah* or among the "*imams*"[49] that Allah is the Legislator and that there must be a *khilafah* (state)'.[50] Similarly, al-Mawardi (d. 450/1067) stated that

> Imamate is prescribed to succeed the Prophethood as a means of protecting the religion and managing the affairs of this world. There is a consensus of opinion that the person who discharges the responsibilities of this leadership must take on the contract of *Imamate* of the *ummah*.[51]

Likewise, Ibn Hajar al-Haythami (d. 974/1585) pointed out the importance of an Islamic state, saying, 'you must know that the companions of the Prophet agreed upon the idea that the Islamic State of the Prophet must continue and they elected their leader before the burial of the Prophet'.[52] Similarly, al-Juwayni (d. 478/1094) stated that 'Muslims must have a leader to lead their State and that is the consensus of the *ummah* and *imams*.'[53] Likewise, Ibn Khaldun (d. 808/1421) pointed out that *khilafah* is obligatory and that it represents 'the consensus of the opinion of the Companions of the Prophet'.[54]

The current scholar of al-Azhar Muhammad 'Umarah (b. 1931), emphasizes that 'Islam is a State in which Allah is the highest governmental and legal authority and its constitution is the Qur'an and the *sunnah*.'[55]

Muhammad 'Abduh (d. 1905) himself stated that

> Islam is a religion of sovereignty (*siyadah*), of authority (*sultan*), and of unity between this world and the Hereafter. Islam is a spiritual, social, economic, political, civilian and military system. Its military force is to protect the application of Islamic law, the general guidance, the freedom of the *ummah*, and not to force others to embrace Islam.[56]

Muhammad al-Khidr Husayn, Shaykh al-Azhar in the 1930s,[57] stated that 'separating religion from State is an act of desecration of the truth of the religion. It is the kind of act that a Muslim cannot perform while remaining a Muslim'.[58] Similarly, Mustafa Sabri, Shaykh al-Islam in 1918 in Turkey, pointed out that separating Islam from politics is more than a conspiracy against Islam. He went on to state that

> separating Islam from State, in Muslim countries, is a heresy[59]; that it was brought about by those modernists imitating the foreigners, and thus an act of rebellion against Islam. This kind of attempt is effectively a revolution by the government against the creed of the people. This is

> a deviant act because the right course is that the revolution should be by the people against the government to enforce the law of Islam. Nevertheless, if rebellion occurs against Islam initially by the government, and then by the people, nothing remains but *kufr*.[60]

According to Khalid Muhammad Khalid, scholar and member of Egyptian Parliament in the 1960s,

> Islam has a legal and governmental duty, that is, to order human life and organize public affairs through its Islamic state, which must be established and must remain as long as there is Islam in this world. The constitution of this State is the Qur'an and the *sunnah* of the Prophet and the consensus of the *ummah*.[61]

Similarly, the Egyptian Shaykh Muhammad al-Bahiyy, professor at the University of Montreal in the 1950s and then Minister of Islamic Endowments in Egypt in 1960, referred to the Qur'anic verse 66: 9 and pointed out that 'Islam is also an organized force that should protect the creed at any time...'[62] The current President of the Academy of Jurisprudence in Makkah, Shaykh Bakr Abu Zayd, echoes this with these words: 'Islam in its very nature is an organized state, therefore, you cannot separate Islam from politics. This is the basic principle of *da'wa* (call: Islamic outreach).'[63] Likewise, Professor Gad El-Haq 'Ali Gad El-Haq, Shaykh al-Azhar (d. 1996) says,

> Separating Islam from the motion of society is undoubtedly wrong and wrong thought does not differ from materialistic Western thought. Separation of religion from human life in the West is a matter which has its roots in the past when the Church exercised its power (*tasallut*) over those it ruled. This has resulted in social and political misery that are known to us all. Islam, by contrast, is a social system involved with human affairs...[64]

These opinions represent a wide spectrum of Islamic thought whether medieval or modern, Islamist, conservative, or modernist. All of these opinions indicate that Islam is a Religion and State, of which its sovereign is Allah. The notion of the *hakimiyyah* of Allah is the fundamental principle in Islamic belief. According to the *Gamal Abd al-Nasser Encyclopaedia of Islamic Jurisprudence* 'There is no *hakim* (sovereign) but Allah; there is no rule but the rule of Allah, and there is no law but the law of Allah. This is the consensus of Muslims...'[65]

Linguistic origin of the term *hakimiyyah*

The Arabic term *hakimiyyah* is derived from the Arabic root *h.k.m* from which the substantive *hukm* (rule) and the *nomen agantis*, *hakim* (ruler), the singular of *hakimun* and *hukkam* are derived. The word *hakimiyyah* can be seen as a *nomen verbi* (verbal noun), because: (i) it is an abstract substantive that expresses the meaning of the verb without any reference to object, subject or time of the verb; and (ii) it can also be used without changing its form when it refers to singular or plural. For example, one can say, *hakimiyyatu* al-dawlah (sovereignty of the state – singular), *hakimiyyatu* al-dawlatan (dual – two states), and *hakimiyyatu* al-duwal (states, plural: more than two) without change in the form of the word *hakimiyyah* (sovereignty).[66]

Since *hakimiyyah* works as a *nomen verbi* (verbal noun), it can also be seen, in English grammar, as an infinitive (*masdar*). In this regard, one should note that *hakimiyyah* is not a regular *masdar* (infinitive).[67] The word *hakimiyyah* can be defined through Wright's note that

> the feminine of the relative adjective serves in Arabic as a noun to denote the abstract idea of the thing, as distinguished from the concrete thing itself; and also to represent the thing or things signified by the primitive noun as a whole or totality. It corresponds therefore to German substantives in *heit*, *keit*, *schaft*, *tham*, and to English ones in *head*, *dom*, *ty*, etc.[68]

Here, Wright's definition emphasizes that Qutb's Arabic terms of the rhythm of *uluhiyyah* (divinity), *hakimiyyah* (sovereignty), *'alamiyyah* (worldwide), *'ubudiyyah* (servitude), *insaniyyah* (humanity), *'aqlaniyyah* (rationality), *kawniyyah* (universality) all are of this category. Based on Wright's definition, one could define the term *hakimiyyah* as an 'abstract noun of quality'.[69]

According to Ibn Durayd (d. 321/939), 'the *hakim* is the one who exercises judicial authority; a ruler or governor... and Allah the highest governor, the ruler and the supreme legal authority'.[70] According to Edward Lane (1955),

> *hakim* is the one who exercises judicial authority, rule, domination, or government; a ruler, or governor. The *hakim* between people is so called because he restrains people from wrongdoing. The plural is *hukkam* and *hakimun*. The *hakim*, as meaning 'The Supreme Judge', is one of the names of God... He is *Ahkam al-Hakimin* 'The most qualified to judge of those who judge': or 'the most knowing and most just of them'.[71]

In referring to the word *hukm*, Ibn Manzur (d. 711/1325) stated that 'Allah is the sovereign of sovereigns and His Qur'an is the *hakim* for you and among you'.[72] According to Wright (1979), 'the term *ahkam* is a noun of preeminence that is to express the greatest force and intent of the term *hukm* to mean that the Sovereignty of Allah surpasses the sovereignty of others'.[73] This supports the view that the word *hakim* in classical Arabic signifies the highest governmental and legal authority. The infinitive of the root *h.k.m* is *hakimiyyah*, which means 'governorship, rule, command, dominion and authority'.[74] The other infinitives of the root *h.k.m*, in addition to *hakimiyyah* is the word '*hukman*' (a ruling period; judgment; verdict; sentence)[75] and '*hukumah*' (government).[76] According to Wehr, '*hakimiyyah* [is] domination, dominion, rule, sovereignty; judgeship, judicature, jurisdiction'.[77] These lexical origins are sufficient to indicate the legal and political connotations of both *hukm* and *hakimiyyah*.

As for the meaning of the word *hukm* in the Qur'an, it is important to remember that the Qur'anic terms have their own connotations. Among the notions relevant to this study and which would help us to better understand Qutb's Arabic terms including *hakimiyyah* is that *jahiliyyah* does not mean ignorance and cannot be seen as an antithesis of knowledge but of Islam in general, and of sovereignty in particular. Although, the term '*ubudiyyah*, which is usually translated by the word 'servitude or worship', is not confined to only ritual duties service such as prayer and fasting. Every act of human conduct done with the purpose of winning the approval of God and for the benefit of humanity comes under its purview.[78] Although the term '*din*' is always translated by the word 'religion', the Qur'anic term '*din*' also means system.[79] It is a certain kind of system, with its own characteristics that distinguishes Islam from other systems. Likewise, the term '*shari'ah*' is usually translated 'Islamic law'. However, according to the consensus of the Muslims,[80] including Qutb,[81] *shari'ah* has never only meant Islamic law. Everything that God has prescribed to order human life is part of *shari'ah*. Intellectuals stress that

> The *shari'ah* is not, strictly speaking, a legal system, for it reaches much deeper into thought, life and conduct than a purely legal system can aspire to do. It replaces the individual in his relationship to society, the universe and his Creator.[82]

Similarly, the Qur'anic term *hukm* has its own connotation. The term *hukm* and its derivations appear in the Qur'an more than 250 times.[83] For example, the Qur'an (4: 105) says, 'We have revealed to you [Muhammad] the Book with the Truth, so that you may *tahkum* (Rule and Judge) among people by that which Allah has shown you...' According to al-Maraghi, 'The Prophet was a leader and a judge by virtue of his divine appointment. Hence he possessed complete judicial power.'[84] Although the command is for the Prophet, the *hukm*, according to al-Qurtubi, must be based on the text (*nass*). If there is no text explicitly relevant to the matter, 'the Prophet gives his own legal opinion on the basis of the general spirit of the *shari'ah* as Allah has shown him'.[85] Elsewhere, the Qur'an says: 'We said: David, We have made you a vicegerent on earth, *fa-uhkum* thou between people in truth (and justice)...' (Qur'an, 38: 26). The word *hukm* here is a verb that commands the leader to 'Judge'[86] and to 'Rule'[87] with justice. These Qur'anic texts indicate that the term *hukm* has both governmental and legal connotations. Thus, the word *hukm* is to rule and to judge according to the law.[88] This implies that, if the judge is also the ruler or governor, he is commanded to rule and to judge on the basis of the law. This was the case with the Prophet; he was the judge and the ruler. If the ruler is not the judge (the two positions are separate), the Qur'an commands both the ruler and the judge to observe their duties on the basis of the law. This means that, whether the term *hukm* is to judge or to rule, the law stands sovereign over the rulers and the judges. It commands them to facilitate the application of the law. In this sense the Qur'an says, 'He who does not judge (*yahkum*) in accordance with Allah's revelation, is indeed an unbeliever.'[89] 'He who does not judge (*yahkum*) in accordance with Allah's revelation, is indeed a transgressor',[90] and 'He who does not judge (*yahkum*) in accordance with Allah's revelation, is indeed an evil-doer.'[91] Thus the rule and judgment must be in accordance with the command of Allah.

The word group of *hukm* is always used to declare that the authority and the right to command rest only with Allah.[92] In support of his view, Qutb cites Qur'anic verses including *surah* 35 verse 5: 'He governs all affairs from the Heavens to the earth.'[93] He used verse 25: 2 which states 'He to whom belongs the domination of the Heavens and the earth, no son has He begotten, nor has He a partner in His sovereignty.'[94] Finally, a verse from *surah* 6 reads 'The command rests with none but Allah.'[95] The Qur'an (18: 110) also declares that the Prophet of Islam is not above the law of God. The Prophet is commanded accordingly: 'Say: "I am but a man like yourselves. It is revealed to me that your God is One God." '[96] Verse 18: 57 reads 'We sent not a Messenger, but to be obeyed, in accordance with the Will of Allah.'[97] According to these Qur'anic verses, the ultimate Sovereignty (*hakimiyyah*) belongs to none but Allah. He is the Creator and Sustainer of the universe. He is the One in whom rests all authority, political or other.

These Qur'anic verses, suggest at least the political implications of the term *hakimiyyah*. According to the English translation of the meaning of the Qur'an approved by the Supreme Sunni Council and the Supreme Shi'i Council of Lebanon in 1980, the term *hakimiyyah* means sovereignty in which rests the highest legal and governmental authority. The two Supreme councils agreed that the term sovereignty was the title of *surah* 67.[98] The title of this *surah* (67) has also been translated by the word 'Dominion' in the *Mushaf al-Madinah al-Nabawiyah* that was revised and edited by the Islamic Researches of Saudi Arabia (1410 AH/1990 AD).[99] George Sale (1679–1736) translated the word '*al-Mulk*' (the title of *surah* 67) by the English word 'Kingdom',[100] but translated by Pickthall it reads 'Sovereignty'.[101]

These translations also indicate that the term *hakimiyyah* is synonymous with the term *mulk* (dominion, power, rule, supreme power of authority), and that the *nomina agantis hakim* is synonymous with the word *malik* (have power or domination over property).[102] In dictionary terms 'The *malik* is the sovereign'.[103] This is one of the ninety-nine special attributes of Allah. He is the Dominion of the Heavens and earth. He is the King, the Ruler of Mankind. This means that the *hakim* (sovereign) is the *malik* (sovereign) and that the *hukm* (sovereignty) is synonymous with the *mulk* (sovereignty). In the Qur'an, the term *hukm* (and its derivations) and the term *mulk* (and its derivations) are repeatedly used.

According to Arabic lexicographers, exegetes and grammarians such as, Ibn 'Amr (d. 50/671), 'Asim (d. 127/747), Hamzah (d. 156/776), al-Kisa'i (d. 189/808), Ya'qub (d. 205/824), Qurtubi (d. 671/1285), Ibn Manzur (d. 711/1325) and Ibn Kathir (d. 774/1383) '*mulk* means sovereignty over everything'.[104] In this regard, I should note that the word *malik* could also be used to refer to humans. For example, Man might possess things, so that he is *malik* (proprietor). In this, he has sovereignty in handling what he possesses. Man can also be *malik* (king). In this, he has sovereignty in handling the affairs of his kingdom. However, The *al-Mulk* refers to both the *malik* (proprietor, king etc.) and what he possesses. Therefore, when the Qur'an says Allah is the 'Malik al-Mulk', it means that Allah is the Proprietor of humans and what is in their possession. In other terms Allah is the Sovereign of all sovereignty. Both terms sovereignty (*mulk*) and sovereign (*malik*) are mentioned in *surah* 3, verse 26: 'Say: "Lord, sovereign (*malik*) of all sovereignty (*al-mulk*). You bestow sovereignty on whom You will, and take it away from whom You please; You exalt whomever You will and abase whomever You please. In your hand lies all that is good; You have power over all things" '.[105] This absolute sovereignty over the universe, life and humankind, is the sovereignty that Qutb speaks about.

If the term sovereignty and/or dominion are the translation of the Arabic term *hakimiyyah* and/or *mulk*, in both cases, according to the verse 3: 26, there is no one in the entire creation who can rightly claim to posses the dominion status or the sovereignty of *hakimiyyah*. According to Qutb, 'any quarrel or wrangle about this point is only an attempt to run away from the truth'.[106]

Sovereignty and the great unity

For many a scholar, Qutb arrived at the concept of Sovereignty only in his later writings of the mid-1960.[107] This however is not the case. Qutb developed the concept of Sovereignty (*hakimiyyah*) over many years. Its seeds can be traced back to his early works of the period 1925–1935, and its genesis took place gradually since then onwards, until this concept finally appeared in his *Social Justice in Islam* and the later writings (1949).[108] In the first edition of *Social Justice in Islam* (1949), Qutb emphasized, *inter alia*, a comprehensive and integrated conception of Islam. He expressed Islam as a perfect and harmonious system of life. It is a complete system 'rooted in the nature of the universe'.[109] Islam came to unify all forces and powers, to blend together desires, inclinations and sympathies and to harmonize all tendencies, thus recognizing the integrated unity of the universe, the self and life.[110] This surely is, Qutb says, the true unity which 'establishes lasting peace between the universe, and life, between life and living being, between the group and the individual, between the desires and aspirations of the individual, and finally between this world and religion, between the heaven and earth'.[111] In 1951, Qutb also admitted that

> The comprehensive theory of Islam about the universe, life and humankind is not the subject of this book [*Islam and Universal Peace* – 1951], nor it was the subject of the book *Social Justice*. However... we have reviewed this theory before discussion 'the nature of social justice in Islam'....[112]

Thus, the idea of unity, which unifies heaven and earth and which explains the nature of the relation between the Creator and His creation, the universe, life and humankind, was outlined in the first edition of *Social Justice* (1949), not after that as perceived by others.[113]

This idea of the relationship is rooted in what Qutb calls 'the great unity', which emerged in his poetry of the period 1925–1935.[114] The idea of the 'great unity' developed with him, from 1939 onwards, to form his ideological response and position in the debate on Egypt's Islamic heritage, culture and identity.[115] It was through the prism of this ideology that he viewed the works of Taha Husayn, Yahya Haqqi (d. 1992),[116] Naguib Mahfuz and others.[117] The idea of the great unity reappeared again in *Taswir* (1945) and it was expressed explicitly:

> The Qur'an unites the heaven and the earth in one system, and unites the scenes of nature with the scenes of life in a 'broad unity' instead of a 'small unity'[118]; The Qur'an stresses the unity of God, [*Taswir*, p. 144]; the unity among all revealed religions in their source [*Taswir*, p. 146]; the unity of the basis of all religions [*Taswir*, p. 149]; and the unity of the means of the *da'wa* of all Prophets [*Taswir*, p. 149].

From 1945, the idea of unity appeared again in *Mashahid al-Qiyamh* (1947). Since the subject of *Mashahid* is the 'Other World', Qutb's discussion of the idea of unity links the 'Other World' with the 'present world', on the basis of the Qur'anic texts. Qutb says that

> The Qur'an connects between the present world and the Other World, between the scenes of happiness and of torments. The style of these scenes communicates with the souls and the feelings in order to achieve a religious aim.[119]

The idea of unity is frequently presented in a way relevant to the subject of the book *Mashahid*. For example, Qutb comments on the Qur'an 50: 19–30 and states that 'this scene begins in "this world" and ends in the "Other World". The present world and the Other World are not separated and the distance between them is not that great any way'.[120]

From 1947 until Qutb finished his book *Social Justice* in 1948, the concept of the 'great unity' was developed and has come to be one of the basic principles of his thinking on Sovereignty and the nature of the relation between the Creator and the creation, the universe, life and humankind: 'There is no supreme authority anywhere except in Allah.'[121] Thus, the religious theme of the idea of the great unity, as appeared in his poetry of the period 1925–1935, was then developed to become, in 1948, one of the essential principles of Qutb's thinking on Islamic issues, political or other. In Qutb's view, all the teachings of Islam are rooted in this great principle and from it all Islamic theories, laws, commandments, provisions for worship and social relations are derived. In this regard, Qutb says

> Islam has dealt with the relationship between the Creator and the creation; the universe, life and man; and between man and his self, as well as between the individual and the group; between the individual and society; among human groups generally; and between one generation and others.[122]
>
> Islam is the religion of unity between worship and social relations, creed and behaviour, spiritual and material things, economic and spiritual values, this world and the afterlife, and earth and heaven. From this great unity issue its laws and commands, its moral directives and restrictions, its opinions for the conduct of government and finance for the distribution of income and losses, and for [determining] rights and duties. In that great principle are included all the particular and details.[123]
>
> This, then is the unity among the parts and forces of the universe, the unity among all the powers of life.[124]
>
> Behind all this is the everlasting and eternal power, which has no beginning and no end can be attributed. To it is the ultimately authority over the universe, life and humankind. It is the power of Allah.[125]

This was further detailed in the successive editions of *Social Justice* and other writings. In his explanation of the nature and the meaning of Sovereignty (*hakimiyyah*), Qutb maintained that the universe, including life and Man issued from the absolute Will of God and is regulated by His law. Every part is in harmony with all parts in an integrated unity. Every part has a reason for being and that is related to this complete and absolute harmony.[126]

The universe, Qutb explains, is regulated by one single law that binds all its parts in a harmonious and orderly sequence. This systematic arrangement is the creation of *hakimiyyah*. However, the multiplicity of essences or beings leads to a multiplicity of wills and these give rise to different rules, different decisions and judgments. The will is the manifest expression of a willing essence, and law is the manifest expression of the effective will. If that was not so, the unity which regulates the system of the whole universe and harmonizes its course, direction and behaviour would disappear, and disorder would follow to the disruption of the harmony. Even an extreme atheist cannot ignore the reality of this harmonious system.[127]

Man, is a part of this harmonious system; his place, role and his life are ordained by *hakimiyyah*. The law of *hakimiyyah* is 'constant' and deals with man's essence that is also 'constant'.[128] For Qutb, constant (*thabat*) is one of the characteristics of *shari'ah*. To him 'constant' means that the *shari'ah* is firm and stable. This does not, however, mean that it is rigid in its application. Islam's basic doctrines are fixed and they can apply to all human situations; they provide for 'movement within a firm framework and about a stable axis'.[129] Gradual alterations and developments in life in general cannot, Qutb asserts, change man's nature into another being. Thus, people must cooperate among themselves in accordance with the *shari'ah*, the law of *hakimiyyah*, and they must take their place in the harmonious system. The Creator does not leave humanity nor any living being without direct guidance and continual care, since His absolute Will is in continuous and direct contact with the whole universe and with every individual being in it.[130]

The Qur'an is a fact with a constant essence like that of the universe itself. The universe, as Qutb asserts, is the visible book of God, while the Qur'an is His legible book. Both give signs and irrefutable proofs of their Creator, and both exist to function; the universe is still functioning and carrying out its role according to the law of God, and the Qur'an continues to carry out its role towards humanity and has remained the same without changing its essence and identity. Human beings remain human and His quintessence and essential nature remains the same. The Qur'an is God's message to Man, whose instinct has remained essentially the same, and whose 'essential nature has not changed into another being', despite changes in circumstances, and despite his role in the socio-political development. Therefore, the Qur'an is still valid and remains the legible message to Man and will remain so as long as Man's place, role and essence remain the same. The visible message (universe) continues to operate according to the ordained law of *hakimiyyah*. In the conclusion of his argument, Qutb stated that

> If it be despicable for one to say, for instance, that the sun is an ancient reactionary (*raj'i*) star and must be replaced by a new developed star! Alternatively, to say, man is an ancient reactionary creature and should be exchanged for another progressive creature capable to develop the earth! If these and other options are detestable, it would be more detestable to say similar things in respect to the Qur'an the inimitable and final message of God to mankind.[131]

Qutb emphasizes that belief in the sovereignty (*hakimiyyah*) of Allah over the universe, life and humans is a first step to belief in the *shari'ah*.[132] The logic here reflects the logic of Qutb's thought on the relationship between '*tawhid*', '*hakimiyyah*', and '*shari'ah*'. In other words, between '*aqidah* (i.e. creed, faith or belief) and *shari'ah* (law). This in turn implies the importance of the question of which one comes first, the '*aqidah*, that is, the belief in '*tawhid*' (Oneness of Allah), or the belief in '*hakimiyyah*' (sovereignty of Allah over the universe, life, and man), or the practice of the '*shari'ah*' (law of Allah)!

Dealing with this question in his commentary on the Qur'an, 6: 136, Qutb states that 'Islam established its own existence not by first fighting social and moral corruption. This battle came *after* the battle of *hakimiyyah*.'[133] Social and moral corruption in Arabia was corrected gradually, according to the Islamic laws after the belief in the Oneness of God and the oneness of His *hakimiyyah* (Sovereignty) became the sole creed of the society and was established deep in the conscience of the people. To him, practising *shari'ah* (law) in a given society is the natural outcome of the belief that *hakimiyyah* (sovereignty) is the society's sole creed. The logical implication of this is that there is no Islamic life as such before the belief that Allah is the only sovereign (*hakim*).[134]

The nationalist, the reformer and Rector of al-Azhar, Muhammad 'Abduh (d. 1905) concludes that the concept of *tawhid* is 'the belief that Allah is one, in His essence, in His attributes, in His existence, and in His acts'.[135] This scope of *tawhid* encompasses the belief that sovereignty belongs to Allah alone: 'He reigns supreme over His servants... Surely, He is the judgment.'[136] 'Allah has sovereignty over the heavens and the earth and all that lies between them.'[137] Thus the belief in '*tawhid*' (Oneness of Allah) comes first before practicing the '*shari'ah*' (law of Allah). 'Abduh says, 'The *shari'ah* came to affirm these Divine attributes and to forbid man to seek for aid except in his Creator... The *shari'ah* summoned man to set his sights on Allah alone...'[138]

Applying 'Abduh's concept of *tawhid* to his own constructs, in the 1960s, Qutb says

> The Islamic creed declares that there is *uluhiyyah* (divinity), and there is '*ubudiyyah* (servitude). The divinity belongs to Allah alone, whereas anything and anyone other than Him is His creature and servant. Each and every divine attribute belongs to Allah, whereas no creature of Allah can possess any of these attributes. Human life, then, ought to be based on the implications and consequences of this pure and complete belief in the Oneness of Allah (*tawhid*).[139]

Here, the scope of *tawhid* indicates that the belief in the Sovereignty of Allah over the universe, life and humankind is an integral part of *tawhid*. Thus, without the belief that Sovereignty belongs to Allah alone, the *tawhid* is not complete. Qutb says

> *Tawhid* is that Allah is the Lord and Sovereign of people not merely in their beliefs, concepts, consciences, and rituals of worship, but in their practical affairs... There is no God but Allah. There is no one worthy of worship except Allah, there is no creator or sustainer except Allah... There is no one in charge of the universe or even one's own affairs except Allah... Thus, Muslims worship Him alone... Muslims believe that there is no true ruler above them except Allah, no legislator for them except Allah, no one except Allah to inform them concerning their

> relationships and connections with the universe, with other living creatures, and with their fellow human beings. This is why Muslims turn to Allah for guidance and legislation in every aspect of life, whether it be political governance, economic justice, personal behavior, or the norms and standards of social intercourse.[140]
>
> We hope that these two examples from the text of the Qur'an are sufficient to elucidate the relationship between the Oneness of Allah in His Divinity, and in His Sovereignty . . .[141]

These words and language indicate that the belief in the sovereignty of Allah over the universe, life and humankind is one of the essential components of *tawhid*. The practice of *shari'ah* then comes after the belief in *tawhid*, which includes the sovereignty of Allah.[142] This logic of the 1960s had emerged before in Qutb's writings in the late 1940s, and early 1950s, particularly, when he began to write Islamist books. In his first Islamist work, *Social Justice in Islam* (1949), the authority of Allah within the scope of *tawhid* is clearly stated. Qutb says

> Islam is the religion of unity among the all forces of the universe, so it is inescapably the religion of *tawhid*, it recognizes the unity of Allah . . .[143] Islam began by liberating the human conscience from service to anyone other than Allah . . . No one other than Allah has authority over it . . . Allah alone has power, all others are servants who have no power over themselves or others.[144]
>
> The Qur'an continually drives home the creed which liberate the human soul from everything even resembling idolatry (*shirk*), whether in terms of divinity or sanctity . . .[145]

Here, Qutb stresses the Islamic creed's declaration that there is *uluhiyyah* (divinity), and there is *'ubudiyyah* (servitude). The *uluhiyyah* (divinity) belongs to Allah alone, whereas anything and anyone other than Him is His creature and servant, who has no power over himself or other. Thus the belief in *tawhid*, that is, that Allah is one (in His essence, in His attributes, in His existence, and in His acts) is the first step before practising His *shari'ah* (law). In other words, the belief that Allah is one and to Him alone is the ultimate authority over the heavens and the earth and all that lies between them is the integral part of *tawhid*. In this sense, Qutb says

> Behind all this is the everlasting and eternal power, which has no beginning and to which no end can be attributed. To it is the ultimate authority over the universe, life and humankind. It is the power of Allah'.[146]
>
> There is no supreme authority any where except in Allah'.[147]
>
> We call for the restoration of an Islamic life governed by the Islamic spirit and Islamic law, in which the Islam we preach is combined with a genuine Islamic environment.[148]

At that time (1949), Qutb was teaching that Allah is one and to Him alone is the ultimate authority over the universe, life and humankind. Qutb also emphasized that there is no *shari'ah* anywhere except the *shari'ah* of Allah. It is sufficient here to recall a brief statement from his writings of the early 1950s. In 1951, Qutb stated that 'the world is enduring the *jahiliyyah* today as it did in the days of the first barbarism'.[149] The statement makes the battle of *tawhid* the first before *shari'ah*. The *jahiliyyah* does not implement *shari'ah*, before the belief that Allah is One in His existence, in His sovereignty, in His attributes and in His acts. The *shari'ah* cannot be practiced before the belief in *tawhid*. Thus, Qutb's statement of the early 1950s indicates his inclination to put the battle against social and moral corruption second to the battle of *tawhid*, of which the sovereignty of Allah is an integral part.

The battle of *tawhid* can also be seen in Qutb's book *The Battle of Islam and Capitalism* (1951). This Islamist book shows Qutb's inclination to eradicate the social, political and moral corruption on the basis of the Islamic creed.[150] The Islamic creed is *tawhid*. Also, implementing the *shari'ah* of Allah requires belief in the *shari'ah* and in its source: He who is the Sovereign of all sovereignty. It was for this creed the *shari'ah* came, says 'Abduh.[151] Similarly, 'the *shari'ah* is the explanation of the creed' says Qutb.[152] This means that Qutb puts *tawhid* first before practising *shari'ah*. In Qutb's view, 'the Islamic social system emerges from the creed'.[153] This logic can also be seen in his *Islam and Universal Peace* (1951). It is an Islamist book in which Qutb tends to put the battle of social and moral corruption second to the creed of *tawhid*. He bases his discussion on the concept of *tawhid* as in the following:

> Islam begins by establishing the principle of the Oneness of Allah (*tawhid*), as it is from Him that life issues and unto him that it turns. 'Say: God is One...' (Qur'an, 112: 1–4). Accordingly, there is no controversy or doubt about the origin of this universe... Out of the Will of this One God, the whole existence has been created in the same unified manner... There is no intermediary between the Creative Will and the created beings, nor are there multiple ways of creation, but it is the Will referred to in the Qur'an by the word 'Be' that prevails... The One God reigns sovereign over all beings, to Him they turn for refuge in this life, and in the Hereafter... The universe, with its divers ramifications has one origin from which it issued... By one Supreme rule, this universe has been thoroughly administered in such a manner that precludes any collision among its parts...[154]

On the basis of *tawhid*, which included the belief that Divinity belongs to Allah the sovereign of all sovereignty, Qutb went on to discuss the universal peace in Islam. The point then is that Qutb's logic in his Islamist writings in the 1950s and in 1960s puts the belief in *tawhid* first before practising the *shari'ah*. In other words, the belief that Sovereignty belongs to Allah alone is the first before implementing the law.

Qutb's saying, in the 1960s, that belief in *hakimiyyah* (sovereignty of Allah) is a first step to belief in the *shari'ah* does not mean that he separates '*hakimiyyah*' from '*tawhid*', or prefers '*hakimiyyah*' over '*tawhid*', or that the belief in *tawhid* should come second after *hakimiyyah*, as has been understood by some. However, the belief in the Sovereignty (*hakimiyyah*) of Allah over the universe, life and humanity is an integral part of *tawhid*. Therefore, when Qutb distinguishes between Islamic and *jahili* systems, he links his ideas of the concept of *hakimiyyah* to the confession of faith. He expresses this point in the 1960s as follows:

> The theory of government in Islam is completely based on the testimony that there is no god but Allah. The one who confesses that Divinity belongs to none but Allah thereby confesses that *hakimiyyah* in human life belongs to Allah alone. Allah exercises *hakimiyyah* in human life, on the one hand by directly controlling human affairs by His will and determination (*qadar*) and, on the other hand by establishing the fundamental order of human life, human rights, duties, relationships and mutual obligations by His *shari'ah* and His program. In Islam, there is nobody who can be associated with Allah, neither in His will and determination nor in His *shari'ah* nor His program. Any other theory would be *shirk* (idolatry) and *kufr* (unbelief). This obvious basic principle distinguishes Islamic government from *jahili* government.[155]

Ideas basic to the concept of *hakimiyyah* are then justified by means of numerous Qur'anic verses, among which, for example, are the following: 'God keeps the heavens and the earth from falling. Should they fall, none could hold them back but He (35: 41).'[156] 'There is not a creature on the earth whose sustenance is not provided by God. He knows its resting place and its repository (11: 6).'[157] 'We created man; and We know the prompting of his soul, and We are closer to him than [his] jugular vein (50: 16).'[158] 'Allah made for you the night to rest in and the day to (give you) light. Allah is bountiful to men (40: 61).'[159] 'Allah has given you the earth for a dwelling place and the sky for a canopy. He has given you shape and made your shapes beautiful, and has provided for you sustenance (40: 64).'[160] 'It is He who has made the earth manageable for you, so walk about its regions and eat of His provisions (67: 15).'[161] 'Who is it that will defend you like an entire army, if not the Merciful? Who will provide for you if He withholds His sustenance? (67: 20–21).'[162]

Conceptual differences

There is not an English word that I know could translate '*hakimiyyah*' accurately or could do so without the risk of seriously misconstruing or losing the force and intent of this Arabic term. What we can do is only to give the descriptions and characteristics. The nature and the meaning of the *hakimiyyah* that Qutb speaks about are different from the nature and the meaning of sovereignty as known today. The word sovereignty is derived from the Latin word '*superanus*', which means 'super-above or supreme'. In dictionary terms, the definitions of the term sovereignty are varied, but signify human governmental and legal authority.[163]

Since the Ottoman Empire came into contact with Europe, the Ottoman institution came to be compared with the Holy Roman Empire. Terminologies associated with the Holy Roman Empire have come to play a major role as a standard measure that the scholars have used to examine the Islamic institutions. It is not so difficult then to emphasise the confusion that had risen about similarities and differences between the two institutions and that which the scholars are tackling since then. It has been said that 'the Caliph was Pope and emperor in one. The analogy is misleading'.[164] Although, the style of the Ottoman institution is not the only style or form that Muslims must conform to.

Islamic law declares that sovereignty belongs to God; He is the Creator, and He is the Legislator. The nature and the meaning of this sovereignty preclude the two sovereignties known in the Middle Ages (i.e. the Roman Emperor and the Pope) and the later modern absolute and non-responsible single sovereign presented by Bodin, Hobbes or Austin whose concept of sovereignty was the result of special circumstances which swept Europe in the sixteenth century. Because of the revitalization, reformation and the consequent break-up of the Roman Empire, and the rise of national monarchies in the sixteenth century Europe, the political thinking underwent a process of secularisation. The circumstances of 'cleavage between the absolutist rulers' compelled the political thinking to find a new theoretical basis for the new political phenomena.[165]

Jean Bodin, in the seventeenth century, was the first to define the modern concept of sovereignty, as a 'supreme power that is perpetual, undelegated, or delegated without limit or condition, inalienable and not subject to prescription. It is unrestrained by law because the sovereign is the source of the law'.[166] His theory rationally defends absolutism, even though he recognized the limitations imposed by the divine laws and laws of nature on the supreme power of the sovereign.[167]

Thomas Hobbes maintained that 'sovereignty must be unified and absolute. Men must choose; they were ruled or they were free; they could not be both; liberty went with anarchy and security with civil obedience'.[168] This definition led to the great Leviathan, the holder of the ultimate power, whom he called 'Mortal God'. His power is irreversible, absolute, indivisible, and unlimited.[169] This is also another exponent of absolutism.

In reaction to the theory of absolutism, the monarchomachs used the Greek-Stoic concept of 'contract' to defend popular sovereignty.[170] Locke used it to defend the English constitutional movement. Rousseau, however, unified the absolute sovereignty of Hobbes and the 'popular consent' of Locke into the philosophical concept of sovereignty that is the general will. It is in this sense that Rousseau's *Social Contract* may be read as an answer to Hobbes and Locke.[171]

John Austin, however, was the one who established the legal theory of Sovereignty, which was long accepted. According to Austin (1790–1859), 'If a determinate human superior, not in the habit of obedience to a like superior, receives habitual obedience from the bulk of a given society, that determinate superior is sovereign in that society, and the society (including the superior) is a society political and independent'.[172]

In this context, one may conclude that sovereignty has varying definitions, but all signify human governmental and legal authority. The nature of this sovereignty signifies the nature of the sovereign will and the nature of the law issued by this sovereign will. The nature of this legal authority implies that the sovereign will is not constant and the law issued by this sovereign authority is not stable. This concept of sovereignty, logically, implies multiplicity of authority, multiplicity of will, and different rules and judgements.[173] The nature and the meaning of this sovereignty is not the Sovereignty (*hakimiyyah*) that Islam envisages or that which Qutb speaks about.

In Islam, according to Qutb, *hakimiyyah* is the Sovereign of sovereignty. *Hakimiyyah* is the characteristic of divinity Whose rule is immediate, and Whose commands, as in the Qur'an, embody the law and constitution of the nation of Islam.[174] The attributes of this Sovereignty can be best ascertained also from the Qur'an, where reference to God is expressed in terms that are suggestive of one or other aspects of His sovereignty. Qutb refers to a number of Qur'anic verses such as these: 'To whom belong the earth and that all that it contains? (23: 84).'[175] 'Who is it in whose Hands is the sovereignty of all things... Who protects all but is not protected of any (say) if you know (23: 88).'[176] 'Who is the Lord of the seven heavens, and the Lord of the Mighty Throne? (23: 68).'[177] 'Say: O Lord, Sovereign of all sovereignty. You bestow power on whom You will, and take it away from whom You please (3: 26).'[178]

According to these Qur'anic verses, the nature and the meaning of the Sovereignty (*hakimiyyah*) in Islam is completely different from the concept of the sovereignty that is known in practice today. Therefore, translating the term *hakimiyyah* by the term sovereignty is not really accurate and it is not safe without a proper definition concerning the nature and the particulars of the term.

Sovereignty and the system of governance

Qutb's concept of *hakimiyyah* thus indicates the following characteristics:

- The system of government in Islam is not similar to any other systems.
- It is distinct from all forms of government in secular democracies.
- It is constitutional.
- It is not inherently theocratic or autocratic.
- The form of Islamic government has no impact on the Islamic identity of the state.

Taking the first point, the theory of government in Islam is based, in Qutb's view, on two fundamental ideas upon which the Islamic system, in general, is based. First is the unity of human beings in race, nature and origin. Second, Islam has universal applicability since God 'accepts only Islam to order and govern human life'.[179] To Qutb, these two ideas are fundamental since they are applied to the political, economic, social, intellectual and moral spheres of the Islamic system.[180]

Qutb then binds these ideas to the concept of *tawhid* (Oneness of God). Thus, any one who confesses that divinity belongs to Allah alone, thereby confesses that *hakimiyyah* (sovereignty) in human life, belongs to Allah alone. Allah is the only '*hakim*' or sovereign who has the right to ordain a programme for human life.[181]

After accepting the Sovereignty (*hakimiyyah*) of God in human life, it follows that government in Islam, according to Qutb, be based on justice on the part of the rulers, obedience on the part of the ruled, and consultation (*shurah*) between the rulers and those ruled. These are the broad basic lines from which all principles branch and provide the foundation of government, its form and nature. The implication of this chain is that the Islamic system cannot be compared with any other systems, and cannot be called anything other than 'Islam'.[182]

The political system in Islam can be understood as a rule by *shurah* (consultation). *Shurah* is a basic principle in the *shari'ah* and essential to the organs of the State and its overall Islamic identity.[183] Consultation, according to Qutb, is mandatory, by virtue of it being the subject of a Qur'anic command (42: 38 and 3: 159), as are obligatory prayers and *zakah* (alms).[184] Qutb did not insist on a particular form of *shura* since there is no specific form prescribed either in the Qur'an or in the *sunnah* (i.e. the traditions of the Prophet). He pointed out that the time of the Prophet and that of his companions after him is a period that preserved variable methods and procedures of consultation. Such procedures, Qutb asserts, are also not the only forms of consultation: 'The Muslim community must devise its own methods to facilitate consultation according to environment, social circumstances, and requirements.'[185] This view practically means that the Chief Executive (can also be called President)[186] of the State is elected, but it is also up to the community to choose a successful means to facilitate the principles of election.[187]

Similarly, consultation (*shurah*) is applied to all cases and affairs in which Revelation does not provide a specific method or the necessary guidance.[188] This implies that the form of government can be altered from time to time without any compromise to its Islamic nature.

Islam, as Qutb asserts, does not impose a specific form of government. The universality of Islam is based on its suitability for all time and place. This requires that matters, which will always be changing according to circumstances, be left to human reason to shape, according to the public interest and within the framework of the general principles of *shari'ah*.[189]

The *shurah* appears to be different from that known today as parliamentary government of any type or form of democracy or other system. *Shurah* is, in fact, an act of worship, divinely inspired, and based on the principle that *hakimiyyah* (absolute sovereignty) belongs to Allah alone. Secular democracy, by contrast, is based on the principle that sovereignty belongs to the people, that is, the majority of them. In this secular form, as Qutb says, one group of people legislates for the rest of the people. Overall, the State enjoys the right of absolute authority.[190] Secular government in general and democracy in particular have the power to enforce the desires of a group of people. This secular democracy or party rule, according to Qutb, usurps the *hakimiyyah* of God on the earth and the absolute right implicit in that notion. Submission to individuals or groups, even as a majority or all people of society constitutes violation, and opposition to the divine law. For Qutb, it is a reversion to the days of *jahiliyyah*. This kind of submission is contrary to the doctrine of *tawhid* upon which the Islamic system is based.[191]

Qutb stresses that the Islamic *shari'ah* is the 'founder' of the Islamic 'community'. It was in the shade of *Shari'ah* that the Islamic community developed its own civilization which signified the shape and identity of their society. This means that Islamic *shari'ah* did not exist from the evolution of Islamic society. The *shari'ah*, however, has existed in its complete and constant form since it was divinely revealed. Therefore, the system of government in Islam is not commensurate with any other system in general.[192]

The point that automatically arises rests in the question of whether or not the government in Islam can be constitutional. In this regard, Albert Venn Dicey pointed out the constitution used in England as follows:

> Constitutional Law, as the term used in England, appears to include all rules which directly or indirectly affect the distribution or exercise of the sovereign power in the state. Hence it includes (among other things) all rules which define the members of the sovereign power, all rules which regulate the relation of such members to each other, or which determine the mode in which the sovereign power, or the members thereof, exercise their authority.[193]

Similarly, Charles Frederick Strong defines the intent of a constitution in these words: 'The objects of a constitution, in short, are to limit the arbitrary action of the government, to guarantee the rights to the governed, and to define the operation of the sovereign power.'[194]

In the view of these definitions, Muslims have no written constitution to govern, or a constitution that is agreed upon by 1.3 billion people of different ethnicity, languages and cultural backgrounds. They however have the Qur'an as the unwritten constitution that is agreed upon by all Muslims and, currently, governs to some extent their daily life according to its rules without a law enforcement body. This constitution answered the concept of Sovereignty and its relevant issues as well as the rules that regulate the relationships between all members in the state, as outlined in the above injunctions.

According to al-Mawardi and Qutb, governmental activity is restricted within the limits of the law, which is ordained by the highest governmental and legal authority (*hakimiyyah* or Sovereignty). Thus, the government acts only within a limited framework. This principle, as Qutb asserts, is a Qur'anic order lucidly expressed in terms of law such as 'do this and do not do that'. In his *Zilal*, for instance, Qutb demonstrated that the Prophet himself was not empowered to exceed or over-step these limits.[195] Qutb based his argument on Qur'anic verses such as these: 'These are the limits ordained by Allah, so do not transgress them. Those that transgress the limits ordained by Allah, those indeed are the unjust' (2: 229). 'O you who believe, obey Allah and obey His Apostle and those from among yourselves who hold authority. Then if there is any dispute between you concerning any matter, refer it to Allah and His Apostle if you truly believe in Allah and the Last Day. This is the better course and most just' (4: 49).

Based on these and other Qur'anic verses, Qutb argues that government in Islam is limited to regulations laid down in the Qur'an and the *sunnah*, the primary sources of *shari'ah*. One could argue that the Qur'an and *sunnah* are sources of *fiqh* (jurisprudence) and expressions of the *shari'ah*. This matter will be detailed later, but here it should be remembered that *fiqh* (jurisprudence) is only personal opinion concerning the *shari'ah*. In addition, all Muslims are agreed on the Qur'an but not on *fiqh*. According to Qutb,

> Muslim jurists are not a specific group like the 'clergy' of the Christian Church, but people grounded in the science of religion in addition to their expertise in other fields. Muslim jurists can differ in their understanding of the texts and on the derivation of the relevant legal opinions. This also occurs in the jurisprudence of the human-made law.[196]

The legal implication of this is that the government in Islam is limited to a constitution that is divinely inspired and that all Muslims are agreed upon it. Islamic government, then, is not absolute government, nor it is an autocratic or authoritarian.

According to al-Zalabani, 'the limitation of governmental power in regulating the affairs of the people is the central principle of constitutional rule.'[197] This means that the government in Islam is constitutional since it is limited to the *shari'ah*, the constitution of the Muslims.

Consequently the limitation of Islamic government to *shari'ah* does not imply that Islamic government is theocratic. Theocracy has been defined as a 'State which has either an overt or covert religious basis'[198] and is 'run by a priestly class. Here a particular class of chosen mortals alone claims to understand the Will and Utterances of God, and it has therefore the final say in all matters of life'.[199] Whatever may be the different forms of theocracy, there is one thing common in them. For example, theocracy is a type of government wherein 'the person or persons at the helm of affairs are regarded as superhuman beings who are raised above the common people by the Almighty God

Himself. The elevation of the Government is thus divine and, therefore, absolute...'[200] Thus, in theocracy those who govern the affairs of the people are considered to be infallible since

> they are the manifestations of God Himself on the earth and are directly dictated by Him. The people have, therefore, no right to advise or instruct them and if they do so, they are insulting the Almighty God Himself. Advice is a sin in theocracy. This is not the case in the Islamic State.[201]

By contrast, according to Qutb, there is no priesthood in Islam. The Chief Executive is not a divine or divinely chosen, but chosen by the absolutely free choice of the community.[202] Unlike the head of theocracy, the head of the Islamic State is required to take counsel from the consultation council (*Majlis al-Shura*) in all important matters of the State.[203] Overall, in the Islamic State, the ruler and the ruled are not considered as divine or as having the right to claim divinity for themselves. Qutb says:

> The chief executive[204] of the Islamic State has no religious authority that he receives directly from heaven as was the case with some European rulers of the ancient times when there was a form of government called theocracy. This is not in Islam since the chief executive assumes his position only by the free choice of Muslim citizens.[205]

To Qutb, the Muslims are theoretically not bound by the Will of the former Chief Executive, or predecessor, nor is the position inherited. The authority of the Chief Executive derives from his undertaking to implement the law (*shari'ah*). He does not claim any personal authority to initiate legislation. These characteristics also distinguish Islamic State from theocracy. In the Islamic State the Chief Executive, as Qutb asserts, can only rule as long as he applies the law and recognizes that the Sovereignty belongs only to Allah.[206]

Loyalty or obedience to the government, in Islam, is subjected to the obedience of government to the constitution, that is, the Qur'an and the *sunnah*. Qutb articulated this argument in clear cut terms saying

> Every government that is based on the principle that *hakimiyyah* (absolute sovereignty) belongs to none but Allah and then implements the *shari'ah*, is an Islamic government. Every government that is not based on this principle and does not implement the *shari'ah*, cannot be called Islamic, even if the government is run by official religious organizations. The obedience of the people is to be given only if, and as long as, the government recognizes that *hakimiyyah* belongs to Allah alone and then implements the *shari'ah* without any qualification other than justice and obedience.[207]

As to the form of government, Qutb's view reveals two concepts. The first is the source of authority. The second is the administration of authority. He noted that, in Islam, there is a distinction between the source of authority, and its administration. This differentiation is critical to Qutb's theory since it explains the importance of Sovereignty (*hakimiyyah*) in terms of its purpose and so elucidates the difference between Islamic government and the government of *jahiliyyah*, whether this latter be theocratic, autocratic, democratic or some other.[208]

For Qutb, the source of governmental authority in the Islamic State is not the Muslim community or the result of election, but the activity of implementing the law (*shari'ah*). In other words, the activity of facilitating the application of the law is the only source from which the government derives its authority. He has dealt with this idea before his detention. In the first edition of *Social Justice* (1949), Qutb pointed out that the political theory rests on the basis of justice on the part of the rulers, obedience on the part of the ruled, and consultation between rulers and ruled. The ruler must implement justice 'which cannot be swayed by affection or by hatred.... This is the pinnacle of justice which no international law and likewise no national law has as yet achieved.'[209] As for the obedience on the part of the ruled, Qutb refers to a number of Qur'anic texts, such as (4: 59), to emphasize the nature and the limits of obedience. He says

> The fact that this verse groups together Allah, the Messenger, and those who hold authority means that it clarifies the nature and the limits of this obedience. Obedience to one who holds authority is derived from obedience to Allah and the Messenger. The ruler in Islamic law is not to be obeyed only by virtue of holding his position through the law of Allah and His Messenger; his right to obedience is derived from his observance of that law, and from no other thing. If he departs from the law, he is no longer entitled to obedience, and his orders need no longer be obeyed. Thus one authority says that, 'There can be no obedience to any creature which involves disobedience to the Creator.'[210] 'An absolute obedience such as this is not to be accorded to the will of the ruler himself, nor can it be a binding thing if he abandons the law of Allah and His Messenger. This tradition indicates the necessity of getting rid of a ruler who abandons the law by deed or by word, but with the minimum use of force.'[211]

Similarly, in his book *Islam and the Universal Peace* (1951), Qutb says 'The Islamic political system can be explained as rule through consultation... Obedience to the ruler depends on his fidelity in adhering to the Islamic laws.'[212] Thus, the legitimacy of the authority of the government is subjected to the government's obedience to the law. If the government departs from the law, the authority of this government is not legitimate and it should be removed from office. This view, in the later writings, remained unchanged.[213]

In the earlier and in the later Islamist writings, Qutb's view concerning the nature and the limits of obedience to the Chief Executive is as follows:

(a) Through the law, the chief executive gets his right to the public office by the free choice of the people.
(b) Obedience to the chief executive is not legitimate unless he facilitates the application of the law.
(c) Obedience is due to him not because of the result of election but because of implementing the law.[214]

Thus if the Chief Executive is elected today, for example, but abandons the Islamic law in the following day, no obedience is due to him.[215] The scope of obedience due to the rulers is clearly determent in the tradition of the Prophet and the Muslims after him. According to 'Awdah the former Judge at the Supreme Court and the author of Islamic criminal law, the first four rulers and jurists are unanimously of the opinion that there is no claim of obedience to the ruler unless his commands are issued for the purposes of facilitating the application of the law; the ruler is not entitled to any obedience if he commands disobedience to the law, such as permitting what is unanimously considered to be prohibited (i.e. adultery, consumption of alcohol and foregoing Islamic penalties).[216]

According to Qutb, God orders the rulers and ruled to implement His law. The ruler has no right to claim that he is divinely chosen or has divine authority for remaining in Office if he departs from the law.[217] Logically, the law would not legitimize the authority of anyone who departs from the law.

To summarize these in terms other than what Qutb actually uses, the Chief Executive enters the public office by free election or on the proviso that he will implement the law. Here, the people participate in decisions concerning their political life. Election gave the elected president a mandate to govern his people according to the law. The result of the election, then, can be seen as a contract between the elected president and the people that he will implement the law. One authority says, 'the contract (vocal or written . . . etc.) is the law of the contracting parties (say i.e. president and the people). This is called by Muslim jurists "*'aqdu al-imamah*" (the contract of leadership)'.[218] The contract here is signed by three: (i) the elected president, (ii) the people and (iii) the law (i.e. the Just witness). As to the law, it

- gives people the right to elect their president who will implement the law;
- gives the elected president the right to enforce the law among the people;
- instructs him to consult the guidance council (consultation: *shurah*);
- gives people the right to impeach the president from office if he departs from the law.

Thus, the law can be seen as a fundamental tenet above the State and citizens. This is Qutb's thinking on Sovereignty (*hakimiyyah*).

To him, Allah is the Sovereign and His Sovereignty (*hakimiyyah*) is the *shari'ah* (law), as Qutb himself admitted.[219] Thus, believing that there is no *hakimiyyah* other than God's *hakimiyyah* means that there is no law other than God's law. The law (*hakimiyyah*: shari'ah) regulates those items, above, and its relevance. A president, 'has no rights other than those which belong to any individual of the Muslim community – except that he can claim obedience to his command, advice, and help in the enforcement of the law'.[220] Neither the elected president nor his consultants or advisers are divine or divinely chosen. The point then is that the government in Islam legitimizes its authority not through the result of election but through its activity to facilitate the application of the law the sovereignty (*hakimiyyah*) of Allah.[221] According to Qutb,

> In the Islamic system the *ummah* chooses the ruler and gives him the legitimacy to administer his government on the basis of Islamic law. The *ummah*, however, is not the source of *hakimiyyah*, which gives the law its legitimacy. The source of *hakimiyyah* is Allah.[222]

Qutb means that Allah is the source of *hakimiyyah* (sovereignty = *shari'ah* = Islamic law); and He gives law its legitimacy. Thus the result of the election is not considered to empower the ruler to adopt laws that lack the legitimacy of *hakimiyyah* (sovereignty = *shari'ah* = Islamic law), or are in conflict with it. The point then is that the *hakimiyyah*, in practical sense, is not Allah but His *shari'ah*. The source of *hakimiyyah* is Allah, neither the party nor the whole community. This is not the case in any other form of government, whether it is a democracy or a theocracy. Speaking of sovereignty in England and Scotland, Green (1956), emphasizes that 'King James I [1566–1625] had said that "kings are not only called God's lieutenants but even by God himself they are called gods." '[223] In Islam, however, if Muslim citizens do not accept the Chief Executive, he simply has no authority. If they do accept him (through election or any other device), and he abandons the *shari'ah* (*hakimiyyah* of Allah), no obedience is due him.[224] According to Qutb, those rulers who do not facilitate the application of the law (*shari'ah*), are called by Islam '*taghut*' (transgressors). Islam commands Muslims to rebel against such rulers.[225] Islamic government does not mean that the ruler should be a religious or military organization.[226] For Qutb, Islamic government is any form of rule in which the law is implemented and in which the Chief Executive recognizes that Sovereignty belongs to Allah alone and accepts that his rule does not exceed implementation of the law.[227]

For those trying to establish some similarity between the Islamic social system and others or for those who have described Islamic system by varying concepts such as imperialistic, socialistic or democratic systems, Qutb had to say

> It may happen, in the development of human systems, that they coincide with Islam at times and diverge from it at others. Islam, however, is a complete and independent system and has no connection with these

> systems, neither when they coincide with it nor when they diverge from it. For such divergence and coincidence are purely accidental and in scattered parts. Similarity or dissimilarity in partial and accidental matters is also of no consequence. What matters is the basic view, the specific concept from which the parts branch out. Such parts may coincide with or diverge from the parts of other systems but after each coincidence or divergence Islam continues on its own unique direction.[228]

Consequently, the Islamic system cannot be associated with or named by anything other than 'Islam'. This and *jahiliyyah* are the only categories recognized by Qutb.[229] The difference between Islamic system and the systems of the twentieth century will be detailed in Part IV in the present text.

Shari'ah and *Fiqh* in the concept of Sovereignty

What is meant by *shari'ah* in the context of Sovereignty (*hakimiyyah*) is of critical importance in Qutb's thought. In the last edition of *Social Justice* (1964), Qutb pointed out the concept of *shari'ah* in relation to *hakimiyyah* as follows:

> The meaning of *hakimiyyah* (sovereignty) in the Islamic conception is not limited to the issue of accepting and following the *shari'ah* in government. Consequently, the *'ubudiyyah* (servitude) to Allah alone does not merely mean accepting the *shari'ah* from Him alone and following this *shari'ah* alone, if we limit the meaning of *Shari'ah* to the principles of government (*hukm*) and its laws, for this alone does not represent the meaning of *shari'ah* in the Islamic conception. The *shari'ah* of Allah is everything that prescribed by Allah to order human life. This takes the form of fundamentals of belief, the fundamentals of government (*hukm*), the fundamentals of behavior and the fundamentals of knowledge. It takes the form of the creed and the conception and all the components of this conception. It takes the form of legislative decisions and it takes the form of principles of ethics and behavior. It takes the form of the values and standards that rule society and by which people, things and events are evaluated. Then it takes the form of knowledge in all its aspects and of all the fundamental principles of intellectual and artistic activity.[230]

Qutb emphasizes that, the limits placed on Islamic government by the *shari'ah* essentially militate against potential dictatorship, despotism, autocracy and similar abuses of power.[231] How this works, is a comprehensive question encompassing the concept of Islamic religion and State.[232] Briefly, in the Islamic State, as Qutb says in 1951,

> justice comes from the law itself... For correct application of this law, Islam relies on its clear codes, the conscience of the judge and society's observation of its injunctions. Every individual in the Muslim society is

obligated to prevent injustice, to admonish the ruler whenever he exceeds his limits and to advise the judge whenever he errs. In Islam the individual sins if he does not testify or if he allows wrong or, at least, does not draw attention to it when he becomes aware of it.[233]

Qutb pointed out that the *shari'ah* provides protection through a number of channels such as that of the guarantees of security, the guarantees for material requirements, social equilibrium and the belief in law.[234] Islam takes into account that society can function effectively when all its members feel safe and secure. Guarantees of security are an important part in Islamic law. In this regard, Qutb pointed out a number of guarantees, which can be summarized as follows:

(1) Preservation of life.... Every human being is included...
(2) Guarantee of honor and property.... The guarantee of honor is implied in the penalties for adultery, fornication and accusation.... As for lawful acquired possession, a guarantee is implied in the penalty for wanton theft...
(3) Guarantee of the inviolability of the home. Nobody has the right to enter another's home without permission...
(4) Guarantee of privacy, spying is prohibited...
(5) Guarantees against slander and perjury. Individuals must be safeguarded against false indictments, verdicts and evidence. To this end Islam provides almost fool-proof rules and procedures... By applying the Islamic law all the personal and social guarantees of human rights to life, honour, property and justice are secured for the individual by his society.[235]

As for the requirements of living, Qutb pointed out that

> Islam appreciates the importance of material requirements but does not unduly emphasize their role in man's total welfare, for in Islam man is physical as well as spiritual being. Recognition of spiritual needs that must be satisfied differentiates Islam from materialistic doctrines... Islam is quite aware that laws and guarantees are not effective if the individual cannot supply his needs... Islam guarantees everyone a decent standard of living to ensure social equilibrium in the community. In Islam, the first of the means which enables man and provides him with his livelihood is work... There are social securities...[236]

Social equilibrium is 'easily discerned in the Islamic political system, in its legislation, in its judicial structure and in its system of social security'.[237]

In his view,

> the ruler therefore has no rights that do not belong to an individual Muslim except for obedience to his command, advice, and assistance in

> enforcing the *shari'ah*. The Prophet was not only a ruler, but also the one who brought the *shari'ah* and set the legal limits for the ruler within the sphere of the rights that Islam gives him, and his successors followed his prescriptions... he allowed people to take retribution from him when they had the right to it, unless they chose to forgive him.[238]

Thus 'the ruler has no legal or financial rights beyond those of the ordinary Muslims, nor does his family'.[239]

In the Islamic system, family structure and individual rights for all citizens are also central to the *shari'ah*.[240] Thus, in Qutb's words, the *shari'ah* functions as a 'protective shield in defence of the rights and liberties of citizens against arbitrary power'.[241]

The nature of the *shari'ah* differs from what is known as *fiqh* (jurisprudence). The *shari'ah* and *fiqh* 'are not equal in their source and argument'. The *shari'ah* comprises no more than those clear commands and prohibitions conveyed through the Qur'an and explained in the *sunnah* of the Prophet.[242] This, however, is not the case for *fiqh*. Muslim jurists practising *fiqh* were considered

> great scholars who, after deep and conscientious study of the Qur'an and the *sunnah*, enunciated important legal principles concerning many problems. Their work facilitated the application of *shari'ah* principles to specific problems faced during their time. Their findings were influenced by their personal approach to the legal sources of *shari'ah* as well as by the social environment of their time.[243]

With time, precedents of interpretation have acquired in the public mind a kind of divine authority like that of *shari'ah* and have come, erroneously, to be regarded as part of the divine *shari'ah* itself. However, as Qutb comments, '*fiqh* cannot be a divine part of the *shari'ah* which is laid down by the Qur'an and the *sunnah*. Any sources of *shari'ah* [rulings] other than the two sources, namely the Qur'an and the sunnah, is *fiqh*.'[244]

The major branches of *fiqh* concern *'ibadat* (ritual duties) and *mu'amalat* (transactions) both of which are interconnected on account of the complex nature of Islamic teachings. *Ibadat* involves Islamic rites that cannot be affected by any special requirements of time, place or a particular people. For this very reason, *'ibadat* is more constant than that of *mu'amalat* which deals with issues that are subject to change in accordance with human requirements and social conditions.[245] What is irrefutable, as Qutb asserts, is that important figures like Abu Bakr, 'Umar, 'Ali, Ibn 'Abbas, Ibn Umar and other Companions of the Prophet were masters of *shari'ah*. Because of the Prophet's influence, they became grounded in the knowledge and practical enunciation of the legal principles of the *shari'ah*. They facilitated the application of *shari'ah* to specific issues and dealt with questions arising from the change of social conditions of their time. Social conditions, according to Qutb, are unrepeatable in history, although they may be similar. Therefore, replicating a judgment or legal ruling of the past is not part of the order of *hakimiyyah* and not of the way of the Prophet.[246]

Qutb does not mean to disregard *fiqh* or disregard its sciences, but he does distinguish *shari'ah* from *fiqh* and advocates research in the field of *fiqh*. In this sense, Qutb says,

> It is better to continue [the discussion] of the distinction between the two great rivers of *fiqh*: The river of *'ibadat* (ritual duties) and that of *mu'amalat* (transactions) – despite the firm connection between them in the nature of Islamic Creed (*'aqidah*)...[247]

He also went on to say '...the rules of *fiqh* can be used as guidance [in the field]...'[248] He added that 'we should be guided by how the Muslim Jurists [enunciate rules] in such cases...'[249] The implication of these quotations indicate that Qutb celebrates *fiqh* as a great and important Islamic source of past rulings and decisions that have provided useful guidance for the present generation. The enunciation of accurate legal principles based on similar cases from the *shari'ah* has thus been possible, but Qutb emphasizes *fiqh* as no more than a human opinion concerning the *shari'ah*, not the *shari'ah* itself.[250]

The *shari'ah* cannot be made dependent on scholarly deductions or inferences of a subjective nature. It lays down the definite ordinances of the Qur'an and the Sunnah. It is the explicit directives of the Qur'an and the Sunnah and these alone, that, collectively, constitute the primary and the constant law of the *shari'ah*.[251] On this point, Qutb is quite categorical: there are no schools (*madhahib*) or 'systems' for Muslims to choose from. There is only one system, the system of the *shari'ah* of *hakimiyyah*. Any system based on or ruled by laws other than the law of *hakimiyyah* is a *jahili* system.[252]

Qutb's distinction between *shari'ah* and *fiqh* that is based on *hakimiyyah* brought an end to the confusion of slogans designed by secularists wanting to separate religion from worldly affairs. In so doing, these secularists consciously fuse *shari'ah* with *fiqh* to support their claim that establishing an Islamic State ruled by the *shari'ah* means implementing the rules of *fiqh* that dealt with social conditions very different from our modern era. Those who hold this view, the so-called Muslims, according to Qutb, 'fuse *shari'ah* with *fiqh* in a ridiculous way to mean that the Islamic rule means to implement *fiqh*. They then say that the legal rulings of *fiqh* were influenced by personal and social environment of the past, and that the Islamic rule is inconsistent with modern society.'[253]

In the early period, Qutb was more concerned about spelling out the details of Islamic order. In the later period, however, he was more concerned to assert its theoretical authority. Nevertheless, in both periods, theocentrism of his writings are present since he began to write Islamist books and increased in the later period.[254] In both periods, also, Qutb does not involve himself in complex legal discussion that overly engaged in *fiqh* (jurisprudence). His view as appeared in all editions of *Social Justice* is that

> Islam enunciates for men a complete theory of life. This theory is always liable to growth by development or by adaptation; it is not open to change or to adulteration, either in its fundamentals or in its general aims. Therefore, in order that this complete theory may bear its full natural fruits, it is necessary to make a complete application of it.[255]

Thus complete application of Islamic order will bring about natural development of legal opinions, *fiqh* or (jurisprudence). In the last edition of *Social Justice*, Qutb says, 'When Muslim society in fact exists, the field will be wide open for *Ijtihad* (legal opinion)...'[256] This view is further detailed in *Zilal*: 'When the Islamic society in fact exists, the fundamentals of the Islamic system will be tested and the society itself will begin to legislate what is required for its actual life...'[257] The point is that in the earlier and later writings Qutb's view of the existence of an Islamic society is crucial for the growth and development of Islamic jurisprudence.

Sovereignty and the existence of Islam

The concept of *hakimiyyah* stands in relation to Qutb's argument that the Muslim *ummah* does not exist and Islam no longer exists. This theme can be seen in the first edition of *Social Justice in Islam* (1949), when he says, 'The Islamic society today is not Islamic in any true sense...'[258] 'The spread of the Islamic spirit came to a halt a short space after the time of the Prophet...'[259] Qutb's 'serious'[260] topic is mentioned in all editions of *Social Justice*,[261] in *Zilal*,[262] in his last book *Ma'alim* (1964),[263] and in his testimony to the Court in 1965, one year before his death. In his answer to the question of whether he 'agrees that the Muslim *ummah* has not existed for a long time and must be reconstructed?', Qutb answers,

> The concept of the Muslim *ummah* needs to be explained. The Muslim *ummah* is the *ummah* which governs all aspects of life – political, social, economic, moral and so on as well as, the *shari'ah* of Allah and His program (*manhaj*). In these terms, the Muslim *ummah* does not now exist in Egypt, or in any place on the face of the earth. But this does not mean there are no Muslims. This is because, an individual is governed by his creed and his morals, but what governs the affairs of the *ummah* is the sociopolitical system.[264]

Thus, one could argue that, if the Muslim *ummah* does not exist, how and in what sense can individual Muslims exist, when Qutb also says that Islam is no longer existing.[265] Qutb's view is that the *ummah* cannot be called *ummah* if it does not firmly establish itself on the '*shari'ah* of Allah and

His program'. In the sense of this definition, Qutb says, the *ummah* does not exist, and thus Islam is no longer existing as a system governing the affairs of the *ummah*. In this context, Qutb distinguished between the *ummah* and individuals and emphasized the reason for this, as in his testimony to the Court. To him, the *ummah* dos not exist, but there are individuals and every individual is 'governed by his creed and his morals'. Following is the question of what Islam individuals can practice in a society where *shari'ah* is not implemented. One might also ask what Qutb means by 'Muslim individuals' and by the idea that 'every individual is governed by his creed and his morals'. Qutb explains this point in his writings of the 1950s and of the 1960s, such as the early and the later editions of *Social Justice*, *Zilal* and *Ma'alim*.

In regard to *Social Justice in Islam*, Shepard notes, 'The early editions make the point that "this religion cannot be rightly practiced in isolation from society. Its people cannot be Muslims if they do not put it into effect in their social, legal and economic system." '[266] Here Qutb implies two points: (i) that the individuals cannot practise Islam[267] in isolation from an Islamic society, that is, the society which practices Islam in the 'social, legal and economic system'; and (ii) that there are two categories of individuals, Muslim individuals and individuals who think of themselves as Muslims. Every individual of these two categories, as Qutb says, is governed by his creed and his morals.

As to these two categories, the individuals who are struggling to 'put Islam into effect in their social, legal and economic system' are Muslims, but the individual who does not stand for this cause cannot be called Muslim. Whether or not to stand for the cause of Islam, in this sense, depends on every individual's perception of his creed and his morals. Thus in the absence of the Muslim *ummah*, as Qutb emphasizes, Islam as a system governs the affairs of the absent *ummah* as well. This does not mean there is no Islam at all, but that there is Islam in the Mosques, in the books, and in the teachings of the scholars, but not in the socioeconomic, legal and political systems which govern the affairs of society.[268] In this context, there are Muslim individuals existing side by side with individuals who think of themselves as Muslims. The Islam, which is available to the former category, is also available to the latter one. Thus, in that sense these two categories exist.

Furthermore, as for the category of Muslim individuals, those individuals are Muslims because they are practising from Islam what is available to them, such as prayer, *hajj* and other ritual duties, but they are also struggling in the cause of making what is not available in society. What is not available to them is out of their hands, which they find unacceptable, but they are struggling to 'put Islam into effect in their social, legal and economic system'. In this sense, Muslim individuals can exist in a society where Islam has disappeared from the socioeconomic and political spheres. This is what Qutb means by 'the *ummah* does not exist, but there are individual Muslims'. Those Muslim individuals, in Qutb's view, are 'liberals' (*ahrar*) distinguished from the flock (*al-qati'*).[269]

As for the category of those individuals who think of themselves as Muslims, Qutb says, 'People cannot be Muslims if they do not put it [Islam] into effect in their social, legal and economic system.'[270] Thus the individuals who do not try to 'put Islam into effect in their social, legal and economic system cannot be called Muslims'. The individuals of this category also might take from Islam what is available to them such as prayer, *hajj* and other ritual duties, but they do not try to bring what is not available and make it available in society. What is not available to the individuals of this category is also out of their hands, but they accept the situation as it is. They do not seek to put Islam into effect in the sphere of government, or economics, and they do not work to bring Islam into effect in the legal sphere. Thus within Qutb's theme of the disappearance of the *ummah* and the disappearance of Islam as a system governing the affairs of society, there are Muslim individuals existing side by side with individuals who might think of themselves as Muslims. They also have the right to claim what they think is right. This right is granted by Islam, as Qutb says.[271] To possess the right to think, however one may, is one thing, but to escape the consequences of one's thinking is another.[272] With this in mind, in the society where Islam is excluded from the socioeconomic, legal and political systems, there are individuals who might think of themselves as Muslims. This is their right, but they cannot escape the consequences of their thinking. They should know that they cannot practise Islam because Islam is one whole entity, that is, that Islam cannot be divided into parts to be practised and parts to be neglected. In the early 1950s, Qutb says 'Take the whole Islam or leave it all.'[273] In other words, the importance of prayer and *hajj* is on a par with the importance of the social, legal and economic system. Thus, individuals who are practising from Islam what is available to them, such as prayer, *hajj* and other rituals, but do not struggle to 'put Islam into effect in their social, legal and economic systems, cannot be called Muslims'.[274] This is what Qutb means by 'this religion cannot be rightly practiced in isolation from society. Its people cannot be Muslims if they do not put it into effect in their social, legal and economic system'.[275]

Echoing Qutb's view is Rashid Rida (d. 1935) when he emphasizes, with words similar to Qutb, that 'Muslims cannot truly think that their religion exists without a strong and independent Islamic State based on the laws of Islam.'[276]

To Qutb, Islam does not confine itself to morality, or ritual duties, or salvation of the individual as an isolated entity.[277] In Islam, the individual *ego* is, no doubt, of paramount value, but it lives, moves and has its being in society; it is society that generates self-consciousness and develops it. All Islamic teachings have a social reference.[278] Islam always deals with Man in society, and social justice is the cornerstone that guides and elevates him to higher horizons.[279] Islam has not left the individual with only teachings of kindness and love for his neighbour. High morality had been preached by all great religions, but no religion before Islam had attempted to organize the individuals into a welfare society. On Islamic ideology, Islam founded a society and made it a model welfare society. The point then is that Islam cannot work, or in Qutb's words, 'exist', in isolation from society.[280]

From the first to the fifth edition of *Social Justice*, Qutb emphasizes that the Islamic society does not exist in the modern era. In this regard, he draws on Qur'anic authority to stress his reason, as in the following:

> The present Islamic society is by no means Islamic. We have already quoted a passage from the Qur'an which cannot be interpreted away, 'Whoso judges not by what God revealed – they are the unbelievers.'[281] In present-day society we do not govern by what God has revealed, for we have institutions based on usury (*riba*) that are the foundation of our economic life, we have laws permitting prostitution and not punishing it, and *Zakat* is not obligatory and of course not spent in the requisite ways . . .[282]

From the first to the fifth edition of *Social Justice*, Qutb pointed out that

> We call for the restoration of an Islamic life governed by the Islamic sprit and Islamic law in which the Islam we preach is combined with a genuine Islamic environment. We have presented the historical foundations for societies as portrayed by the Qur'an and the Hadith and then we have presented glimpses of actual Islamic societies as portrayed by history.[283]

In Qutb's view, 'It is not sufficient that Islam once lived in the past and created a complete, soundly structured society in the age of the Prophet and the early caliphs.'[284] Here Qutb indicates that the reality of the existence of Islam and its societies left its characters on the pages of the history of humankind. Thus, when Qutb says that Islam is no longer existing, he means that Islam is no longer existing as a system that governs the affairs of society.

In the sixth edition of *Social Justice*, which was the last edition published in 1964, two years before his death, Qutb's view of the claim that Islam is no longer existing shifted and was expressed in a harsher and more challenging tone. He says,

> We call for a restoration of Islamic life in an Islamic society governed by the Islamic creed and the Islamic conception as well as by the Islamic *shari'ah* and the Islamic system (*nizam*). We know that Islamic life – in this sense – stopped a long time ago in all parts of the world and that the 'existence' of Islam itself has therefore also stopped. And we state this last fact openly – in spite of the shock, alarm and loss of hope it may cause to many who still like to think of themselves as 'Muslims!'[285]

Here, Qutb clearly and directly connects the existence of Islam with the existence of Islamic society. As the existence of the latter had ceased, the existence of the former had also ceased. Explaining why Islam no longer existed, Qutb pointed out his reasoning based on the authority of the Qur'an and emphasized his awareness of the danger behind his claim that Islam

> cannot exist as a creed in the heart nor as a religion in actual life unless people testify that there is no god but Allah, that is, that there is no *hakimiyyah* (sovereignty) except Allah's *hakimiyyah*, a *hakimiyyah* represented both in his foreordaining and determining of events (*qada' wa qadar*) and in his law (*shar'*) and command. All of these are equally part of the foundation of the creed that can, from the very beginning only exist in the heart through this foundation. Likewise this religion can only exist in actual life as a 'religion' if the creed takes shape in an actual system of life which is 'the religion', so that the *shari'ah* of Allah alone supervises people's lives both in general and in detail. In such a system the ruler does not make and the ruled do not accept any claim to 'divine' right by means of claiming '*hakimiyyah*' and then in fact legislating what Allah does not permit, that is systems, usages, rules and laws which humans adopt for themselves but which are not derived from the *shari'ah* of Allah, either by an authoritative text (*nass*) if one exists, or by *Ijtihad* – within the bounds of the general principles – is a text does not exist [Qur'an, 4: 59] . . .
>
> We do not define the meaning of 'religion' or the concept of 'Islam' in this way on our own authority. In so serious a matter as this, upon which our concept of the religion of Allah depends, as does also the judgment that the 'existence' of Islam has stopped in today's world and the reconsideration of the claim of hundreds of millions of people that they are 'Muslims' – in such a matter it is not permissible for man to pass judgment (*fatwa*), as it is a life-and-death issue both for this world and the next . . .
>
> The One who defines the meaning of 'religion' and the concept of 'Islam' is none other than Allah, the God of this religion and the Lord of Islam. Allah does this in decisive texts which cannot be reinterpreted or misinterpreted [Qur'anic texts] . . . .[286]
>
> All of these [Qur'anic texts] establish one truth. There is no Islam and no faith without confession that *hakimiyyah* belongs to Allah alone, that we must refer to Him on every point of disagreement – where there is no authoritative text (*nass*) – since there is no scope for opinion or debate where there is a text. Judgment must be based on what has been revealed and on nothing else in all the affairs of life, and there must be full acceptance of it in our hearts after we have submitted to it in our actions. This is 'The right religion' and this is the 'Islam' which Allah wants from people . . .
>
> When we examine the whole face of the earth today in the light of this divine definition [referring to the Qur'anic texts] of the concept of religion and Islam, we cannot see that this religion has any 'existence'. This existence stopped when the last group of Muslims ceased to give

> *hakimiyyah* over human life to Allah alone, when they ceased to govern all the affairs of life by His *shari'ah* . . .[287]

This clearly defines what Qutb meant by Islam no longer 'existing'. In his last book *Ma'alim* (1964), two years before his death, Qutb pointed out that 'The Islamic society is not the society which contains people who call themselves "Muslims," who pray and perform *hajj*, but the law of their society is not the Islamic *shari'ah*. The Islamic society is not the society which creates an Islam for themselves, calling it "developed Islam," other than the Islam ordained by Allah . . .'[288]

> Islam cannot rightly execute its rules unless Islam takes shape in a society or *ummah* . . . The Muslim *ummah* has not existed for a long time. The Muslim *ummah* is not the 'land' (*ard*) where Islam once lived. The Muslim *ummah* is not the 'people' (*qawm*) whose ancestors, in an age of the ages, were living in accordance with the Islamic system. The Muslim *ummah*, however, is a group of people whose life and conceptions, systems and values, are all derived from the Islamic program (*manhaj islami*). This *ummah* – with this qualification is not exist since the rule by the *shari'ah* disappeared altogether from the face of the earth.[289]

Thus when Qutb says that Islam does not exist, he means that Islam is no longer existing as a social, legal and economic system in society. In other words, Islam stopped to exist as a system governing the affairs of society, since the *hakimiyyah* of Allah was replaced by the *hakimiyyah* of man.

Concluding remarks

1. Lexical origins of the term *hakimiyyah* suggest that this is 'abstract noun of quality'.
2. Lexical and religious meanings of the term *hakimiyyah* signify the highest legal and governmental authority, clearly defined in several places in the Qur'an (i.e. 67: 1).
3. Translating the term *hakimiyyah* by the political term sovereignty as used in practice without further definitions is not appropriate.
4. Qutb's concept of *hakimiyyah* suggests that Islam is a Religion and State in one.
5. The government in Islam is not theocratic or autocratic or any form, but it is a constitutional government specifically designed to implement Islamic law and administer justice in accordance with its decrees.
6. Government in Islam is constitutional and limited to a constitution that is divinely inspired and that the Muslim community has agreed upon it.
7. In an Islamic system of government, there is a difference between the source of authority, and administration of that authority.

8 The source of governmental authority, in the Islamic state, is not ruling party or all political parties, nor the Muslim community; authority derives from the activity of facilitating the application of Islamic law.
9 The concept of *hakimiyyah* implies that there is difference between the concept of *shari'ah* and that of *fiqh* (jurisprudence).
10 Practising *shari'ah* is the natural outcome of belief in *hakimiyyah*. There is no Islamic life prior to believing that Allah is the only *hakim* (sovereign).
11 In the present-day, the *ummah* does not exist and Islam no longer exists as a political, social, legal or economic system in modern society, but there are individual Muslims.

2 Servitude (*al-'Ubudiyyah*)

Introduction

Similar to *hakimiyyah* (sovereignty) the term *'ubudiyyah* (servitude) is used by Qutb conceptually and intellectually to foster his political discourse. He uses this concept also as an essential principle in articulating his concept of sovereignty. In his analysis, Qutb argues from the Qur'an, emphasizing that the Qur'an lends the concept of *'ubudiyyah* great importance as a basic principle of Islamic creed. He then employs the relation between the two concepts *hakimiyyah* and *'ubudiyyah* in his confrontational theory and uses them both as a means in the distinction between Islamic and *jahili* societies.

Critics claim that *'ubudiyyah* is not a Qur'anic term at all and that what is mentioned in the Qur'an of the term *'ibadah* refers only to ritual duties. This simply means that the concept of the Qur'anic term *'ibadah* is not *'ubudiyyah*. Kepel (1985) supports this view and argues as follows:

> Both terms, *'ubudiyyah* and *hakimiyyah*, are not Qur'anic terms. The former is derived from a root meaning to 'adore' or 'worship', the latter from one meaning 'to govern' or 'to judge' . . . Neither *'ubudiyyah*, nor *hakimiyyah* are Qur'anic terms, a point made against Qutb, by al-Hudaybi the Supreme Guide of Muslim Brotherhood . . . . The Qur'anic term *'ibadah*, for instance, is understood by Muslims today in the light of the time-honored commentaries of the treatises of the Tradition. In this interpretation, it means 'ritual'. This means in Islam the profession of faith, prayer, fasting, the giving of alms, and pilgrimage.[1]

The relevance of this opinion concerning the concept of *hakimiyyah* (sovereignty) and the position of al-Hudaybi and others were detailed in Chapter 1. The present chapter investigates the grammatical, lexicographical, political and religious specifics of the term *'ubudiyyah* (servitude) so as to explain its conceptual and intellectual relationship to the concept of *hakimiyyah* (sovereignty), demonstrate the ideological value of this relation, explore the force and intent of these concepts and their impact on political establishments with special attention to the confrontational theory of *jahiliyyah*.

Lexical origin of the term *'ubudiyyah*

The Arabic term *'ubudiyyah* is derived from the Arabic root (*'a.b.d*). The substantive is *'abd*; its plural, *'ibad* and *'abid*; the *nomen agentis*, *'abid; the nomen patientis*, *ma'bud*; and the infinitives are *'ibadah*, *'ubudah*, *'abdiyyah*, and *'ubudiyyah*.[2] According to the second Caliph Umar Ibn al-Khattab's narration concerning redemption the literal meaning of the word *'abd* is human being (*insan*), and all human beings are *'ibad* or *'abid*.[3] The Arabic grammarian Sibawayh (d. 180/799) pointed out that the word *'abd* (*insan*: human being) is not a noun but 'an adjective used as a noun denoting submission and obedience to someone other than oneself, and that this action of submission is *'ibadah*, *'ubudiyyah* and *'abdiyyah*'.[4] The term *'ubudiyyah* then means 'acknowledging someone other than oneself as holding authority; of abdicating one's freedom and independence in their favour; of relinquishing any resistance to or disobedience of them; of surrendering oneself totally to their authority'.[5]

This physical and mental state of submission and obedience means, according to the Muslim lexicographer Ibn Manzur (d. 711/1325), ''*ibadah* (service), *'ubudah* (servitude), and *'ubudiyyah* (servitude), or *'abdiyyah* (servitude)'.[6] Earlier, al-Razi (d. 666/1280) has shown that ''*ibadah* is *'ubudah* and *'ubudiyyah* or *'abdiyyah*' and that the literal meaning of *'ibadah* is 'obedience (*ta'ah*) with complete submission (*khudu'*).'[7] Likewise, in his book *al-'Ubudiyyah*, Ibn Taymiyyah (d. 728/1342) points out that the ''*ibadah* is *'ubudiyyah*, and that the true nature of *'ibadah* is *'ubudah* and *'ubudiyyah*'.[8]

Furthermore, the condition of the *'ubudiyyah* (servitude) that distinguishes Islam from *jahiliyyah* reveals that the Qur'anic conception of the term *'ibadah* (service/worship) abolished all forms of *'ubudiyyah* (servitude) among human beings themselves. The concept of *'ibadah* (service/worship) in the Qur'an is declared in such a way that all human beings are servants (*'abid* or *'ibad*) and their *'ubudiyyah* (servitude) must be conferred only upon Allah.[9] According to the book *Preachers not Judges* which is attributed to al-Hudaybi 'the meaning of the word *'ibadah* is complete submission and obedience'.[10] This complete submission and obedience will include submission and obedience to God's order, laws and codes in general and in details. Accordingly, if al-Hudaybi, the Supreme Guide of Muslim Brotherhood, was the author of *Preachers not Judges*, then he did not confine the specifics of *'ibadah* to rituals or rites (i.e. prayers, fasting etc.) as Kepel seems to suggest.

Similar to al-Hudaybi and those earlier and contemporary scholars, Qutb argues that the Qur'anic term *'ibadah* means complete submission to God's order. This is the key point of Qutb's political discourse with its unique character of linking all his constructs to promote his theory of society, his confrontational theory and fostering his concept of sovereignty. In his commentary on *surah* 12 verse 40 where the term *hukm* (to govern and to judge) and *'ibadah* (worship) occur together with the concept of *jahiliyyah*, Qutb emphasizes the given term *'ibadah* (worship) as *'ubudiyyah* (servitude), that is complete submission to Allah alone. Qutb then draws on the chronological aspect of this verse to support his point. He states that

> The triliteral perfect (*'abada*), means to submit, to obey, to surrender and to be subject to someone other than yourself. This is the very meaning used by the early Muslims precisely when this verse was revealed. At that time, there was nothing yet revealed of the rites (*sha'a'ir*: spiritual duties/service). Therefore, the Muslims understood *'ibadah* as complete submission to Allah and obedience to His order in everything in general and in detail whether the order was rites, behaviour, or laws.[11]

This brief etymological history suggests that the term *'ibadah* is not confined to 'adore' or worship such as prayer, *zakat*, fasting and other ritual duties. The context of the Qur'anic verse 12: 40, shows the intellectual and the conceptual relationships between the concept of *hakimiyyah* (sovereignty) and the concept of *'ubudiyyah* (servitude); and it emphasizes the link between these two concepts and the concept of *jahiliyyah*. Therefore, Qutb expresses the relation between these three concepts ideologically. This ideological value was expressed by al-Qurtubi (d. 671/1285) and Ibn Kathir (d. 747/1361). The link between these conceptions (*'ubudiyyah*, *hakimiyyah* and *jahiliyyah*) in the Qur'anic verse (12: 40) was explained by Ibn Kathir as follows: 'This verse is a declaration that (i) the *'ubudiyyah* of all humanity is due to Allah; and (ii) Allah is the highest governmental and legal authority; and (iii) other than this declared order is *jahiliyyah*.'[12]

To Qutb, the Qur'an emphasizes *'ubudiyyah* as the purpose of existence. Qutb bases this on a verse in which God says 'I only created humankind and the jinn that they might worship (*ya'budun*) Me.'[13] According to al-Qurtubi, Ibn Taymiyyah, Ibn Kathir, and al-'Asqalani (d. 852/1465), in this verse, the term *'ibadah* is covered by the word *al-'ubudiyyah*. This is 'the task of all the prophets, and [it was] for the purpose of *'ubudiyyah* that all the Prophets worked'.[14] In the Qur'anic verse 16: 36 God says 'We raised an apostle in every nation, saying, "Serve (*'u'budu*) Allah and avoid the *Taghut*..."' Here the concept of *'ibadah* appears to be antithesis of the concept of the term *taghut*.

This term *taghut* is repeatedly used by Qutb in his analysis. The referent of the word *taghut* elucidates Qutb's concept of *'ibadah* and *'ubudiyyah* in his analysis of *jahiliyyah*. According to Qutb,

> *taghut* is a symbolic representation that denotes all tyrannical and oppressive forces that oppress consciousness, feelings and awareness, perception, comprehension and knowledge. The *taghut* is any form that oppresses the right (*haqq*) and transgresses the framework laid down by God for His servants. *Taghut* is a form that has no criterion or standard of belief in Allah and His *shari'ah* and program (*manhaj*). Any system or program based on, or derived from, other than the principles of *shari'ah* is *taghut*. Any conception, ideas, literature (*finun*: arts), philosophy derived not from the principle of *shari'ah* is *taghut*.[15]

According to al-Qurtubi '*taghut* is a noun that derives from oppression and transgression'.[16]

This implies that the concept of the term '*taghut*' and that of the term '*'ibadah*', mentioned in the previous verse 16: 36, are opposite each other. The concept of *'ibadah* is not limited to ritual duties such as prayer and fasting but complete submission and obedience to the ordained order of *hakimiyyah* in all aspects of life. The Qur'an (17: 23) does not confine *'ibadah* to worship. In (39: 12–14, 64) the term *'ibadah* is antithesis of *jahiliyyah*.[17] In (109: 1–5) the term *'ibadah* is antithesis of unbelief.[18]

In view of the grammatical, lexical and Qur'anic injunctions, the term *'ubudiyyah* is like the term *'ibadah*. Both are infinitives (*masdar*), that is derived from the same root and from the same basic form of the triliteral verb *'abada*.[19] Also, the term *'ubudiyyah* is a synonym of the Qur'anic term *'ibadah* and means complete submission and obedience to Allah the sovereign of all sovereignty. Complete submission and obedience to Allah means to submit to Him and obey His *hakimiyyah* (sovereignty).

As appeared earlier, the term *'ibadah* in the Qur'an has a general or comprehensive meaning. Every act of human conduct with the purpose of winning the approval of Allah and for the benefit of humanity comes under the purview of *'ibadah*. The true nature of *'ibadah* is but *'ubudiyyah*.[20] The Qur'an says: 'Praise be to Allah, Lord of the Universe, The Compassionate, the Merciful, Sovereign of the Day of Judgement! You alone we worship (*na'bud*), and to you alone we turn for help...' (Qur'an, 1: 1–5). Here, the word *'ibadah* is not confined to prayer or *zakat*, but 'submission and obedience in general and in details. It is a testimony of Lordship (*rububiyyah*)'.[21] Elsewhere, the Qur'an, says 'I created the jinn and mankind only that they might worship (*ya'budun*) Me...' (Qur'an, 51: 56), Here, the word '*ya'budun*' means submission and obedience.[22] Thus, the Qur'an does not confine the concept of *'ibadah* to ritual duties.

Critics could argue that the term *'ibadah* in the Qur'an has a general meaning, but in the 'tradition' it came to be restricted to ritual, so the synonym *'ubudiyyah* is used by Qutb to convey the more general idea. This argument is important as it implies two points; (i) that there is contradiction between the Qur'an and in the tradition on the general concept of *'ibadah*; and (ii) that there is difference between the concept of *'ibadah* in the tradition and in the modern use of the term. Dealing with this argument, there are two points that should also be remembered.

The first is that the true nature of the Qur'anic term *'ibadah* is *'ubudah*, *'ubudiyyah*, and *'abdiyyah*, as discussed earlier. In other words, the word *'ibadah* (worship) refers to various types and forms of *'ibadah*. In this sense, prayer, charity, *zakat*, work, submission to God's law and order, all are *'ibadah*. Because, the true nature of *'ibadah* is *'ubudiyyah* (servitude), the word *'ubudiyyah*, then, refers to the true nature of *'ibadah* of all types and forms or in one word *'ibadat* (plural) in all spheres of human life. Thus the word *'ubudiyyah* is used by Muslims to refer to the nature of *'ibadah*, not to convey the more general meaning of *'ibadah* or to limit it to rituals as such.

The second point in the argument, implies the importance of the definition of the word 'tradition'. What is meant by 'tradition'? Dealing with this matter also implies three further points:

(i) If the 'tradition', specifically, meant hadith, the hadith of the Prophet should not contradict the general meaning of the term *'ibadah* in the Qur'an.[23] Since, 'both the Qur'an and the hadith of the Prophet are inspiration (*wahy*), the hadith is in line with the Qur'an'.[24] The Qur'an (53: 2–4) says to the Muslims that 'Your Companion [refers to Muhammad] is neither astray nor being misled, nor does he say (ought) of (his own) desire. It is no less than Inspiration sent to him.' Thus there is no contradiction between the Qur'an and tradition, if the tradition meant to be the hadith of the Prophet. In one authority attributed to the Prophet, the Prophet says, 'After me, if there is difference between you [Muslims] about what you have received from me [i.e. hadith], consult it with the Qur'an. What was in harmony with the Qur'an take it as authority, but what is in conflict with the Qur'an disregard it, as it was not from me.'[25] According to Shaykh Muhammad Abu Shuhbah, 'Any hadith that contradicts the general meaning of the Qur'an is a fabricated hadith (*hadith mawdu'*). This type of hadith was not considered as authority.'[26] Similarly, Muhammd 'Abduh, the Rector of al-Azhar (d. 1905), called on to reject any hadith contradict the general meaning of the Qur'an. He also says that 'The characteristics of the fabricated hadith (*hadith mawdu'*) is its conflict with the general meaning of the Qur'an.'[27] Similar words were repeated by Shaykh Muhammad al-Ghazali. He says, 'Among the signs of a fabricated hadith text (*matn*), is its conflict with the Qur'an.'[28] He concludes that 'The hadith of the Prophet is explanation of the Qur'an. It is impossible (*mustahil*) that the hadith can contradict the Qur'an in any status.'[29] The point then is that if the word 'tradition' means 'hadith', there is no contradiction between the Qur'an and hadith of the Prophet on the concept of *'ibadah*. In other words, because the Qur'an does not restrict its word *'ibadah* to ritual, the hadith also does not, and should not, restrict the word *'ibadah* to ritual. If there is contradiction between the Qur'an and hadith, then, the Qur'an is the authority.

(ii) If 'tradition' meant *fiqh* (jurisprudence), the jurists themselves did not confine the term *'ibadah* to rituals or contradicted the Qur'an by claiming that the concept of the term *'ibadah* was only ritual duties such as prayer and *zakat*.[30] The matter, for the jurists, is only one of classification. The jurists classified their rulings, which were also based on the Qur'an and hadith, into two major branches: *'ibadat* (worship) and *mu'amalat* (i.e. transactions, social and economic relations and dealings between people). Under the category of *'ibadat* came prayer, *zakat* and other ritual duties. As time passed, *fiqh* (jurisprudence), with its classification and rulings, came to be regarded as divine law and continued to acquire in the public mind a kind of divine authority, up to the present.

(iii) If 'tradition' is used in a general sense, not *fiqh* or hadith, the discussion in the previous pages illustrated that other than the Qur'an and the authentic hadith is but human opinion about the Qur'an and hadith. For intellectuals and in particular, specialists, the term *'ibadah* is comprehensive and means *'ubudiyyah*. In other words, according to Wajdi, 'The act of *'ibadah* itself is but *'ubudiyyah*'.[31] This nature of *'ibadah* was further illustrated by *Imam* and Jurist Ibn Taymiyyah in his book *al-'Ubudiyyah*.[32] The point is that the Qur'an does not restrict *'ibadah* to ritual. The tradition, whether it meant to be *'hadith'*, *'fiqh'*, or something else, should not contradict the Qur'an. In this regard, Qutb says:

> The division of human actions into *''ibadat'* (worship) and *'mu'amalat'* (transactions; social relations, dealings between people), which we find in the books of *fiqh* (jurisprudence), was introduced in the beginning merely for technical reasons in order to present different topics in a systematic manner. Unfortunately, with the passage of time, this produced the erroneous impression in people's minds that the term *''ibadah'* (worship) applies only to those actions that are included under the title *'fiqh al-'ibadat'* (jurisprudence of worship). The application of the term *''ibadah'* to 'transactions' gradually faded in their thought. Undoubtedly this was a grave distortion of the Islamic concept, which eventually resulted in producing deviations in the Muslim society...
>
> In the Islamic concept there is not a single human act to which the term *''ibadah'* is not applicable or its property is not desired. Indeed, the ultimate aim of the Islamic program (*manhaj*) is the realization of the meaning of *'ibadah* from the beginning to the end.... If we refer to the Qur'an concerning the acts that [Muslim] scholars have called *''ibadat'* we find that such acts are not discussed separately from the other that they have termed *'mu'amalat'*. Indeed, both kinds of activities are intimately connected in the text of the Qur'an, as both form parts of the *''ibadah'* that is the purposes of human life, *'ibadah* signifying total submission and obedience (*'ubudiyyah*) to Allah alone and the ascription of Divinity (*'uluhiyyah*) to Him alone...[33]

The other point that should be noted here is also that Muslims, usually, use *'ubudiyyah* in both positive and negative connotations: positive, when the term *'ubudiyyah* means submission to Allah alone, negative, when the term *'ubudiyyah* applies to submission to anybody or anything other than Allah. Qutb used the term *'ubudiyyah* in a both negative and positive sense.[34] To Ahmad Lutfi al-Sayyid, the *'ubudiyyah* to the government is paganism.[35] Similarly, Tawfiq al-Hakim used the word *'ubudiyyah* in its negative connotation as follows: 'In fact, our economic and financial problems is the product of our "political system" (*nizamuna al-siyasi*) and this "parliamentarian handcraft" (*al-hirfah al-barlamaniyyah*) which accommodates the *'ubudiyyah* and despotism (*istibdad*).'[36] According to 'Abduh, 'the *tawhid* freed man from the *'ubudiyyah* to anything except to Allah alone'.[37]

Socio-political specifics

The discussion now turns to the specifics of *'ubudiyyah* in relation to the whole spectrum of human life. To emphasize sovereignty, Qutb links the concept of *'ubudiyyah* to that of divinity and points to the Qur'an which revealed specifically at Makkah (in early Islam) to support his claim that the case of *'ubudiyyah* holds true for all the Qur'an, whether revealed early in Makkah or later at Madinah where the first Islamic state was established. This is because, in both cities, 'the Qur'an emphasizes the concept of real divinity (*uluyiyyah*), and divine will (*mashi'ah*) and determination (*qadar*); and the ultimate legal and governmental authority (*hakimiyyah*). It emphasized the concept of *'ubudiyyah* and its conditions so people submit themselves only to Allah, believing in His overlordship and His sovereignty'.[38]

Here, Qutb employed a few, not one, comprehensive concepts as tools to promote his ideological use of the term *'ubudiyyah*. He sees it as a fundamental principle of human responsibility in the development and renewal for their well-being and happiness on earth. In his exposition of verse 51: 56 in which God says 'I only created Mankind and the jinn that they might worship (*ya'budun*) Me', Qutb asserted that

> *'ubudiyyah* is the function that connects both the jinn and humankind with the law of existence. In view of this important fact, the referent of *'ibadah* must be broader than just ritual. This is because the jinn and humans spend their life on other than ritual obligation. Moreover Allah does not ask, on one hand, the people to spend all their life in prayer or fasting and, on the other hand, charging them with various activities encompassing most of their life. This means that the jinn and humankind were charged with duties regarding rituals and other activities. We do not know what were for the jinn but we do know the limits of the activities for humans. We do know this from the Qur'an. In the Qur'an God said to the angels 'I am placing on earth one that shall be my Vicegerent.' The function of the vicegerent implies varying activities concerned with the life on earth.[39]

Qutb's view is simply that true worship (*'ibadah*) is (i) submission (*'ubudiyyah*) to Allah alone in the conscious; and (ii) every action in this life must be physically and mentally fulfilled as an act of worship.[40] This view sees *'ubudiyyah* as having a dual purpose: belief and practice, or theory and practice. Thus in this life (the whole existence) there is no more than worshippers and worshiped: 'One Lord and all to Him are servants. There is divinity (*uluhiyyah*) and servitude (*'ubudiyyah*).[41] This dual purpose exhausts the meaning of *'ubudiyyah*. Hence "work will be ritual duty, rituals will be development on earth, development will be *jihad*, *jihad* will be forbearance and acceptance of God's will and determination. All these are *'ibadah* (worship) and all fulfill the first function for which Allah created humankind.

These all are forms of submission to the general order which manifests in the *'ubudiyyah* of the universe, life and man to Allah alone." '[42]

Qutb interwave the concept of *'ubudiyyah* with that of *hakimiyyah* (sovereignty), liberty, justice and equality and based his argument on the testimony of faith. Here is another cluster or bunch of comprehensive concepts, all of political connotations and those which reflect the character of Qutb's style. To him, when God is recognized as One, the theory and practice of worship will be united and all humankind turn to Him only and give no authority or sovereignty to any other than He so that no human being shall make another lord other than God, and no human being shall have higher status than another, except on the basis of good deeds and piety.[43] In this system, Qutb continues, the ruler does not make rules or claim sovereignty and those ruled do not accept divine right by means of the claim sovereignty nor render what is not permitted by Allah.[44] Qutb concluded his argument, saying that

> The most specific divine quality is *hakimiyyah* (sovereignty), so that those [individual or group] who legislate for the people, represent the Divinity (*uluhiyyah*) and reflect its attributes. In this case, the people [the entire people] are servants (*'abid*) of those individual(s) or the group(s) [legislators] rather than of Allah, and their creed is also the creed of this individual or this group, not the religion of Allah. The People are servant (*'abid*) of the people. However, when Islam recognizes *Shari'ah* as the right of God, it liberates the people from submission to the people, declaring the liberation of humankind ... A human being is not a human being unless he is liberated from the rule of another human, and is equal in this affair with all people before the Lord of all people ... The case of *uluhiyyah* (divinity) and *'ubudiyyah* (servitude) is a case of justice and piety, liberty and equality, and of the liberation of mankind. Therefore, *'ubudiyyah* is a case of belief or unbelief, a case of Islam or *jahiliyyah*.[45] [In Islam], 'there are no capitalist ethics, nor socialist ethics, nor ethics pertaining to a bourgeois society and others pertaining to democratic society. There are only Islamic ethics and *jahili* ethics, Islamic society and *jahili* society.'[46]

In his analysis of Islamic and *jahili* societies, Qutb considers *jahiliyyah* a condition, not a period in time. He notes that 'when we examine the whole face of the earth today, in the light of this definition, we cannot see that Islam really exist at all'.[47] He continues, 'societies have returned to the *jahiliyyah* from which Islam picked them up'.[48] Qutb notes that

> In all societies, the *jahiliyyah* takes varying forms emerged from the belief and conception. It takes the form of belief [creed]; of government; of behaviour; of ethics; and of knowledge. It takes the form of legislative decisions; of values; of standards that governs society and that evaluates

> people, things and events. *Jahiliyyah* takes the form of knowledge in all its aspects and of all basic principles of intellectual, philosophical and artistic activities... the *jahiliyyah* differs in its types and forms, its flags and symbols, its names and descriptions, its allies and adherents, its systems and ideologies...[49]

One might conclude therefore that the necessary and sufficient criterion which determine whether a given society is Muslim or *jahili* society is that society's understanding of *'ubudiyyah*.

Concluding remarks

The term *'ubudiyyah* is used to refer to the nature of *'ibadah* in general. The *'ubudiyyah* means complete submission to the highest authority, both legal and governmental. Qutb restores the full connotations of the term *'ubudiyyah* as he does with the term *hakimiyyah*. Thus the complete submission to Allah and His sovereignty apply to all situations and conditions. To Qutb then there is no *'ubudiyyah* without *hakimiyyah* (sovereignty); the one implies the other. Both have universal implications while being fully integrated and logically derived from the Islamic system.

3 Universality of Islam

Introduction

The notion of universality combines comprehensiveness and applicability. With regard to Islam, universality is based on the nature of the relationship between the Creator and His creation, the universe, life and all humanity. Qutb emphasizes the universality of Islam as a characteristic of the Islamic system ordained by *hakimiyyah* (sovereignty), the ultimate legal and governmental authority of the universe, life and humanity. He uses the universality of Islam as a conceptual tool in developing his theory of society.

This chapter investigates Qutb's ideas concerning the political particulars of Islam. It will elucidate and recapitulate the relationship of the concept of *hakimiyyah* (sovereignty) and *'ubudiyyah* (servitude). This is followed by an examination of the ideological significance of the universality of Islam in Qutb's analysis of Islamic and *jahili* societies.

In Qutb's view, the concept of universality has legal implications for the confession of faith. Thus, the political implications involve Man's material and spiritual forces and relate to Qutb's ideas regarding sociopolitical interaction (as one global community), the nature of systems (one overarching system), laws (one ultimate law) and religions (one comprehensive religion). The ideological function of the claim to universality by Qutb should be noted. Universality is attributed to the concepts of *uluhiyyah* (divinity), *'ubudiyyah* (servitude) and *hakimiyyah* (sovereignty). This highlights potential freedom, justice and equality for Muslims and non-Muslims alike. It renders an Islamic state available to all. As will be argued, the potential impact of the universality of Islam on the New World Order and Western domination is highly significant.

Etymological aspects

The Arabic word 'Islam' is derived from the Arabic root (*s.l.m.*), pronounced *silm* or *salm*. According to the Muslim etymologist Ibn Manzur, it means physical and mental peace, peace of body and mind.[1] Similarly, Hans Wehr (1971) describes it as 'entering into a state of *silm*, *salm*, or *salam* that signifies physical and mental peace'.[2] The verb *sallama* and *aslama* means 'to surrender, to obey, to submit and to yield'.[3] According to Ibn Kathir, the Arabic expression '*aslama amruhu li-Allah*' means 'he surrendered and completely submitted his whole-self to Allah'.[4] In this expression, the perfect verb '*aslama*' alone means he surrendered his cause to God's order and became a Muslim.[5] Thus, 'Islam' signifies that the nature of the relationship between the Creator and the creation, the universe, life, and humankind is but a complete submission and obedience to the order of the *hakimiyyah* (sovereignty of all sovereigns). The condition of complete submission and obedience to the law implies peace (*salam*) on all levels between individuals and groups: 'peace of conscience, peace at home, peace in society and the world'.[6]

Socio-political specifics

In Qutb's view, Islam projects unity onto all forces in the universe. It is inescapably the religion of *tawhid* (oneness, unity). Islam recognizes the unity of God, the unity of all religions in the religion of God, and the unity of the source of the law that governs the world. Islam recognizes the unity of the messengers in preaching this religion of oneness, and the unity of all humankind in their origin and in their destiny.[7] Qutb explains that the unity emphasized in Islam is a unity that encompasses all elements from a single particle to the most advanced form of sophisticated life. It is the unity of the motion of all existence: the universe, life and humanity. These varying worlds follow their eternal law. It is the law of *hakimiyyah* (sovereignty). Human souls, for instance, are a world that follows the law of *hakimiyyah*, while they respond to their natural inclinations to acquire knowledge and implement justice. There is unity among all these human energies whether they represent the physical striving for necessities or the spiritual craving for elation. There is unity among all living beings, all generations and everything encompassed by existence.[8]

To Qutb, all living things on the earth constitute one big family; that which had the same origin is interrelated with all inanimate things and that the universe, life, and the position of man therein all are not of an accidental occurrence. The universe and its laws, according to Qutb, have been so preconceived and designed as to allow life to emerge, to provide the living beings with their needs and to allow continuity through renewal.[9] All beings have been collected into groups to form communities. The Creator has given each community a specific character, system and a specific programme for life. All communities are living according to the programme ordained by the Creator. In verse 6: 38, the Qur'an states that 'there is not an animal [that lives] on the earth, nor a being that flies on its wings, but [form part of] communities like you'.[10]

Humanity is one of these living communities, and that human, though the highest form of all beings on the earth, is made of the same basic substance that comprises the most primitive life forms. All human beings are equally related to the same origin. Those differences in colour and language, as Qutb asserts, are some of the prejudices that human communities use against each other, but this difference is not a reason for dispute and clashes among themselves. These differences, as in Qutb's analyses of the Qur'anic verses 30: 8–32, are seen by Islam as a manifestation of God's will.[11] The Qur'an says: 'And of His signs is the creation of the heavens and earth and the variety of your tongues and lives. Surely in that are signs for all living beings.'[12] Therefore, Qutb emphasizes that these very differences should be a reason for clashes but rather for mutual acquaintance and cooperation among all humankind. Islam strongly repudiates segregation and apartheid.[13]

Qutb argues that God gave human society one faith. This is Islam the self-sufficient orbit of culture, the spiritual attitude of mind and the social system of clearly defined features. It incorporates the faith of all prophets and messengers of God. The Qur'an (42: 13) says: 'He [God] has ordained for you the faith which He enjoined on Noah and which We have revealed to you, and which We enjoined on Ibrahim, Moses and Jesus, (saying): "Observe this faith and be not divided therein." '[14]

The Qur'an addresses itself, on the whole, to the totality of humankind and emphasizes the universality of Islam as a basic principle of the Qur'anic message.[15] The Qur'an points to the universality of Islam, contrasting it with the local and limited nature of other historical religions.[16] The Qur'an also charges believers of the other religions to follow God's order ordained in the Qur'an and the Sunnah.[17]

It follows that Islam is not a temporal system limited by historicity. Nor is it merely a system for a certain generation or a particular environment and with only local appeal.[18] Islam has a mandate to order the life of humanity through a programme that expounds the nature of the universe and determines the position of man and his ultimate objectives therein.[19] To Qutb, Islam is not a religion in the common, distorted meaning of the word that confines it to the private life of man. It is a complete way of life that 'provides a systematic guidance for all spheres of human life; private and social, material and moral, economic and political, legal and cultural, national and international'.[20]

Universality of Islam, to Qutb, therefore, means universality of *uluhiyyah* (divinity), of *'ubudiyyah* (servitude) and universality of *hakimiyyah* (sovereignty). These concepts are interdependent, comprehensive and universal in their applications, and reflect *jahiliyyah* in a universal sense. According to Qutb, Allah is not the God only of the Arabs, nor is He the God only of the Muslims. He is the God not only of the Heavens, nor is He the God only of the earth. Allah is the God of all: 'the Arabs and non-Arabs, the Muslims and non-Muslims, the East and the West, the Heavens and the earth.'[21] Allah is the essence of existence. Nothing in creation happens except through God's will. His knowledge encompasses the whole universe. He is the Creator and Sustainer of the universe, the heaves and the earth and everything therein.[22] This reveals that the key to understanding Qutb's concept of the universality of Islam rests in the integrated conceptions of *uluhiyyah* (divinity), *'ubudiyyah* (servitude) and *hakimiyyah* (sovereignty). The intellectual and conceptual relationship of this interdependent and comprehensive *trio* implies the concept of *tawhid*, the bedrock of Islam.

Tawhid can be simply defined as the wholehearted conviction and declaration that 'there is no god but Allah'.[23] This brief statement carries within itself the richest and most profound meaning in the entire creation. The *tawhid* or the testimony that there is no god but Allah, means that the *uluhiyyah* (divinity) belongs exclusively to Allah, while creatureliness is common to everyone and everything else. Since Allah is the only Divine Being, it follows that His *hakimiyyah* (sovereignty) and all the Divine attributes belong to Him alone. And, since everyone and everything else is Allah's creation, it follows that they are all devoid of Divine attributes, as they are all *'abid* (slaves) or servants before Him.[24]

The Islamic concept of *tawhid* entails the distinction between *uluhiyyah* (divinity) and *'ubudiyyah* (servitude). There is one Sovereign Creator and there are creations. Thus God's sole *uluhiyyah* (divinity) necessarily entails His sole *hakimiyyah* (sovereignty).[25] According to Qutb,

> The consequence of *tawhid* is that Allah is the Lord and Sovereign of humans not merely in their beliefs, concepts, conscience, and rituals of worship, but in their practical affairs. The Muslim believes that there is no god except Allah, that no one is worthy of *'ibadah* (submission and obedience) except Allah, that no one is Creator or Sustainer except Allah, that no one can do benefit or harm except Allah, and that no one except Allah is in charge of the universe or even of one's own affairs. Accordingly, the Muslim worships Him alone, and turns to Him alone with hope and fear and with the sincerity of his heart. In the same way, the Muslim believes that there is no true *hakim* (ruler) above him except Allah, no legislator for him except Allah, no one except Allah to inform him concerning his relationships and connections with the universe, with other living creatures, and with his fellow human beings.[26]

The relationship between *uluhiyyah* (divinity), *hakimiyyah* (sovereignty) and *'ubudiyyah* (servitude) emanates from the concept of *tawhid*, the cornerstone of Islamic faith. Indeed, this is hardly surprising in that 'the *tawhid* is a belief ingrained in our being, the ultimate explanation of human existence and a way of life in itself'.[27] From this standpoint, this basic creed can be said to have embraced in the clearest and lucid terms the principal ideas of the Islamic system. From the brevity of this basic creed, Qutb says, branch out all the doctrines and systems, knowledge and teachings, learning and understanding, culture and wisdom, and actions and intentions of the religion of Islam.[28]

In this context, the reality that Qutb emphasized (the reality of the Creator and that of the creation) is of two generic origins. The first is that there is only One Eternal ultimate Sovereign: Allah remains infinitely unique without partner or associates. The second is the creation, the universe, life and humankind. The ontology of duality separates and distinguishes the two basic orders of the Creator and the creation. These two orders are utterly and absolutely disparate, and it is impossible to unite, infuse, or confuse one with the other. There is also no possible transformation of the nature of each order. The Creator infinitely remains the dominating absolute Sovereign; and the creations will always be His servants and subject to transient, ephemeral existence.[29]

This relationship between the Creator and the creation is basically intelligent and ideational in its essence. Everything in the universe is created voluntarily and with a purpose. The whole universe is unified and issues from one Will. Since human beings are part of the universe that cooperates and acts in harmony with other parts, there must be cooperation and harmony among all human beings. Therefore, argues Qutb, the Islamic conception 'makes humanity a unity whose parts separate in order to come together, who differ in order to harmonize, who hold various opinions so that they finally cooperate with each other'.[30]

In this existence, a human being is a unit and can never cease to be a well-planned unit in the perfect balanced harmonious sequence of the infinite universe. The internecine warfares that have gone on between individuals, groups, communities, nations, and sects appear to stem from Man's inveterate desire to uphold not what is right, but merely to decide who is right.[31] Division and schism that disrupt the universal peace are the result of Man's attempt to disregard the fact of his own constitution. The universality of Islam blocked all avenues that could lead to schisms or develop the spirit of partisanship and racial pride.[32] It could be argued that this is not historically true. This argument can be supported by the dispute and the civil war between 'Ali and Mu'awiyah in the early period of Islam. Of this, Qutb in 1960 says,

> At first sight, this argument appears to be valid. Many writers have attempted to implement this idea in people's minds, to persuade them that the path of Islam is impractical and unrealistic . . . They have found, in the disorders that began with murder of Uthman, the subsequent conflict between 'Ali and Mu'awiyah and related events, a fertile ground for attempting to prove their vile contention, sometimes by implication and sometimes explicitly, as circumstances dictate. They are unintentionally helped in this aim by those sincere believers who are disturbed by the fact that these events should have interrupted the rise of Islam in that glorious period of history. There involved too a deviation from the concept of government that prevailed in the time of the Prophet and his first two successors. Similarly the conduct of some leaders of the community thereafter deviated from Islamic norms.[33]

This means that unity is the rule while division and schism are not. Division and schism are not the natural situation foreseen by Islam.

According to Qutb's writings in 1960, 'Islam is a realistic system, and it therefore supposes that the people who live according to its path will be living in an Islamically governed society.'[34] Deviation from the Islamic order will bring about division or schism. In the first edition of *Social Justice* (1949), Qutb says, 'With the coming of Mu'awiyah the caliphate in Islam became a monarchy, or a tyranny, confined to the Umayyad family. This was characteristic, not of Islam, but of the *jahiliyyah*...'[35] This statement appeared in the last edition of *Social Justice* (1964): 'When the Umayyads came, and the Islamic caliphate became a kingdom based on force in the line of the Umayyad clan, that was inspired not by Islam but by the *jahiliyyah*...'[36]

This means that division, schism, and conflicts are not the rule. In 1951, Qutb states,

> Peace is the rule in Islam...and emerges as the preamble to the principle of harmony. Peace means harmony in the universe, the laws of life and the origin of man, while war is the result of violations of harmony, such as injustice, despotism and corruption.[37]

Divisions among human community are clearly disparaged by Islam in the declaration that all people come from Adam and Adam was made from dust. Satan is exhibited as an accursed one precisely because he argues, for the superiority of his high origin as contrasted from what he believes is the lowly origin of Man. Satan says of himself 'he was created of fire but Man was created of dust'.[38] The exclusivism exemplifies the human desire to claim superiority of high birth and is denounced by the Qur'an in unmistakable terms. Indeed of all creeds, Islam alone has successfully devalued the importance of race, colour, language and privilege in general. It has admonished its followers not to put human beings into categories or groups on racial, ethnic or geographical contiguity or any particular privilege that they might claim for themselves. Islam exalted only the *muttaqi*, that is, those who fear God, completely submit themselves to Him and surrender to His law. This sort of *'ubudiyyah* is the only legitimate means of differentiating between individuals of the human race. All other trimmings and personal trappings of individuality are incidental and ultimately meaningless.[39]

This form of total submission reveals that the core ideas in universality with regard to Islam are freedom, justice and equality. The just society in Islam means, according to Qutb, the society that secures and maintains respect for persons through various sociopolitical arrangements that are in the common interests of all members. A man, as viceregent of Allah on the earth, must be treated as an end in himself and never merely as a means. This cannot be found in system other than the Islamic system which 'widely opens its society for all people irrespective of their race, colour, or language, and irrespective of religion or creed'.[40] This logic, specifically about the freedom of non-Muslims in the Qutbian state, has been detailed in a separate article[41] and will also be discussed in some details in Chapter 4,[42] but it is sufficient here to note that this logic of the 1950s was repeated in his last book *Ma'alim* (1964) as follows:

> Since that day [when Islam came] the homeland (*watan*) of Muslim is not the land, but the homeland of Islam. It is the land that is dominated by the Islamic creed and governed only by the Islamic law... It is the homeland for everyone whose faith is Islam and accepts its law as his way of life. It is also for everyone who accepts to live there – even if they are not Muslims, such as those non-Muslim others who are living in the homeland of Islam.[43]

In *Zilal*, Qutb views the Qur'anic verse 24: 32 as one of the Islamic milestones in the journey to liberty, which establishes a just order between all humanity, Muslims and non-Muslims, black and white.[44] This universality does not mean and never meant to force others to embrace Islam, or discriminate against others because of their belief, colour, language or other privileges but means universal justice and equality among all humankind.[45]

In the Islamic State, according to Qutb, the *hakimiyyah* grants the non-Muslims complete political and religious freedom and protection to practise their religious duties. The sensitive concern of *hakimiyyah* for the freedom of non-Muslims rests also in the difference between *jizyah*[46] and *zakat*.[47] Islam imposes tax (*zakat*) and *jihad* only on the Muslim and takes from the non-Muslim only an annual tax (*jizyah*). This is utilized with the tax (*zakat*) paid by the Muslim for general defence and administration. Non-Muslims share with Muslims the protection provided by the state and thus must share in its expense.[48]

Islam does not impose *zakat* or *jihad* on the non-Muslim. To Qutb, *zakat* and *jihad* are a form of worship specifically for the Muslims. Therefore, Islam does not want to compel the non-Muslims to perform a specifically Muslim act of worship.[49] To this extent the sensitivity of *hakimiyyah* to the universal justice extends throughout the human family. Islam excludes the non-Muslim female from paying tax (*jizyah*). In the case of males (non-Muslim), Islam excludes from paying *jizyah*, children under age, the aged, the poor and those with all forms of illness or disabilities. All other non-Muslim men, eligible for *jizyah* will be only those who are physically qualified for military service. However payment of *jizyah* will exonerate them from military service and from fighting in the cause of Islam or on behalf of an Islamic State. Other than that, according to Qutb, Muslims and non-Muslims are equal before the law in every aspect. An Islamic state should grant financial support and benefit for the needy of the non-Muslims, Qutb concludes.[50]

Islam imposes on the Muslims of both genders of any age taxes other than *zakat*. These, for example, are *'ushr*,[51] *sadaqat* (charity) and other financial dues such as *zakat al-fitr* (a form of tax that must be paid during the month of *Ramadan*). In addition, Muslim men will still be required to take up military service and charged with *jihad* as necessary for the protection of all citizens, Muslims and non-Muslims.[52]

In summary, the rights that are guaranteed by the *hakimiyyah* to the non-Muslims are '(i) protection from all external threats. (ii) Protection from persecution, assault or violence or unlawful detention by any hostile party operating within national boundaries.'[53]

These rights are of an irrevocable nature. They derive from the Muslim's religious duty to protect life, property and honour of the non-Muslims since this action forms part of faith and an act of worship in itself. The distinction between 'Muslim' and 'non-Muslim' thus remains one of political administration and not of human rights. In granting non-Muslims freedom in this way, Islam, according to Qutb, is influenced by its broad universal spirit indicating that the non-Muslims are not beyond the reach of the *hakimiyyah*'s jurisdiction. Allah, the Sovereign, the Lawgiver legislates for the human community regulating its life, duties and relationships. The Lawgiver charged all humans to adhere to the law and gave them the faculty of free choice. Those who decide to live by the law of *hakimiyyah* in its entirety are, according to Qutb, the true Muslims. Those who refuse to adhere to the law of *hakimiyyah* in its entirety or subjected themselves partly to it are the *jahiliyyah*.[54]

The universality of Islam also has another dimension which Qutb forsaw: the end of the domination of white rule. This calculation was also made by the English philosopher Bertrand Russell. According to Qutb, 'Russell in 1950 pointed out that "the white man should maintain his domination indefinitely is not in the natural scheme of things".'[55] Despite the difference in their analyses, Qutb and Russell agreed on the fact that infinity is not of the nature of creatures such as people, systems and others.[56]

From his historical position as a social critic in the 1940s, 1950s and 1960s, Qutb emphasizes that the sociopolitical systems of the colonialists are 'exhausted' and has no more pragmatic conceptions to provide the current development with humanitarian ideas and values. Western systems, argues Qutb, became sterile long ago, as long ago as the British 'Magna Carta' in 1215 AD.[57] This Charter legalized the *'ubudiyyah* (servitude: complete submission) of people to people. It guarantees more rights only for aristocrats, not the ordinary people that form the majority of the population of the United Kingdom. The ideas that underlie Magna Carta also inspired American aristocrats to compose the American Constitution.[58]

Similarly, the principles of the French Revolution and the rights of individual freedom, according to Qutb, were hammered out at the beginning of what Westerners call the 'American experiment of democracy'. Despite its values, this was never developed or fully implemented. Democracy flourished during specific intervals and under restricted circumstances. Its values however remain insufficient for a progressive humanity whose needs go far beyond the accumulated achievement of those democratic values as evolved by the European sociopolitical and economic systems.[59] These systems were based on ideas and methods that are repulsive to the nature of life and have no roots attached to the depth of the nature of human beings and their human needs. These systems are temporal and the leadership of the Western systems has come to end. It is now the turn of the Islamic system.[60]

Concluding remarks

To Qutb, the universality of Islam is clearly significant in his analysis of *jahiliyyah*. Its significance rests on his comprehensive treatment of conceptions of the universality of *uluhiyyah* (divinity), *'ubudiyyah* (servitude) and *hakimiyyah* (sovereignty). The universality of Islam is comprehensive because it incorporates all aspects of human life. Doctrinal and ideational construction based on *tawhid* (divine oneness), to which the Qur'an lends greater importance, constitutes an integrated conception of the confessional faith. Through these doctrinal structures and their social ramifications, Qutb emphasizes that Islam is not a temporal system for a specific age or for a particular nation but a universal system that appeals to humankind at all times.

Part II

Philosophical discourse

Introduction

The influence of philosophy on Qutb's ideological position is turned through his notion of *hakimiyyah* (sovereignty), *'ubudiyyah* (servitude) and the universality of Islam as detailed in Chapters 1–3. Employing these interdependent conceptions in his discussion of the theory of society, Qutb focussed on the concept of Sovereignty (*hakimiyyah*) and made it the heart and the mind of not only his political discourse but also his philosophical dialogue.

The task of Chapters 4–6 will then endeavour to explore the position of the concept of sovereignty (*hakimiyyah*) and its political connotations in Qutb's philosophical discourse and how he used this concept to develop his theory of society. These chapters intend to provide an exposition of Qutb's thought regarding *al-fitrah* (the unchangeable constitution that Allah made innate to the universe, life and man); the nature and the role of human intellect (*al-'aql*) in relation to text; the ideological and political significance of the relationship between the universe (*al-kawn*), life and man; and consequently, how Qutb employs these ideas intellectually and conceptually to develop the conceptual framework of the polity (*hakimiyyah*: sovereignty) and overall the role of Islam in the state.

Qutb argues that human beings have lived through many years without even arriving at a comprehensive concept of human nature or the relationships between human beings and the universal powers. With all of these philosophies concerning human life, human beings have failed to arrive, with their own knowledge and authority, at a comprehensive conception that expounds the nature of man and its potentials, the harmonious relationship between the nature of man and his surrounding universe and the purposes of man therein.[1]

The ultimate goal of the Greek philosophers was to remove the misunderstanding and disputes that characterize human affairs. These philosophers, Paul Davies tells us, 'sought a means to formalize human reasoning to establish some sort of common ground for belief. But this goal has never been achieved'.[2] Bertrand Russell who puts philosophy in no man's land between theology and science, pointed out that

> philosophy failed to answer the questions of most interest to speculative minds. Is the world divided into mind and matter, and, if so, what is mind and what is matter? Is mind subject to matter, or is it possessed of independent powers? Has the universe any unity or purpose? Is man what he seems to the astronomers, a tiny lump of impure carbon and water impotently crawling on a small and unimportant planet? Or, is he what he appears to Hamlet? Is he perhaps both at once? Is there a way of living that is noble and another that is base, or are all ways of living merely futile? If there is a way of living that is noble, in what does it consist, and how shall we achieve it? To such questions no definite answer can be found in philosophy.[3]

The factor that most distinguishes human beings from all other beings is human intellect. Rationalism, Qutb asserts, is an outlook that emphasises human reason and the ability to address basic questions, such as the meaning of life, birth and death or the nature of eternity and the place of humanity in the universe (*al-kawn*).[4] Philosophical rationalism seeks to discover the nature of truth and knowledge. Some were concerned with ethics, while others were concerned with the role of the government and relationship of the individual to society.[5] Whoever attempts to address these issues, by means of reasoning alone tends to come to a halt.[6] In the 1770s, rationalism relied on reason rather than on religion in creating a theory of human life and destiny. Voltaire and Thomas Paine were the advocators of this movement.[7] The Age of Reason considers human mind the sole source of learning truth.[8] This has been swept away by Darwinism which saw man as part of the 'animal world' and now in serious danger of following both dinosaur and the dodo to extinction.[9] This was followed by Freud in the nineteenth century. He believed that most of man's thinking processes lay behind a barrier. Man's decisions were often taken there and then surfaced for implementation. In implementing his decisions concerning his material needs such as sex or food, man does not distinguish between his own internal mind and the outside environment. To Freud, for example, the *id* stimulates the sex drive or the need for food. The *id* makes no distinction between a mental image of food and the food itself.[10] In this case, man, like animal, has no sense or such a faculty enabling him to distinguish between lawful and unlawful ways in his response to his own inclination for material needs.

According to Qutb, human beings continue to differentiate between spiritual and material powers, denying the existence of one of these to establish the other. If human beings admit the existence of both, they were presented in a state of opposition and enmity. Man then, Qutb continued, based his sciences on the presumption that there was a basic conflict between the spiritual and material powers, and that the superiority of one depends on belittling the other. Human being held that such superiority on the one hand and inferiority on the other, were inevitable, because he thinks that conflict was inherited in the original nature (*fitrah*) of the universe and humankind.[11] This means that secular thought fails to analyse the *fitrah* and fails to realize the nature of the relationship between humankind and the universal powers.[12] The reason for this failure may be that secular thought rejects beliefs in a higher being as the only source of truth. Second, it separates man's body from his spirit, rejecting the *fitrah* and the metaphysical order of reality. Third, it ignores the transcendent dimension of human nature.

The divergence between religion and secular thought, on the one hand, and misunderstanding and dispute by secularists, on the other, results in a multiplicity of theories about human life. Beliefs and conceptions, ethics and behaviours, decisions and judgements, and systems and laws together feud to tear human life into fragments of contradictory opinion.[13] This fragmentation is characterized by Qutb as totally antithetical to the notion of *al-fitrah* (the unchangeable constitution that Allah made innate to the universe, life and man), *al-kawn* (universe) and *al-'aql* (human intellect). He finally connects secular thought concerning these concepts to a *jahiliyyah* that is similar in its basis of belief and conceptions to the historical *jahiliyyah*.[14]

4 The innate character and moral constitution (*al-Fitrah*)

This chapter investigates the lexical origin of the term *fitrah* and its implications with regard to the relationship between the Creator and His creations, the universe, life and man, explores the conceptual relationship of *fitrah* to sovereignty (*hakimiyyah*), servitude (*'ubudiyyah*) and the universality of Islam, and overall the theory of society. This will be followed by a discussion of the socio-political and religious connotations of the given conceptions and their bearing on the Islamic theory of human nature.

Lexical origins of the term *fitrah*

The word *fitrah* is a Qur'anic term derived from the Arabic root (*f t r*) from which the strong triliteral verb perfect *fatara* and the *nomen agantis fatir* are derived. The root action of '*f t r*' means to create, originate, split, cleave or to slit and crack.[15] Accordingly, a *fatir* is one who enjoys origination (*al-ibtida'*) and creation (*al-khalq*), or one who brings something into being, or causes something to exist for the first time. When Arabs say '*Ana fatartu al-shay*', it means 'I created the thing'. Thus '*fatara*' means he originated or created (it). Likewise '*fatiri al-samawati wa al-ard*' means, 'the Originator/or Creator of the Heavens and the Earth'.[16]

The second use of *fatara* in strong triliteral verb perfect form is *fattara*. The verbal noun of *fattara* is *taftir*,[17] which denotes repetition, quantity and frequency of the action in question. These are also applied to the verb *fatara* and its derivations such as *tafattara*, *infatara* and *infitar*. All these forms are mentioned in the Qur'an. For instance, 'I have set my face, firmly and truly, towards Him Who created (*fatara*) the Heavens and the Earth.'[18] Similarly, '*idha al-sama'u infatarat*, when the Heaven is cleft asunder'[19] '*Takadu al-samawatu yatafattarna minhu*, the Heavens are about to burst'[20] '*Tafattarat qadamahu*, his feet are cleft'. '*tafattarat al-ardu bi al-nabat*, the seeds broke through the ground.' Although, '*futira 'ala shay*' means, he was created with a disposition to a thing'.[21]

The passive form of *fatara* is *futira*. This form is also synonymous with '*tubi'a*' (stamped or impressed upon), '*khutima* and *khatama*' (stamped or sealed), and with '*jubila*' (be ingrained with primordial and unchangeable disposition). These forms clearly signify that the natural constitution of every human soul is part of the essential self of a person and cannot be changed by anyone other than the Creator. This natural constitution is signified by the words *sajiyyah*, *jibillah*, *khaliqah*, *tabi'ah* and *fitrah*. These are also names for the primordial self inherent to every human being and, like the soul, is fixed. Thus, the term *fitrah* literally means originating or creating a thing with an unchangeable natural constitution. In the case of humans, *fitrah* thus signifies fixed or unchangeable natural constitution, the legacy of every created being.[22]

The religious implication of the term *fitrah* concerning humans is clear: every human being is born in a state of *fitrah*, which includes knowing his Creator. In creating humans and endowing them with a certain constitution, Allah distinguished them from other beings on earth. Allah endowed all human beings with a quality, which enables them to know the Creator. Every human being is born in a state of complete submission to the Creator.[23] This meaning is repeatedly affirmed by the Qur'an, for instance 'Set your face in sincerity (*hanif*) to the true faith, the *fitrah* with which Allah has endowed mankind (*fatara al-nasa 'alaiyha*). There is no change in the creation of Allah. This is surely the true religion, although most people do know not.'[24] In referring to this verse, Muslim commentators usually speak of Islam as the religion of the *fitrah* born with every child. The implication here is that all children are born pure, sinless and in a state of complete submission to their Creator. The child will remain on this *fitrah* until he/she attains maturity. If he/she dies prior to attaining physical and mental maturity, the child retains the *fitrah* of complete submission to the Creator. External circumstances may intervene and cause the child to deviate from the *fitrah*. Deviation will express itself in the affairs of his/her daily life. With no outside influence, the child will remain on in the state of *fitrah* and then be able to decide for himself/herself whether to confirm his or her *fitrah* of submission to the Creator or to go astray.[25]

Conceptual differences

The next point, which rests in the concept of *fitrah*, is complex. This is because Qutb's argument is comprehensive and expressed in one of the finest prose styles of Arabic. To Qutb, the concept of *al-fitrah* means something more than human nature.[26] In the secular pattern, there are philosophical theories and opinions concerning 'nature' (*tabi'ah*), the universe and 'human nature'.[27] In the traditional Islamic construct, however, there is only one notion, that is, the *al-fitrah*. It is a comprehensive concept that expounds the nature of the relationship between the Creator and His creation – the universe, life and humanity.[28] The principles of the Islamic conception of *al-fitrah* and other notions such as *al-kawn* (universe) and *al-'aql* (human intellect) all differ from that of secular paradigms.[29] The difference between Islamic and secular patterns rests with the tools that are employed in the exposition of these and other ideas. With this in mind, Qutb prefers to use the Islamic conception instead of philosophy and its dry language.

Explaining the Islamic view of *al-fitrah*, *al-kawn* (universe), *al-'aql* (human intellect) and similar ideas, one should take into account the basic principles of Islamic conception as a safeguard to maintain a clear distinction between what Qutb calls Islam and *jahiliyyah*. Without the safeguard of the Islamic conception, a kind of fusion may occur and that may lead to deviation from the basics of Islamic belief.[30] Islamic concepts are comprehensive and do not separate the nature of the universe from the nature of life or the nature of man. Rather, there ought to be a well-balanced, harmonious and firm relationship between all of them. The use of philosophical language in the discussion of Islamic ideas such as the concept of *al-fitrah* may lead to confusion.[31] According to Qutb

> There exists a genuine disharmony between the methodology of philosophy and the methodology of religious creed (*'aqidah*), between the style of philosophy and the style of the creed, and, in particular, between the great and sublime truths of the Islamic faith and the petty, artificial, and confused efforts that go under the headings of metaphysical philosophy and scholastic theology.[32]

Muhammad Yasien (1996), for instance, interpreted *al-fitrah*, but the methodology of philosophy that he employed led his interpretation away from the basic principles of Islamic faith and belief. He considered *fitrah* to mean human nature, while *fitrah* is more than to be limited within human nature, which is but a miniature in the nature of the infinite universe, the nature of life and the comprehensive nature of the harmonious relationship between man, and the universal powers. Yasien however tried to shape his opinion along Qutb's comprehensive lines. The difference between the two was more complicated, as Yasien employed philosophical language to interpret some points of Qutb's view. Overall, Yasien's analyses lack due attention to the socio-political context. Briefing on Yasien's interpretation, then, is a preferable attempt to highlight Qutb's view that the use of philosophical language in the analysis of Islamic concepts may lead to confusion. Observing Yasien's view will highlight the difference between his use of philosophical language and Qutb's use of Islamic conception in the interpretation of Islamic notions, in general, and *fitrah*, in particular. The concept of *fitrah* is one of the most sensitive areas of Muslim belief. It touches upon the Islamic concept of God's will and determinism; and is concerned with questions such as good and evil; the human, freedom, reason and human will; Sovereignty; the divine rule and judgement.

Yasien uses the concept of *fitrah* as interchangeable with the notion of 'human nature' and concludes that 'humans are innately good and evil'.[33] Yasien drew on the Qur'anic analogy of earthern clay being embodied by the spirit by Allah to support his presupposition. He interpreted this as clay being associated with the innate evil, and the spirit with innate good, 'clay and spirit are equal proportions'.[34] Yasien bases this on the word *sawwa* (upright and perfect balanced tendencies),[35] mentioned in the Qur'an 15: 29 and 91: 7–10, which dealt with human creation. Yasien tried to shape these views of his along Qutb's comprehensive theory and claimed that

> Sayyid Qutb drew on this verse [91: 7–10] to support his dual view [of human nature], but his interpretation of the *ayah* [verse] is questionable because he ignored the significance of the word *sawwa* (moulded) and rendered an inaccurate translation of *alhama* (inspired).[36]

Yasien says Sayyid Qutb incorrectly translated [*alhama*] as to create a disposition, natural disposition or natural preparedness for right and wrong.[37]

However, there are both linguistic and religious reasons to support the view that Qutb did not limit *fitrah* to mean human nature. To Qutb, the *fitrah* encompasses the universe, life and man, and alludes to the nature of the relationship between them as well as between them and their Creator. Also, when Qutb speaks of human nature as part of *fitrah*, he did not associate matter with evil in any Manichalism or gnostic sense, as Yasien does. According to Qutb, there is nothing in the Qur'an and the Sunnah that considers that matter corresponds to or represents innate evil in human nature. Yasien's claim that the human being is an 'admixture of clay with equal proportion of spirit' cannot also be derived for Qutb.[38] The ideas implied by the keywords 'admixture' and 'proportion' are not ideas that Qutb would use, since Qutb considered human nature as 'a nature of a compound (*murakkab*) rather than a mixture (*khalit* or *mazij*)'.[39] Qutb has also defined the word proportion, admixture and others as follows:

> Philosophers and commentators increasingly talk of the creation of heaven and earth. They speak of anteriority (*qablyyah*) and posteriority (*ba'dyyah*). They talk of straightness (*istawa'*) and equal proportion (*taswiyah*). They forgot that the words before (*qabl*) and after (*ba'd*) are human expressions which have their meaning in the context of human actions, not in the context of the sovereign Will. They also forgot that the word straightness (*istawa'*) and the word equal proportion (*taswiyah*) are no more than idioms that approximate to the limited human image of the infinite. Philosophical argument of *kalam* among Muslim scholars about Qur'anic expressions and idioms was an contagion (*afah*) from Greek philosophy . . . Let us not today make the same mistake.[40]

Furthermore, Yasien claims that human nature is made up of 'equal proportions of good and evil' represented by spirit and matter, respectively.[41] Thus, natural tendencies to material or bodily needs are evil. This implies that man's natural desire for food, drink and sex is evil. The claim that 'the good in human nature is only the spirit' implies that monasticism is good and denial of body needs is good. Therefore, human effort for material need or the cultivation of industry and the like, of development and civilization, all are evil.

None of these tally, in general and in details, with Qutb's ideas, which are grounded in the perception of a perfect balance of the material and spiritual in life. For Qutb, there is no separation between religion and human affairs. Qutb's position on the unity between matter and spirit in human nature goes back to 1935 and was first raised in the introduction to a volume of his own poetry.[42] He also expressed his ideas of human nature in a poem written in 1934 and published in this volume of poetry in 1935.[43] There he emphasized that Islam deals with Man as he exists in reality, not with Man as an intellectual concept. In contrast with Idealism, Positivism and similar notions, Islam, according to Qutb's later writings, does not deal with propositions of no practical reality.[44] Islam does not view human beings as spirit only or as matter only. Humans are not pure mind but integrated beings whose faculties are part of a unified, functional whole.[45]

Moreover, Yasien claims that the

> material component of Man shares no part at all in the *fitrah*. *Fitrah*, in its entirety, is vested in man's spirit. Since Allah has breathed His spirit into clay [matter] to generate the spirit of Man, *fitrah* itself must be good, because Allah is good and the source of all good.[46]

This also diverges from Qutb's view, according to whom, Yasien clearly places matter in the subordinate position, much as Plato had.[47] Yasien, therefore, makes the following claims: (a) Allah is the source of spirit only and spirit is *fitrah*. (b) Allah is not the source of matter and matter is not *fitrah*. (c) Allah is the source of the spirit in humanity only, and this is *fitrah*. (d) Allah is not the source of the material constituent of Man, and this is *fitrah*. (e) Unity of matter and spirit as Man is not *fitrah*. (f) Allah is not the source of the material universe, and the universe is therefore not *fitrah*.[48] These claims elucidate and support Qutb's view that the use of philosophical language in the discussion of Islamic concepts may cause confusion.[49]

The use of philosophical language drove Yasien to a position that suggests a lack of understanding the concept of the word 'spirit' (*ruh*) and the lack of a thorough reading of Qutb. His claim appears to be based on Qur'anic verses 15: 28–29 and 38: 72, in which God says to the angels 'When I have perfected him [Man] and breathed into him of My spirit (*ruh*), kneel down and prostrate yourselves before him.' In his analysis, Yasien does not clarify the 'source of all good' when he states

> The material part of man's constitution shares no part at all in the *fitrah*. *Fitrah*, in its entirety, is vested in man's spirit and since Allah has breathed of His spirit into the clay [matter] to generate the spirit of man, *fitrah* itself must be good, because Allah is good and the source of all good.

The very words suggest that 'spirit' is part of Allah. The spirit, Yasien says, 'will return to its origin which is Allah (Qur'an 96: 8)'.[50] This means that the spirit is part of Allah, not His creation. This is another point of the confusion that Yasien could avoid if he said that the spirit will return to its Creator or Originator, instead of saying the spirit 'will return to its origin which is Allah, Qur'an 96: 8'.

The other point that needs to be noted here is his reference (Qur'an, 96: 8). He uses this verse to support his claim that the spirit will 'return to its origin which is Allah'. The verse does not speak of the spirit and the word spirit is not mentioned at all. The verse says 'To your Lord is the return [of all].' This means that 'everything; spirit and matter will return to the Lord'.[51] If we consider Yasien's claim that 'the spirit will return to its origin which is Allah', the question, then, will be to whom should 'matter' return? If Allah is the origin of spirit only, as Yasien says, then who is the origin of matter? This confirms that Yasien's philosophy made him think that the spirit is part of Allah. If he thinks otherwise, he should say that the spirit will return to its Originator or Creator, which is Allah. If Yasien considers the spirit to be God's creation (as repeatedly mentioned in commentaries, including Qutb's *Zilal*) the spirit then will be the equivalent of matter and, like the universe, life and humanity, issue from Allah, the source of all creation. To the Creator all creation will return. There is the Creator and there are His creations. There is Divinity (*uluhiyyah*), which belongs exclusively to God the Creator, while servitude (*'ubudiyyah*) is common to everyone and everything else.[52] Like the universe, life and Man, 'spirit' has an existence separate from Allah's existence.[53] This is *tawhid*: 'Allah is one in His essence, in His existence, in His attributes (i.e. *uluhiyyah*, *hakimiyyah*), and in His acts.'[54]

Nevertheless, the word 'spirit' (*ruh*), according to al-Qurtubi, is like 'a subtle being among the beings created by Allah'. In the Qur'an the word *ruh* is used also as an appellation. The word is linked to various objects as a means to symbolize sanctity in conjunction with ordinary things [matter] in the mundane world. Examples abound: *'ardu Allah* (the earth of Allah), *sama'u Allah* (the heaven of Allah), *naqatu Allah* (she-camel of Allah), *shahru Allah* (the month of Allah), *rusulu Allah* (Messenger of Allah), *mala'ikatu Allah* (angels of Allah), and *ruhu Allah* (spirit of Allah). The spirit (*ruh*) is by Allah's command'.[55]

The point here is that the spirit is a being created by Allah. Thus, spirit, matter, human beings, the universe, angels, death and life all issued from the sovereign Will. Both death and life are created by Allah 'He who created death and life' Qur'an (67: 2). In guiding the Prophet about the spirit (*ruh*), the Qur'an (17: 85) advises that if 'They ask you concerning the spirit. Say: The spirit is by my Lord's command.' This means that the source of the spirit, whether angelic or not, is Allah. This linguistic analysis is helpful in interpreting Qutb's view of *fitrah*.

Yasien also claims that Qutb ignores the significance of the word *sawwa*.[56] He says

> Sayyid Qutb drew on this verse [91: 7–10] to support his dual view [of human nature], but his interpretation of the *ayah* [verse] is questionable because he ignored the significance of the word *sawwa* (moulded) and rendered an inaccurate translation of *alhama* (inspired).[57]

Yasien says Sayyid Qutb incorrectly translated [*alhama*] so as to create a disposition, natural disposition or natural preparedness for right and wrong.[58]

One should note that Yasien translates the word *sawwa* into the phrase 'moulded and proportioned'.[59] With this in mind, Yasien's claim and argument about this specific word *sawwa* is based on the Qur'anic verse (91: 7–10). This verse is present at the end of the last volume of *Zilal* and is referred to only in brief by Qutb. Thus, one might take the criticism seriously. However, Qutb defines the word *sawwa* elsewhere in *Zilal*[60] and in similar verses that deal with human creation and human nature. Therefore, it seems appropriate to clarify the meaning and implications of the word (*sawwa*).

The word *sawwa* is a verb whose referents include: upright, complete, even, level, flat, straight, ripe and mature. Each of these meanings depends on the context. In Arabic, for instance, according to Arabic grammarians and scholarly exegetes, one says about a man, '*istawa al-rajul*' to denote that he fulfilled his 'highest physical and mental potential'.[61] *Sawiyy*, the noun is derived from the verb (*sawwa*). *Sawiyy* is not only a noun, as Yasien claims, but is also adjective (*sifah*) and expressive of the conditional (*hal*) meaning upright or straight. For example, the Qur'an describes a man as *sawiyy* (19: 27), refers to the 'straight path' as *sawiyy* (19: 43) and upright behaviour as *sawiyy* (67: 22). Based on these and other Qur'anic verses, linguists Tha'lab (d. 209/905), Abu 'ubaydah (d. 209/824), Ibn Sidah (d. 458/1065), al-Zajjaj (d. 311/924) and Abu al-Haytham (d. 316/929) translate the saying '*rajulun sawiyy*' as 'his being (*kaynunah*) is upright'.[62] Thus, the verb *sawwa* includes the meanings upright, complete, straight, ripe and mature as a connotation of upright. The verb *sawwa*, according to Ibn Kathir, gives rise to the word *sawiyy*.[63]

The use of the verb *sawwa* is evident in the Qur'an and varies according to the verses' context. It is used in verses speaking of origination and creation of the Heavens and the earth, for example. Purpose and intent is evident in these verses. In referring to the origination and creation in general, the word *sawwa* is used; 87: 1–2 which says 'Praise the name of your Lord, the most high, who has created [all things] and *sawwa*.' In this verse, the word *sawwa* means, 'upright and perfect balanced tendencies'.[64] Therefore, the translation which fits the Arabic text of the verse would be 'Praise the name of your Lord, the most high, who has created and completely perfected His creations.' This meaning is arrived at after a careful study of the interpretation of this word in various commentaries, including Qutb's *Zilal*.[65] This suggests that Qutb did not ignore the various meanings of the word *sawwa* but refined them.

Furthermore, Yasien's interpretation of the word *sawwa* as equal proportions implies equality between two or more things, either actually or in a figurative sense. However, in various places in the Qur'an, the word *sawwa*, sometimes, refers to one thing only. In the case of human creation, for instance, the word *sawwa* refers to matter, before its transformation by spirit. This is mentioned in 15: 29 in which God says to the angels 'When I have perfected him (s*awwaytuhu*) and breathed into him of My spirit, kneel down and prostrate yourselves before him.' Similarly, the word *sawwa* is mentioned before spirit in 38: 72. The word is also used to refer to the human being after God created him as in 75: 38 and 82: 7.

Likewise, the word *sawwa* is used in the Qur'an also to refer to Heaven (singular) as in 79: 28. The word *sawwa* in 2: 29 refers to Heavens (plural). The origin of Heaven is unknown. Therefore, to interpret *sawwa* to mean equal proportion of things is nonsense, particularly if other words such as 'perfect' are appropriate. In these and similar verses, according to al-Qurtubi, *sawwa* means 'created' (*khalaqa*).[66] I therefore conclude that the word *sawwa* in the case of creation does not necessarily mean 'equal proportions' but rather means 'created and perfected'.

To briefly recapitulate, in response to Yasien's philosophical interpretation of *fitrah* and his critique of Qutb, I have argued on the following:

1. Qutb does not ignore the significance of the meaning of the word *sawwa*, rather he redefines it and other terms, according to context.
2. Qutb and early Arabic sources show the verb *sawwa* does not necessarily mean equal proportions.
3. Qutb does not interpret the word *sawwa* as proportion or moulded, as it has been claimed.
4. Consequently, according to Qutb, 'proportion' and 'moulded' are associated with heat, shape, size, before or after and other questions prefaced by how, where, why, what and when. These and similar questions do not fit in the case of creation.[67]
5. The meaning of words such as 'proportion' and 'moulded' when associated with the human intellect and various fields of knowledge, even figuratively, cannot be applied in the same way to the case of origination and creation of the universe, life and human beings.
6. Spirit is not part of Allah or associated with Him but is created by Allah.
7. There is nothing in Islam to indicate that matter constitutes or exemplifies innate evil in man.
8. Allah is the source of all matter and spirit.
9. There is no separation between matter and spirit in human nature or human conduct.
10. Human beings are both matter and spirit and this is the *fitrah*.

I conclude that the use of philosophical idioms or language in the discussion of Islamic concepts such as *fitrah* may cause confusion. Qutb's position on human nature is consistent with his view of *fitrah*. Human nature is part of the *fitrah* with which Allah has endowed His creation – the universe, life and humanity.

Socio-political specifics

Qutb emphasizes the potential of Islamic conception, in the face of philosophical challenge, of interpreting *fitrah* and providing a rationale. To Qutb, the 'Islamic conception' is more workable and practicable than philosophy in interpreting *fitrah* and similar ideas where philosophy has failed to provide satisfactory answers to the Muslims.[68] His view of *fitrah* is manifestly based on the Qur'an.

The word *fitrah* is mentioned in the Qur'an in several places among which are a variety of circumstances of social, political and religious contexts.[69] Thus, *fitrah* has a variety of connotations. Therefore, when Qutb discusses the Qur'anic concept of *fitrah*, he presents the concept as a comprehensive one that covers the nature of the relationship between the Creator and His creation – the universe, life and humanity.[70] He examines *fitrah* as it applies to discussion of human nature and human affairs in general. To Qutb, *fitrah* is the unchangeable nature of the universe, life and humanity created by Allah.[71] This means human nature is *fitrah*. Human *fitrah* is thus a part of the universal *fitrah*. Thus, when Qutb speaks of *fitrah* without qualification, he means the universal *fitrah*, which envelops human nature. Similarly, when he speaks of human nature, he means the unchangeable constitution Allah has bestowed on Man. Universal *fitrah* encompasses the physical and psychological nature of Man.[72]

Qutb's view of *fitrah* has four dimensions all of which are related to the Qur'anic use of the term. First is the linkage with the concept of *khilafah* (vicegerency) of Man on earth. Second, Qutb emphasizes *fitrah* within the context of Man's free will. Third, *fitrah* has a direct link to human life affairs and the human responsibility for development and renewal. Fourth, *fitrah* reflects the perfect and harmonious relationship between humanity and the universe.[73] These four dimensions complement Qutb's comprehensive constructs of Sovereignty (*hakimiyyah*), servitude (*'ubudiyyah*) and the universality of Islam. These notions are related, in turn, to what Qutb calls the 'great unity' (*al-wahdah al-kubra'*). This entails the comprehensive and integrated conception of the nature of the relationship between the Creator and the creation, the universe, life and Man. Qutb then, firmly binds these ideas to the concept of *tawhid*, the cornerstone of Islamic faith.

To Qutb, Islam is a comprehensive system, an ideological ideal and a convincing concept that expounds the nature of the universe, the nature of Man, and determines Man's position in the world, as well as the ultimate objectives of existence as a whole.[74] Qutb believed that there is a strong correlation between human nature, the nature of life, and the nature of the social order and the nature of the ideological ideal. The social order, with all its characteristics is but an offshoot of the ideological ideal. This social order grows biologically and naturally, and is completely adapted according to necessity, as this is expressed in human nature, circumstances and goals of humanity in this life. Growth and evolution are in the nature of these things.[75]

Therefore, Islam, according to Qutb, does not deal with or treat the various aspects of human life as separate parts. This also alludes to the discussion of the *fitrah*'s dimension, outlined earlier. This is because Islam has an overall, integrated concept of *uluhiyyah* (divinity), life and humanity. The approximate meaning of the testimony that there is no god but Allah is that the *uluhiyyah* (divinity) belongs to Allah alone. The first aspect of *uluhiyyah*, as Qutb says is 'The right of absolute sovereignty (*hakimiyyah*), whence arises the right to legislate for His worshipers, to ordain programs for their lives, to prescribe values on which their lives should be based.'[76] Islam is the only system in harmony with the system of the universe, life and man. Man should not follow a system not in harmony therewith, since he is obliged to live within its framework, and to cooperate in every respect with the universal system.[77] Qutb emphasizes the harmony between the *fitrah* of man and the *fitrah* of the surrounding universe. He then stresses that any system other than Islam is one that conflicts with the *fitrah* of man and the *fitrah* of the universe. Such conflict will lead man to misery and affliction. In this regard, Qutb uses his ideas to stress the *jahiliyyah* of the present world:

> This religion [Islam] is a divinely ordained program for human life. Its realization in the life of mankind depends on the exertions of men themselves, within the limits of their human capacities and the material realities of human existence in a given environment. Working for this aim starts at the point where mankind finds itself on being given the leadership, and it continues to the end of the path within the bounds of human capacities, insofar as these are put to work.[78]
>
> Is Islam not revealed by Allah? And does not Allah have authority over everything? Why, then, does this religion [Islam] operate only within the boundaries of restricted human abilities?... Naturally, Allah is capable of transforming human *fitrah* (nature), by means of this religion or any other method. But – may He be exalted! – He has chosen to create man with his present *fitrah* in accordance with His own wisdom. He has chosen to make divine guidance the fruit of exertion and desire for it... None of Allah's creation has the right to ask Him – may He be exalted – why He has chosen all this and willed it to be....[79] None of Allah's creation has the right to ask why He has chosen to create man with the *fitrah* he has; why He has chosen to make the operation of this *fitrah* permanent and uninterrupted; and why He has chosen to make the divinely ordained program for human life be realized through human existence, rather than enforcing it miraculously, through obscure, hidden means.[80]

> Human legislation, as laid down by a ruling individual, family, class, nation or race, cannot possibly, in the light of human *fitrah*, be unaffected by the desires and interests of the legislator.[81]
>
> It is only harmony between the program for human life and that of the universe and life that guarantees for man the cooperation of the awesome forces of the universe (*al-kawn*), and guides him to avoid conflict with them. If he opposes them, he will be destroyed and annihilated, and he will not fulfill his duty of vice-regency (*khilafah*) on earth. If, however, he conforms to the norms of the universe, he will possess knowledge of its secrets and know how to make use of them in his life. Then fire does not consume him; instead, he will use it for cooking, heating, and light. The *fitrah* of Man conforms basically to the norms of the universe. When man's way of life disregards this norm, not only will he come into conflict with the awesome forces of the universe, but also with his own *fitrah*. He will be miserable, bewildered and anxious, living like present-day man in acute torment, despite all the triumph of modern science. Present-day humanity is afflicted with misery, anxiety, bewilderment and confusion; it flees from its true self by taking recourse to opium, hashish and alcohol, to a desire for speed, to idiotic adventures . . . This bitter emptiness pursues man like a fearsome ghost. He flees from it, but inevitably it overtakes him . . .[82]
>
> When one compares the concept held by a 'civilized' man of the purpose of human existence with the Islamic concept, present-day civilization appears as a curse dragging human feelings down into the morass. For example, in America, new gods are worshipped, which are thought to be the aim of human existence – the god of finance (*al-mal*), the god of pleasure, the god of fame, and the god of productivity! Thus it is that in America men cannot find themselves, for they cannot find the purpose of their existence. The same is true of other *jahiliyyat* (singular *jahiliyyah*), where similar gods are worshipped, and people cannot find the true God.[83]

According to Qutb, Islam is the religion of unity in this great universe. The universe, life and man have all issued from one Sovereign. By one Supreme rule, the universe, with its divers ramifications has been thoroughly administered in such a manner that precludes any collision among its spheres.[84] Life is not an accidental occurrence. The universe and its laws have been so preconceived and designed as to allow life to emerge, to provide the living with their needs, and to allow continuity through renewal.[85] It is from this harmony that the psychological aspects of Islam are derived, for the essentially harmonious relationship between human *fitrah* and the *fitrah* of the universe or between human nature and the nature of the universe has psychological implementation.[86] The law, which governs the nature of the universe also governs the nature of Man and his life. This is one aspect of the *fitrah*. Allah created human beings in such a way as to ensure their perfect balance and harmony with the ultimate plan. This is the plan for the social order ordained by the Creator.

The nature of the relationship between the Creator and His creation, the universe, life and humankind, follows directly from the sovereign Will that has created all things, including humanity. The sovereign Will keeps and sustains all existing things. Existence issues from the sovereign Will as an integrated whole, every part of which is in harmony with all other parts. Everything has a reason for its existence since it relates to this complete and observable harmony.[87] Thus, all life is conducive to harmony and to the existence of humans who are the highest form of life. The universe is thus in a perfect balance and harmony with human nature: the same law governs both. It is the law of existence.[88] In Qutb's words

> The universe is not an enemy to Man, nor is *al-tabi'ah* (nature) the expression of the contemporary *jahiliyyah* or an adversary that Man struggles with and conquers. The universe, life and Man are simply part of God's creation. The universe is a friend, whose tendencies are not radically differed from those of life and Man.[89]

The legal and moral implications of Qutb's words are that material and spiritual forces converge to make the Islamic system unilaterally purposeful. Everything in the infinite universe is created for a purpose. The realization of that purpose, according to Qutb, must be possible in space and time.[90] The realization of absolute divine objectives for creation must be attained. For that purpose, all creation including Man's physical, psychic and spiritual functions must be capable of realizing the divine purpose. The realization of that purpose demands man's total capacity. Man's nature must become, Qutb asserts, malleable, transformable and capable of exposing its substance and its structures so as to lend itself to the patterns and purpose of creation.[91]

Therefore, God has endowed Man with faculties that enable him to perform functions of observations, selective analysis, comprehension and so on. Allah endowed every human being to enable him to realize the sovereign Will, expressed in the nature of Man or in the nature of the surrounding universe. Allah has created the universal forces to be, as Qutb puts it,

> Man's friend, helper and companion. The way for Man to cooperate with the natural forces is to observe them carefully, and become acquainted with them. If they sometimes harm him it is because he does not approach them properly and does not know the laws by which they operate.[92]

Since the divine Revelation teaches and guides humans to realize the sovereign Will in themselves and in the surrounding universe, Man has no excuse for revenge. He must come to terms with his responsibility as *khalifah* (vicegerent) of Allah on the earth.

Acknowledging the oneness of God is the *fitrah* engraved on the universe as well as upon the soul of every human being. According to Qutb, 'belief in the oneness of God is the basic principle of life'.[93] This is based on the Qur'anic verse 7: 172,

> when your Lord brought forth descendants from the loins of Adam's children, and made them testify against themselves, [He said]: 'Am I not your Lord?' They replied: 'We bear witness that you are.' [This He did] lest you should say on the Day of Judgment: 'We had no knowledge of that', or: 'Our fathers set up partners with Allah; but will You destroy us, their descendants, on account of what the followers of falsehood did?' Thus We make plain Our revelations so that they may return to the right path.[94]

Concerning this Qur'anic assertion, Ibn Kathir and al-Qurtubi represent the opinions of Muslim commentators and refer to numerous Qur'anic verses and *Sunnah* attributed to the prophet. According to Qutb, Ibn Kathir and al-Qurtubi, the dominant view was that each individual from the time of Adam made a Covenant that is binding on each individual. The words of the given verse (7: 172) refer to the descendants of Adam, that is, to all humanity, born and unborn.

Allah has given humans certain abilities and faculties to enable them to fulfil their obligations arising from this Covenant. According to Ibn Kathir, al-Qurtubi and Qutb, this Covenant is as follows:

> We acknowledge that Allah is one. He is our Creator, our Lord, sustainer and sovereign, to Whom we acknowledge our duty. When we testify concerning ourselves, the obligation is assumed by us. It follows from our very nature when that is upright, pure and sinless.[95]

Taking his argument a step further, Qutb emphasizes that

> *tawhid* is the *fitrah* engraved into human nature and with which every child is born. The child will remain on his *fitrah* of *tawhid* unless he deviates from it, under social influence. The principles of *tawhid* are interwoven not only into human nature but are also bound firmly into the nature of the universe. The *fitrah* with which Allah created human beings is but a part of the *fitrah* of the whole of existence and governed by the same law that governs existence.[96]

This means that the centre of *tawhid* lies at the centre of human nature and forms the *fitrah* to which human natural tendencies are firmly bound. In other words, the *fitrah* is the faculty that organizes human natural forces, keeping them in balance and harmonizes their outcome behaviour in the real world. Thus, deviation from *tawhid* will disrupt the arrangement of natural human tendencies and will result in maladjustment to the real world.

The moral implication of this is that, according to Qutb,

> human life will not be rightly ordered until the balance and harmony of the *fitrah* is fully instituted, in accordance with the law that organizes and governs natural constitution of the universe, life and Man. Balance and harmony must be accomplished, for the welfare of humanity. Therefore, it is permissible to use force to bring those who deviate from *fitrah* back on to the path of *fitrah*.[97]

Qutb base this on the Qur'anic verse 5: 33 which says 'Those who make war against Allah and His Apostle and spread disorder in the land shall be put to death or crucified or have their hands and feet cut off on alternate sides, or be banished from the land.'

Using the Qur'anic image of the clay of the earth (matter) and spirit from Allah, Qutb emphasizes that the human being is a unitary creature with a dual nature. His exposition of the origin of humanity, human nature and human responsibility is based on Qur'anic verses 15: 26, 28–29 and others dealing with human origin.[98] The origin of Man, according to Qutb is matter and this is derived from the sounding clay. Matter is the origin not only of human beings but also of all created things on the earth. There are stages of creation between elementary matter and a human being. This is denoted by the word '*sulalah*'[99] as in 23: 12; 32: 8. Qutb goes no further to explain stages of creation. He refers to Qur'anic verses and points out that

> this is the end of all texts. Further assumptions . . . are unnecessary. Scientific research then can make further . . . theories and assumptions. The results can be verified and can be changed. Either way, elementary matter from which Allah created Man remains *fitrah* the only reference and guidance for all. How does the inorganic matter developed from an elementary nature to an organic, living matter and then a human being? This secret and that the secret of life in the first cell is part of the realm of the unknown.[100]

Human nature, according to Qutb, is not only spiritual as are the angels.[101] It does not express itself only in the direction of bodily needs like animals.[102] Thus, in the 'Sound State' (*sawiyy*) Man's response to material needs is different from that of an animal. Nor is it like that of angels. As a free being and a decision maker, Man differs from all beings. Man, says Qutb, 'conducts his life and activities as a compound or one unit of a dual nature and dual ability'. There is no separation between his material and spiritual tendencies in any activity. According to Qutb,

> he who interrupts his material ability is like he who interrupts his spiritual ability. Both attempts are deviations from the *fitrah*. He who deviates from *fitrah* harms himself because of his doing what Allah asked him not to do. Man is a trustee and a guardian of the pure aspects of his *fitrah* and he is responsible for it.[103]

Taking his argument a step further, Qutb then outlines his view concerning the psychological nature of Man, basing this on the Qur'anic verses 91: 7–10 which say 'By the soul and Him that perfected it and inspired it with knowledge of wickedness and piety. Successful is the one who keeps it pure, and ruined is the he who corrupts it.' Qutb referred to these verses in conjunction with an earlier one 90: 10 which states: 'Have we not given him two eyes, a tongue and two lips and shown him the two paths [of good and evil].' These verses and others (76: 3; 38: 72) according to Qutb, point to the duality of Man. His responsibility and accountability for his decisions are defined in 74: 38 and 13: 11. These denote Allah's attitude with regard to human behaviour.

Verses 90: 10 and 91: 7–10 indicate that Allah inspired (*alhama*) Man with knowledge to enable him to distinguish between right and wrong, so that he can choose either way. Taking this point in conjunction with verse 74: 38, the decision then is up to him and he is therefore responsible for his decision. According to Qutb, this dual ability is denoted by the word inspired (*alhama*) in 91: 8 and in 90: 10 which states '*hadaynahu al-najdayn*'. (We have shown him the two paths.) Qutb adds,

> Man is a creature of dual nature, of dual ability and of dual dimensions. He is able to follow Divine guidance and to go astray. He is just as capable of recognizing good, as he is of recognizing evil. He is equally capable of directing himself one way or the other. This dual ability is deeply ingrained in his being. Divine messages and external factors do not create this natural potential but serve to awaken it and help it to go one way or the other.[104]

In addition to these abilities, Qutb believed that Man is equipped with '*quwa wa'iyah*' (conscious or decision-making faculty). This faculty enables Man to perceive, comprehend, analyse and determine his line of action.[105] Allah does not leave Man up to the impulses of his *fitrah* and his decision-making faculty. Allah helps Man by

> sending him messages with certain signs that help him to choose the right path . . . and clears the way of obstructs that he may see the truth. Thus, Man's decision-making faculty functions with full knowledge of the direction it chooses, and the implications of that choice. This is what Allah willed for Man and whatever takes place within this framework is a direct fulfillment of His will.[106]

This means that Man is assigned a definite task that is related to the power of freedom and capabilities given to him by Allah.

The socio-political implications of *fitrah* are Qutb's next focus. He points out that human nature is originally upright, a coherent unity of material and spiritual tendencies. The natural domination of the spirit is the *fitrah* that enables Man to move and act as one unit, to develop and fulfil his responsibility as *khalifah*.[107] This means that the natural domination of spirit over man's physical, psychic and mental forces is *fitrah* and this is the purest way. The domination of spirit over these forces makes Man act according to his *fitrah*. His spirit guides him to respond to his *fitrah*. When man's material nature dominates over his spirit, man's ability to distinguish between right and wrong will be disrupted.[108] Domination of matter over spirit is not of man's nature. This means that deviation from *fitrah* disrupts man's ability to distinguish right from wrong. It is a condition that indicates that man's physical, psychic and mental forces are torn apart. In this context, the state of *fitrah*, in Qutb's view, rests on the question of what guidance is available. If guidance is dominated by the spiritual nature, Man will behave according to his *fitrah*, and that is, his material and spiritual tendencies will be balanced. If Man's material nature is dominated, man's physical, psychic and mental forces will respond to their needs anarchically. Consequently, he will go astray.[109]

Humanity needs a coherent system of guidance that inspires behaviour and sentiments in daily life. The very system must take in its account the natural, material and spiritual forces of Man, unite all forces and help Man to develop and conduct his life as a human being whose Maker assigned him the responsibility of *khalifah*.[110]

The system should be based on *tawhid* because, according to Qutb, *tawhid* is the nucleus of reality to which human natural forces are linked. Islam provides such reality because 'the system instituted by Islam for people is the trustee and guardian of the purer nature created by Allah for this very purpose'.[111] A system that encompasses all human activities is preferable to a system that deals with only a part of human life. Thus, a strong and firm relationship exists between all spheres of human action: physical and mental, practical and ritualistic, social, political and economic, spiritual and intellectual, involving an individual or a group.[112] Qutb's view of socio-political implications of *fitrah* is based on the concept of *tawhid*. His comprehensive concept of *tawhid* is significant in this context. He believed that the structure of human nature which is based on *tawhid* constitutes an inherent reality of primordial belief that Allah made innate to humankind.[113] This natural endowment is the *fitrah* which is universal and immutable and upon which the revealed knowledge as well as acquired knowledge rests. This *fitrah*, according to Qutb, refuses to subject human life to any system other than the divine code.[114] This means that the principles of *tawhid* are *fitrah* and they enable Man to fulfil his responsibility as vicegerent of Allah on earth. The human being who is not able to know his perfect balanced natural constitution, cannot fulfil the obligation. Nor can he balance between the material and spiritual needs of his life.[115] Therefore, messengers and revelations are necessary guides to help human beings to project their perfectly balanced natural constitution onto the reality of their daily life activities.

Islam is a means of projecting Man's perfectly balanced nature onto the real world. Second, deviation from Islam causes disruption of the harmony of human life. This suggested that human nature manifests a dualism in the real world. This means that the external reality of following the Islamic social system is a reflection of the perfectly balanced human nature as provided by the Creator, whereas the external reality of following the systems of *jahiliyyah* is a reflection of corrupt human nature. Qutb articulated this very point in his commentary on the Qur'anic verse 103: 2–3 as follows:

> Faith is a sign of health in a person's nature and soundness in his disposition. It also indicates Man's harmony with the whole universe; a sign of mutual effect with Man and the world around him. Because Man lives within the universe, his life, as long as his behavior is straightforward, brings about an orientation of faith because the universe itself possesses signs and testimonies about Allah.[116]

Thus, following any other system not based upon the Islamic code ordained in the Qur'an and the Sunnah is a sign of deviation from the *fitrah*. Deviation from the *fitrah* is a *jahiliyyah* similar to historical *jahiliyyah* as defined by Qutb.[117]

Concluding remarks

Qutb emphasized *fitrah* as the unchangeable constitution with which Allah created the universe, life and Man. It was God's Will to create the universe and make it suitable and available for Man. The perfect balance and universal harmony of this relationship reflects the sovereign authority of Allah. Therefore, Qutb views *fitrah* within the context of the concept of *hakimiyyah*, *'ubudiyyah* and universality of Islam and bases all these on the concept of *tawhid*.

Man is part of this universe and originated from its origins. Qutb views human nature as an indivisible part of the universal *fitrah* thus elevating Man to position of being responsible for his action; yet allowing him freedom of choice. Qutb's view reflects the dignity with which Islam endows humanity; a position worthy of the creature to whom God has given preference over all other. Islam emphasizes that Man's fate is in his own hands and the responsibility for that rests completely with him. Therefore, Man is in charge of the means of production. He is not a slave to anything or any one other than Allah. This imbues Man with awareness, with caution and with *taqwa*, that is with fear of God the sovereign of all sovereignty.

Qutb also emphasizes that Islam seeks to remind Man of his spiritual and material nature; Islam reminds Man of his permanent need to refer to behavioural criteria fixed by God. These provide framework and standards that God has revealed to Man enabling him to demonstrate his true nature, and his framework within which his desires can be contained to avoid leading him astray and manoeuvring him into *jahiliyyah*.

5 Human intellect (*al-'Aql*)

Like *al-fitrah*, the concept of *al-'aql* (human intellect) is one of the important conceptual tools that Qutb has used to articulate his socio-political theory. This section investigates Qutb's concept of human intellect or in his words – *al-'aql* as it relates to the concept of Sovereignty (*hakimiyyah*) and other of Qutb's comprehensive constructs such as *'ubudiyyah* (servitude), the universality of Islam and, overall, the confrontational theory which expounds Qutb's view on the *jahili* predominance in the world. Rationality and the relationship of human intellect (*al-'aql*) to Revelation (*al-wahy*) are also examined in the context of Qur'anic text (*nass*), and then to various other concepts, such as the universe, humanity and life, including the socio-political realm.

Revelation and human intellect

The relation between human intellect and revelation is one of the most contentious issues in our modern world. It holds a central position in every public debate over rationality, freedom of intellect, religion, modernity and human rights. At times the force and intent of the issue also make their presence felt in bilateral and regional relations. In this sense the relation between religion and human intellect are always with us, just as the relation of the spirit to matter in man.

To Qutb, the function of human intellect (*al-'aql*) is limited in time and place, and it is therefore not the sole source of truth. The function of human intellect is obviously subject to human circumstances and environmental factors that characterize the transience of human affairs.[1] Human intellect cannot provide a well-balanced system for human life or serve, in absolute sense, in place of the revelation (*al-wahy*).

The critical view is of two dimensions: while the first has concerned itself with the relation between religion and intellect, the focus of the second is the understanding and interpretation made by others. While the former argues that both Man and the Revelation issue from the sovereign Will and thus human intellect is equal to Revelation,[2] the latter thinks that Qutb is one of those who sees 'human intellect as a means and container (*wi'a'*) for what is already exist and has no role to bring about the existence of what is not exist of conceptions that are not linked to the revelation (*wahy*).'[3] This view claims that Qutb considers human intellect as a receiver and has no role to think, to accept or reject religious decrees. As this is not Qutb's view, it could suggest a lack of understanding of the topic and lack of thorough reading of Qutb. Qutb's ideas are grounded in the perception of complete freedom and the balance between spiritual and material need. A brief summary of Qutb's view is legitimate:

1. Revelation is the supreme source that is able to guide human intellect and enable man to distinguish right from wrong.
2. Revelation does not consult human intellect and is not subjected to scholarly deduction.
3. Human intellect might change in relation to a given concept or problem, but Revelation does not. This does not mean that Islam is rigid in its application: 'while its basic doctrines are fixed they can apply to all human circumstances; they provide for "movement within a firm framework and about stable axis." '[4]
4. Human intellect is required to follow Revelation; but the decision is freely chosen and man is responsible for his decision.
5. Revelation is not required to follow human intellect. It does not follow that there is conflict between human intellect and Revelation. This means, however, that if human intellect (it is but a creature created Allah) could guide, in absolute sense, humans to right belief and action, Allah would not have sent His messengers with a Revelation.[5]
6. A harmonious relationship exists between human intellect and Revelation.
7. Revelation was not sent in vain, but to guide human intellect to the truth for the welfare of intellect of human individuals, of the society and humanity at large.[6]

These brief comments imply that the source of authority is the revelation, not human intellect. Equally they also substantiate that the role of human intellect is free to confirm or to reject the revelation but not to judge it, or to label it right or wrong. Qutb notes that 'after human intellect confirms the Revelation was from Allah and understood the literal and technical dimensions of the text (*nass*); the role of human intellect then is not to judge the Revelation.'[7] To Qutb therefore, the attempt of human intellect to create, on only human authority, theories concerning the universe, life and man as to create systems and laws for human life will lead to 'disorder and barbarism'.[8] To him, these attempts surely lead to nothing but 'hideous schizophrenia'.[9] He views such attempts as a direct result of deviated notions such as Rationalism, Idealism, Positivism and dialectical materialism and the like of which separate human life from the straight path of religion.[10]

To Qutb, the ignorance prevailing in the world today is the direct result of the interference of human intellect on religion.[11] He points out that when

Europe speaks about the contradictions between human intellect and religion, they meant a specific religion and specific circumstances that continued for centuries in Europe. This long history witnessed rational disputes and philosophical arguments, all trying to find the source of truth. Theories regarding the importance of each abounded as did theories as to the basis of knowledge itself. To Qutb, the involvement of human intellect in religion, in Europe, distorted religious conceptions about divinity, the universe, life and man. It was from these distortions that 'Western thought developed since the fourteenth century up to modern times'.[12] Qutb pointed out four stages of European thought since the fourteenth century. These stages were to justify one or another of the three sources of knowledge known in the history of humankind up to modern times, religion, human intellect and Nature. Initially, religion held the monopoly as the source of truth in the European context. Qutb says

> in the medieval period, religion was predominant in guiding human affairs; organizing institutions and explaining to man the nature of the surrounding universe. The religion here was Christianity; and Christianity meant Catholicism; and Catholicism meant Papism, that is to say, as the Vicar of Christ, the Pop was the final authority. The interpretation of the 'Holy Book' was strictly limited to the Pope and the highest council of cardinals, so 'what the Book says' meant 'what the Catholic Church says'. Then, Trinity was formulated, confession and indulgences were introduced and whatever related to Catholicism.[13]

This state of affairs, as Qutb says, continued until the fifteenth century, by which time the ideas about freedom, equality and justice of the 'heavenly law, not the law of the papacy or the law of the landlord of Europe', which the Crusaders had brought back from the Muslims to Europe had gradually changed European thinking.[14] Here, Qutb shares Hegel's view that 'the domination by the papacy of Europe continued until the fifteenth century'.[15] Martin Luther (1483–1546) led the reformation against Catholicism, stood against the concept of Trinity, Papal infallibility, declared the Holy Book the final authority, demanded limited freedom to study the Book and declared the priority of faith over other matters including human intellect.[16] This was then enhanced by John Calvin (1509–1564). Commenting on the result of these events, Qutb says

> The philosophers who rejected religion rejected the authority of the Pope. He who pointed to the contradictions between human intellect and religion they meant contradictions between human intellect and the catholic teachings (Trinity, sacraments, indulgences). He who defended Christianity among the philosophers, as for example, Hegel, defended the 'pure Christian teachings' as explained by Luther, in contrast to catholic teachings. This is a religion subjected to rational debate and philosophical

> conflict. It was a particular type of religion: he who accepts its teachings accepts them in the name of rational philosophy. He who rejects some of its teachings does so in the name of rational philosophy. This is the result of the interference of human intellect in religion in Europe.[17]

The religion here was not Islam. So when some speak of the contradiction between religion and human intellect they mean a specific type of religious behaviour and specific circumstances known in history. Under these circumstances, in the second half of the eighteenth century, human intellect was generally accepted as the most reliable source of truth, by philosophers. The period is commonly referred to as Enlightenment or the Age of Reason. According to some observers, this marked the beginnings of 'a refusal, and in some respects an antithesis of much of Church belief'.[18]

The Age of Reason, as Qutb asserts, is characterized by German, English and French thought at the time. Its philosophers were concerned with three spheres of knowledge: 'religion, human intellect, and the natural world (*al-tabi'ah*). This formulated a kind of thought that distinguished the Age of Reason from other ages.'[19] The leading Enlightenment thinkers saw human intellect as far more conductive to solving life's problems than a doctrine concerning Revelation. Human intellect (*al-'aql*) became sovereign and was considered as central to the planning of human affairs and the future life of society. This was coupled with emphasis on empiricism, and knowledge was derived from sense perceptions.[20] Works that were widely read included, for instance, Berkeley (1685–1753), Locke (1632–1704), Hume (1711–1776) and Kant (1724–1804) which have played a significant role in arousing general doubt about God, about the Revelation, immortality of human soul, moral values and about life after death and the relevant religious conceptions. Hume described such religious beliefs and conceptions, for instance, as 'sophistry and illusion'.[21]

The intellectual climate dominated by rationalism in Europe facilitated a growing deviation from revealed truth in areas concerning the universe (*al-kawn*), life and human affairs. Qutb notes that 'those who do not know Allah', understood His Will (*mash'ah*) and determinism (*qadar*) through their own human standards and measures. They look around and find that the human being is but one creature among many on this planet and see the earth as but a small atom in the galaxy; while the galaxy, in relation to the visible universe, is perhaps the size of a speck of dust in this vast universe. So they said 'it is not rational (*ma'qul*) that man was created for such a purpose'.[22] In addition,

> they think man has no value in this vast universe. What can he do? Man's existence appears accidental, and the universe around him is his enemy. This blind *jahiliyyah* is the direct result of the small mindedness established by human intellect (*al-'aql*) to measure God's Will and determinism concerning the universe, life and man.[23]

These deviant concepts concerning the relationship between the Creator and the creation, the universe (*al-kawn*), life and man have paved the way for the acceptance of the Newtonianism which reduced God to 'watch maker, who had to exist to set the Newtonian universal machine in motion, but who did not interfere with its harmonious operations'.[24]

In the *Keeper of Genesis*, Robert Bauval (1979), analysed the thought of ancient Egyptians concerning the universe. Bauval considered that, despite the genius of the ancient Egyptian thought and the modern intellect, the human mind is limited. Comparing the ancient Egyptian intellect with the modern, Robert Bauval cites John Maynard Keynes on Newton:

> Newton was the last magician – why do I call him a magician? Because he looked at the whole universe and all that is in it as a riddle, as a secret that could be read by applying pure thought to certain evidence, certain mystic clues which God had laid about the world to allow a sort of philosopher's treasure hunt to the esoteric brotherhood. He believed that these clues were to be found partly in the heavens . . . partly in certain papers and traditions handed down by the brethren . . . By pure thought, by concentration of mind, the riddle, he believed, would be revealed to the initiate . . .[25]

Intellect thus helps man to think that God can be of any form or shape. Man can even invent Him. According to Voltaire 'If God did not exist, it would be necessary to invent him.'[26]

Supposing that man owned this vast universe, what could he do with it? asks Qutb. Man's capacity is limited, his intellect is limited but

> the man's problem is that when he deviated from the guidance of Allah and followed his own intellect, he called it knowledge (*'ilm*). He believed that development means to forget Allah, or to understand Him on the basis of human standards. This is the problem of man: bragging and boasting about his limited knowledge of the truth.[27]

In the *Mysterious Universe*, James Jeans (1931), the writer tried to find his place in the mysterious universe but, Qutb notes, 'Sir Jeans found that it was alien to human feelings and aspirations, knowledge, arts and all religions.'[28] Jeans concludes that

> It is perhaps right to say that there is a strong enmity between the universe and our life. This is because most parts of space are very cold, to the degree that life cannot continue – and the heat of most of the matter in space make also life impossible . . . Our circumstances brought us to this universe. If it is not true that our existence occurred as a result of a mistake . . . there is no less than to be a result of what is described rightly as accident.[29]

This mechanical concept of the universe devised by pure reason, also facilitates similar mechanical explanations of the nature of man and the purpose of his existence. According to Owen (1975), Litter and Robin defined human nature as 'anatomically, the functions of the neck and spinal column; physiologically, the sum of functions of the power of perception in the brain'.[30] Similarly, Julien La Mettrie (1953) concludes that the 'soul is clearly an enlightened machine . . . the soul is therefore but an empty word of which no one has any idea, and which an enlightened man should use only to signify the part in us that the mind'.[31]

In a mechanical pattern, Qutb says, human intellect observed man, in a similar way as he observed the universe, as a 'chance product of a blind and purposeless nature who came to this planet accidentally'.[32] Man is then treated as an unconscious product operating through accidental variations in a self-designed and self-propelled evolution. Human intellect puts man at the mercy of brute forces that, as Bertrand Russell says, 'unknowingly happen to throw him into being'.[33]

Rejection of religious ideas concerning the nature of man and his purpose in this life and the harmonious relationship between man and his surrounding universe has also engendered the social sciences, where the attempt is to explain the individual and social behaviour by analogy with the principles of Newtonian physics. Human actions were observed also as due to 'chemical causes and processes'.[34]

Positivism, for instance, rejected religion and exalted intellect and science without realizing their limitations. Explaining the function of a human being in mechanical terms, according to Qutb, tended to make the social sciences materialist and determinist.[35] Materialism is, Qutb says,

> a direct result of deviation from religion, since it holds that the universe is primarily and fundamentally governed by Nature (*tabi'ah*) and that the Nature determine the final cause. The result was that the existence, human nature, feelings, values and standards, wealth and body needs, became to be explained in material terms and material processes.[36]

Consequently, the facts in the physical universe, life and human history and behaviour are explained in terms of dependence upon their psychosocial causes. Locke (1632–1704), Marx (1818–1883), Freud (1856–1939), and Watson and others such as Skinner (1904–1990), all considered that human beings are conditioned by their environment or by factors outside their conscious control.[37] Watson (1878–1958) and Skinner, for instance, explained human behaviour as determined by mechanical and automatic responses to external stimuli as in animals.[38] For Freud, human behaviour was determined by unconscious mental states.[39] For Marx, socio-economic conflict and class struggle determined human behaviour.[40] A lack of focus on moral responsibility for individual behaviour tends to undermine the role of religion as a collective force in society. Consequently as the power of religion in society diminishes, the process of secularization increases.

Secularism, however, does not mean the absence of religion. Part of the process of secularization is, according to Qutb, 'when man separates himself from the constant source of truth (religion) to rely on and trust only his intellect. He then becomes ignorant (*jahil*) as regards his purpose in this world, afraid of his surrounding universe, anxious about his life affairs, and worried about his future.'[41] Qutb, therefore, labelled the Age of Reason 'the Age of Deism, that is, the age of philosophical belief in a god who has no creation and has no Revelation (*wahy*).'[42] According to Bertrand Russell (1953), the purpose of Man in this universe is observed by reason 'in a scientific sense and that the ultimate concept of life gradually disappears from social thought'.[43] This will continue as long as man continues to restrict himself to the paradigm box of his intellect, afraid to even try to get out and rethink the available knowledge around him.

Freedom and the role of intellect

In Islam, the role of human intellect in human development cannot be denied. According to Qutb, human intellect has scored great triumphs in science and medicine in the cure of physical diseases. Science has lead to the discovery of new drugs and means of diagnosis and treatment. Almost miraculous results have been achieved in the sphere of industrial production and improvements occur daily. Similar achievements are visible in the exploration of space, the construction of satellites and space stations.[44] However, Qutb asks, what is the effect of all of this on human life and on the spiritual life of humanity? Has humanity found security? Has it found peace? According to him, 'humanity has certainly found misery, anxiety and fear'.[45] Human intellect, Qutb asserts, has crowned new gods to be worshipped – the god of finance, the god of pleasure, the god of fame, and the god of productivity? Human intellect cannot find himself for he cannot find the purpose of existence.[46] Conveying the philosophical view of the universe, Bertrand Russell stated that

> all the labors of the ages, all the devotion, all the inspirations, all noonday brightness of human genius are destined to extinction in the vast death of the solar system, and the whole temple of Man's achievement must invariably be buried beneath the debris of a universe in ruins.[47]

In response to this, Qutb writes

> The attempt of intellect to interpret existence and man's place in it and the purpose of his existence results in an assortment of answers, mostly naïve and ridiculous in their idiocy . . . One is surprised that such ideas can emerge from a philosopher until one remembers that this philosopher too is but a man equipped with only human intellect. This is not the realm of intellect, yet he has strayed into a region where he has no lamp

> to guide him other than that candle which is called intellect and was granted to him by God for use for different matters and in different realms – matters wherein the candle may be of some use, a realm where it will shed some light. That realm is the viceregency of God on earth, in accordance with the divinely ordained path, depending on the grace and assistance of God, as is understood from a comprehensive interpretation on the basis of which a healthy human way of thought may arise, a system of human life with natural roots.[48]

The role of human intellect, then, according to Qutb, is not to judge the rules of the Qur'an, saying this is right or wrong. Qutb points out that Islam is the religion of intellect, that is that Islam speaks to the intellect on all religious issues and made *al-'aql* responsible to understand the implications of a given text (*nass*).[49] According to Qutb, Islam grants human intellect the freedom to think of religion, but the role of intellect ends at the point of understanding the meaning and the implication of the text on the bases of linguistic and technical principles. After that, the true meaning of a given text cannot be subject to scholarly deduction or judgement or any form of decision; as to say this is right or this is wrong. Such decision is above human intellect which is limited in time and place. This is simply because the text (*nass*) descends from God and human intellect is not God to judge God's rule. This is the point at which numerous arguments occur between those who promote intellect as their authority and those who relinquish the role of intellect in the hope of divine guidance. Between the two which are extremes, the right way, in Qutb's view, is the middle path, that is, Islam. Therefore Islam speaks to intellect in a way that the intellect can understand the message. Human intellect is guided through the right way of observing these decrees for the whole affairs of life.[50]

Qutb then emphasizes that if human intellect perceived the decrees of Islam, that is, understood the meaning of the text, there is nothing for intellect to do but to accept, conform, submit and practice. Explaining this important point, Qutb states that 'the message of Islam does not force intellect to implement the message's decrees whether or not intellect understands them.'[51] In other words, Islam does not force human *intellect* to implement the rules of *shari'ah* even after intellect understands them.

This statement should be considered carefully or it may lead to error. Qutb means that if intellect fully grasps the religious decrees, the decision then is a free one, that is either to conform and practise the decrees or not. Due to this freedom, intellect has no right to judge the decrees; that is, intellect is not allowed to assess 'this decree as wrong or that as right, or this decree fits our time or that does not fit our time.'[52] Qutb says

> In Islam, human intellect has the complete freedom to accept or reject the decree of religion – to reject it, or to practise it completely or incompletely. Islam does not force anyone to implement the rules of *shari'ah*

> even after he has understood them. After understanding the decrees (*muqarrarat*), the decision then is a free one, that is either to conform and then practise the decrees, or not. Everyone is responsible for his decision. Everyone, Muslim or non-Muslim, has the right to belief or to claim that whatever he believes is right. This is the freedom granted by Islam. Because of this freedom, human intellect has no right to judge the decrees; that is, intellect is not allowed to assess this decree as wrong or as right, or that this decree fits our time or that one does not. This is because 'Allah knows best'. The creature cannot judge the rules of his Creator.[53]

The decision then is for human intellect to choose. The decision must be free (no compulsion of any type or form).[54] In Islam, human intellect is the foundation of responsibility or obligation (*taklif*). Islam does not charge Muslims to carry their Islamic duties before they attain maturity and are able to decide for themselves. Therefore, those who have mental illness are not obligated to observe the precepts of their Islamic faith. As long as there is intellect and freedom of decision, there is responsibility, and everyone is responsible for his decision. This is important and stable in Qutb's analysis. In his last book *Milestones*, which brought him to the gallows, Qutb says 'Man has the power (*yamlik*), with his free-will, to change his faith (*'aqidah*), his conception (*tasawwur*), and his thought (*fikr*), and the program of hs life (*manhaj hyatuh*).'[55]

Sovereignty and the freedom of intellect

Taking Qutb's argument a step further, I now return to the concept of sovereignty (*hakimiyyah*): that Allah is the highest governmental and legal authority in human life and in the universe. In the context of sovereignty, Qutb's view of the freedom of intellect implements questions about the rights to freedom, in general, and to the freedom of belief, in particular. The ultimate goal of Qutb is to establish an Islamic order, that is, an Islamic state supervised and governed by *hakimiyyah*. The *hakimiyyah* (sovereignty) in practical application, as Qutb says, is the *shari'ah*:

> The *shari'ah* of Allah is the foundation of legislation. Allah Himself does not descend to govern, but sent down his *shari'ah* to govern. The Qur'anic texts say that the *hakimiyyah* of Allah will be implemented by the implementation of the *shari'ah*.[56]

The *shari'ah* comprises the clear-cut commands and prohibitions conveyed in the Qur'an and the traditions of the Prophet of Islam. With those commands, the *hakimiyyah* (sovereignty; *shari'ah*) deals with individuals and groups, links them to the state and the society at large, and defines the individual's rights within the limits of the community. In Qutb's view, the non-Muslim minority in the Islamic state is not outside of the jurisdiction of the '*hakimiyyah*' which regulates the relationship between the State and its citizens, Muslims and non-Muslims, individuals and groups.[57] Thus the freedom of belief in relation to Qutb's view of sovereignty (*hakimiyyah*) and intellect (*al-'aql*) can be seen as one of the pressing and 'sensitive' issues.

Qutb stresses the freedom of belief that all citizens, Muslims and non-Muslims would enjoy in the Islamic state as an issue of personal conviction, and relates to personal perception and apprehension, not to force or compulsion. To him, Islamic teachings have been based on an appeal to the mind and the conscience. Qutb is in the view that

> Islam has abstained from all forms of compulsion, even the mental compulsion implicit in the miracles that accompanied the earlier religions. Islam is the religion that respects the cognitive and emotional faculties of man and is content to address them without compulsion and without miracles that break the laws of nature.[58]

Qutb supports his view by quoting the Qur'anic commands 'There is no compulsion in religion' (Qur'an, 2: 256); 'Invite them to the path of your Lord with wisdom and comely admonishment' (Qur'an, 16: 125); and also 'You [Muhammad] are not a magistrate over the people' (Qur'an, 88: 22); 'We know best what they say; and you [O Muhammad] are not a tyrant over them [to force them to belief]' (Qur'an, 50: 54).

Qutb views these verses as a declaration of human liberation in the seventh century. He contrasts these declarations with the behaviours of the Byzantines and their use of brutal force to convert the occupied countries to Christianity, particularly, after Christianity became the official religion of the Byzantine Empire. Qutb pointed out that the non-Christians were not the only oppressed people, but also the Christians who differed in their opinion from the opinion of the Empire. From the examples given by Qutb were the Christians in Syria, Jordan and the Christian Copts in Egypt. He referred to Sir T. W. Arnold's book *'Preaching of Islam'* and quotes some of his accounts about the opinions of the Christian inhabitants of these territories toward Muslims. In short, the inhabitants of these territories 'preferred' Muslims and wrote to them 'O Muslims, we prefer you to the Byzantines, though they are of our own faith....'[59] Against this background, the command in the Qur'anic verses above declared the freedom in its widest sense including the freedom of human intellect.[60] Qutb says

> The right to freedom of belief is the basic characteristic of human liberation. Without the freedom to think of religion, man cannot be identified as a human being. The freedom of belief is the first right that gives to and secures for this creature [man] his human quality and human identity.[61]

In relation to universality and rationality, freedom in its widest sense is a just order, but compulsion is injustice. In addition, the just order is not confined to a specific race, generation, or place. Qutb stresses firm relationship between the rights to freedom of belief and both the universality and rationality of Islam. Echoing views of earlier Muslim exegetes, Qutb pointed out that the Qur'an demonstrates the universality of its teachings by addressing all human moral, social and religious problems of man, irrespective of race, colour, creed or nationality.[62] Islam also 'gives man his rights in complete measures and elevates him to a position of being responsible for his decision, yet allows him freedom of choice. Islam grants for the individuals their freedom to think about their religion'.[63] It is necessary therefore that those Islamic teachings should have the potential of universal application with an appeal to universal human nature. The proclamation by the Qur'an that Muhammad is a universal Prophet with a universal message, is in itself tantamount to declaring that the religion of Islam is founded on rationality. No religion with any element of irrationality can be acceptable to the universal conscience of man.[64] In declaring the universality of the Prophet Muhammad, the Qur'an says 'And We have not sent you but as a bearer of glad tidings and a Warner, for all humankind, but most people know not' (Qur'an, 34: 29).

Qutb points out that the Qur'an manifestly acknowledges the role of rationality for the attainment of truth.[65] For him, truth is the religion of Islam, Islam is the religion of truth – truth requires no compulsion for the transmission of its message – the only instrument it needs is rationality. As such, Islam invokes human intellect to investigate the truth of the Qur'anic teachings with reference to the study of the comprehensive concept of the Nature of the relationship between the Creator and the creation, the universe, life and man.[66] Here, Qutb recalls a Qur'anic warning and stresses that the inquiry by itself is not sufficient. To draw the right conclusion from the Qur'an, 'absolute liberation of the conscience' of man is essential in the processes.[67] The conscience should be freed from *ubudiyyah* (servitude) to anything and to anyone except to Allah alone. This principle of fundamental importance is dictated in the beginning of the Qur'an as follows: 'This is that perfect Book; there is no doubt in it; a guidance (*hudan*) for the righteous (*muttaqin*)' (Qur'an, 2: 2). Regarding the keyword *muttaqin* in this verse, Qutb draws special attention to the comprehension of its underlying message. He argues that the divine teachings are obviously expected to guide the unrighteous to the right path. What, then is the significance of the claim that this Book guides only those who are already righteous? Qutb's response is this: 'The seeker after the truth, in the Qur'an, must necessarily be true himself or his inquiry will prove futile. The discovery of the truth depends essentially on the honesty and the freedom of the inquirer's conscience and intent.'[68] This profound wisdom is reflected in this short simple Qur'anic statement *hudan li al-muttaqin* 'a guidance for the righteous'.

Furthermore, regarding the freedom of intellect and the rights to freedom of belief that all citizens, whether Muslims and non-Muslims, would enjoy in an Islamic state, Qutb draws further attention to the Qur'an 88: 21–22; 6: 109; 2: 112, 256; 16: 125–126; and 50: 45. Regarding these verses, Qutb stresses that when Islam grants every individual the 'freedom' in its widest sense, it does not leave the use of freedom to 'human impulses' but guides it in the best way that secures a 'decent life' for the 'welfare' of both the 'individuals and society'.[69] For Qutb, to possess the right to believe in whatever one may is one thing, but to escape the consequences of one's belief is quite another. He argues that the fundamental right and freedom to hold any belief is not a licence to violate the rights and freedom of others. In this regard, Qutb says

> There can be no decent life if every individual seeks to enjoy his absolute freedom without limit. Such behaviour is guaranteed to destroy both the society and the very individuals. Society has a higher interest which must limit the freedom of the individual, and it is in the individual's own interest to have definite limits to his enjoyment of freedom so that he does not get carried away by his instincts, desires and pleasures to the point of destruction, and also so that his freedom does not clash with the freedom of others, resulting in endless quarrels, turning freedom into a torment and a hell, and arresting the growth and perfection of life in the interests of a shortsighted individualism. This is what has happened with the 'freedom' of the capitalist system.[70]
>
> Islam grants the non-Muslims the fundamental right to believe in whatever they may and to claim that their beliefs are right. While they are livening within the Islamic state, the non-Muslims have the right to practice their beliefs openly and publicly, day and night. Yet Islam does not, in any way, permit any human, ruler or ruled, Muslim or non-Muslim, to impose his personal convictions on others, nor does it grants him any right to punish others for the crime of their wrong beliefs as he judges them. Man is only answerable to Allah, and it is He alone Who knows the hidden intricacies of the human mind and heart.[71]

In connection with those statements, Qutb stresses that the Muslims should comply with the Qur'anic teachings and should not 'revile' the gods of others.[72] He pointed out that the Qur'an warns Muslim not to combine in himself the role of a judge or magistrate and that of an executioner, as even the prophet of Islam is demanded 'you are merely an admonisher, you are not a magistrate over them [non-Muslims others]' (Qur'an, 88: 21–22).[73] Qutb further outlined that the Qur'an forbids Muslims to vilify the imaginary gods of idolaters:

> Do not revile those whom they worship besides Allah, lest in retaliation they revile Allah. So have We made the practice of everyone to appear to be attractive in their view. Then their return will be to their Lord who will then inform of what they had been really doing.
>
> (Qur'an, 6: 108)[74]

The Qur'an further teaches 'If it had been Allah's Will, they [non-Muslims] would not have taken false gods. We have not made you [Muhammad] one to watch over their doings nor are you one to mange people's affairs' (Qur'an, 6: 107).[75]

Qutb draws on the previous verses 88: 21–22 and 6: 107, 108 to emphasize the relationship between freedom of human intellect, the right to freedom of belief and the human nature. He stresses that every human is assigned a definite task that is related to the power of freedom and capabilities given to him by God. Based on verse 6: 107, Qutb argues that if it had been God's will, all people in the world will adopt 'Islam'. Allah is also able to 'create humankind from the beginning like angels; know only the right path'.[76] Regarding the freedom of human intellect (*al-'aql*), the rights to freedom of belief and human nature, Qutb says

> Allah's Will is to create man with dual nature of dual ability and dual dimensions. Man is able to follow divine guidance and to go astray. He is just as capable of recognizing good, as he is of recognizing evil. He is equally capable of directing himself one way or the other. This dual ability is deeply ingrained in his being. Divine messages and external factors do not create this natural potential but serve to awaken it and help it to go one way or the other. Man is also equipped with a decision-making faculty. This faculty enables man to perceive, comprehend, analyze and determine his line of action. However, Allah, the Compassionate, does not leave man up to the impulses of his natural tendencies and decision-making faculty, but helps him by sending him messages which lay down accurate and permanent criteria, clear the way of obstructs so that he may clearly see the truth. Messages point out to him the signs that should help him to choose the right path. Thus, man's decision-making faculty functions with full knowledge of the direction it chooses, and the implications of that choice. Allah granted man the freedom to think of religion, to choose and he is responsible for his choice. The responsibility of man and his freedom of choice, make man the honored creature of this world. This is what Allah willed for man and whatever takes place within this framework is a direct fulfillment of His will.[77]

The Qur'anic message does not foster any of the dual nature of man, but guides him onto the right path. Thus, the Prophet's role is, essentially, to convey the message to the people and let them decide. Whether or not the people follow the message, the decision is a personal one, and everyone is responsible for his decision. Qutb stresses that 'Everyone has the right to claim that he is absolutely true in his inner bearing. Everyone; Muslim or non-Muslim, has the right to claim that his belief is good. Punishing others for their wrong beliefs is not of human responsibility.'[78] Islam grants the non-Muslims who preferred to live within the Islamic state complete political and religious freedom and 'protection' to practise their religious duties. Islam 'grants the non-Muslims protection against all threats, persecution, confiscation of their property, assault or violence or unlawful detention by any hostile party operating within national boundaries'.[79]

Qutb concludes that

> those who claim that human intellect (*al-'aql*) is able to replace the Revelation (*wahy*) – those who claim that philosophy is able to make human intellect qualified to replace religion – those who claim that science (the product of intellect) is qualified to guide humanity in place of religion, are saying something has no justification or practical reality.[80]

Concluding remarks

Elevating human intellect to be the highest legal and governmental authority is directly opposite to the Islamic notion of *hakimiyyah* (sovereignty), *'ubudiyyah* (divinity) and the Islamic conception of *al-'aql* (human intellect).

Islam does not abolish the role of human intellect in human life, but human intellect is limited and is incompetent to be the highest legal and governmental authority in place of *hakimiyyah*. Qutb opposed Western philosophy's concept of Rationalism and the ideas that views human intellect as the sole source of knowledge or truth in the place of divine Revelation.

6 The universe (*al-Kawn*)

Qutb's concept of the universe (*al-kawn*) is a result of his comprehensive view of Islam. He views all Islamic spheres as part of a comprehensive and integrated concept. Qutb does not separate man and his life from the surrounding universe. He interweaves the concept of universe, of life and of man with his ideological argument concerning the secular socio-political and economic systems, its theories and procedural practices. He prefers not to use the term Nature (*tabi'ah*), but uses the word '*al-kawn*' (universe), highlights the frame of its Islamic sense and emphasizes the failure of philosophy in arriving at a comprehensive concept of universe. In short, Qutb provides the Islamic conception concerning universe (*al-kawn*) in place of the philosophical conception of Nature. In this sense, the concept of *al-kawn* is one of Qutb's concerns and relates to his theory of *jahiliyyah* in all spheres.[1]

This chapter focusses on Qutb's concept of the universe (*al-kawn*) and its socio-political and religious implications for the concept of sovereignty (*hakimiyyah*), servitude (*'ubudiyyah*) and the notion of universality. It will also examine the significance of the concept of *al-kawn* in the articulation of his theory of society. This will entail a brief outline of Qutb's ideas and methods with regard to the observation of the universe, taking into account differences between his concept of the universe (*al-kawn*) and that of Nature (*tabi'ah*). Qutb's ideological view as regards man and his responsibility will then be outlined.

Conceptual differences and implications

In his works, Qutb prefers to use the word '*al-Kawn*' (universe) instead of using the word '*tabi'ah*' (Nature). The word 'Nature' in English dictionary terms means 'the power that regulates the world, the established order of things, the external world, esp., as untouched by man'.[2] The Arabic dictionary defines the word '*tabi'ah*' (Nature) as 'the world of beings, the force in the universe or the individual, the essence (*jawhar*)'.[3] In referring to humans, Ibn Manzur notes that '*tabi'ah* is the natural disposition: *fitrah* . . . the Qur'an says "*taba'a 'ala qalbihi* (sealed his heart)" '.[4] Thus, in the traditional Islamic construct, the word '*tabi'ah*' (Nature) means everything in the world except those made by humans. This means that '*tabi'ah*' (Nature), as Qutb says, is '*al-kawn*' (Universe).[5] Also, the word '*tabi'ah*' (Nature) can be used in various ways: '*tabi'atu al-insan*: nature of man' and '*tabi'atu al-kawn*: nature of the universe'. In the sense of the former, *tabi'ah* is one part among other parts existing in *al-kawn* (universe). Thus *tabi'ah* (Nature) which means force or essence, is a force or an essence among the forces and essences existing in this vast universe (*al-kawn*). In this way, man himself is a universe (*kawn*) within this vast universe (*al-kawn*). Every creature itself is a universe within the vast universe. It follows that Nature (force and disposition whether of the individual or of the vast Universe) is regulated by God's order (i.e. law). The point is that Nature, in Qutb's view, 'is the Universe.'[6] If so, why does Qutb prefer to use the word 'Universe', not 'Nature', and how does he take this concept as one of his important tools in his analysis of the theory of *jahiliyyah*?[7]

One reason may be the historical background of the word Nature and its ideological use. As Qutb says 'numerous intellectuals recognize *tabi'ah* (Nature) as the sole source which engraves the truth on only human intellect'.[8] This view implies the following propositions:

(i) Nature is the source of truth.
(ii) Therefore, Revelation is not the sole source of truth.
(iii) The Creator the ultimate sovereign is not the ultimate source of truth.
(iv) Consequently, there is no relationship between Nature and other living beings.
(v) The creator of human intellect is not the creator of other living beings. Therefore, there is no relationship between human intellect and other living beings.
(vi) Further, there is no relationship between man as a creature and the Creator.
(vii) Nature is the ultimate authority in the universe, life and man.
(viii) Nature is not a creature of God but an ultimate power.

The moral implications of the above are that numerous intellectuals 'set up Nature as a god rather than make God the criterion of reality'.[9] Here, Qutb refers to the ideological role of Positivism as a cultural heritage of Darwinism, which developed into the dialectical materialism of Marx and other thinkers.[10]

According to Qutb, the secular concept of Nature is evident in various spheres of contemporary writings.[11] The term Nature has come to be used in the West without awareness of its historical background. Moral and socio-political implications of the term Nature are also two of the significant spheres in which the theory of *jahiliyyah* actively operates.[12] Consequently, the term *tabi'ah* (Nature) has come to be used in the Muslim world without the realization of its secular implications.[13] In explanation, Qutb referred to Alexis Carrel (1873–1944), the French Nobel Prize winner for contributions to surgery in 1912. Carrel was one of those who rendered judgment against the present materialistic civilization. He, however, expressed Nature as the only source of all forces latent in humankind. Qutb cited from Carrel that 'there are millions and millions of human beings that successively dwelled in this world but only a few individuals, from time to time, are born whom the Nature has engraved them with unusual powers'.[14]

Perhaps Carrel did not realize the significance of his words: 'Nature engraved them with unusual powers'. Qutb notes that

> Carrel's belief in Allah . . . was based on his observation of the facts in his field of medical science. However, his cultural heritage facilitates, to him, the application of the term Nature wrongly. It causes him to violate the truth by his expression of 'Nature engraves': This expression makes no sense to the believers, since it is only Allah the Bestower of bounties. The Nature is universe which is created by Allah. Nature has no power of endowment because nature is not Allah.[15]

According to Qutb, cultural heritage plays a significant part in the application of the term Nature wrongly as, for example, in expressions like Mother Nature or *Man Stands Alone*.[16] The latter celebrates human autonomy over Nature in a secular way: Man is seen to have conquered Nature (*al-insan qahir al-tabi'ah*).[17] These expressions are in fact titles of books, which Qutb, as a literary critic, commentated upon. He says

> Westerners – the inheritors of the Roman *jahiliyyah* – accustomed to express their use of the power of Nature by their saying: '*qahir al-tabi'ah*' [conqueror of Nature]. This expression has its clear evidence on the view of the *jahiliyyah*, which has no connection at all with Allah and the spirit of the universe, which submitted itself to Allah.[18]

The word '*qahir*' (conqueror) in those latter expressions has connotations of dominant, conqueror, forceful, tyrant and dictator. Thus, Qutb states

> The mind of materialism, which sprang from the pagan myths of the ancient Greece and Rome, was nourished by the concept of imperial power that dominated Europe. Thus, all relationships in the European sense are based on *qahir* (conqueror) and *maqhur* (conquered). There is no relationship of *tafahum* (mutual understanding) or *sadaqah* (friendship).[19]

Islamic connotations of the word '*qahir*' or dominant also means the Omnipotent, the Almighty Allah, who created the universe (*al-kawn*) and made its Nature a friend to man, who gave man the programme and means whereby man can make and develop his friendship with the surrounding universe. The notion implied by the word '*qahir*' or dominant is completely different in materialistic thought from that in the Muslim context. This may be why Qutb distanced himself from using the word Nature but uses the Arabic word '*al-kawn*' universe frequently. This does not mean that Qutb avoids the word nature totally, but when he does use it, he specifies clearly, what he means, for example: 'the nature of things', 'the nature of man' and 'the nature of the universe' or 'the nature of life'. He also speaks of the nature of religion and the nature of political, economic and social systems.[20] Thus, clarity is a significant feature of Qutb's view concerning Nature and other subjects.[21] Qutb sometimes points out what he means by his use of particular words. For example, in using the term '*waqi'iyyah*' (Realism), Qutb notes that he 'uses the term in its meaning which has been given to it by Arabic expression, free from whatever meaning attached to this term in another environment.'[22] This confirms Qutb's intention of distinction between those conceptions in words and specifics.

Some of Qutb's works, when translated into English, consequently suffer in the process due to these constraints. This was one of the reasons (not the exclusive reason) why William Shepard attempted to correct the extant English translation of Qutb's book, *Social Justice in Islam*. In preparing his own translation, Shepard noted that

> The first edition of *Social Justice in Islam* was translated into English some years ago and this translation has been widely used by scholars since then. I have, of course, consulted it in preparing this translation. Unfortunately, however, it is not always as accurate as one might wish, so the present translation will also serve to provide a more dependable version of the first edition, as well as making the later editions available to the reader of English.[23]

This means that inaccurate translation of the first edition of *Social Justice in Islam* was one among several reasons also indicated by Shepard.[24] He also cited two examples 'where later scholars have quoted badly translated passages' from the first edition.[25]

In the first edition of *Social Justice*, Hardie translated Qutb's phrase '*hamiyyah diniyyah jahiliyyah*' as 'ill-informed religious zeal'.[26] In this translation the word *jahiliyyah*, which is ideologically significant, is not mentioned. This translation implies something rather different, as it does not reflect Qutb's intention of the term *jahiliyyah* (that Qutb speaks about and mentions explicitly in the phrase). Regarding this phrase, Shepard sees the more accurate translation in this: 'ignorant religious fanaticism'.[27] Here also the word *jahiliyyah*, which is technical, was not mentioned in Shepard's technical translation. In this phrase, the word *jahiliyyah* does not mean that simple ignorance implied by such translation intended to be technical.

Another example that abounds is in the phrase '*Siyasat al-Hukm fi al-Islam*', which is a title of a chapter in Qutb's '*Social Justice in Islam*'. Translating this phrase, Shepard pointed out that

> Hardie translates [it] 'political theory' which reflects the author's intention [Qutb's] fairly well but suggests a different Arabic phrase (*al-nazariyyah al-siyasiyyah*), which he [Qutb] might conceivably have used but did not (he does use *nazariyyat al-hukm* in paragraph 29).[28] It also suggests perhaps something more complex than what this chapter contains.[29]

In the sphere of government, Qutb's phrase *'al-ra'i wa al-ra'iyyah'* was translated by Shepard as 'shepherd and the flock'.[30] This also is an accurate translation, but, in the context of government and for the reader of English, Hardie's translation, 'the ruler and his subjects' is clearer and points to Qutb's idea of government.[31]

Muhammad Moinuddin siddiqui, who translated Qutb's book *Khas'is al-Tasawwur al-Islami* into English, translated Qutb's phrase *'nizam al-hukm:* [system of government]' as 'system of justice'.[32] Such translations moved the government and its system to the court of justice. He also translated the phrase *'al-manhaj al-Rabbani* [Divine program]' as 'Islamic way of life.'[33] Qutb's phrase 'ifrad Allah bi *al-uluhiyyah* wa al-i'tiraf lahu wahdahu bi *al-'ubudiyyah'* was also translated by siddiqui 'for the sake of Allah alone and with recognition that He alone deserves to be worshipped.'[34] These translations are accurate in their own right but do not reflect the force and intent of those key phrases (the system of government, the divine programme, *uluhiyyah* and *'ubudiyyah*), which are of ideological importance in Qutb's thinking.

Furthermore, the literal translation of Qutb's word *'al-kawn'* as 'cosmos'[35] is accurate in its own right, but it does not fairly fit Qutb's thinking of *al-kawn*. The word 'cosmos' is the physical universe as an embodiment of order. In this sense of physics, 'cosmos is a term used to refer to everything that exists, from the smallest atoms to the most distant celestial bodies. It comes from the ancient Greek word *kosmos*, which means order, the universe, or the world.'[36] 'The universe consists of all matter, light, and other forms of radiation and energy [these also are matter].'[37] In short, cosmos is the universe, but the universe is matter; thus, cosmos is matter. If the word cosmos, which is the physical or material universe, includes humans and, furthermore, alludes to the orderly nature of the universe, it, excludes the non-physical or immaterial world, the world of spirit which exists in this vast *al-kawn* and is significant in Qutb's thinking on the subject. In other words, the cosmos includes the matter in man, not his spirit. This implies some questions about the nature of the relationship between man and his surrounding forces in the universe. It implies questions about the relationship between matter and spirit. Implications like this are numerous and indicate that the word cosmos, as a translation of Qutb's word *al-kawn*, does not fairly fit his thinking on this subject. Qutb's idea of *al-Kawn* reflects the relationship between the Creator and the creation, the physical and non-physical universe, life and humankind (spirit and matter).[38] The point is that the Islamic concept of *al-kawn* has its own connotation and particular style of expression.[39] Qutb's view is comprehensive; that is, he does not separate this world from the other, heaven from the earth, cosmos from life, life from man, or man from his spirit and the rest of the universe.[40]

Qutb calls upon people to implement Islam in their lives. In so doing, he explains the relationship between the Creator and the creation, the universe, life and man. He emphasizes that it is not a question of the conqueror and the conquered; there is only one dominant power that is the sovereign Will. From Him issue all things, the universe, life and man. Man does not, and cannot, stand alone in the universe, but he does have friends. Accordingly,

> the existence suited for and conductive to the existence of life in general and the existence of man the highest form of life in particular. Thus, the universe is not an enemy to man, nor is Nature; the expression of contemporary *jahiliyyah*, an adversary that man must struggle with and conquer, but is part of God's creation. It is a friend, whose tendencies do not differ from those of life and man. It is not the task of living things to struggle with Nature, since they have sprung from its very heart.[41]

The Creator has pressed into man's service all the known and latent properties of the universe: physical and non-physical, material and immaterial. It is Allah Who foresaw all the possible requirements 'this small creature – man' could ever need during all the ages of his spiritual, material, scientific, economic and cultural advancement. The Qur'an says 'And He has pressed into your service whatever is in the heavens and whatever is in the earth, all of it entirely. In that there are Signs surely for a people who reflect' (Qur'an, 45: 13).[42]

A more wonderful gesture of encouragement for limitless exploration could not be conceived. It is underwritten that everything that man would discover would be of service to him. But that is not all. The following verse speaks not only of the visible heavens and earth but also of that something which fills the space between the two – the heavens and the earth – to be of benefit to man. The message is clear that the apparent void in the interstellar space is in reality filled with some form of existence of which man has no knowledge. 'We have created the heavens and the earth, and whatever lies between them, according to the requirements of truth and wisdom' (Qur'an, 15: 85). These words of 'wonderful expression are of deep meaning and implication. It inspires that the truth is rooted deeply in the design of this existence.'[43]

Qutb also emphasizes that there is a harmonious relationship between Islam and the universe because both issued from the Omnipotent, the sovereign Will. He says

> It is not natural and not in the nature of Islam to be segregated from life in this universe, nor is it natural for the Divine system to be confined to conscientious feelings, ethical rules and ritual duties. Nor is it in its nature to be immured in a restricted corner of human life and labelled a 'personal affair'.[44]

Qutb's method and ideas, then, are reflected in what he says of the universe. His objective is to promote the purpose of human life. He expounds on the universe within a comprehensive theory that covers religio-political, economic, social, intellectual and moral spheres together with other issues relevant to the affairs of human life. Among his fundamental concerns are *hakimiyyah* (sovereignty), *'ubudiyyah* (servitude) and universality of Islam. These are interwoven with others, such as *fitrah* (the unchangeable constitution of the universe, life and man as laid down by Allah). To this he ties his concept of human intellect (*al-'aql*) and human thought (*al-fikr*), and his theories about civilization, culture and philosophy. He then uses all these ideas as one comprehensive and integrated conception to examine various cultures, civilization, religious conceptions, systems and laws, human life in general and man's aims and obligations within this universe in particular. Finally he shapes his arguments to the concept of *tawhid* and some Qur'anic verses. In this way, Qutb deals with the universe as a subject in his theory of society. The complexity and comprehensiveness of Qutb's ideas with theological, socio-political, economic and intellectual dimensions make it worthy of further studies.

Socio-political and specifics

To Qutb, Islamic concepts of the universe, life and man all are themselves in harmony in their witness to the nature of reality. Allah has created the universe. He knows these historical and general socio-economic circumstances of man. Therefore, Allah provides the Islamic framework within which life can develop peacefully and harmoniously with justice and equity.[45] For Qutb, Islam is not only a religion but also an integral part of a perfectly balanced universe. According to Qutb,

> Islam issues from the sovereign Will to unify all forces of the universe, life and man; to blend together desires, inclinations and sympathies into a harmonious whole. Islam came to unite the Heavens and the earth in a universal order; this world and the Hereafter in the religious order; spirit and body in the human order. Islam then leads them all along a unified road of complete submission to Allah and subjects them all to one authority, the authority of Allah.[46]

It is impossible for man to reside in this infinite universe as a straying atom without a special bond securing his life, his stability and his peace, and guiding the motion of his life in general. To Qutb, there is and must be an "*aqidah* (religious creed) to explain the world to man and his relationship with it; to reveal the purpose of his life within this universe.'[47] The creed must be able to provide man with a

> comprehensive explanation of all that exists, on the basis of which he relates to the world. This explanation brings him closer to an understanding of the great realities that confront him, and of the nature of the relationships and connections that exist among these realities, namely, the reality of the *uluhiyyah* (divinity) and the reality of *'ubudiyyah* (servitude) the latter including the reality of universe, the reality of life, and the reality of man.[48]

Qutb means, by the creed, the divine revelation. In contrast with intellectual knowledge, the knowledge of the creed is characterized by truth and integrity, validity and vitality, constancy and universality. It does not violate the nature of the universe and of life, and does not violate the nature of humankind.[49] The need for this creed is universal and a *fitrah* that Allah has made innate to the universe, life and man. Therefore, the constant need for a creed transcends particular circumstances, time, race and place. This is simply because the nature of the universe, of life and the nature of man remained with no change.

According to Qutb, there is a relationship between the nature of the social system and the nature of the ideological ideal. No social system has emerged and established itself in the universe randomly, that is, without background of ideological ideal. The social system, Qutb claims, is an offshoot of the ideological ideal. It grows biologically and naturally, and is completely adapted in accordance with the assessment of life that is relative to the human situation and goals in this world.[50] The objectives of social order are stabilization and fulfilment of human existence. This cannot be achieved unless man harmonizes the motion of his life with the motion of the universe. The rights assumed by man by virtue of his function in this life serve to determine his course of action and to determine the means he is entitled to use for reaching his goal. It also determines the tenor of his relations between his human race, institutions and all that encompass the term social order.[51] A social order that is established on any basis other than Islam is for Qutb merely arbitrary and lacking in social harmony. Such secular systems, therefore, are short-lived. According to Qutb, when the balance of harmony is absent, man is an destined for misery and hardship regardless of the material and industrial facilities such systems may offer him. Thus any society based on a system that cannot explain the harmonious nature of the relationship between the Creator and the creation, the universe, life and man, is an arbitrary and short-lived system.[52]

Because human beings cannot comprehend universal laws, which regulate the motion of the universe, life and man, humans, they cannot create a system for the regulation of human life. It is beyond the ability of man to create a system to regulate his visible life with his invisible and unknown tendencies.[53] The Creator of the universe, life and man, has created the programme which regulates and harmonizes their life and stability. This programme is Islam. For Qutb, the *Shari'ah* regulates the relationship between the Creator and the creation, the universe, life and man.[54] In contrast to secular ideological constructs the Islamic social system emanates in the conscience and interacts with the soul. This system is able to establish a balanced life for all humanity and leads them towards development and renewal. Qutb has emphasized the stages of progress of the conscience (*damir*), the soul (*ruh*) and the stage of practical implementation as an integrated quality that characterizes the Islamic socio-political system and distinguishes it from the systems of *jahiliyyah*.[55]

Detailing this process, Qutb points out that the practical implementation of Islamic laws and concepts cannot be rightly followed unless conviction supports it from within. This is what Islam expresses by moral exhortation and in legislation. According to Qutb, some people believe that liberating the self from domination by the pleasures and passions of life and turning towards a heavenly kingdom will grant man the freedom of his conscience and blessings for his soul. On the contrary, Qutb argued, the impulses of life cannot be contained in all circumstances. The necessities of practical life cannot be overcome. Man must submit to them most of the time.[56] The Creator has not created these impulses for no purpose. Man should not seek to paralyse that life, or stop its expression. Qutb considers that,

> it is good for man to rise above his needs and passions but it is not good to destroy life itself in the process. If there is a way by which the forces latent in human nature can be released, and man rise above humiliating submission to his needs, that way is the soundest and the safest. That is what Islam aims when it unites the needs of the body and the desires of the spirit in one system and provides for the freedom of the self at the deepest level and in the most practical way.[57]

Thus, Qutb argues secular systems and calls them *jahiliyyah*. He argues Communism and its philosophical attempts of explaining the universe and the responsibility of man therein. Economies and human life in general cannot be separated from the universe and its phenomena. However, communist philosophy separates man from religion and from the universe. It claims that human freedom means economic freedom.[58] According to Kamenka (1983), Communism 'abolishes the eternal truth, abolishes all religions and separates man from his surrounding universe and from his humanity.'[59] Thus, 'in Communism, the universe became determined by Nature and man became determined by economy'.[60]

From Marx's philosophical perspective, as outlined in the communist manuscript *Alienated Labor* (1848), Marx has alienated man not only from the universe but also from his natural tendencies, as stated by Kamenka in the followings:

> What, then, constitutes the alienation of labor? First, in the fact that labor is external to the worker, that is, that it does not belong to his essential being; that in his work, therefore, he does not affirm himself but denies himself, does not feel well but unhappy, does not freely develop his physical and mental Energy but mortifies his body and ruins his mind. The worker, therefore, feels himself only outside his work, and feels beside himself in his work. He is at home when he is not working, and when he is working he is not at home. His work therefore is not voluntary, but coerced; it is forced labor. It is therefore not the satisfaction of a need, but only a *means* for satisfying needs external to it. Its alien

> character emerges clearly in the fact that labor is shunned like the plague as soon as there is no physical or other compulsion. Externally labor, labor in which man is externalized, is labor of self-sacrifice, of mortification. Finally, the external nature of labor fore the worker appears in the fact that it is not his own, but someone else's, that it does not belong to him, that in that labor he does not belong to himself but to someone else. Just as in religion, the spontaneous activity of human imagination, of the human brain and the human heart, operates independently of the individual, i.e. as an alien divine or diabolical activity, so the worker's activity is not his spontaneous activity. It belongs to another; it is the loss of his self. The result, therefore, is that man (the worker) feels that he is acting freely only in his animal functions – eating, drinking, procreating, or at most in his shelter and his finery – while in his human functions he feels himself nothing more than an animal. What is animal becomes human and what is human becomes animal. Eating, drinking, procreating, etc. are, of course, also genuinely human functions. But taking in abstraction, separated from the remaining spheres of human activities and turned into sole and ultimate ends, they are animal.[61]

This account of Kamenka echoes Qutb's view of Marx's philosophical attempts of explaining the universe and the responsibility of man therein. Qutb says

> Between human being (*al-ka'in al-insani*), animal beings (*al-ka'inat al-hayawaniyyah*), and materialistic beings (*al-ka'inat al-maddiyyah*) some common qualities for which those of the '*jahalah* of science' (*al-jahlah al-'ilmiyyah*) labelled human being as an animal like other animals, or a matter like other matters! However, human being has the qualities, which distinguished him and made him a unique being . . .[62]
>
> The idea that the human is an animal developed from an animal is the idea which inspired Marx to announce that the essential need of man is food, drink, shelter, and sex! These, in fact, are the essential needs of animals! Human beings will never be in a lower position than in this theory. All his rights, which are based on his difference from animals, will be outlawed. He will have no right to the freedom of belief. He will have no right to the freedom of thought and opinion. He will have no right to choose the type of work and cannot choose the place where he wants to dwell. He will have no right to criticize the regime and its intellectual and ideological bases. He will have no right to criticize the activity of the 'Party' or any of the rulers of those odious regimes, which oppress the people, for these people in the eyes of the materialistic philosophy are, but animals. They call all of this misery 'Scientific Socialism' (*al-ishtrakiyyah al-'ilmiyyah*).[63]

Marx's idea firmly binds the motion of human life with the motion of production. In this regard Kamenka says, 'All these consequences are contained in the fact that the worker is related to the product of his labor as to an alien object.'[64]

By contrast, the Islamic conception sees Nature and social relations differently, that is in harmony of human life and the function of the universe. According to Qutb, The Islamic system sees the motion of the universe as responding to all human needs. This response also is not limited to a particular age or generation. In addition, the Islamic system offers a stable (*thabit*) programme for human life. This does not, however, mean that the programme is rigid (*jamid*) in its application. It enables humanity to develop within a framework that does not separate the motion of human life from the motion of the universe.[65] In this regard, Qutb states

> Motion, it appears, is a law of the *al-kawn* (universe) and it also is a law in the life of man who is part of this universe. But this law of motion is not free of restrictions or without some control, if only because it is a coherent system. An analogy to the life of a man is a planet with an orbit and an axis. This Divinely-revealed Islamic concept is like the sun around which the life of all mankind is to revolve. There is plenty of rooms for mankind to grow, progress, advance, and evolve, while still remaining in the field of attraction of this central concept. Moreover, this concept is perfect and complete. It does not require any 'spare parts' from outside or any change for completion. Since it is given by Allah, nothing from a source other than Him can fit it. Man is incapable of adding anything to it or making any corrections in it. Indeed, it has come as a gift to man in order to make him grow, correct him, and propel him forward. It has come to enrich his heart, his intellect, his life, and his world.[66]

According to Qutb, disrupting this harmonious motion by means of political, economic or social means is *jahiliyyah*.[67] To him, any society not based on Islamic conception is *jahiliyyah*.[68] He says

> The Islamic concept stands firm on the basis of the policy that for the life of man there are but two states of being, and that these states are independent of time and place. Their respective values are intrinsic to them, because they are determined by Allah's just balance, which remains unaffected by temporal and spatial changes in man's condition. There are only two possibilities for the life of people, no matter in what time and place they live. These are the state of guidance (*huda*) or the state of error (*dalal*), whatever form the error may take; the state of truth (*haqq*) or the state of falsehood (*batil*), whatever may be the varieties of falsehood; the state of light (*nur*) or the state of darkness (*zalam*), regardless of the shades of darkness; the state of *shari'ah* or the state of following whims, no matter what varieties of whims there may be; the state of *Islam* or the state of *jahiliyyah*, without regard to the forms of *jahiliyyah*; and the state of belief (*iman*) or the state of unbelief (*kufr*), of whatever kind.

> People live either according to Islam, following it as a way of life and a sociopolitical system, or else in the state of unbelief (*kufr*), *jahiliyyah*, whim (*hawa*), darkness (*zalam*), falsehood (*batil*), and error (*dalal*).[69]

Thus, his observation of the universe brought him to the same result of one way or the other: Islam or *jahiliyyah*. The point here is that in the face of philosophy and secular thought, Qutb gives the Islamic conception of *al-kawn* (universe) great importance and he views the Islamic system as a central part in the harmonious universe.[70]

This turns our attention to the failure of philosophy to provide a stable and comprehensive concept of the nature of the relationship between the Creator and the creation, the universe, life and man. Permitting people to give free rein to their natural appetites covered the failure.[71] According to Qutb, Positivism

> recognizing Nature not only an independent source of knowledge but also the sole source of truth. Nature is the only source that engraving the truth on human mind, revealed the truth to human soul and shaped the truth's basic frame in human conscience.[72]

The logical conclusion to draw here is that Nature is the only source forming human intellect. This means that human intellect is dominated only by Nature and not by the sovereign Will who created the Nature, the mind and the whole of existence. Positivism's view, according to Qutb, implies that any knowledge coming from what is beyond Nature and the whole of existence cannot be true knowledge, since it lacks certainty. For Positivism, the truth is dictated by what is called 'Mother Nature'.[73]

Qutb argues that engraving the truth on the human mind by Nature means that Nature creates the human mind. Qutb asks,

> why Nature, then, does not create the mind of animals? Why does Nature engrave the truth only on human mind? Does Nature have a distinctive will that is able to choose? If the essence of Nature manifests itself on only human thought, the process of manifestation, therefore, depends on the existence of human mind. How can Nature then be the creator of mind while, on the contrary, Nature manifests itself on the mind only after its existence?[74]

In this regard, Qutb argues

> what is this Nature? Is it the primary matter of the universe? If so, what is the essence of this primary matter? They themselves admit they do not know what this thing, which they term 'matter' and consider to be something permanent, really is. When they claim that 'matter' is unchangeable or constant, they called it 'Nature', but it became apparent to them that

> matter is not constant.... In which form then and at which stage does the creative power appear which imprints truth on human mind? At which stage this 'god' acquire the creative power?[75]

For this Qutb's argument goes further and asks

> which truth that the Nature imprints on human mind? Is it the truth when human mind has determined matter is the solid thing or when human mind has determined matter the accumulated energy that can change from one state to another? Is it the truth when human mind has determined Nature is the product of the mind, or when human mind has determined that the mind is but the product of Nature? Which one of these rational decisions was the truth, which was engraved on the human mind by Nature?[76]

According to Qutb, the truth, which is engraved on the human mind by Nature, was not stable or constant but changed from time to time, from mind to mind and from generation to generation.[77] This character of inconstancy and instability of knowledge is a reflection of the limited power of the human mind. Instability of knowledge confirms the failure of philosophy to provide a stable explanation of Nature and its relationship with existence, life and man. The logical implication here is that the origination of life and its truth cannot be revealed through matter and that the infinite universe (*al-kawn*) cannot be reduced to material forces. Similarly, human life cannot be reduced to the cycle of economy or the motion of the machine and production, that is, the will of economy cannot be the only dominant force in human life.[78]

Allah has created matter and subjected it to man and enabled him to use it in varying ways and forms according to his understanding.[79] Allah does not leave man to deal with matter according to the impulses of his own conscience, but provides him with the programme to guide him to use the matter rightly. The individual who follows the revealed guidance is *sawyy* (person in sound state). The *sawyy* will use the power of matter in the right way to develop and facilitate its application in all aspects of his life. The corrupt person, however, will use the power of matter to destroy, to conquer and to oppress others.[80]

Islam, philosophy and science

Science says matter itself is neutral. From here Qutb develops his argument to assert that the function of pure science, technology, theories and research are all also neutral in themselves, but they can be used for good or evil. The choice is man's. He is a free being and a decision maker, but his freedom is coupled by responsibility, that is he is responsible for his decision.[81]

The concept of mechanical universe, of life and man is manifested in Western civilization where, Qutb asserts, material development, power and prestige have become the most desirable things in life. Most of Western intellectual and material resources are directed towards the development that can secure access, to any place in the world, for their material objectives. Believing in materialism, the Western machine then subjugated the world to Western material demand. Western invention of science has lost all regard for mental and spiritual values. Therefore, Qutb says, irresponsible use of worldly power, irresponsible concepts and erroneous philosophical ideas are evident in many fields and disciplines in the West.[82]

By contrast, Islamic conception concerning scientific invention is positive, encouraging scientific development. It does not reject science or knowledge for its own sake.[83] Qutb argues that the Islamic conception emphasizes science as a branch of knowledge that should not be separated from religious belief.[84] This means that man should use the power latent in matter – subjected to him by the Creator – to broaden life and make it rich in all its aspects. To Qutb, science and technological progress should facilitate human life and strengthen man to understand and recognize the possibility of a harmonious relationship with the universe and the Creator who controls all material forces and makes them available to man.[85]

The point that should be noted here is that Qutb does not reject scientific invention and the modern technology but rejects their use for evil. He firmly rejects the use of science as a means of political, social, intellectual and moral domination of man over others.[86] Qutb does not reject science for its own sake but rejects its philosophical theories which attempt to explain the origins of existence, the meaning of life and human responsibility in this world on only Rational authority or sensual grounds rather than in the light of Revelation.[87] To Qutb, science should not destroy, corrupt or pollute life, but help man to recognize the Creator and fulfil the responsibility of man as *khilafah* (vicegerency of Allah) on Earth.[88]

Therefore, Qutb rejects all Western philosophical ideas such as Rationalism, Positivism, Sensualism and other philosophies of science that recognize it as the supreme path to truth.[89] To Qutb, philosophy has failed to provide humanity with knowledge to enable man to establish a universal socio-political system to harmonize human life with the universal powers, and not violate the universal law of life and its highest goals.[90] Therefore, philosophy and science cannot replace Islamic conception. According to Qutb, philosophy and science have replaced religion in some places in the world. This was because of conflicts between religion, science and philosophy there. Islam, however, was not one of those religions. Islam stands on its own.[91] There is no inherent conflict between Islam and science. According to Qutb, there is not a single 'scientific fact' that contravenes Islam and its basic creed.[92]

To Qutb, philosophical knowledge is but 'frozen knowledge': it has no practical vitality.[93] By contrast, 'Islam is a program of a proper practical motility that does not deal with hypotheses. Islam deals with the reality of the universe, of life and the reality of man living on this planet.'[94] This makes Islam a worldwide system for all humanity regardless of time, ethnicity or place.[95]

Qutb emphasizes the *shari'ah* of Islam as part of this vast universe and in harmony with it. Therefore he calls it *shari'ah kawniyyah* (i.e. universal law). This translation reflects Qutb's intention as in the following:

> The *shari'ah* is part of the General Divine Law, which governs the nature of man, the nature of general existence and harmonizes all parts together... The *shari'ah* prescribed by Allah to organize human life – hence – *shari'ah kawniyyah*. It means that [the *shari'ah*] is connected (*muttasilah*) to the General Divine Law and in harmony with it.[96]

Thus, the *shari'ah* in Qutb's view is rooted there in the General Divine Law which governs and harmonizes the universe, life and man. The position of human thought here, as Qutb asserts, is only a means that should facilitate the processes of understanding and facilitate the practical application of the revealed knowledge without adding to it or taking away from it.[97] Man's function is thus to receive the revelation, to understand it and then to implement it with no need to philosophize its characteristics and foundations.

Qutb rejects claims for culture (*thaqafah*) as a human heritage not located in territory, ethnicity or religion.[98] This claim implies that the phenomenon of human thought is universal and thus, that Western civilization, culture and philosophy – both classical and modern – are commensurable with Islamic culture or Islamic civilization, that is, both are equally human processes. Qutb, rejects this although with some qualifications:

> This claim is true insofar as it relates to pure sciences (*al-'ulum al-bahtah*) and their practical applications but does not go beyond this area. It should not apply to philosophical explanations of the results of these sciences, nor philosophical explanation of the human self and its activity and history, or to the arts, literature and expressions of human feelings. Beyond the pure sciences and its practical application, Islam considers that there are only two kinds of culture, Islamic culture and *jahili* culture. Islamic culture is based on Islamic conception, and *jahili* culture is based on various but reducible to one basic principle, that of setting up human thought as the divine and not making God the ultimate truth.[99]

Islamic culture therefore includes, as Qutb asserts, all fields of human intellectual and practical activity. Islamic culture has its unique principles, methods and characteristics that guarantee the growth of both practical action and continued vitality. In support of this proposition, Qutb draws from the Muslim and Western history and even from Western intellectuals:

> according to Western intellectuals who do not deny historical facts, industrial civilization is the offshoot of Islamic scientific invention and experimental orientation that began in the early Islamic universities in Spain. Experimental science upon which present industrial civilization

> rests, derives its roots from the Islamic concepts and teachings concerning the universe, its nature and its resources. Europeans adopted these methods, developed and improved them. Then, Europe separated the methods it had borrowed from these Islamic origins and took science as far from God as possible. Europe then broke loose from the Church which had dominated people with oppression and hostility in the name of God.[100]

According to Qutb, there is a connection between faith and the sciences of astronomy, biology, chemistry, physics, medicine, agriculture and other sciences connected with the law of the universe, of life and man. All of them lead to God, and his law when they are not distorted by a perverse desire to disregard God, as became the tendency in European method in the scientific revival.[101] In some of his published works, Qutb detailed the philosophical ideas that separated human life from religion and its concept of the universe.[102]

Thus correct Islamic thought concerning the universe cannot be taken from philosophy in general, or even from what is known as 'Islamic philosophy'. According to Qutb 'Islamic philosophy is but a shadow of pagan Greek philosophy.'[103] Therefore, works by al-Kindi (d. 246/860), al-Farabi (d. 339/951), Ibn Sina (d. 429/1037), Ibn Rushd (d. 595/1198) and others represented a misguided adventure. Understanding the Islamic conception of the universe, according to Qutb, comes not through ideas or methods imported from outside Islam but only from within: from the Qur'an and the Sunnah the natural roots of the programme that expounds the nature of the universe, of life and man.

Concluding remarks

Qutb's view of the universe rests on an Islamic concept: existence represents a unity whose parts are integrated and harmonious in character, organization and orientation. The position of man in the universe witnesses the relationship between man and the universe. In precise language, this means that a harmonious relationship between the universe, life and humankind exists. The source of this relationship cannot be the universe or life, and cannot be human mind, or Nature. This is because the universe and its being, life and man are all created from non-existence. Because the universe, life and man cannot create themselves, they cannot create their relationship with others, nor the programme that maintains their harmonious motion and orientation. The sole source of the relationship between the universe, life and man is the sovereign Will and from Him issues all created things. Therefore, Qutb's concept of the universe simply means the relationship between the Creator and the creation.

The Creator is the One Eternal Sovereign; Allah remains utterly unique, without partner or associates. The universe, life and man will always remain Allah's creation, subjected to transient ephemeral life. The two orders cannot be united, absorbed or confused with one another. Thus, the divine programme that governs the universe, life and man cannot be coterminous with a man-made programme, because the programme reflects its author.

Consequently, Qutb rejects all ideas trying to blend the divine programme with human made programmes. The nature of both mutually excludes this. Qutb does not oppose science but he believed that science is a means to the knowledge of Allah. He opposes philosophy in general, including Islamic philosophy, because its knowledge has no practical vitality, and because it is based on the philosophy of Ancient Greece and Rome.

Part III

Face to face

7 Sovereignty and political establishments

Introduction

The relation between religion and politics has been a focus of debate among scholars. Focusing on Islam, its place in the polity is one of the most controversial issues in Muslim countries. It holds a central position in any public debate over constitution, laws and codes and national and cultural identity. The nature of the debate, in one way or the other, is revolving around the conceptual framework of Sovereignty. At times this issue makes its presence felt in world politics in bilateral and international relations. In this sense, the similarity and the difference between the pulses of the Islamic and other systems is critical.

Some of those who discuss Islam and its system, whether social or political, economic or intellectual, make an effort to establish relationships or similarity between Islam and other systems.[1] Therefore, we can find numerous intellectuals who consider Islam a capitalist system, while others call Islam 'democratic'. In either case, they mean to imply that there is no difference between Islam and capitalist or democratic systems found in our modern world.[2] There is also a perception of Islam as a socialist system,[3] while for others Islam is a communist system, or Communism is the latest version of Islam. The latter tends to be accompanied by the view that imitation of Communism is appropriate, that is, Muslims should imitate the Communist experiment of the Soviet Union.[4] Some thinkers have considered Islam as an imperialist system.[5] According to Muhammad 'Abduh (1849–1905), 'there are some thinkers still whispering that Islam has the elements of dictatorship in it and that Muslims should review the order of obedience to the leader.'[6]

With regard to the above opinions, Qutb argues that labelling the Islamic system by any name, other than Islam, is but a reflection of the condition of inward defeat in the face of the human systems that humanity have formed for themselves in isolation from the system of Allah. In his view, Islam gains nothing when told there are similarities between it and these ideas, and it loses nothing if there are not.[7]

This chapter, in its five sections, intends to bring Islamic system face to face with other political establishments. It examines the power of Sovereignty (*hakimiyyah*) in relation to Nationalism, Capitalism, Socialism, Communism and Democracy. Analysis will involve Qutb's religio-political and philosophical constructs and how he employs them, conceptually and intellectually in each of these topics, to promote his polity and the theory of society.

Discussion will begin with nationalism because of its sociopolitical implications; the influence of the Western nationalistic movement and the creation of a nation-state in the Eastern world.[8] The Muslims came into contact with the West through Western military, commercial and colonial expansionism in the eighteenth century. This aroused in Muslims a general emotional response that resulted in the later nationalistic governments. They have viewed nationalism as an important means that would strengthen their cause for self-government and secure freedom from Colonialism. As to the Arabs, nationalism was seen as a step on the way to unity that never materialized.[9]

NATIONALISM

This section investigates the sociopolitical and religious basis of Qutb's concept of nationalism and examines the relevance of Qutb's key ideas to the concept of nation-state, Arab nationalism, Islamic language and Egyptian nationalism. It will also trace Qutb's concept of nationalism during the period of his involvement with the Free Officers prior to and after the Egyptian Revolution of 1952. It will finally analyse the conceptual framework and sociopolitical implications of *ummah* and Nation.

The major religious basis for Qutb's rejection of secular nationalism is the three concepts *hakimiyyah* (sovereignty), *'ubudiyyah* (servitude: complete submission to Allah) and universality of Islam. These are related to *ftrah* and its connotations of the original nature of the universe, life and man. A brief outline of how his view of nationalism develops from these religious concepts is appropriate.

Taken the concept of *fitrah*, for Qutb,[10] as for al-Qurtubi,[11] Ibn Taymiyyah,[12] al-'Asqalani[13] and Muhammad 'Abduh,[14] Islam is the religion of *fitrah* (the unchangeable constitution that Allah set as innate to the universe, life and man). Qutb received this idea from his pioneers and linked it to his construct of *'ubudiyyah* (servitude) to result in the conceptual framework that every human being is born in a state of complete submission (Muslim) to the Creator. This means that the nationality of all human beings at birth is Islam.[15] This relationship facilitated to Qutb the link to the concept of sovereignty and hence, laws and codes and the affairs of human life in general. Since all human beings at birth are Muslims in a state of complete submission (*'ubudiyyah*), then he who affirms his *'ubudiyyah* to Allah alone thereby acknowledges the sovereignty (*hakimiyyah*) and authority of Allah over everything in his life.[16] Thus he who affirms this sovereignty thereby adheres to its laws and codes. This decision is a personal one but coupled with responsibility, that is every person is responsible for his decision.[17] As this briefly reflects the connection between Qutb's key ideas, it also indicates that these ideas including sovereignty are all one integrated concept that characterizes the comprehensiveness of Qutb's concept of Nationalism.[18]

Consequently, Qutb thinks of Islam as a universal system of life meant for the whole world.[19] This also brings the notion of Islam as the primary identity of all human beings of different ethnicity, languages, territories and beliefs.[20] Thus, Qutb's concept of nationalism is not regional but 'supra-national' (*al-qawmiyyah al-'ulya*). In this regard Qutb quoted Leopold Weiss

> No sign is available that mankind, in its present stature, has outgrown Islam. It has not been able to produce a better system of ethics than that expressed in Islam. It has not been able to put the idea of human brotherhood on a practical footing, as Islam did in its supra-national concept of *ummah*.[21]

This type of nationalism is not the secular one, which is regional. Secular nationalism, by definition, is not universal: 'The spirit of nationalism is still far stronger than the spirit of world community (Emory S. Bgardus)'.[22] In Qutb's view, secular nationalism is regional and he rejects it as *jahiliyyah*.[23] The other type of nationalism that Qutb stands for is connected to Islam. Those who testify that there is no god but Allah thereby affirm that their identity is Islam. Rejecting Islam does not change its universality.

Qutb's view of nationalism in connection to Islam, which appeared in the later writings of the 1960s, is rooted in his earlier writings of the 1950s when he lifted the idea of nationalism from its piece of land to be a piece of mind. For the purpose of this study, a brief outline may illustrate the development of Qutb's position.

(a) In the 1950s, Qutb's view of nationalism in connection to Islam begins by his idea that the homeland (*watan*) is an idea in the consciousness, not a geographical place limited in time and space. In this sense, he says

> In the Islamic view, all human beings are one nation. Thus there is no race, or homeland (*watan*) that can exploit other races or the homeland of others ... When Islam abolishes both those geographical bounds and racism, upon which the idea of the national homeland is established, it does not abolish the idea of homeland completely but preserves its righteous meaning, that is the meaning of association, brotherhood, cooperation, system, and the meaning of the common goal with which the group is associated. This makes the idea of homeland an idea in the consciousness, not a piece of land. In the shelter of this idea, the peoples of all races, colors, and territories can associate as people of one homeland. They are brothers in the name of Allah, cooperating for their welfare and the welfare of humanity as a whole. This idea is Islam – 'The true believers are brothers' [Qur'an, 49:15] ... Here the idea of Islam replaces the idea of homeland in its righteous meaning ... What emerges from this [idea]

is the feeling that every territory under the shelter of Islam is the homeland of all Muslims and they are all its citizens . . .[24]

The patriotic creed itself is not enough, because it cannot stand in the face of the communist creed in many countries. In social life, the idea of social justice between individuals prevailed over the slogan of patriotism in the countries where the people were divided into masters and slaves. No system other than Islam is able to establish the two ideas [patriotism and social justice] altogether, without contradiction or conflict between them. Islam has the capacity to establish both ideas: the idea of patriotism, in the bigger Islamic homeland exists wherever Islam extends its shade; and the idea of complete social justice in this vast homeland.[25]

The way that we are calling for is the way . . . that leads to the establishment of a society with its own independent identity . . . Islam must govern . . . .[26]

(b) In the 1960s, Qutb defines the concept of the term *ummah*[27] to serve his ideological view of nationalism in connection to Islam as follows:

The basis for association is Creed . . . Humanity must associate on the basis of its most noble attributes, not on the basis of fodder, pasture, and enclosure like the animals. There are, on the face of the earth, two parties: that of Allah and that of Satan . . . The *ummah* (nation) is the group of people bound together by belief, which constitutes their nationality. If there is no Creed, there is no *ummah*, for there is nothing to bind it together. Land, race, language, lineage, common material interests are not enough, either singly or in combination, to form an *ummah*.[28]

The Muslim has no homeland other than that which implements the *shari'ah* . . . The Muslim has no nationality other than his Creed which makes him a member of the 'Islamic *ummah*' in the Islamic homeland.'[29] 'The homeland is a place governed by Creed, and a program of life and the *shari'ah* of Allah. This is the meaning of the homeland appropriate for human beings. The nationality is Creed and program of life. This is the bond appropriate for human beings.'[30]

These accounts are sufficient, here, to indicate that Qutb connected nationalism to Islam in his writings of the early 1950s and not only in the late 1960s. To him, nationalism is no longer a piece of land but a piece of Islamic mind. It was in this sense that Qutb's view of nationalism was being understood by his critics (i.e. Judge Muhammad Sa'eed al-'Ashmawi) as 'Islamic Nationalism, which 'Abd al-Nasser replaced by Arab Nationalism'.[31] Thus the idea of 'Islamic nationalism' is not outside the frame of Qutb's ideas in the 1950s and 1960s.

Among the Qur'anic basis for Qutb's concept of nationalism is 30: 30 'set your face in devotion to the true faith, the upright nature with which Allah has endowed man. Allah's creation cannot be changed. This is the dominant religion (*al-din al-qayyim*).'

The Arabic word *qayyim* means 'straight, as opposed to crooked, standard, as opposed to irregular, definite and permanent, as opposed to casual or temporarily. The master of command or leader who legislates for the people is *qayyim*'.[32] Ibn Manzur refers to earlier sources and Qur'anic verses such as 30: 43, 18: 2, 98: 5 and 9: 36. The latter verse, for instance, states 'This is the dominant (*qayyim*) religion. So wrong not yourselves.' Similarly, the Qur'anic verse 6: 161 commanded the Prophet, 'Say: "My Lord has guided me to a straight path, to a dominant religion (*dinan qayyiman*)." ' The word *qayyim* commonly means dominant and power. Since Islam possesses 'domination and power (*qayyim*), therefore, Islam is nationalistic (*qawmi*)'.[33] To Qutb then, Islam is the nationalistic identity applicable for all human beings.

With regard to Arab and Egyptian Nationalism, I now turn to Qutb's own involvement in this movement. His general ideological position meant that Qutb rejected Arab nationalism as a form of those regional forms that are dismissed as *jahiliyyah*.[34] The reason for that can be concluded in two points as follows:

1 Arab nationalism is based on principles that regard Islam as secondary to ethnic identity.
2 Arab nationalism may oppose in some cases, universality of Islam, that is, universality of *uluhiyyah* (divinity), universality of *hakimiyyah* (sovereignty of Allah) and universality of *'ubudiyyah* (complete submission) of all humanity to Allah alone.

Qutb's perspective clearly considers the integration and ascendancy of Islam in any theory about the mundane world. Qutb argued that the sovereign law, the *shari'ah*, aims to bring together all mankind into one moral and spiritual framework guiding people to be mutually assisting one another on a universal scale. Islam presents to all humanity a social system of justice and piety based on a creed and a specific morality. Islam invites all humans towards it. The Islamic order applies to all spheres of human life (politics, economics, civics, legal rights etc.). Those who accept this system are not divided into categories of nationality based on language, birth or belief.[35]

By contrast, secular nationalism makes distinctions that create bitterness and hatred through racial and national distinction, between nations. These end up fighting, even exterminating rather than helping one another.[36] In his explanation of the Qur'anic verses 3: 164–179, Qutb emphasizes the similarity between modern Arab nationalism and the *jahiliyyah* of the Arabs in pre-Islam times. He comments

> The *jahiliyyah* is the *jahiliyyah*, and each *jahiliyyah* has its types and forms of abominations, atrocities, enormities and taboos. The form of *jahiliyyah* of a particular time or place is not important. If there is no *shari'ah* governing the daily affairs of the people, there will be nothing but *jahiliyyah* in any of its varying forms and shapes. The nature of the

> *jahiliyyah* of the world today is not different from the nature of the *jahiliyyah* of Arabia or the *jahiliyyah* of the world before Islam. The Arabs know that nothing transferred them from the stage of the tribe, the interests and revolts of the tribe, except Islam. Islam made them not only a nation (*ummah*) but also a nation to lead humanity to the ideal program and system of life. They know that nothing gave them their national existence (*wujud qawmi*), their political existence (*wujud siyasi*), their international existence (*wujud dawli*) and, their humanity, except Islam. Islam gave the Arabs a message to be delivered to the world, a theory for human life, and a distinctive system for humanity. This was Islam: its concept of existence, its view of life; its social laws, its organization of the life of humanity; its ideal *shari'ah* for establishing a system for every human being to live in happiness. This was Islam with all its particular characteristics, the identity card by which the world has come to know the Arabs and to whom it has handed over leadership. Today, the Arabs have nothing more than this card. They have no message other than this message to address themselves to the world. If they carry it [the identity card: the message], the world will recognize them and respect them. If they do not carry it [identity card: the message], they will return to their status prior to Islam, when nobody recognized them. They do not have anything other than Islam to present to humanity. Only Islam is the identity card.[37]

These in words and language indicate how Qutb conquers with Samuel Huntington the view that the existing Arab states, without their Islam, are lacking legitimacy and have identity problems. Nationalism then divided them to small entities labelled by Huntington 'tribes with flags'.[38] Similar to Qutb's words and language Huntington says:

> In the Arab world, existing states have legitimacy problems because they are for the most part the arbitrary, if not capricious, products of European imperialism ... These states divided the Arab nation, but a Pan-Arab state, on the other hand, has never materialized. In addition, the idea of sovereign nation states is incompatible with belief in the Sovereignty [Qutb's word is *hakimiyyah*] of Allah and the primacy of the *ummah*. As a revolutionary movement, Islamist fundamentalism rejects the nation state in favor of the unity of Islam.[39]

For Qutb as for Huntington the expression 'Arab Nationalism' stands against not only the 'belief in the sovereignty of Allah' but also against *tawhid*.[40] During the time of Qutb, the official title of many Arab states was not linked with Islam and the word Islam was not included in any title. After independence, Arab states identified themselves simply as 'Republics' or 'kingdoms'. Arab nationalism has served to signal language, territory, territorial culture and racial and sub-racial distinctiveness. The logical implication of this is that 'Arab Nationalism' implies division, not *tawhid*.[41]

Nationalism generally signifies the special relationships that link certain individuals to one another. Social values, language, culture and history lead individuals to come together in a social bond that is ultimately called nation. The desire of 'each nation, which is proud of its history and language, to govern itself, has been an important movement which led the change in the European map several times and resulted in the separation of state from religion'.[42] Nationalist movements in the Muslim world sprung out of the desire for unity and self-rule but resulted in their division and the creation of nation–state that separated religion from state.[43] Arab Nationalism, then, has separated the Arab countries from each other and separated the countries from the rule of *shari'ah*.

For Qutb as for 'Abduh 'Arab nationalists are well-informed by Western culture but, like their counterparts in the West, Arab nationalists lack sufficient information on the side of the nationalistic trend of the Islamic heritage, which is human and universal in nature.'[44] The Arabs know that the term 'Nationalism', in practice today, is of a secular nature. Adding the term Arab, which denotes a particular race, to the term 'Nationalism', resulted in a complex secular expression called 'Arab Nationalism'. This is why Qutb calls such expressions complex *jahiliyyah*.[45] Arab nationalism is the centre of the debate between Islamists and nationalists in the Arab region.[46] Al-Dawalibi (1984) argues that

> the nationalist bond in any nation is under the threat of division and apathy under the influence of various factors, especially people migrating from their motherland, unless they had a stable and permanent social, and human value to unite them in carrying a message to mankind wherever they reside. This has happened to the Arabs themselves when they migrated outside the peninsula and spread in Iraq and North Africa from Egypt to Morocco. This was what happened, for instance, to the Babylonians, the Assyrians, the Phoenicians and the Ancient Egyptians. The Islamic message which had reached them through their Arab cousins, was the only thing which united them and brought them back to the mother tongue thanks to the language of the Qur'an . . .[47]

According to Maspero (1910), the Babylonians, the Assyrians, the Phoenicians and the Ancient Egyptians were all Arabs departed from their motherland and then from their mother tongue with the passage of years.[48]

Consequently, Qutb notes that 'the return of these people to their original Arab identity and language, could not have been possible without the "language of Islam."' To Qutb the 'Islamic Language' carried to these different nations a new life system that meant freedom of belief and culture for all and the right of everybody to an honourable life without making any distinctions. Islamic language brought to the Arabs the necessity to be good to those who differed from them in faith under the new universal and humanitarian system which is unique to the message of the Qur'an.[49]

Qutb lends what he calls 'Islamic Language' great importance as he states that

> the victory of the Islamic Language in the battle with ancient countries is a remarkable phenomenon that, unfortunately, has not received systematic study or analysis. From my view the victory of the Islamic language is more remarkable than the victory of the Creed and its establishment. Change the language, which interweaves all social life of the people, Arabs and non-Arabs, is a complete miracle! The factor behind this matter of change was not the 'Arabic Language'. Arabic Language was in Arabia long before Islam... The new energy, which has renewed Arabic Language, was only Islam... Therefore, I call it [Arabic Language after Islam] 'Islamic Language'. The language, which has changed the history, was the Islamic Language...
>
> In the countries liberated by Islam, the geniuses went on to express themselves, not by their original languages but by the new language, the 'Islamic Language'. They produced works in every field of knowledge. The Islamic language became, actually, the mother tongue for these geniuses. This was because the energy of Islam and the nature of the obligation that this language [Islamic language] is carrying were closer to the soul of these geniuses than their ancient cultures and languages. This energy were only Islam....[50]

In Qutb's view, Arabic is elevated as the language in which Allah revealed the Qur'an to mankind. This position implies that no other language is to be preserved unchanged and alive or to remain perfect as the exalted standard of the highest and excellent expression as Arabic. The Qur'an made the Arabic language the language of Islam, and no language of any Muslim group, whether or not it has achieved a lofty rank in civilization, is without the influence of Arabic.[51] With regard to Arabic language, the Qur'an made art of clear expression (*bayan*), with primary quality and proclaimed clarity, in adjectival style (*mubin*), as one of its most important virtues.[52]

The Arabicity of the Qur'an raised the Arabic language from regional to international status. To Qutb the Arabicity of the Qur'an does not contradict the universal status of Islam as a religion of mankind.[53] In other words, the concept of 'Islamic Language' does not contradict the Arabicity of the Qur'an and its universal message. The Qur'an 34: 28 states: 'We have not sent thee but as a bearer of glad tidings and a Warner, for all mankind, but most men know not.' It also says 'We have indeed sent it as an Arabic Qur'an in order that you may learn wisdom' (Qur'an, 12: 2). In order to understand the wisdom of the message of this Qur'an and the traditions of the Prophet, knowledge of Arabic became essential. Thus Arabic became the official language of Islam,[54] but the message of Islam has been embodied in all languages of Muslims. Many of these languages have preferred to adopt Arabic Islamic terminology in religious and related discourse. This also illustrates what Qutb meant by calling the Arabic language 'Islamic Language'.

The Qur'an raised not only the Arabic language, but also the Arabs, and the Muslim *ummah* as a whole, to international status. Qutb emphasizes that the Qur'an raised up this *ummah* and made it a 'unique *ummah*' in the history of humanity 'You are the noblest *ummah* ever raised up for mankind' (Qur'an, 3: 110). This was a 'new birth' for the Arab nation and all mankind. The 'Jahili Poetry' and other texts scattered here and there, all have been considered as a record of the pre-Islamic life of the Arabs and their conceptions of creation, the universe, behaviour and ethics before Islam. Comparing those concepts in the Arab's record before Islam with that in the Qur'an 'we will know that the Qur'an is the unique gift to this *ummah*.'[55]

The Qur'an points out that the Arabs could not have received the message and become the vehicles for its promulgation, if it had not been sent in Arabic tongue and delivered by an Arab person. The Qur'an (26: 192–199) says: 'Verily this is a Revelation from the Lord of the World... In the perspicuous Arabic tongue... Had We revealed it to any of the non-Arabs, and had he recited it to them, they would not have believed in it.' In this regard, Qutb notes that 'this is the tongue of Salman the Persian, and 'Abdullah Ibn Salam.'[56] Here Qutb implies two points: (i) that the energy of Islam renewed the Arabic language and raised it from regional to international status. This could not happen without Islam. Arabic became the 'Islamic Language' of the Muslims, Arabs and non-Arabs. (ii) Islamic Language is not merely an alphabet, letters, or words, but it can be seen as '*The Lingua Franca*' of the Muslim *ummah*. Huntington notes that during the whole 500 years of the 'Abbasid Caliphate's existence, Arabic was the *lingua franca* of the whole area extending from Soviet Central Asia to Spain and Portugal inclusive.[57] The reason is that Arabic became the language of the Qur'an, hadith, prayers and main references on Islam. Precisely because of this, it is supposed to be learnt by every Muslim with some degree of proficiency.[58] Therefore, Qutb emphasizes that, because of the energy of Islam, the Arabic language became 'Islamic Language' and the mother tongue of the 'geniuses who went on to express themselves, not by their original languages but by the new language, the 'Islamic Language'. They produced works in every field of knowledge.'[59]

Many of those whom Qutb calls 'geniuses' were not Arabs. As to this fact, Ibn Khaldun (d. 1406) emphasizes that 'Most of those who established and developed the science of Arabic and the science of jurisprudence, hadith and other sciences related to the Qur'an were not Arabs.'[60] This implies that Islam freed the Arabic Language from regional or racial restriction and from regional nationalism. This means that the criterion for a language affiliation is fluency and perfection in using it and not blood or racial relations with a language community. The Prophet was reported to have said:

> Oh mankind, verily the Lord is only one, and the father is only one, and the religion is only one, and Arabic is not of any of you through maternal or paternal relations, it is an act of tongue, and whoever speaks Arabic is an Arab.[61]

This tradition frees Arabic from regional limitations and raises it to the universal status which corresponds to the universality of the message of Islam, the identity of Muslims. Many of the nations that embraced Islam abandoned their native languages to speak Arabic, while others use its form of writing for their languages. Individuals from the new Muslim nations, as Qutb asserts, excelled in Arabic Islamic sciences to the extent that the majority of early Muslim scholars were not Arabs.[62] Explaining this phenomenon, Ibn Khaldun emphasizes that the natural acquisition of a language has no connection with the racial origin of the learner. In his view, being non-Arab in language is something different from being non-Arab by racial origin.[63]

Thus Qutb notes that the Arabs cannot be united on the basis of merely their Arabic language or through the slogan of 'Arab Nationalism'. The present Arabs cannot attain their unity on the basis other than on the message which united the Arabs and non-Arabs in the first place. This echoes Muhammad 'Abduh's view that 'the nationality of the Muslims is only their religion'.[64] 'Abd al-Rahman Tajj (1896–1975), a Western educated professor, who became Shaykh al-Azhar in 1952 after the Revolution states that 'Arab nationalism is a heresy appeared to remove the Arabs from Islam. It considers Islam as a factor of weakness, not strength...'[65] Qutb describes Arab nationalism as an idolatrous expression and a pagan slogan. He states that

> the pagans have a variety of idols that sometimes called homeland (*watan*) and race (*jins*) or nation (*qawm*). These forms of idols appear from time to time – once under the name of popularity, once under the name of Hittite nationalism, and once more under the name Arab nationalism and sometimes under various names and flags...[66]

Consequently, Qutb views the modern 'nation-state' like a 'tribal entity', similar to the pre-Islamic period of *jahiliyyah*.[67] In his commentary on the case of the *qiblah*[68] in the Qur'anic verses 2: 42–45, Qutb states that 'Islam has come to liberate the hearts and the souls from all historical, racial, and earthly circumstances, and to liberate them from tribalism, and all *jahili* slogans. Islam came to link the hearts and the souls directly to Allah and unite the *ummah* in the belief of the One Allah, one religion, one system and even one *qiblah* to which the Muslims in the world turn in prayer. Islam has established this unity on neither racial or language basis nor other similar *jahili* slogans. Unity under Islam is appropriate for human beings...The unity of human beings is the unity of their hearts and souls in one direction, one path and to follow one law in a complete submission to the One Sovereign'.[69]

Qutb argues that the concept of nation-state is a reflection of multiplicity of wills that give rise to different rules and judgements that lead to conflicts between individuals, groups and nations. The Prophet himself rejected the the concept of the nation–state based on language, race or colour.[70] Critics, however, could argue that nationalism is a modern concept and that the nation-state was not an issue during the time of the prophet.[71]

However, the nationalist movement, in general, can be traced back to the Ancient Egyptians of 3100 BC.[72] This point will be briefly outlined later in this section. Nevertheless, the Arab Nationalists of the seventh century perhaps were considering themselves modern when they were looking at the Egyptian Nationalist movement of 3100 BC. Similarly, the Arab Nationalist movement of the twentieth century considered itself modern in relation to the Arab Nationalist movement of the seventh century.

Qutb emphasizes that Arabia of the seventh century witnessed two Nationalist movements in Makkah: the Islamic Nationalist movement led by the Prophet and the Arab Nationalist movement led by Abu Sufyan.[73] The sociopolitical particularities, development and obligations of these two movements are familiar ground in the literature.[74] In AD 616, soon after the beginning of the Revelation in AD 611, Abu Sufyan (father of Mu'awiyah d. AD 680) established the Arab Tribal League to lead the opposition of the Arab Nationalist movement against the Islamic Nationalist movement in Makkah. The leading council of the Arab Tribal League raised the idea of Arab Nationalism, since they tried to persuade the prophet, through his uncle, to accept their proposal of Arab nation-state. Their plan provides the kingship for Muhammad but he must stop the activity of the Islamic Nationalist movement. They agreed to make Muhammad the king of Arabia. They agreed to leave under the sovereignty of Muhammad, not under the sovereignty of Allah. The Prophet rejected their proposal, and made his position clear in a well-known speech preserved in the history.[75]

Arab nationalism in the seventh century Arabia, as appeared earlier, was based on language, history and racial essence. The dispute between the Arab and Muslim Nationalists was also moved from the phase of dialogue to enter the phase of military confrontation in the second year after the *hijrah* (AH 2/AD 623).[76] The end of this conflict is marked by the conquest of Makkah (AD 629) by the Muslim nationalists. Then the members of the Arab Tribal League including its leaders became Muslims by their free choice, and joined the Islamic Nationalist movement led by the Prophet.[77] In this regard, Qutb notes

> It was easier for the Prophet to establish Arab Nationalism based on the Arab language and history. He then can launch a war of national liberation to liberate the Arab land from the Romans in the north of Arabia and to liberate the south from the Persians. He was able to raise the Pan-Arabism up high and establish a strong Arab state to unite all Arab tribes in the Arabian Peninsula. This, however, was not the right path and was not the message of the Qur'an. The Qur'an delivers the Islamic Revolution against the earthly rules and earthly ties...
>
> Regional nationalism was not the right path, as it would liberate the Arabs from the sovereignty of the Roman *dictator* or from the sovereignty of the Persian *dictator* to be under the sovereignty of an Arab *dictator*. The *dictator* is but *dictator*. The earth is under the sovereignty of Allah and it

> must be liberated for the sake of Allah. Liberation of the earth means to raise the word 'there is no God but God', and to liberate the people from the *servitude* to anything other than God. The Arabs of that time know their language and know that the phrase 'there is no God but God' means there is no *sovereignty* other than the *sovereignty* of Allah, and there is no *shari'ah* but the *shari'ah* of Allah . . .[78]
>
> The nationality that envisaged by the Qur'an is the *Creed* in which the Roman, the Persian, the Arabian and all races and colours are equal under the law of Allah. This is the only bond which linked the Arabians, Persians, Babylonians, Assyrians, Phoenicians, Egyptians, Moroccans, Turks, Chinese, Indians, Romans, Greeks, Indonesians, and the Africans and so on to the end of races and tongues. They were all united, their specialties cooperated and harmoniously worked to build the Islamic society and Islamic civilization. This great civilization never was, at anytime, Arabic but was always Islamic.[79]

Turning the discussion to focus on Egyptian Nationalism, there is a tendency among intellectuals to locate the origin of the Egyptian Nationalist movement in 1798. The time when three months after the French invasion more than a thousand persons led by Shaykh Badr marched towards the house of community government known as '*Bayt al-Qadi*' (house of the jurist) shouting anti-French slogans.[80]

Critics would argue that Egyptian nationalism could be traced back to the time of the Ancient Egyptians. King Menes led the Egyptian Nationalist movement, united the South with the North of Egypt and established the Egyptian nation-state in 3100 BC.[81] This Egyptian State, in fact, had its national capital city,[82] national court of 42 jurists,[83] national flag, national anthem and a national official sign.[84] All these are among the significant characteristics of the modern state and its sovereignty in the twentieth century world. In his speech to the government concerning the expected war with the Hittites (present day Turkey), King Ramses stated that

> Egypt is our mother, our past and our future. She gives without calculating, at every moment she offers us her bounty. Shall we answer her with ingratitude, selfishness and cowardice? If need be, Pharaoh himself will lay down his life in order that Egypt may live.[85]

These words constitute the sociopolitical implications of the modern concept of Nationalism. This means that if the term Nationalism is modern, its implications are, at least, ancient.

The difference between the ancient concept of Egyptian nationalism and the modern concept of Egyptian nationalism is that the ancients did not separate their Creed from their state but based their nation–state totally on their religion.[86] By contrast, the modern concept of nationalism gave raise to a modern state in which religion became second important to language and history.[87]

In twentieth century Egypt, according to Muhammad Hasanayn Haykal, the eminent writer and journalist of the Nasser era,

> the revolution of 1919 was a nationalist movement separated religion from the state. Islamic nationalism was also not addressed by the Revolution of 1952. Egyptian thinkers such as al-Tahtawi, Taha Husayn, Tawfiq al-Hakim, Muhammad Husayn Haykal, and al-'Aqqad did not address Islamic nationalism because of the sensitivity of the issue . . .[88]

Haykal was perhaps trying, through the revolution of 1919, to justify the secularization processes of the Revolution of 1952. According to Jeremy Salt, 'the Revolution of 1952 modified the concept of nationalism into ideas in which Islam has come to be the second important to language and history.'[89] This implies an important question about Qutb's concept of nationalism during his active participation with the members of the Revolution of 1952 in Egypt.

Concerning this question, one should note that Qutb was one among those who planned for the Egyptian Revolution of 1952.[90] The Revolutionary Council called Qutb 'the tribune of the Egyptian Revolution.'[91] They may have recalled the French Mirabeau Comte de (1749–1791) who prepared for the French Revolution and was called the tribune of the people.[92] On Egyptian Radio, in a series that lasted for about six months, Qutb personally explained the Islamic aim of the Egyptian Revolution of 1952.[93] Qutb's acceptance of nationalism at that time was due to its Islamic aim and that Egypt was, for him, the starting point or a step towards the unity of Muslim nations. In an article 'The Principles of the Free World' (January 1952) and republished, with other articles, in the book *Islamic* Studies (1953), Qutb pointed out his ideological position about Egyptian and Arab nationalism in 1952 (six months before the Revolution):

> The flag which unites us in our struggle is the flag of Islam. Among us, a number of people prefer to be associated under the Arab flag. I have no objection of this association being transitory as a step on the road of a wider association. There is no opposition between Arab nationalism and Islamic Patriotism; only if we understood Arab nationalism as a step on the road. All the Arab land is part of the land of Islam. If we liberate the Arab land, it means we liberate part of the body of the Islamic homeland, which could be used to help in the liberation of the rest of the Muslim land. The point is to get it started.[94]

Qutb's view of Nationalism, as appears in the article given, became the subject of the debate between intellectuals on the pages of *al-Risalah*. Muhammad 'Asim wrote an article entitled 'Our Problems in the Light of Islam'. 'Asim provided some materials from the nationalists themselves, and in his analysis he appeared to be in agreement with Qutb's view on the subject. Qutb also responded. With regard to this, Qutb's publisher, al-Shuruq, published Qutb's book *Islamic Studies* which consisted of some of Qutb's articles, a single article by Muhammad 'Asim and Qutb's response entitled 'Without Comment'. In his article, 'Asim says:

> In the previous issue of *al-Risalah*, the eminent writer 'Sayyid Qutb' wrote in his article 'The Principles of the Free World' that 'Among us a number of people prefer be associated under the Arab flag. I have no objection that this association to be transitory as a step on the road of a wider association. There is no opposition between the Arab nationalism and Islamic Patriotism, if we understand Arab nationalism as a step on the road....' But do the 'nationalists' understand nationalism to be a step on the road to a wider 'Islamic' unity? This is the question. The reality is that 'nationalists' neither understand Nationalism, nor do they do anything for it on this basis... Sati' al-Husari – who is one of the leading thinkers of Arab nationalism says that the reason for 'Antuwan Sa'adah'[95] walking away from 'Arabism' is the association of Arabism with Islam in his mind. If he knows that 'Arabism' is something independent from Islam and unattached to it, he would not charge Arabism and call it primitive, reactionary, retardation, and fanaticism... These mirror the creed of most nationalists. They say that Islam answered the need of the Arabs in specific time and specific space, which are different from the present.... The nationalists do not understand 'Arab Nationalism' in the way that the eminent writer 'Sayyid Qutb' understands it. Their Nationalism, therefore, is not a step on the road...[96]

Qutb's response entitled 'Without Comment' was this:

> The text presented by brother Muhammad 'Asim from Sati' al-Husari – if accurate – to portray the idea of the advocators of Arab Nationalism, does not require comment from me. The text indicates the deep *jahl* about both Islam and Arabism. It will be nonsense to discuss this level of *jahalah* of those who lack the alphabet of Islam and Arabism. As you have seen – the Arab *ummah* is but a part in the body of the Islamic homeland.[97]

Thus, Qutb's ideological position that involves the concept of Nationalism, in his writings before or after the 1952 Revolution, is Islam and 'Islamic Patriotism'.[98] Soon after 1952, when Qutb found the Revolutionary Council was not ready to carry on the Islamic reform, he distanced himself from them and pointed out that the concept of nationalism after 1952 changed and lost its historical basis.[99] Later, in his detention, Qutb also emphasized regional nationalism as a slogan of *jahiliyyah*. In his words:

> In their *jahiliyyah*, the Arabs were glorifying the Sacred House [Ka'bah] and considered it the great symbol of their Nationalism. Because Islam aims to free the hearts from anything but Allah – and from any slogan related to anything except the Islamic program – therefore, Islam pulled them out

> from the direction of the Sacred House and declared for them the direction of the farthest Mosque [in Jerusalem], for a period of time to free their souls from the precipitates of *jahiliyyah*, and to distinguish between those who would follow the Messenger from those who would turn on their heels with pride to the *jahili* slogan related to race, lineage, land, and history.[100]
>
> The *qiblah* does not mean mere place or direction to which the Muslims turn in the prayer. The place or direction is but a symbol meant for distinction and specification. Distinction in the conception, in the identity, in the goal, in the interests, and distinction in the entity.[101]

In his last book *Ma'alim* for which he was hanged, Qutb's position was this:

> Islam came to this humanity with a new conception about the bonds and connections . . . Islam came to declare: that there is only one bond connecting the people in the name of Allah; that there is only one party of Allah but the others are of Satan and tyranny; that there is only one road that leads to Allah but the others lead not to Him; that there is only one system, that is the system of Islam but the others are systems of *jahiliyyah*; that there is only one *shari'ah*, that is the *shari'ah* of Allah but the others are whim; that the truth is only one, not numerous; and that anything other than the truth is error; and that there is only one homeland, that is the homeland in which the Islamic state is established, and the *shari'ah* of Allah is dominant.[102]

This indicates to us that Qutb's position was not the result of detention, as such, but rather a result of his avid reading and studying in the mid 1940s.

Qutb's concept of nationalism in connection to Islam was similar to Muhammad 'Abduh and al-Banna. These three Muslim thinkers have emphasized that the nationality of the Muslim is his creed. They also stressed that the responsibility towards nationalism should be first the responsibility of the Arabs and that the other Muslim communities are the Arab's partners.

'Abduh notes that

> The nationality of the Muslims is only their religion.[103] Allah has guided the Arabs by the Qur'an and guided by their Islam the powerful nation of Persia and led the world to the liberation of man. Guided by the Qur'an, the Arabs liberated the land, liberated the soul and demolished the authority of the Persian and Roman Empires . . .[104]

Similar to Qutb, 'Abduh described modern nationalism *jahiliyyah* and emphasized Arabic Language, after Islam, Islamic language as follows:

> In the early period of Islam, all those who became Muslims believed that they were brothers. Every one of them feels that he is brother to all Muslims and his nation is not the Arab nation, nor the Persian, the

> Coptic or Turkish but the nation of Islam . . . The unity of the *ummah* cannot be established without the unity of the language. There is no language uniting the Muslims and connecting them together except the language of the religion which made them brothers in the name of Allah. This language is the Arabic language which became unrestricted to the Arab race . . . The nationalism of the *jahiliyyah*, which was prohibited by Islam, prevailed in the Muslim world after the Muslims became weak in their language and belief.[105]

Here, in this statement of 'Abduh, the language of the Muslims cannot be Arabic or Persian but the Islamic Language. This also does not differ from Qutb's view as detailed earlier. Similarly, al-Banna stated

> Islam emphasizes that every Muslim must do as much as he can for his *ummah* where he lives and he must defend it. Islam has commanded the Muslim to begin with his nearest relative and then the nearest neighbour and so on, in that order. We are Egyptians by this precious piece of land on which we were born and grew up . . . Why do we not work for Egypt and defend it? We are proud of our beloved native place, working for it, defending it and we will remain believing that Egypt is the first step on the way to the nation of Islam (*ummah*).[106]

The point is that Qutb, like al-Banna and 'Abduh, believed that Egypt his native home, as part of the Arab world, was the first step on the road to one Muslim nation whose identity is Islam.

Turning the discussion to focus on Qutb's concept of the term *ummah*, we should note that the term *ummah* is usually translated as *nation*. To examine his view, the concept of the term *ummah* in the Qur'an and in the Sunnah will be investigated and compared to Qutb's view.

The term *ummah* is mentioned 64 times in the Qur'an,[107] and establishes a variety of concepts that have been the driving force of the Muslims in political, social, economic, intellectual and moral spheres of their life. According to Muhammad Asad (1980), the establishment of the Muslim State by the Prophet, and later that of the Caliphate, represents one of the basic reasons why the meaning of the term *ummah* and the identity of the *ummah* itself is considered a political one.[108] In his *Political Islam*, Nazih Ayubi (1991), pointed out that the term *ummah* is primarily a political term.[109] In fact all life (political and otherwise) of the *ummah* is confined to its specific constitution, that is, the Qur'an and the *Sunnah* upon which the *ummah* (Muslim community) was established in Madinah.

The sociopolitical implications of the term *ummah* are obvious, for instance, in the document which was agreed upon among the inhabitants of Madinah (Yathrib) and the new immigrants (from Makkah) to the city. The document named the Prophet Muhammad as the Chief Executive of the city. The document declares itself

> a document from Muhammad, the Prophet, among the believers and Muslims of Quraysh [the Makkan Muslim immigrants] and Yathrib [Muslims of Madinah], and those who followed them and lived with them and went with them to *jihad*. They constituted one single *ummah* to the exclusion of all other people.[110]

The document goes on to show the regulations concerning the administration and security of the city of Madinah. Among the implications of this document is the fact that the Muslims received and enjoyed recognition as a distinct community and in which the city of Madinah became a confederation. This means that the word *ummah* is a comprehensive term with political, economic, social, intellectual and moral connotations.[111] Therefore, Muslim scholars and the *'ulama* usually used the term *ummah* to refer to the nation of Islam in the political sense. According to the Qur'an, the term *ummah* signifies a united nation (not nations) that is the nation of the Islamic Creed.[112] Islamic Creed legislates for the Muslims and the non-Muslims alike.

Critics could argue that the term *ummah* is synonymous with the term *nation*. However, practical application of the two terms indicates the difference between the concept of the term *ummah* and that of the term *nation*. The two concepts, according to Qutb, are different in their ideological particularities and historical context.[113] Throughout Islamic history, the '*ummah*' has been, as Samuel Huntington says, 'the principal foci of loyalty and commitment, and the nation state has been less significant'.[114]

According to Qutb, 'the *ummah* is not a group of consecutive generations of specific race, but a group of believers, no matter what their race, country or colour are.'[115] The term '*ummah*' was revealed in Makkah and Madinah to declare the new basic principles of the socio-political bond which should tie people of all races, colours and languages.[116] In the context of the Qur'anic verses 21: 92 and 23: 52, this bond is only the Islamic Creed. The term *ummah* then, Qutb claims, is totally based on *tawhid*, *'ubudiyyah*, *hakimiyyah* and the comprehensive Islamic conception concerning the nature of the relationship between the Creator and the creation, the universe, life and man.[117] Thus the term *ummah* implies the unity of people of different races, colours and languages under the law of the one sovereign who brought them to life and legislates for them and to Him they all will return.[118] Living under one law means, according to Qutb, unity in the direction and in the source from which the *ummah* derives the values and the considerations in all aspects of life.[119] As these principles cannot be implied by the modern term *nation*, interpreting the Qur'anic term *ummah* by the term modern nation state is not appropriate. For according to Qutb, the application of the term *ummah* to denote a secular nation is not appropriate.[120]

Therefore, secular nationalists, according to Qutb, should not use the term *ummah* because the *ummah* cannot exist on a secular basis. The Islamic Creed is the only social bond that ties language, history and others to form the *ummah*.[121] This implies that the use of the term *ummah* to refer to the Arab nations is not appropriate. This expression does not mention the term Islam. If the term Islam were mentioned, the Arabs would be part of the nation of Islam.

Concluding remarks

In his writings of the 1950s and 1960s, Qutb connects nationalism to Islam. To him, nationalism is a creed that is Islam. He also calls for 'Islamic Patriotism'. He provides Arabic Language after Islam as 'Islamic Language' and emphasizes the need for further studies concerning this matter. His ideological position projects responsibility onto Arabs to carry their responsibility towards one Muslim nation, not nations. All other Muslim communities are the Arab's partners. In this sense, Qutb's position is similar to that of Muhammad 'Abduh and al-Banna. The term *ummah* is an Islamic term of Islamic particular. Therefore, the application of the term *ummah* to denote secular nationalism such as Arab nation, or Arab nationalism is not appropriate. For Qutb, secular nationalism is simply *jahiliyyah.*

CAPITALISM

Islam has been labelled by many a term, one of which was Capitalism. However, Qutb argued that the Islamic system is different from all known systems before and after Islam, and that it cannot be called anything other than Islam. To him, any system other than the system of Islam is *jahiliyyah.*

This section intends to investigate Qutb's view on the difference between the Islamic system and Capitalism. This is not an easy task particularly in the context of Qutb's method of observation which emphasizes the comprehensiveness of the Islamic system. To him it is difficult to separate one part from the other in a divinely balanced system encompassing the whole affairs of human life. The Islamic system is one whole entity; its parts do not work separately. Therefore, I will briefly examine some specifics of the socio-political particularities of Capitalism and Islam, then brief on the basic principles of the two systems, and the mechanism that characterizes the differences between them and why Islamic system cannot be called a capitalist system. Commencing with a brief outline of the reasons behind the existence of Capitalism (human, economic and other factors) the chapter will then examine the influence of the Age of Reason on Capitalism and then similarities and differences between Islam and Capitalism particularly in relation to the right to private ownership.

To Qutb as for Rodinson and Weber, Capitalism in its classical *laissez-faire* sense does not exist anywhere, for it has been modified over the centuries.[122]

Qutb notes that the seeds of Capitalism were planted by the Crusaders in the eleventh century when Westerners came in close contact with the system of Islam. According to Qutb,

> Crusaders saw a *Shari'ah* that governed all people; the ruler and the ruled, the wealthy and the poor, the owner and who owns nothing, the landlord and the laborers who are working in his land; all are equal before the *Shari'ah*. A *Shari'ah* that is not of the will of the master or the landlord, and it is also not of the will of the kings or princes, but a *Shari'ah* that came to them from Allah the Sovereign and the governor of all the existence.[123]

After the Crusaders had returned to their countries, Qutb says, they rejected feudalism and its domination in their societies. Opposition of Crusaders to feudalism, as Qutb asserts, was ignored mostly by the materialist theorists who are not interested in recognizing the contribution of the human factor in the history of social evolution. Materialist theorists emphasize only economic factors. This is because economy was the factor that coincided with the Crusades and the establishment of market cities in the south of Europe.[124] Qutb also emphasizes the impact of the Islamic system on Western thought in general in the period after the Crusades. This period was, Qutb asserts, an opportunity for the West to compare feudalism with the system of Islam. This is Qutb's attempt to express the importance of the human factor in social evolution and to point out that Muslims and the Islamic system was an influential factor in social evolution and development.[125]

In addition to the human factor, Qutb emphasizes also the economic factors. He demonstrates the freedom that was granted by Islamic system. He then outlines the influence of Islamic freedom on the Crusaders.[126] In short, Qutb means that the factors which contribute to social evolution are not only economy, but there is also a human factor, and that the Muslim's contribution in social evolution cannot be ignored. According to Arnowitz Stanley (1990), the materialist's interpretation of social evolution and development is based on only economic factors.[127]

The worldview of Capitalism was then greatly influenced by the Enlightenment that extended from the early seventeenth century to the beginning of the nineteenth century. This period is known by the term 'Age of Reason' and, in some respects, is the antithesis of much of the Church belief.[128] There is no attempt to go into the many reasons for the anti-religious posture of the time. One of them was, according to E. A. Burtt[129] and Voltaire,[130] corruption, despotism and, as Durant asserts, 'so much laxity of morals among the clergy that a thousand testimonies could be adduced to prove it'.[131] The point is that the existence of Capitalism is the result of European circumstances. This is completely different from the line of the history of Muslim society and its Islamic laws, which existed and were in practice for about ten centuries before Capitalism. The circumstances that brought about the existence of the Islamic system and that of Capitalism are different. If there is similarity between the two systems, as claimed by some intellectuals,[132] it does not mean that Islam is a capitalist system or imitates Capitalism.

Each political or economic system has its characteristic elements, but one of these elements could dominate and determine the function of the others. The dominant characteristic of Capitalism is the right to own and manage private property, but the mechanism of the whole system is based on *riba* (usury or interest), monopoly and exploitation, which are completely prohibited in the Islamic system.[133] This is another point of the basic principles that distinguished Islam from Capitalism.

However, according to Qutb, there is similarity between Islam and Capitalism in the right to private property, the right of investment and the right of inheritance, but as will be detailed later this similarity is immediate and lacks legitimate justification.[134]

In Islam and in Capitalism there is freedom to own and to manage private property, but the means by which an individual or group owns property and the ways of management of the property are completely different.[135] In addition, these rights were in the Islamic *Shari'ah* ten centuries before the existence of Capitalism. The *Shari'ah* has never been subject to scholarly deduction and modification or influenced by historical factors as it was the case with Capitalism. There was no coexistence between *Shari'ah* and the capitalist thought.[136]

The existence of nation-states, as Qutb asserts, was one of the political reasons that gave rise to Capitalism. According to Qutb

> the existence of nationalism which is but racism was among the factors that gave rise to colonialism and its exploitation and incessant conflicts among different nations over markets and raw material resources. Therefore, Lenin used to say that 'colonialism is the most developed form of Capitalism'. Islam, however, is universal. Islam rejects regional nationalism and its earthly borders. Islam does not confine itself to land borders but made its perimeters the perimeters of the theory, established the freedom of humanity and fought colonialism and exploitation. Thus, universal justice and equality are the aim of Islam and the means for achieving this goal are an antithesis of much of the practice of Capitalism and the capitalist thought at any time.[137]

The Islamic system may have influenced other systems, since they existed after it. Logically, it is not legitimate to think that Islamic *Shari'ah* was influenced by a system or systems that existed ten centuries after *Shari'ah*.[138] Therefore, similarity between the Islamic system and Capitalism cannot be justified. The historical circumstances of the existence of the Islamic system and Capitalism (basic principles, the mechanism, the aims and obligations of the two systems) are completely different.[139]

The difference between Islam and Capitalism with regard to the right of ownership, Qutb claims, is that Islam establishes the right of the individual to legally own property. This right is the basis of its system. Preserving property and protecting it from theft, robbery, looting or fraud is also a right. Its confiscation for public good with adequate and genuine compensation is permitted.[140] Islam also sets punishments to ensure the mentioned rules are respected and to provide moral guidance to restrain people from coveting what is not theirs. In addition, Islam focuses on other rights such as the right to free disposal of the property by sale, rental, pawning, gift or bequest, as well as other rights of legitimate use within the limits that it has laid down for such activities. These basics of Islamic life and the Islamic economy differ markedly from Capitalism.[141] Qutb supports his view with Qur'anic verses such as 4: 2, 32.

Qutb then emphasizes the difference between the reasons for which the right to private ownership was established in Islam and Capitalism. Here also Qutb uses his ideas such as *hakimiyyah*, *'ubudiyyah* and *fitrah* and others as detailed earlier.

Unlike Capitalism, the Islamic system is ordained by God, not by the Capitalist owners. It is based upon the principle that *hakimiyyah* (sovereignty) belongs to Allah alone, and He alone legislates.[142] Capitalism, in its classical purity, as weber says, is free from all relationships to religion and 'the religious root of modern economic outlook is dead'.[143] Capitalism, and all Western systems, in Qutb's view,

> might be compatible with the environments in which they were conceived – the environment of Western materialistic civilization. There any objective other than immediately utilized ones are by-passed and any human element other than the ego is not recognized. Where the whole life is dominated by such materialism, there is no scope for laws beyond provisions for labour and production. The result is class struggle, which becomes inevitable and visibly evident. But when our social life is governed by the Islamic laws as enjoined by Allah and not ruled by self ordained lawmakers, the inevitability of materialism and class struggle never surface. Materialism and conflicting class interests are inherent in non-Islamic social systems because these societies are dedicated to materialistic abundance that is devoid of any sublime objective.[144]

Islam proceeds in the management of wealth on the basis of its general view and comprehensive idea. In this management – management of wealth – it undertakes first to implement the idea of *'ubudiyyah* (servitude) to Allah alone, in that it subjects the circulation of wealth to the law of Allah. This law achieves the welfare of the individual and achieves the welfare of the community, standing between them as a guardian who harms neither the individual nor the community. It does not contradict the *fitrah* and does not violate the authentic laws of life and its highest and most far-reaching goals.[145]

Among the justification of the right to ownership in Islam is the just balance between effort and reward.[146] To Qutb, the right to private ownership is in agreement with the *fitrah* of man and with the genuine tendencies of the human soul.[147] Man naturally loves wealth for himself: 'And you love wealth with inordinate love!' (Qur'an, 89: 20). Man likes to pile wealth 'thinking that his wealth makes him last forever' (Qur'an, 1.4: 2–3). According to Qutb,

> the individual is created with a natural love of good things for himself: 'Surely he is passionate in his love of good things' (Qur'an, 100: 8). 'Say, "If you possessed the treasuries of my Lord's mercy, yet would you withhold for fear of expending'" (Qur'an, 17: 100). 'And souls are very prone to avarice' (Qur'an, 4: 128). He likewise has a natural love for his posterity and a desire to pass on to them the results of his labor. The wealth which he saves for them is but his work stored up in the form of wealth. By means of it a man gives preference to his posterity over his own personal pleasure in his life. There is no harm in going along with these natural tendencies, so that the individual will expend his fullest energy in productive activity and work, because thus he serves his own desires and needs. He does not feel that his work is being exploited, nor does he expend his effort unwillingly and without hope. Beyond this, it is the community that profits from his effort and labor. Islam sets the basic principles which give the community this profit and assure that no harm will come from granting individual freedom and establishing the right of private ownership.[148]

Qutb emphasizes that destroying natural and reasonable incentives cannot produce any good for the individual or for the community. This is because, according to Qutb, justice is the fundamental principle of Islam and cannot always be at the expense of the individual. In Islam, justice is meant for the individual as much as it is meant for the community.[149] This balance between the right of individual and that of the community 'requires a balanced social order that deals with Man as a human being',[150] rather than as a mechanical object at the mercy of brute forces that, as asserted by Russell, 'unknowingly happen to throw him into being'.[151] Justice demands the social order to serve the needs of the individual and satisfy his inclinations (*fitrah*) within limits so that they do not harm him or harm the community.[152] As this implies the role of government in the system of economy, it also reflects the strategy of Islamic system as a completely different one to Capitalism. Unlike Capitalism, the Islamic system is based on its own concepts of human well-being and the good life that give utmost importance to human brotherhood and socioeconomic justice. It thus seeks the balanced satisfaction of both the material and the spiritual needs of all human beings.[153] Therefore,

> if man's way of life disregards the Islamic system, he will come in conflict with his own *fitrah*. He will be miserable, bewildered and anxious, living like present-day man in acute torment, despite all the triumph of modern science and all the conveniences of material civilization.[154]

Islam does not leave the right to private property absolute without restriction or limitation, as does the Capitalist system. According to Qutb, Islam realizes the community's welfare and the welfare of individual owners.[155] Owners are also subject to specific ways of maximizing their property, expending it or circulating it. This is a religious filter mechanism for Islamic economy. This mechanism is essential in the Islamic system but not in the basic of Capitalism.[156]

According to Qutb, Islam does not accept a capitalist system that accelerates the wealth of society with no plans for distribution of wealth.[157] Critics could argue that Socialism addresses this point and assert the relationship between the forms of production and distribution. This will be detailed later, but what should be noted here is that socialists affirmed that the distribution of wealth is continually subordinated to the form of production.[158] Islam does not accept such subordination because whatever was the dominant form of production, Islam grants a sufficient amount of money that is enough for every individual to live. After that, the right to private property will be as a reward that is equal to his effort. The point here is that the motivating factors in the Islamic system are justice, equality and a balanced social development.[159]

By contrast, the motivating factor in Capitalism is the objective to maximize production and interest in order to promote wealth.[160] This often, as asserted by Qutb, leads to the amassing of wealth in the hands of capitalist owners and a relative diminution of the properties owned by working class.[161] This in turn increases unemployment and its consequences of social problems and, at least, enables capitalist owners to pay workers low wages.[162] The outcome of this, according to Qutb, is reduction in the consumption rate and accumulation of surplus production leading the capitalist countries to look for new markets. This may lead to monopoly, exploitation and even war.[163] Furthermore, the capitalist system is characterized by periodic crises resulting from depression caused by low wages and low consumption in relation to increasing production.[164] Focusing on certain points of distinction between Islam and Capitalism, one may point out Qutb's view about the following:

The first principle distinguishing Islamic system from Capitalism is that the individual, in the Islamic system, is virtually the community's agent in relation to his property. His tenure of it is more like social employment than ownership. Ownership in general is fundamentally the right of the community, and the community has this as a delegation (*mustakhlafah fihi*) from Allah the only true owner of everything.[165] Private ownership then arises from the particular effort by the individual to acquire title to part of the general property over which Allah has delegated stewardship (*istakhlafa*) to the human race.[166] The point here implies *hakimiyyah*. The basic principle of the Islamic system in respect of property ownership is that wealth in all its possible forms is a thing created by Allah, and is, in principle, His property. He alone is the true owner and has the right to lay down the rules as to how it is to be acquired and used. Man is, no doubt, the owner of the reward which he gets in return for his endeavour, but it is Allah who gives him the ability to make this endeavour and it is He who created this wealth. Thus, man is not altogether free to put his property to any use he likes but is bound by the commands of Allah. Man is hence under the obligation to acquire, and increase, and spend his wealth in accordance with Allah's command. Here enters the idea of *'ubudiyyah*. Submission to Allah alone implies submission to His command in all affairs including the affairs that relate to the acquirement of wealth and its management. Qutb says,

> Because the only true owner of wealth is Allah. The wealth, then, is subjected to all the rules that decreed by the true owner to regulate all matters related to the wealth and the means to acquire it, or increase it, and the ways of spending it. This is the principle of the Islamic theory of wealth management.[167]

Qutb bases this proposition on numerous Qur'anic verses such as 4: 5 and 57: 7. The latter states 'Believe in Allah and His Messenger and expend from that of which He has made you stewards (*mustakhlafina fihi*).' Similarly, Qur'anic verse 24: 33 declares that the true owner of wealth is Allah 'Give them of the wealth of Allah that He has given you.' Qutb emphasizes that the words of these verses do not require a deep interpretation (*ta'wil*) to yield the meaning that the property in the hands of humans is the property of Allah and that they are stewards (*khulafa'*) of it, not the original owners.[168]

Thus, the right to private ownership, in Islamic system, is but the right of control and benefit. Ownership of things does not have any value without the right of control and benefit. This right, as Qutb asserts, depends on sound judgement and functional ability. If the owner cannot fulfil this condition, his right of control and benefit is terminated. This principle, according to Qutb, is supported by the fact that the ruler (*Imam*) is the heir of anyone who has no heir.[169] The legal consequence of this is that the property returns to the community. This does not mean communism of property.[170] This is because, Qutb maintains, the right of private property is a clear and basic right in the Islamic order before the existence of any of Capitalism and Communism. The idea behind this basic principle is, Qutb notes, to make the individual aware that he is merely an employee in relation to the wealth that is in his hands, and that it is basically the property of the community.[171] The awareness makes the individual accept the obligations that the system places upon his shoulders and accept the restrictions by which the system limits his freedom of actions. Likewise, when the community is aware of its basic right to this wealth, this makes the community bolder to impose obligations and set the limits without violating the principles of the Islamic order. This finally leads to principles that achieve complete social justice in the use of this wealth.[172]

The second principle of distinction between Islam and Capitalism is that great wealth, in Islam, cannot be retained in the hands of a particular group of people, or a monopoly group.[173] This principle is based on the Qur'anic verse 59: 7 which says of wealth '...it [should] not be circulating [merely] among the rich....' The aim here is to establish a mechanism for social balance in society. According to Qutb, the accumulation of wealth by a minority in the community makes for corruption.[174] Excess of wealth is like an excess of vital energy in the body that, according to Qutb, must find an outlet, and there is no assurance that the outlet will be pure and safe. This might take the form of gambling, drinking, prostitution, luxury, white slavery and other forms that are found in the imbalanced society of Capitalism.[175] On the other hand, those who are deprived and who cannot find support may suffer. Deprivation is also a great force for theft, robbery, looting and fraud. These criminal activities are usually committed by deprived people who feel worthless in an imbalanced social order where extremes of wealth and poverty exist. Such people become worthless also in their own eyes, as well as in the eyes of the wealthy. They become small miserable human fragments with no role except to satisfy the capitalists.[176]

Conditions and limitations thus surround property in the Islamic order. In addition, some property is collective, that is, no one has the right to own it, but all benefit from it. Some of the collected property that is in the hand of the community by right is also given by right to those who are in need of it, for their welfare and for the welfare of the community.[177]

The third principle concerns the means of acquiring private property. Unlike Capitalism, Islam sets out conditions of acquisition. These conditions do not violate the interests of the community or that of the individual, and do not separate the individual from the community.[178] To Qutb, 'a right does not arise from the nature of things. All rights including the right of possession, arise out of the permission of the Lawgiver and His making the cause legally productive of its effect.'[179] In the Islamic system work approved by the *Shari'ah* is the only means of acquiring the right of possession.[180] This principle implies the just relationship between effort and reward. It also means that certain professions, trades or industries are forbidden as a source of earnings. Prostitution, for instance, is legal in the Capitalist system, permits and licences are issued to those who enjoy this trade and prostitutes enjoy rights similar to other professionals.[181] The Islamic system, however, forbids this very mean of earnings and forbids sexually exciting dancing and similar erotic activities and industries.[182] Islam forbids all kind and forms of gambling, liquors, intoxicant drugs, and idol industries. In Islam, improper earnings or illegal ownership of property are forbidden.[183] These and similar prohibited industries are not among the mechanisms of the Islamic economy. Thus, the nature mechanism of the Islamic system, its aims and obligations are totally different from that in Capitalism.[184]

The fourth principle of ownership impacts on the mechanism of inheritance. In Islam, transferring one's wealth through inheritance is regarded as an act of social solidarity (*takaful ijtima'i*). To Qutb, Islam establishes the principle of solidarity and mutual respect and responsibility in all its forms. There is solidarity (*takaful*) between the individual and his self, between the individual and his immediate family, between the individual and the wider group and between one generation and successive generations.[185] Inheritance means passing one's wealth to heirs in accordance with the Islamic principles explained in the Qur'an (4: 11–12, 176). Death removes control over one's wealth. It passes on according to a set system. In Islam, there is no 'bequest to an heir' and no bequest of more than one-third of the estate is permitted.[186] This also prevents the problem of accumulation of wealth. Inheritance is thus a tool for division of accumulated wealth over generations since a single property passes to numerous descendants and relatives.[187] Comparing this system with, for instance, the Capitalist system of England, which leaves the whole estate to the oldest son,[188] reveals the wisdom of the Islamic system and the justice that the Islamic system provides for the other heirs.

Critics could argue that Qutb's own family had lost its wealth in part because of the Islamic law of inheritance. As to this personal matter, Qutb himself emphasized this in his own biography. The wealth of Qutb's grandfather was divided between members of the family in accordance with Islamic rules of inheritance. The share of Qutb's father was significant, but was decreasing all the time since 'the eminence of the family meant he was responsible for the maintenance of its social status and rural presence'.[189]

As a mayor of his village, Qutb's father could not thus abandon rural tradition in what can be considered a wealthy village. Qutb's father also was a local leader of the Wafd Party in Asyut province, and spent most of his wealth propagating the Party and its newspaper. His family home was a centre for daily meetings of nationalists.[190] This indicates that the Islamic law of inheritance did not drive the reduction in the wealth of Qutb's father. On the contrary, Qutb's father benefited from the system of inheritance and received what was rightfully due to him. This was a form of what Qutb later came to call social solidarity and mutual responsibility between one generation and successive generations.[191] Thus, the case of Qutb's father was a case of financial responsibilities, requirements and wealth management in general, not the Islamic law of inheritance as such.

If we consider the injunctions of the Qur'an,[192] it would appear that the system for the distribution of wealth laid down by Islam envisages the difference between Islam and the materialistic systems of economics in the world. The system of inheritance prevalent today in most of the European materialistic economics is the rule of primogeniture, that is to say, all the property of the deceased goes to the eldest son and all the other children male and female are totally deprived of it.[193] This, as Qutb emphasizes, is similar to the 'rules of the *jahiliyyah* prier to Islam.'[194] Moreover, at certain places in the materialistic systems, a man can if he so wishes dispose of his whole property by will to any person, thus depriving even his male offspring of a share in the inheritance. As a result of this system, wealth gets concentrated in one hand instead of being circulated. In other systems such as in the Hindu Code, the male members of the family jointly inherit the property, and the women are totally deprived from inheritance. This obvious injustice to women is also an act similar to the rules of *jahiliyyah* before Islam.[195] The sphere of the circulation of wealth is even here narrower than what it is under the Islamic system.

On the contrary, the system of dividing inheritance laid down by Islam does away with all these rules of injustice. The characteristics peculiar to this Islamic system are as follows:

1 Based on the idea of social solidarity, there is a long list of inheritors that has been prescribed in accordance with the degrees of relationship, because of which the inherited wealth gets a very wide circulation.[196] It should be noticed here that, in order to give a wide circulation to wealth, it could be as well enjoined that the whole inheritance should be distributed among the poor or be deposited in the Bayt al-Mal (Public Exchequer). But, in that case, everyone would have tried to spend all his wealth during his own lifetime, and this would have only upset the economy. It is for this reason that Islam has laid down a system which requires that the inheritance should be divided amongst the relatives of the deceased – an arrangement which should be the natural desire of the owner of the wealth.[197]

2 As against capitalism and all other materialistic systems of inheritance in the world, Islam has given to woman also the right to inherit property. The Qur'an (4: 6) says

> There is a share for men from what is left by parents and kinsmen, and there is a share for women from what is left by parents and kinsmen, whether it be little or much – and it is a determinate share.

In this regard, Qutb says

> This is the general principle by which Islam, since began fourteen century ago, gave women the right to have a share in the inheritance and men, and preserved the right of those under age who were oppressed in the *jahiliyyah*.[198]

3 The deceased has not been given the prerogative to deprive a legal heir of his or her share, nor to make any form of modification in the prescribed share of any heir. None of the heirs, individually or collectively, is allowed to do any form of modification to the shares or to the property left by the deceased. This injunction puts a complete end to the possibility of a concentration of wealth resulting from inheritance. The Qur'an (4: 10) says 'You do not know which of them, among your fathers and your sons, is nearer in profit to you. This is the law laid down by Allah.' This implies the *hakimiyya*, the *'ubudiyyah* and the universality of the law that all Muslims must abide to:

> Allah is the Creator of the parents and their offspring. He is the Giver of the livelihood and wealth. He is the One who divides the wealth and declares the shares. He is the One who legislates for the welfare of the individual and groups.[199]

4 No distinction has been made among children on the basis of priority of birth. An equal share has been allotted to the elder and the younger.[200]
5 It has been forbidden to make a bequest in favour of an heir, in addition to the prescribed share. Thus no heir can receive anything from the estate of the deceased over and above his or her own share of the inheritance.[201]
6 A part of the property can be bequeathed to one who may not be an heir. This also helps in the circulation of wealth, for a part of the property is given away as legacy before the sharing of inheritance takes place.[202]
7 A testator cannot dispose of all his property by will. He is allowed to bequeath up to one third of his property, and has no legal right to exceed this limit. This injunction thus serves to avoid that danger of the concentration of wealth that would arise if a man were allowed to dispose off all his wealth by will. At the same time, it also safeguards the rights of the near kindred. This is not subjected to the condition of an individual or group, or subjected to the circumstances of the place where Muslims are living.[203]

Thus the Islamic system of inheritance has a basic importance in the Islamic system of the distribution of wealth. It is not really to expatiate upon the inequity produced in the distribution of wealth by the restricted forms of inheritance. One of the greatest causes of the inequity that is found in Capitalism and other materialistic systems in this sphere is just this, and many economist have admitted this fact.[204]

The fifth principle with regard to how wealth is maximized focuses on individual freedom within the legal limits that expound the welfare of the individual and the welfare of the community in Islam.[205] An individual may cultivate the land, turn raw materials into manufactured goods or engage in trade to increase his capital, but he may not cheat or engage in a prohibited trade. There is freedom of competition in the marketplace but hoarding, manipulating the price of goods, exploitation and fraud are all prohibited.[206] A Muslim may not buy any article that he knows to have been obtained by unlawful means.[207] This ratifies methods that

> generally do not vastly increase capital to the point where this create classes. This happens only with that exorbitant increase of capital that we see in the Capitalist system, through cheating, usury, consuming workers' wages, hoarding, exploitation of need, theft, robbery, dispossession and usurpation . . . and all the other crimes that underlie contemporary means of exploitation.[208]

The sixth principle that distinguishes Capitalism from the Islamic system is *riba* (usury or interest). *Riba* is the basic principle that interweaves and characterizes the economic interactions in Capitalism. *Riba* of all types and forms are forbidden in Islam.[209]

For Qutb, the Islamic system cannot be identified with Capitalism, nor should it be called Capitalism. Islam is Islam, and Capitalism is Capitalism.

To Qutb, 'any system other than Islamic system is but a system of *jahiliyyah*.'[210]

Concluding remarks

Liberal Capitalism has been found to fulfill the desires of the individual with minimal restrictions. Unlike Capitalism, Islamic system is divinely inspired as a perfect balanced system. Among the points, which distinguish between Islam and Capitalism are the right to private property, the right of investment, and the right of inheritance. Islam grants Man the right to private property and guides this right by the rules of *Shari'ah*. Qutb emphasizes the limitations, referred to by the *Shari'ah*, as safeguards for the individual and the community.

The *Shari'ah* also guides the individual to earn and maximize his wealth through lawful means, rather than through theft, gambling, prostitution, liquour and other activity such as *riba* (interest). The social impact of these illegal pursuits on both the individual and on society cannot be ignored.

Limitations on the right of private property or inheritance thus reflect the fact that there is nothing absolute in the universe, even life and human affairs. This is the universal law, the *fitrah* with which God created the universe, life and Man. This harmonious relationship is the characteristic of the Islamic system.

Unlike in Capitalism, the freedom of the individual in Islam is limited within the universal law. This guides Man through a safeguard framework to ensure good relations are maintained among individuals and between individuals and the community. This grants liberty for all. This liberty and its safeguards are applied to all spheres in the Islamic system.

SOCIALISM

This section examines Qutb's perception of differences between the Islamic system and Socialism. It will briefly examine sociopolitical particularities of socialist society and compare these with the Islamic law laid down in the *Shari'ah*. It will investigate the origins and mechanism of Socialism and socialist views on Capitalism, Democracy and religion. The concept of Arab Socialism and its genesis will be discussed, together with the ideological response of Muslim scholars.

Socialism is an ideology that seeks to correct and rectify the moral and social problems that were inflicted by Capitalism. Socialism is not a precise term, there being several versions of it. Utopias were conceived of by the ancient Greek philosophers and thinkers such as Plato (427–347 BC).[211] Later the Persian socialist Mazdak expressed another form of Socialism, which dominated Persian politics in the late fifth and early sixth centuries before Islam. Mazdak advocated a social programme that abrogated, among other things, private property and marriage. According to al-Shahrastani (d. 548/479) 'Mazdak proclaimed a community of women, and made wealth and women freely and equally available to all men like fire, water and fodder.'[212] In 528, Crown Prince Chosroes launched a campaign to eliminate the Mazdakites. Among those who were killed was Mazdak.[213]

In nineteenth-century Europe, there were the utopias of Robert Owen (1771–1858) of Great Britain and Charles Fourier and Comte de Saint-Simon of France.[214] There are also Fabian, syndicalist, guild, Marxist, market, democratic, Arab Socialism and others.[215] The definition of Socialism, which became known in England in the 1830s, increased, within less than a century later, to more than 260 definitions.[216]

The details and mutual differences of all of these variants of Socialism require a separate study. What should be noted here is that, according to Qutb, the common characteristics among most, if not all of them, is the basic principle of separating religion from state. Religion has no role in the sociopolitical and economic affairs of society.[217] Socialism, as asserted by al-Badri (1983), holds the view that 'religion is the opiate of the masses'.[218] According to Lichtheim (1978) 'Socialism is generally associated with secularism'.[219] To Qutb, 'Socialism, in its various forms, has the same secularist worldview as Capitalism'.[220]

Socialism offers a social and common critique of the capitalist mode of production and exchange. It argues that free and uncontrolled market economics on which Capitalism rests are bound to bring about an allocation of resources that favour the rich and perpetuates injustices and enormous inequalities of income and wealth.[221] Chapra (1995) pointed out the characteristics of Socialism as follows:

> the characteristics of Socialism considered private property and the wage system to be the source of evil and insisted that social justice cannot be rendered to the poor without socializing private property to varying degrees. They [characteristics of socialism] felt that even democracy was not workable effectively as long as there are inequalities and special interests. They conceived of a future in which masses would either forcibly or democratically take control of the levers of government from the capitalists and create an egalitarian and democratic society, free from class conflict and based on comprehensive planning and public control of the means of production. In other words, [Socialists] attacked capitalism and proposed a different system for allocation and distribution.[222]

The characteristics mentioned, indicate that Socialism is critical of religions, the right to private ownership in both Islam and Capitalism. Socialism has its own system of distribution of wealth. However, according to Qutb, the whole system of Socialism is like Capitalism in that both do not prohibit *riba* (interest).[223] Qutb stresses that 'it is impossible today or tomorrow that the world economy could be based on anything other than *riba*...'.[224] This together with the characteristics above is suggestive of the differences between Islam and Socialism.

For Qutb, the Islamic system is comprehensive, that is, its political realm cannot be separated from economic, social, moral or intellectual spheres of society. It is basically based on the Islamic concept of Sovereignty (*hakimiyyah*) and the relevant constructs. It has a special view about the nature of the relationship between the Creator and the creation, the universe, life and Man. According to Qutb,

> the difference between Islam and Socialism is obvious in their source, their existence, their history, their characteristics and their conceptions and aims. Islam is a universal system of all spheres of life of all humankind, while Socialism is a local system limited to the economic sphere . . .[225]

In the 1950s, Qutb expressed a number of ideas that were considered by a number of intellectuals as socialist. This claim was perhaps because there was similarity between Islam and socialism on a number of points.[226] However, Qutb's expression of those ideas does not mean that he stood for Socialism, or advocated it, or preferred Socialism to the Islamic system. Qutb's ideological position in regard to all systems other than Islam is evident, as discussed, in his writings in the mid 1940s and in further detail in the first edition of *Social Justice in Islam* (1949).[227] Also, in his articles of the 1950s, which were later collected and published in his book *Towards an Islamic Society*, Qutb discussed the similarities and the differences between Islam and other systems such as Capitalism, Socialism and Communism. For example, after discussing Capitalism, Qutb pointed out that

> at this point – and for these reasons – England, in particular, went towards Socialism. But Russia went towards Marxism despite the changes which significantly removed the theory from its first nature. All the principles of Socialism and that of Communism were the result of these historical developments. By contrast, what Islam has in this sphere is rooted in the Islamic system itself and in the *Shari'ah* since it was revealed fourteen century ago. The *Shari'ah* created the society. The *Shari'ah* was not the result of social development but the motive force behind the development. The purposes of Socialism and Marxism will end because they emerged as a result of the development. Those purposes will end when the development reaches a certain stage. But because the principles of Islam are above the transitory requirements of the environment, they will continue to work as a motive force behind the continual development in accordance with the specific program, which was planned since fourteen century ago . . .
>
> There is similarity between Islam and Socialism on many points in the sphere of economy . . . because of this similarity, a number of Muslims

> speak of the 'Socialist Islam', 'Islamic Socialism' and 'Socialism in Islam.' But the reality is that Islam was established earlier before Socialism. This reality rejects any attempt to label Islam with Socialism. This is an immediate distinction between Islam and Socialism. As for the subject, Islam is a complete system in which all these points [of similarities and differences] are based on constant foundations and dependent upon the comprehensive idea which is harmonious in its parts and connected to the belief in Allah. By contrast, Socialism is a materialistic idea of life, addressing no more than the economic affairs in the life of society. Therefore, Socialism is partial and transitory, but the Islamic system is complete and permanent.[228]

This represents Qutb's view of Socialism, whether it could be called Islamic or others, in the 1950s. The point that should also be noted here is that when Abd al-Nasser adopted Socialism as an ideology for the United Arab Republic in 1961, Qutb was in prison. Thus Qutb had limited occasion to discuss Nasser's Arab Socialism in detail. Nasser also was propagating Socialism as Islamic. These factors have shifted Qutb's interest from discussing partial or small points, here or there, to focus closely on his theory of Islamic conception and its characteristics which distinguish Islamic conceptions and systems from all other conceptions, and systems and ideologies of any time and space, as he also admits:

> We will not focus on this or that particular deviation in Islamic thought or practice and let this to consumes our time. Our effort is not to response to a specific deviation or situation in order to correct it, but rather to clarify the characteristics of the Islamic concept and the truths of Islam in their entirety in the way the Qur'an contains them – complete, all-inclusive, balanced and harmonious.[229]

With this in mind, he revised a few volumes of the second edition of *Fi Zilal al-Qur'an*, and published it in 1961. In 1962, he published *The Characteristics of Islamic Conception*; and *Islam and Problems of Civilization*. In 1964, he published his last *Milestones*. Thus, since 1961 when Nasser adopted Arab Socialism and described it as Islamic, Qutb published three major books and several revised volumes of *Zilal*, from prison.

This tells us that imprisonment isolated Qutb physically, not intellectually. To reflect his awareness of what was going on outside the walls of the prison, Qutb says, in the revised parts of *Zilal* (i.e. second edition 1961), that 'despite the obvious differences between Islam and Socialism, there are attempts at labeling Socialism as Islamic'.[230] Elsewhere in *Zilal*, and in response to those who were trying to link Socialism to Islam, Qutb concludes his analysis in these words: 'therefore, the saying that "the Scientific Socialism" is an ideology independent from materialistic ideology is but a *jahalah*, and nonsense. Following the "Scientific Socialism" is a departure from Islam: belief and conception, program and system.'[231] In the last book, *Ma'alim* (1964), he says:

> The Islamic society is not the society which contains people who call themselves 'Muslims', who pray and perform *hajj* while the law of their society is not the Islamic *Shari'ah*. The Islamic society is not the society which creates an Islam for themselves, calling it 'developed Islam' other than the Islam ordained by Allah. The '*jahili* society' takes many forms – all are *jahiliyyah*. It takes the form of a society which denies the existence of Allah, explains the history on dialectic and materialistic bases, and follows what is called 'Scientific Socialism' as a system. It takes the form of a society which believes in Allah but does not implement His *Shari'ah*.[232]

Thus, The difference between Islam and Socialism of all types and forms was addressed and meant, to Qutb, the difference between Islam and *jahiliyyah*.[233]

Arab Socialism is the form that was devised by Gamal Abd al-Nasser (1918–1970) in Egypt (the United Arab Republic). Nasser officially took power in 1954 on the basis that all the Egyptians and the Arab supporters were agreed on a framework of broad national objectives. As soon as Nasser came to power, the socialist propaganda machine began to prepare the ground for Socialism. Arab socialists published a considerable large number of literature that advocates a general assumption that Arab Socialism is the Arab goal.[234] Then, Socialism was adopted by Nasser and it was officially embodied in the Socialist laws of 1961 the year of the dissolution of Egypt's union with Syria.[235] The collapse of the union with Syria indicated that the proposed assumption of general agreement concerning Arab Socialism by the masses was unjustified. Nevertheless, in his book *Arab Socialism*, published in 1967 and sponsored by the Egyptian regime and bearing Nasser's photograph, 'Abd al-Majeed states

> Arab Socialism has been recognized in the United Arab Republic [then Egypt]. Arab Socialism was found on the bases of the social philosophy heralded by the Revolution, embodied in the Socialist laws of 1961 and the principles of the National Charter of 1962. The introduction of Socialism was a response to the actual demands of the Arab nation [not plural], which was influenced by alien factors and reacted in such a way that required immediate action to remove the prevailing conditions and realize the aspiration of the Arabs as Liberty, Democracy and Socialism.[236]

These words of 'Abd al-Majeed emphasize that authorities in Egypt insisted on that Socialism (not Islam) was the most effective means of turning Egypt into a modern industrialized State, ensuring justice and equality for all its citizens.[237]

Nasser's view of Socialism found its institutional expression in the National Union (*ittihad qawmi*), which was a political mass organization, charged with implementing Socialism as a goal of the Revolution. According to Enayat (1982), 'class alliance was eradicated and was then considered feasible only among the working forces of the people'.[238] These working forces, as in the 1964 Constitution, comprised farmers, workers, soldiers, intellectuals and those few owners of national capital. Eradicating class differences was then admitted to be impossible. It was emphasized that there could be no 'peaceful coexistence between the working forces of the people and the exploitative classes whose adherence to imperialism as well as inherited privileges were to be illuminated.'[239] Therefore, the Socialist Union (*ittihad ishtraki*) replaced the National Union, to shift the idea of Socialism to 'social determinism, that is, a belief in the decisive influence of class interests and status on the sociopolitical outlook of individuals'.[240]

This clarification of class, according to Enayat, is 'decidedly Fabian: the rulers always accompanied their statements of the belief in the primacy of class interests with firm denial of the inevitability of class struggle or warfare, or the necessity of the proletarian dictatorship.'[241] Socialists in Egypt continued to claim that the aim of their Socialism was merely to eradicate the differences between classes, liberate the exploited and safeguard their rights without revenge on former exploiters and oppressors. Brigadier 'Abd al-Hamid Mursi listed nine points as basic aims of their Socialism. These aims can be concluded in 'justice, freedom and equality'.[242]

These goals, according to Mursi, did not stem from Islam or any other 'religion' but 'from good socialist plan'.[243] Nevertheless, Nasser attempted to show that his regime was Islamic. According to Judge 'Ashmawi, 'The revolution of July tried to show itself as Islamic in order to overcome the increased Islamic sentiment at the time.'[244] Therefore, most of the published works of Arab socialists celebrated Arab Socialism as Islamic. They quoted passages from the National Charter to emphasize that their Socialism is 'Islamic Socialism' and in harmony with 'Christian Socialism'.[245] Their view of social life was not 'Islam alone'.[246] Arab Socialism is thus not a theory of purely political or economic systems. A group of Arab socialists of the time emphasized 'Socialism is a system of life that takes in its account the circumstances of the environment in which Socialism exists'.[247] According to Hulayq (1965) 'the fact is that no word in the National Charter indicates that Islam is the religion of the state'.[248]

The point of the given statement, as asserted by Qutb, is that Arab socialists were praising Islam, on the one hand, but on the other, declaring that their Arab Socialism was the only system able to solve Egyptian and Arab problems.[249] Nasser himself, in a televised speech to the nation on October 1964, articulated Qutb's point. Nasser proclaimed that 'Socialism is our only road to justice.'[250] Brigadier Mursi interpreted Nasser's claim as follows:

> Our national problems are three types: economic, social and political . . . It is the problems that guided us to Socialism. When we decided to establish the socialist system, we were not demanding philosophy . . . we wanted to

> solve the problems practically. The answer has been found in only one system, that is, Arab Socialism. If someone asks us why Socialism? The answer will be simply that Socialism is the one system suitable to solve our problem.[251]

The words of President Nasser and Brigadier Mursi clarify two points that have been made by Qutb. First, that 'Arab Socialism was not Islam'.[252] The second, that 'Socialism was recognized as the only system of life that is able to solve their problems.'[253] Consequently, Arab Socialism does not recognize Islam as a system of life that has the capacity to solve the modern problems.

Socialists moved Islam to the third priority in the Egyptian and Arab affairs. In his *Philosophy of Revolution*, published in 1955, Nasser identified Islam as one of the three circles centred in Egypt, the other two being, according to Nasser's reign, Arabism and Africanism.[254] Among the Egyptian theorists of Arab Socialism, who in the condition of strict censorship, during Nasser's reign, freely published their views, noted that

> attachment to Islam, although potentially a motive for political dynamism, and an indispensable element in the fabric of the Arab national life, had now become incapable on its own of tackling the problems of the Arab homeland – the ultimate focus of the loyalty and concern of the Arab progressives.[255]

Others considered Islam had proved a failure.'[256] Treating Islam as a second class political system was, without doubt, a point of tension between the Nasser school of Arab Socialism and Qutb's.

Concerning Arab Socialism and its relation to Marxism, when Arab Socialism relegated Islam to second class, it

> legitimized the thoughts of Marx, whether old or new, as an ingredient of Arab Socialism. And from 1961 onwards, while official publications took good care not to mention Marx except in dissociating Arab Socialism from his atheism, officially sponsored political literature showed a distinct drift in the direction of Marxism.[257]

Enayat mentioned two Egyptian authors, in a joint book devoted to a defence of the ideas of the young Marx, as the epistemological foundation of the ruling ideology. They tried to show, rather over-confidently that, of all the existing systems of thought, only Arab Socialism attained the Excellent Mean between Capitalism and Communism.[258] From their book, Enayat cited the following:

> Arab Socialism is based on a completely new balance of thought. If we describe its position as the excellent mean between two extremes, this should not be understood to mean that our Socialism stands midway

> between Capitalism and Marxism, because we are not talking of an arithmetic or geometrical average. What we mean is that while Arab Socialism stands midway between Capitalism and Marxism, it represents a jump forward with regard to these opposite poles...This balance between the two poles has asserted itself of the development of the universal thought which, according to dialectical logic, has proceeded from thesis to antithesis, and then to state [the synthesis], in which the opposites are reconciled. Thus Capitalism gave rise to Marxism, and these opposites gave rise to Arab Socialism.[259]

According to this socialist view, Arab Socialism is the offshoot of Capitalism and Marxism. This means that Arab Socialism is not the offshoot of Islam or takes Islam as its aim. Numerous Egyptian intellectuals openly acknowledged their debt to Marxism and indulged in an 'historical criticism of Islam. Their criticism concerned itself not only with the theological or metaphysical principles of Islam, but also with the false representation of its ideals in conventional literature'.[260] This is one among the reasons for which Qutb described Socialism, in general, and Arab Socialism in particular as *jahiliyyah*.[261]

During the time of Nasser, the response of the *'ulama* to the challenge of the authority of Socialism was only an attempt to prove that Islam by itself contained all the provisions of Socialism. Muhammad Shaltut (1892–1963), a Western educated professor, who became the Rector of al-Azhar in 1958 (during Nasser regime), summed up his concept of social solidarity saying

> Briefly summarized, such is the doctrine of Islam regarding the relations among men, from the point of view of solidarity of members of society. It contains in detail all the solid foundations necessary to make our nation a magnificent stronghold, a haven of happiness for those who shelter there. The doctrine also contains a clear statement of what the Socialism of Islam is, for adoption by those who wish to adopt it. Can Man find a more profound Socialism that that decreed by Islam? It is founded on the basis of faith and belief, and all that is decreed on that basis participates in the perpetuation of life and doctrine.[262]

The response of the *'ulama* to Arab Socialism in Egypt was influenced by the government pressure on al-Azhar to reform itself in 1961. Western educated Shaykh Muhammad al-Bahiyy, was professor at the University of Montreal in the 1950s and then Minister of Islamic Endowments in 1960.[263] Al-Bahiyy was 'anxious to prove that Islam contained all the provisions of Socialism and there is no need for another ideology'.[264] At that time, according to Enayat, an academic summarized the opinion of the *'ulama* in these words: 'While the crypto-secularists in the government and in the intelligentsia [are] striving to justify Socialism through Islam, the shaykhs are trying to justify Islam through Socialism.'[265]

Opposition to official Socialism and, indeed, to all imported ideologies and idioms during the censorship of this crucial period, was not expressed openly with the exception of Qutb. He felt under no obligation to avoid giving offence to the ruler.[266] He presented Islam, according to Cantwell Smith (1977), as an operative force actively at work on modern problems.[267] According to al-Bazzaz (1913–197?), 'Qutb has successfully explained the capability of the Islamic system (political, social, financial, legislation and juristic principles), and the difference between Islam and other systems known before or after Islam....'[268] Qutb also did not use alien idioms to describe Islamic ideals and did not approve of such terms like Islamic Socialism, or Islamic Democracy.[269] He described these systems directly as *jahiliyyah* and pointed out that Islamic system cannot be called by any name other than Islam.[270]

Concluding remarks

Socialism, which sought to rectify the problems created by Capitalism, has lost its way because of the lack of congruence between theory and practice. Like Capitalism, contemporary Socialism is a new edition of various ancient models, and an extension of the secularist philosophy of the Age of Reason. What Socialism has done is not more than some changes introduced to transform human beings to accept state ownership of the means and production and exchange. If the right to private property and profit are embraced by Socialism, then what will distinguish it from Capitalism, particularly when inequalities have risen, and social classes also continue to dominate in the countries in which Socialism has a strong hold. This is evident not only in the West but also in the Arab countries that embraced Socialism.

These reflected the tensions and differences between Arab socialists and Islamists. For Islamists, Socialism is a secular system and its application did not cure economic or other problems. This became evident in the 1970s, during the term of President Sadat, when Egypt diverted its policy from Socialism to the 'open door policy' (*infitah*). Neither Socialism, nor the 'open door policy' cured Egypt's problems. The Islamists noted the fact that Capitalism, Socialism and Democracy had been tried and that none cured the Egyptian problems. This is apparent in all spheres of life in Egypt today. The Islamists, therefore, are asking why do Egypt and Arab countries not try Islam and facilitate its application as they did with secular systems. If by this secular system are meant freedom, justice and equality, Islam is able to perfect these. Qutb notes that 'the Arabs should review their rich Islamic heritage before they go begging for a loan from beyond the seas and across the deserts'.[271]

COMMUNISM

This section outlines Qutb's view of the difference between the Islamic system and Communism. It will compare their sociopolitical theories and assess the mechanisms each uses to analyse and rectify social problems of human communities. The origins and development of Communism will be traced and contrasted to Capitalism, Democracy and religion.

The intellectual roots of Communism, it is sometimes said, lie in, the philosophic substratum of Ancient Greece. Plato (427–347 BC), who wrote *The Republic*, introduced to the world the notion of community in the ownership of wealth and women.[272] His idea, according to Bertrand Russell, was that 'whenever a number of individuals have a common name, they also have a common idea or form.'[273] Plato divided the citizenry into three classes,

> the common people, the soldiers, and the guardians. The last, alone, are to have political power... This idea [of class] is similar to that of the Jesuits in old Paraguay, the ecclesiastics in the States of the Church until 1870, and the Communist Party in the USSR of the present day.[274]

In the view of communists, Communism is a form of government, an economic system, a revolutionary movement, a way of life, a goal and/or an ideal. It provides social analyses of how and why human history has taken the form it has and in what direction it is headed.[275] Many Communist ideas were adopted and developed by Vladimir Lenin (1870–1924) from the writings of Karl Marx whose work, *The Communist Manifesto* appeared in 1848 and *Das Capital* appeared in 1867. Marx was a German social philosopher. Lenin was a Russian leader of the Bolshevik Revolution in 1917, after which he ruled Russia until his death in 1924.[276]

According to Qutb, Communism, in its classical theory, aims to create a classless society in which the state, as a political structure, fades away and the proletariat (workers) control all elements of production and distribution. However, like most utopian analyses these did not translate to reality. The communists, as Qutb maintains, assumed that Communism would replace Capitalism, but in practice, Communism appeared to be like others: class struggle,[277] although its social analysis shows its promised ideal society that cannot be materialized.[278] The 'Soviet calls it Socialism, not Communism.'[279]

Karl Marx (1818–1883) was a free thinker, who, according to Qutb, claimed that criticism of religion is the foundation of all criticism. In Qutb's view, Marx 'denies the very basis of religious thought – belief in God, the Eternal, the Self-Subsisting Creator of the material world. In Marx's view, all religions, because of their very origin, are a curse or "opium of the masses." '[280] Like all social philosophers, Marx sought to diagnose the condition of Man under the capitalist system. Marx developed a theory to explain what he saw as basic features of the capitalist system.

In his analyses, Marx's tools were a few concepts such as alienation, exploitation, balance (surplus value), private property and the class struggle between the proletariat and the bourgeoisie. Economic determinism was fundamental to this analysis of bourgeois monopoly of powers.[281] Qutb pointed out that

> Marx employed the dialectic of the principles of contradiction introduced by the German philosophers Fichte and Hegel before him. But while they employed it in the realm of concepts and ideas, Marx employed this principle in the field of 'economics' in relation to the history of societies. In this view every 'thing' has its opposite and thus every 'thing' annihilates itself. This is the general principle of contradiction, but Marx applies it to the annihilation of classes that based on capitalism just as those classes were annihilated which pre-dated the capitalistic system. The monarchs and feudal systems collapsed, according to Marx, because of their inherent contradictions. Similarly, the new capitalistic system will collapse by producing its opposite or contradiction, the communistic system which will have but one class of workers.[282]

According to this logic, says Qutb,

> the principle of contradiction does not stop after producing the opposite of the 'thing', but continues onwards by a synthesis of the two, which brings about a new 'thing', which again produces its opposite, and so on. But, contrary to its own logic, Marxism expects that after the communistic system comes into being it will not collapse by producing its opposite... The question is why should the principle of contradiction stops its operation at this stage? Why should not the communist system, by the inexorable logic of this principle, produce its opposite, then a conflict of the two, and then a new system?[283]

During 1843–1844, Marx had absorbed the 'materialism of Feuerbach's genetic-critical method'.[284] This method, as Qutb asserts, represents the extension of the 'Fichtean–Hegelian concept of alienation' and its application to religion in the endeavour to 'escape from the Church'[285] and, in Kamenka's words, 'to expose the real secret of Christianity. It is the secret that man made God out of the hopes.'[286] Marx thought that the recent industrial achievements of the humanity, declared man's liberty, as he was able 'to escape from God' and 'to escape from the need and dependence of the Church'.[287] Marx's attempt, as Qutb asserts, was only to 'establish a deity other than the deity of the Church, a deity that has no priests, no clergymen, no pope, and no Church....'[288] This means to Kamenka that 'God then felt into dependence on his own creation, mortified himself before his own fantasy'.[289] For Kamenka, 'Marx had absorbed the mechanism and the method which gave to God what he surely needed for himself and what he must now take back into himself'.[290]

In his *Economico-Philosophical Manuscripts*, published in 1844, Marx applied the mechanism of the materialistic concept of God to show the same mechanism at work in economic life.[291] Now Marx seeks

> to subject the political economy of Capitalism and of all societies based on private property and the division of labour to a fundamental logico-ethical critique – to bring out their theoretical, practical and moral contradictions, summed up in this phrase 'The more riches the workers produces, the poorer he becomes.'[292]

Marx based his historical arguments, as Qutb asserts, on only 'economic determinism'.[293] There is no Sovereignty (*hakimiyyah*) of Allah here, but the sovereignty of economy. There is no *'ubudiyyah* to Allah here but to the economy. The principal concept in Marx's analysis, according to Qutb, is alienation that arises in capitalist society from the exploitation of the proletariat by the bourgeoisie.[294] The bourgeoisie is the capitalist class, owners of the means of production and exchange. The proletarian class is made up of workers who own nothing but their labour and hence became subject to slavery.[295] Marx's view is that all economic production and surplus value come from the workers, who do not get more than a subsistence wage. Therefore, the rich become richer, and the poor became poorer.[296]

According to Qutb, Marx's diagnosis of the condition of Man in society is that the state and the bourgeoisie together function to exploit the proletariat. They each play a crucial role in Man's alienation. Alienation will eventually disappear when a classless society is established and the state and religion have withered away during the various stages of the historical process.[297] Only after the abolishing of private property, money, state and religion can man finally become a true Communist human being. Marx then seeks to find a creative society in which man is not dominated by needs, envy, or desire to possess property.[298]

Marx believed that the independent man 'who escaped from God has a new nature that needs no more than food, drink, shelter and sex'.[299] His main characteristic, as asserted by Marx, is 'a man [who] has no individual human nature'.[300] This hypothetical human is

> a man separated from what he needs, from his very capacity to work, from the products of his work, from his own labour-power, and hence from his own humanity, from other men, from society, and from Nature. He is alienated, reduced to the dependence of an animal, but a dependence that is infinitely more pervasive and horrible in so far as it is the self-created dependence of a conscious and potentially universal being, capable of mastering the universe. Money infinitely intensifies this dependence and at the same time mystifies all economic relationships, conceals their fundamentally human content and purpose.[301]

This means that, says Kamenka, the key to history lies not in Man's ideas but in the economic conditions. The making of history is determined only by economic determinism. Man is a passive creature without a stable nature or inclinations. His will has no functional importance in the face of material and economic forces.[302] This is, according to Qutb, one of the basic differences between Islam and Communism.[303] For Qutb, Islam respects Man and views him as an active being with a free will of his own that is subject to the sovereign Will. In addition, Man has power as the vicegerent (*khalifah*) of God on the earth. The responsibilities of *khilafah* make it clear that Man enjoys power and position on this earth with all material and economic forces according to the programme at his command. The Lawgiver also provides rights to private property and a total programme guide for him to fulfil the obligations.[304] Man has a crucial role in the development of this life economics and others as a whole. By contrast, Communism, in Qutb's view,

> has separated man from his spirit, looks at man in terms of his material needs, and looks at the universe in terms of matter and nothing else. Islam, however, looks at man as a unity in which spiritual desires and physical inclinations are not separated from each other... Islam looks at the universe and life in this comprehensive way of unity. This is where Islam, Communism, and all systems diverge. The divergence arises from the fact that Islam is the pure creation of God, but Communism comes from pure human fantasy.[305]
>
> Life is mutual love and respect, cooperation and solidarity. Its bases are defined and its forms are institutionalized, among Muslims, in particular, and among all human beings, in general. Life from the point of view of Communism is but conflict and struggle between classes ending in victory of one class over another, at which point the great Communist dream will be fulfilled. From this it appears that Islam is the dream of an eternal humanity embodied in a reality living on the earth. Communism which alienated man from his nature has no capacity to continue for more than one human generation.[306]

In the 1950s, Qutb pointed out that 'Communism is the natural end of the European civilization.'[307] Elsewhere, Qutb emphasized that Communism would defeat Capitalism and then Communism and Islam would confront each other.[308] By the time it confronts Islam, 'Communism will be in its final stages... There is no doubt, for a moment, that the outcome will be for Islam.'[309] In Qutb's view, Communism has no capacity to continue after it defeats Capitalism. In the early 1950s Qutb's announced prophecy was in these words: 'I expect the most length of time for the Communist movement will go no further than the time of our generation in which we are, and early in the next, if the situation continue as it is going now.'[310] Thus Qutb's idea stresses that Communism was a temporary system for temporary circumstances of its period and cannot survive more than one generation. In the 1960s in *Islam: the Religion of the Future* (1961), Qutb writes,

> The purpose of life is not and never was only food, drink, sex and shelter, as Marx believed. Marxism is completely ignorant of the human consciousness, human nature, and the nature of history, not to mention

> Marxism's ignorance of the nature of existence and the interpretation of life and the universe. Marxism ascribes all human incentives to the material hungers and to the struggle for material gain. It describes historical events as due solely to change in the means of production. It abrogates the most important human values which distinguish man's history from that of animals and denigrates man's most significant function.[311]

In *The Crisis in Historical Materialism*, Aronowitz Stanley (1981), began his book with the comment 'Theorists have interpreted Communism in various ways; the point however, is to change it'.[312] Aronowitz also refers to Communists as follows: 'In his preface to *Evolutionary Socialism* Bernstein acknowledges that his conclusion were "deviant" in relation to "Marx–Engels" doctrine by which he had been so deeply influenced... For Bernstein, the time had arrived to jettison the theory...'[313] Qutb defined Communism in one word: '*jahiliyyah*'.[314]

Concluding remarks

Communism is another human attempt to establish justice and equality without religious guidance. While Capitalism introduced its temptations – the right to private property – and tried to reform human nature through freedom that nevertheless resulted in extreme selfishness and wars, Communism sought to destroy the selfishness of Capitalism. Despite this, Communism has ended where it started in theory rather than in practice or application. Marx's thought 'displayed the inability of taking any concept of civic values seriously to improve what is there of class struggle and moral degradation characteristic of societies which claim to enjoy freedom and equality'.[315] Communism condemns the entire structure of Capitalist ownership of property, but also introduced changes to reform human nature to accept state ownership. Lenin informed communists that 'people are mistaken when they believe that laws protect the freedom of individuals. Laws are passed to protect the State. It has to be said that the worker in a factory does not own himself. The factory owns him.'[316] Communism began in class struggle and has ended with class struggle.

DEMOCRACY

Democracy was also not spared from Qutb's harsh criticism.

> The world today stands on the brink of an abyss, not because of the threat of imminent destruction – that is the symptom of the decease not the decease itself – but because of its moral bankruptcy, the morals that human life cannot develop rightly without guidance. This is completely evident in the Western world, which no longer has morals to offer to

> humanity, no longer has what could convince their conscious that it deserves to exist since its democracy has ended with bankruptcy and has began to borrow from the Eastern Camp, particularly in economic spheres that fall under the name of Socialism. Similarly, the Eastern Camp and its collective systems, above all, Marxism have retreated from the idea.[317]

With regard to Qutb's style, this section examines his understanding of what could be called secular democracy. Comparisons with this and Islam reveal, once again, that for Qutb, the Islamic system cannot be labelled democracy but remains simply itself – Islam. Qutb's view of the origins, goals and variations of democracy will be traced and compared with his view of the Islamic system. It will examine the identity crises of democracy and highlight the difference between it and Islam as a system of government, a source of authority and the legal bases for social and political relationships between rulers and people and between citizens and institutions.

The word democracy comes from the Greek word *demos* (masses: people) and *karatos* (rule and/or authority). The term democracy thus means the authority of the people. Etymologically and historically, the original meaning of democracy relates to a form of government. Democracy as defined by Herodotus, is 'the rule of the many' and some times translated by 'the multitude's rule' or 'the rule of the people by the people'.[318]

Democracy was a form of political regime that had played a major role in the history of the city-states of Ancient Greece in the fifth century BC. This was a revolution against the authority of 'clergymen and religion'.[319] In this classic form of democracy, according to Marshall (1998), a number of people were allowed to have a voice in decisions that would affect all people. This right was exercised at a mass meeting. The decision was direct in a way that would be called today 'direct democracy'. However, there are three points that should be remembered: (i) that this form of classic age democracy excluded women and a large class of slaves, (ii) that the mass (*demos*) acted as a collective or social body, rather than as separate or isolated individuals and (iii) that this form of collective decision making could work only as long as the citizen body who are allowed to exercise this right remained relatively small and homogenous.[320] In this form of democracy, the number of people 'never exceeded 20,000 persons'.[321] In his *Human Scale* (1980), Kirtpatrick Sale suggested that

> true democracy is difficult in groups larger than 10,000, and impossible in populations above 50,000: most West Europeans and Americans live in towns and cities larger than this. In fact the classic age of Greek democracy lasted only for about 200 years, in city-states of a few thousand privileged citizens, and was destroyed by invasion and war. Its long term durability in the face of population growth was never tested.[322]

The disappearance of democracy continued from the time of the ancient Greeks until the late eighteenth century, when the early modern democracy appeared as a product of what is called 'mental revolution', which reached its climax towards the end of the eighteenth century. Some see the reappearance of the early modern democracy in the Virginian Declaration of Rights and the American Declaration of Independence in 1776, and in the French Declaration of the Rights of Man in 1789.[323] As for the latter, one French historian has called the Declaration 'the death certificate of the old regime'.[324] Some others see that neither the French nor the American Declarations were manifestos of democracy. Thomson (1957) emphasises that the

> French Declaration was not a manifesto of democracy. Even the Americans had not yet instituted universal suffrage and the French contented themselves with stating that 'all citizens have the right to take part, in person or by their representatives', in forming the law and in voting taxes. That they intended neither universal nor direct democracy became clear before the end of 1789, when a constitution was drawn up by the Assembly. This made a distinction between 'active' and 'passive' citizens and withheld the vote from the latter who were defined as those who did not pay taxes equal in value to three days' wages.[325]

This means that democracy did not reappear before 1789 and when it did reappear, it excluded a number of people from having a voice in decisions that would affect all people. In the eighteenth century, according to Green, 'England was ruled by a small class of property-owners . . . Property was the key to government and the basis of representation in parliament.'[326] Therefore, in seventeenth century Europe, according to Dunn,

> there was no one at all, as far as we know, who identified their own political values by calling themselves democrats. The term democracy did not reappear in any Western European language until the late eighteenth century and when it does appear, it appears in political antithesis to the word aristocrat.[327]

By the end of the eighteenth century, 'the dominant view was that the State is the enemy of individual freedom'.[328]

In the nineteenth century, Equality, Liberty and Fraternity were the watchwords of this early modern democracy. The democrats insisted that liberty of speech and writing were fundamental rights.[329] In this regard, John Stuart Mill's essay *On Liberty* (1858) is a classic protest against the tendency of governments to restrict this freedom. Yet 'neither Mill, nor any other leading thinker, taught that speech and writing should be completely free in a democracy. Also, some restrictions on purely political opinions were justified.'[330] The democrats of the time, did not advocate 'economic equality', for that would have run counter to their respect for 'private property'? Thomson emphasizes that, at this time, the historical connection between the belief in freedom of thought and the freedom of action put the concept of democracy, as an idea and form of government, in question. The relationship between the government and the citizens became one of the many pressing questions of the time.[331] In this regard, throughout the nineteenth century, the prevailing view was that 'the less the State interfered in economic life the better for everyone... Thus democracy in politics came to be closely associated with individualism in economic.'[332]

In the twentieth century, there was a growing tendency to insist that democracy involves economic as well as political and civil rights. In a number of European countries the issue of equality, that everyone should be given equal opportunities to make the most of their lives, led to the demand for civil equality, for laws that would be the same for nobles and commoners, rich and poor. In this sense, a citizen has the right to work, the right to basic wages, the right to security and care in sickness and old age.[333] Socialist movements and Islam, as Qutb asserts, have been particularly active in proclaiming these rights.[334] The claim for civil equality led to a gradually increasing demand for political equality, for the principle 'one man one vote'. However, 'property qualification' for voting disappeared only gradually. In 1918, for the first time, all men were permitted to vote, but not until 1928 could all women vote.[335]

Subsequently, the word democracy, according to Marshall, has become virtually 'meaningless' in its everyday use. It has come to be used as a 'label to legitimize every kind of political power arrangement'.[336] There have been several versions of democracy. A liberal democracy is one in which an elected group rules the entire group by means of election in which 'one person, one vote' ensures equity of political right exercised by secret ballot. The United Kingdom and the United States of America exemplify this form of liberal democracy, but these two countries, according to Margolis (1979) 'provide examples of liberalism without democracy'.[337] The second model of democracy is what Hafiz Salih (1992) calls the 'demo administration' form. Here, leadership is exercised by a group of people, but decisions are made through consultation with local officials and senior public servants.[338] The third model, 'industrial democracy', indicates the participation of workers in the administration, planning and supervision of the state. There is 'Demo Centralism', which is a principle basis in Communism and used in the election of all members of the communist ruling party from the community. The Soviet Union exemplifies this form.[339] The theory of modern democracy was, in particular, developed by Mao Tse-tung to explain the situation in China. He believed that his model was the best model for all democracies in the world.[340]

Whether or not these models and others are truly democratic is the point emphasized by Graeme Duncan (1983) in these words: 'democratic practice throws a dark light on democratic theory. In present circumstances it might seem more fitting to come in black, ready to celebrate democracy's last rites'.[341] There is a difference between theory and practice. However what is more significant here, for Qutb, is that theories that take no account of the tendencies which encompass the nature of the relationship between the Creator and the creation, the universe, life and man cannot be considered an 'ideal' system for human life on this earth.[342]

Nevertheless, many people claim democracy as the 'ideal and the world's new universal religion'.[343] This may be, as asserted by Duncan, due to 'the propaganda machine that is going on for quite some time propagandizing the dogmas of liberty, equality, self-determination and human rights that are violated so often . . .'[344]

The claim that democracy is an 'ideal' has been challenged on few grounds. Some of these challenges have appeared in the philosophical and moral critiques of democracy provided by both ancient and modern philosophers. Some other challenges are derived from the institutional and the procedural critique marked by modern critics of democracy.

Plato and Aristotle, for example, both have argued that 'democracy, far from being an ideal political constitution, was not even a form of constitution *sui generis*, but was a distortion or corruption of something else'.[345] The classical critique of democracy is familiar ground in the literature.[346]

If democracy is not ideal, nor a form of constitution, what is democracy then? This is the dilemma to which the modern views turn their attention. John Dunn (1979) characterizes democracy as follows:

> the majority's ambivalence to a comprehensive social justice, the political instability, often tending to war and tyranny. The lack of moral virtues, promoted by a politics of ambition, popular rhetoric, majoritarianism and general licentiousness; the entrenchment of a few in long possession of office; the injustices occasioned by a superficial and the absence of genuine social or moral aims.[347]

Supposing these problems were considered not simply as problems '*in*' democracy, but problems '*of*' democracy, then the point of Qutb is that 'democracy is but a fancy dream, a theory that has no actual existence in the world'.[348] Here Qutb echoes Rousseau's view that 'In the strict sense of the term, there has never been a true democracy, and there never will be. It is contrary to the natural order that the greater number should govern and the smaller number be governed.'[349]

The arguments provided by Marxists and other modern critiques of democracy are not different from classical ones, but a new style with new vocabulary. The basis of Plato's condemnation of democracy is renewed, for instance, by Marx's view of Capitalism and bourgeois life.[350] Plato's criticism of democracy is also 'felt in Marx's views of democratic licentiousness conjured up in his vision of crude Communism'.[351] In this context, Qutb argues:

> Why then do these attempts to present Islam seek to contrast it to failed systems such as socialism, and democracy? Socialism is a socioeconomic system invented by human beings and subject to fallacy. Democracy is

> a system of government made by human beings. It carries with it the characteristics of human beings and subjected to fallacy. Islam, however, is a comprehensive program for human life. It contains the conception of belief, a social system, an economic system, a legal system, and the system of formation and administration. It is a system made by Allah, far above defect and fault. All the *shirk* (polytheism) of the *jahiliyyah* of the pre-Islamic Arabs was their belief in idols as mediators bring them nearer to Allah. If this was their *shirk* as the Qur'an 39: 3 says, – which description then can rightly be said to suit those who believe that Socialism and democracy bring them nearer to Allah. Islam is Islam. Socialism is Socialism. Democracy is Democracy. There is difference between the program made by Man and the program made by Allah who created Man . . .[352]

Qutb's point is that if democracy means a system of freedom, justice and equality, Islam has the inclination and the capacity to provide a better option. In this regard, Qutb's first five editions of *Social Justice* questioned the democratic safeguards in Europe when the Nazi, the Fascist and the Spanish coups took place. He emphasized his doubts about the safeguards for freedom of opinion in the United States where 'the publishing and broadcasting companies monopolize the expression and guidance of opinion, and do not allow any contradictory idea to find its way to the eyes and ears and minds of people'.[353] Qutb asserts that if it is socially wrong and inconsistent with justice for the desires and ambitions of the individual to supercede those of the community, then it is also wrong for the community to supercede the needs of the individual.[354] Justice and harmony between the two sides, in Qutb's view, cannot be achieved unless the Social Contract is under the guidance and supervision of a Divine Law. This point of Qutb is reminiscent of Jean-Jacques Rousseau (1712–1778) when he stated that

> There comes a time when individuals can no longer maintain themselves in primitive independence; it then becomes necessary to self-preservation that they should unite to form a society. However, how can I pledge my liberty without harming my interest? The problem is to find a form of association which will defend and protect with the whole common force the person and goods of each associate, and in which each, while uniting himself with all, may remain as free as before. This is the fundamental problem of democracy.[355]

Democracy in the light of 'rights' has also been challenged and labelled as 'distortion' or corruption of something else, or in Rousseau's words, 'loss of either life or liberty. It would be an offence against both nature and reason to renounce them at any price whatever'.[356] Considering the rights of individuals and groups in democracy, Rousseau says, 'we shall find no more substance than the truth in the so-called "voluntary establishment of tyranny"...'[357]

Rousseau's view of the problem of democracy echoes Plato's and Aristotle's view of moral and procedural corruption of democracy, as in the above injunctions. Both classic and modern thinkers such as Plato, Aristotle, Rousseau, Bertrand Russell, Ortega, John Dunn, Graeme Duncan and others including Margolis and Qutb lamented this dilemma.[358]

Another dimension of modern democracy's philosophical and moral insufficiency concerns political rights. Contemporary thinkers such as Jose Ortega Y Gasset (1961) and Nicolai Berdyaev (1938) outlined the 'dangers', 'destructiveness' and 'moral impoverishment' of societies 'succumbing to democratic revolutions'.[359] This issue could explain the impulse behind a number of not only Qutb's works such as *Social Justice in Islam* (1949) and *The Battle between Islam and Capitalism* (1951) but also Rousseau's works such as his *Discourse on Inequality* (1754), or *Social Contract* (1762) in which he tried to devise a democratic model that would avoid moral corruption of the individual. Rousseau freely suggested the need to adhere to the Divine Law.[360] To achieve justice and equality in the society, Rousseau asserts, 'human governments required a basis more solid than reason alone'. This solid basis, in Rousseau's view, is 'the divine Will'.[361] To Qutb, the divine Will is *hakimiyyah* (sovereignty) and that is perhaps what Rousseau wants to say. According to Bertrand Russell, the sovereign in Rousseau's view is 'not the government... the sovereign is a more or less metaphysical entity...'[362]

By way of summary of the classical and modern views of democracy, including its philosophical and moral bases, Graeme Duncan considers that

> Democracy lacks realistic definitions and legitimization of the consensus. Democracy is but a form similar to Socratic dialogue, addressing questions that constitute a continuous dialogue with political problems, some old and some new, in which actual contact with real problems is possible only by virtue of being unable to bring ideals, aims and moral values into sharp focus.[363]

If democracy is not a justifiable ideal, and is procedurally self-defeating, there must be real doubts about constructing models for practical reform and establishing a comprehensive justice, values and rights. Based on an extensive examination of classic and modern forms of democracy, Duncan concludes that

> Democracy is nothing more than a kind of politics, of procedure in which interests are advanced according to some plan of war, or by a more or less orderly competition. Real, historical democratic constitutions, such as they exist are bold moral and theoretical compromises. The English, American, French and Russian revolutions, which eventually produced such constitutions have produced also a genre of political and historical literature to defend or lament critical moments in the life of each revolution. One would certainly be pressed to discover a consistent adherence to even procedural means, much less moral ideals, in these revolutionary

movements, even in their intellectual and propagandistic dimensions. They were set in real circumstances, with real lives and interests at stake…

Close examination of the writings of the greatest democratic theorists such as Madison, Hamilton and Jefferson; John Stuart Mill; Michels; and more recently Schumpeter, Schattschneider and Dahl. One might even, upon close inspection, make some surprising additions to this list. Aristotle, Locke, Rousseau and Marx each had a direct interest in gaining recognition of the rights and duties of the whole community, but each also has grave doubts about how this might be institutionalized without ruining these rights for the great majority of the people. Democracy, then, whether as a revolutionary movement or a competitive struggle for the people's vote, is essentially a form of political action. It is a means of achieving aims of utilitarian sort, at most, by attacking narrow interests with less narrow ones. This means that democracy is the legitimate province of the theorist or philosopher…[364]

Duncan asks 'Are democratic parties inherently oligarchic? Is political democracy a by-product of liberal capitalist or post-industrial economy? Must electoral politics either be corrupt in an old-fashioned way, or mindless in the sophisticated use of the mass media…'[365]

Duncan maintains that

moral content, human equality, legal justice, natural rights, is not inherent in democratic ideas. The ethical values are not coincident with or derived from the theoretical premises of democracy, but are rather gathered from several theories, Idealism, Roman Law, and others…[366]

Regarding democracy in the public place, Dunn (1979) notes that

there are really two distinct and developed democratic theories – one dismally ideological and the other blatantly Utopian. In the first, democracy is the name of a distinct and very palpable form of modern state, at the most optimistic, simply the least bad mechanism for securing some measures of responsibility of the governors to the governed within modern states. The second democracy (some times called participatory democracy) is close to meaning simply good society in operation, if there less wastefully, better taste, and all social arrangements authentically represent the interests of all persons, in which all live actively in and for their society and yet all remain free.[367]

The type of defects and disability of today's democracy is emphasized by Graeme Duncan as follows:

Democracy is a kind of identity crisis, not only as concerns the frustrations and contradictions and *culs-de-sac*, but in the difficulty one faces in speculating theoretically as to the fundamental nature of democracy. For

> example, when inquiring as to the source of power, its origins, the reply of democratic theory – 'the people' – is trivial and romantic. In trying to examine the ends of power, democratic theory finds itself impoverished, begging for a loan.[368]

The point echoes Qutb's view that 'democracy has ended with bankruptcy and has began to borrow from the Eastern Camp, particularly in economic spheres that fall under the name of Socialism . . .'[369]

The identity crisis of democracy thus reflects its constructs on both theoretical and practical levels. For Qutb as for Tawfiq al-Hakim (1938), Marshall Gordon (1983) and 'Abd al-Hakim khalifah (1961),

> Democracy has become the vaguest of concepts. Hitler's Nazism claimed to be a democracy and great Nazis tried to convince or deceive the world that Hitler had been elected as a leader of the nation by a free democratic vote and that he represented the voice and will of the people. The persecution of the Jews was a demonstration of democracy, because it was the will of an exasperated majority giving its verdict against an alleged anti-national minority. The Fascists also claimed that they had invented a special brand of democracy superior to the Anglo-American type which, according to Mussolini, was the luxury of secure and prosperous nation . . . Russian Communism claimed to be the most democratic of all the existing systems; they called Anglo-American democracy plutocracy, where directly and indirectly capital governed and labour was exploited. The British and the Americans called Russian Communism totalitarianism, where the colossus of state capitalism and the domination of one party had deprived the individual of his fundamental liberties.[370]

All known forms of today's democracy have their own defects and disabilities; thus, none of them is qualified to be the ideal system for human life. In this regard, Rousseau pointed out

> the different masks behind which inequality has hidden itself up to [his] present time and may do so in centuries to come. According to the nature of governments and the revolutions which time will necessarily produce, one would see the multitude oppressed inside society . . . One would see the rights of citizens and the freedom of nations extinguished little by little, and the protests of the week treated as sedition noises.[371]

In the sense of Rousseau's prophecy, John Dunn concludes,

> If we are all democrats, democracy today is not a very cheerful fate to share. Today, in politics, democracy is the name for what we cannot have, yet cannot cease to want. We do need a theory of how the governments of modern states can least badly be controlled.[372]

By contrast, Qutb asserts that from the perspective of 1,400 years of Islam there is almost no one, up to contemporary times, who claims that Islamic system has an identity crisis. The identity of the Islamic system rests on its divine basis. It is a system based on an inspired constitution: the Qur'an and the Sunnah.[373] This logically implies that the nature of the relationship between the universe, life and Man must be stable, well balanced and harmonious with the nature of the divinely ordained system. He who created Man created for him the system that is harmonious and suitable for his life within this universe. This system, according to Qutb, entails the ideological ideal – the convincing concept that expounds the nature of the universe and determines the position of Man and his ultimate objectives therein. It includes 'the doctrine and practical organizations which emanate from and depend upon this ideological ideal, and make of it a reality that impacts upon the everyday life of human beings'.[374]

The Islamic system is, for instance, a creed, an ethical foundation, a sustaining power, a political system with its form and characteristics, a social order with its bases and values, an economic system with its institutional and doctrinal principles and an international organization with its interrelations.[375] All these are interdependent constituents in the Islamic system; that is, there is no separation between the system of government and other spheres in Islamic life. The perfect balanced unity and the harmony between the constituents of the Islamic theory singled out that the Islamic system is the ideal system for human life on this earth. For Qutb, the characteristic of the ideal system rests in the reality that the system counts for. Distinguishing between Islam and democracy, Qutb asserts Islam as *the* universal ideal:

> The reality the Islamic system counts for is not the reality of an individual or the reality of a nation or the reality of a generation. These are small, limited and temporary realties, to which the perception of transient human individuals are limited when their vision cannot take in what is greatest and most complete in the life of the whole of human race, and the life of the whole universe.[376]

An important point to consider is the concept of sovereignty. In all forms of democracy, the people whether a group (political party) or the whole community are the highest source of legal and governmental authority.[377] This in Qutb's view implies the servitude (*'ubudiyyah*) of people to people. Here, Qutb echoes Rousseau's view in words and language. According to Rousseau 'Political distinctions necessarily introduce civil distinctions. The growing inequality between the people and its chiefs is soon reproduced between individuals, and is modified there in thousand ways according to passions, talents and circumstances...'[378] In this regard, Rousseau quoted from Tacitus that 'They call a state of wretched servitude [in Qutb's words, i.e. *'ubudiyyah*] a state of peace'.[379] The *'ubudiyyah* of people to people, implies, Rousseau maintains, that

> The general will (the sovereign body of politic) is not identical with the will of the majority, or even with the will of all citizens. There is often a great deal of differences between the will of all and the general will.[380]

This implies that the 'will' and the 'laws' that are issued by the highest legal and governmental authority (the sovereign body of politic) of all known democratic models are all not constant or stable, but that there is multiplicity of wills, rules and judgements. This illustrates the identity crisis of democracy as previously detailed by Duncan, John Dunn and Michael Margolis.[381] Qutb described such 'multiplicity of wills, rules and judgements as *jahiliyyah*'.[382]

In contrast with all forms of democracy and other systems, Qutb says, Islam declares that the 'highest governmental and legal authority is Allah'. He is the 'Sovereign' of all sovereignty and He is the 'Legislator' for all wills. Qutb asserts that 'there is no place in Islam for arbitrary rule by a single individual or a group (political party)...'[383] The difference between the nature of sovereignty in the Islamic system and that in democracy, echoes the difference between Islam and democracy.[384] The specifics of governance and its implementation in Islamic terms were previously detailed in this text (see Chapter 1).

What should be noted for the Islamic system here is Qutb's emphasis that believing in the oneness of the sovereign Will, means practical obedience and complete submission to the sovereign order specified in the Qur'an and the Sunnah, or, in one word, the *Shari'ah* (Islamic code). This is because *Shari'ah* is the founder of the Muslim community and rules its daily affairs, constantly, with no change since it was divinely revealed.[385] This is not the case with democracy, since it was devised by people, whether theorists or political party, indeed, not the whole community. Democracy was developed over a period of time and subjected to historical evolution.[386]

In contrast with all forms of democracy and other systems, according to Rousseau,

> Mahomet [Muhammad] had very sound opinions, taking care to give unity to his political system, and for as long as the form of his government endured under the caliphs who succeeded him, the government was undivided and, to that extent good.[387]

In democracy, the ruling party, or a group of legislators, not the whole community devises the law for the entire community.[388] The laws are temporary rules enacted by the society to administer its current affairs and meet its proximate needs if possible. Thus, the laws are actually behind the standard of advancing societies, or at the best, suit the date of issue. Of necessity, they become backward after a while as long as they do not change quickly to catch up with the evolution of society. Temporarily, laws would suit the conditions of society at or for a certain time, but they would have to be changed.[389] In addition and overall, the government has the power to enforce the laws made according to the desire of a group (the minority) in the interest of another group (the majority).[390]

By contrast, the basis of all actions in the Islamic system is the *shurah* (consultation). This also is carried out within the framework of the *Shari'ah*.[391] The *shurah* (consultation) is an act of worship like other Islamic institutions such as *salat* (prayer) and *zakah* (tax). The idea of *shurah* is divinely inspired and based on the principle that the sovereignty belongs to Allah alone.[392]

This brings us to another complex point which may account for the distinction between the Islamic system and democracy. Unlike democracy, the Islamic theory of government distinguishes between two fundamental concepts. These are, (i) the source of authority and (ii) the administration of authority. These two concepts, for Qutb, are quite significant in distinguishing Islam from all models of democracy and other systems. This is because, according to Qutb, the source of authority, in the Islamic State, is neither a group of people (political party), nor the whole community or the result of election, but the activity of facilitating the application of the *Shari'ah*. Facilitating the application of the *Shari'ah* is the source from which the government derives its authority. This means to Qutb that if Muslims do not accept the President or the chief executive, his legitimacy is threatened and his authority may be challenged and if he abandons the *Shari'ah*, no obedience is due to him.[393] These details illustrate the difference between Islam and all other systems of government. To Qutb, therefore, the Islamic system cannot be called anything other than Islam.[394]

Concluding remarks

Unlike secular democracy, the divine basis of the Islamic system singled out its identity and nature which means, to Qutb, that it is the only system free of the results of human desires, weaknesses and self-interest. For Qutb, the Islamic system is free from any attempt to gain self-interest by means of legislating for the benefit of that individual, his family or his class. The author of the Islamic system is God. He is the Sovereign and Lawgiver. God does not legislate for His own sake, or for that of one group or a nation or a generation in preference to another.

Qutb sees democracy as a system of government made by human beings. It carries with it the characteristics of human beings. The basis of the Islamic system, its mechanisms and the source of authority are quite significant in the distinction between Islam and secular democracy.

Part IV

Influences and responses

8 Egypt's Islamic movement

Influences and state responses

Introduction

Since the early years of the twentieth century, a number of Islamic organizations have developed in Egypt. This phenomenon of Islamic resurgence appeared as part of a general reaction to the political, economic, social and intellectual conditions, which resulted in the setback to secular liberal ideologies in Egypt. The emerged Islamic organizations seem to have similar targets and ideas; although externally they are invariably different. There are various differences between Islamic groups in Egypt, but this should not obscure their ideological affinity. Their main objective is to establish an Islamic state ruled by *shari'ah*, but they have different approaches to their goal. Their differences rest largely on their understanding of the concept of Sovereignty and the theory of society enunciated by Qutb.

This study seeks to examine the influence of Qutb's ideas upon recent developments amongst Islamic groups in Egypt and the difference between them and Qutb's ideas. It will investigate why and how Egypt's Islamic groups were able to grow in the face of official repression under Egyptian regimes; what religio-political forces motivate the adoption of the method of violence and terror; and what has shifted Islamic groups from the realm of intellectual debate to act in such a violent and terrorist manner.

The main focus is on three major Islamic groups, all of which have come to the scene after the death of Qutb in 1966[1] and all are commonly called Islamic Groups: *Jama'at Islamiyyah* (JIs), or radical, extremist, Jihad and terrorist groups, but each of which is also labelled, in the Arabic media, with a specific label to distinguish the one from the other. These labels are numerous but all go back to three main groups: First, the Military Technical Academy Group, second, the Society of Muslims (later known as *al-Takfir wa al-Hijrah*: practising emigration and charging others with unbelief)[2] and third, the Society of Jihad. These groups currently exist and have a significant influence in Egypt and abroad. I will approach these groups as a sociopolitical movement whose religiosity and theocentrism form the hard core of their aim and objective that is to establish an Islamic state in Egypt.

THE MILITARY TECHNICAL ACADEMY GROUP

The dispute between the Nasser regime and the Muslim Brotherhood (Ikhwan) has left its influential marks on the subsequent development of Islamist movements in Egypt. There also was a growing appetite for the rule of *shari'ah*. Nasser himself was saying that 'The people demands the return to religion and I am with them.'[3] However, according to Shamir (1967),[4] 'the regime seemed unable to satisfy the growing appetite for more religion.'[5] This is the point which was made by Judge Muhammad Saeed al-'Ashmawi, in 1990. Speaking of the Islamist's aim and activity, 'Ashmawi says:

> This is but a reaction to, and a result of, the activity of the revolution of 1952, which attacked liberalism, and the freedom of thought. Liberal intellectual movement was destroyed, and the thought was formulated only in a government model.[6]

The former diplomat, lawyer and eminent writer Yahya Haqqi also made this point, in 1991:

> I never forgive Nasser for beginning the post-revolution period with the hanging of workers in Kafr el-Dawar. Neither can I forgive him for the hanging of Sayyid Qutb [the first critic to write about Haqqi's *The Lamp of Umm Hashim*...end of al-Ahram comment]. And the regime's imprisonment of the left in concentration camps...this was all unforgivable.[7]

After the death of Qutb in August 1966, the Islamists regrouped, and reviewed their infrastructure and ideas. From past experience with the regime, the Islamists had learnt that their security and strength did not lie in one large structure like that of the Muslim Brotherhood (Ikhwan). Based on secrecy reasons the Islamist groups recognized the Ikhwan's large pyramid structure as a point of weakness.[8] Consequently, the large body of the *Ikhwan* was reorganized into small groups, of which each had usually, between a hundred to two hundred members. However, some groups reached two and three thousands or more if necessary. This also implies special considerations for secrecy. The Military Technical Academy Group came to be known by this title in April 1974, when the group attempted to overthrow the government by seizing the Military Technical Academy in Cairo. This group was one of the *jihad* groups. There were several groups with similar names. All of them considered *jihad* the only way to establish an alternative Islamic order. This particular group was formed in Egypt and led by the Palestinian Dr. Salih 'Abdullah Siriyya (1933–1974). He was a member of The Islamic Liberation Party established by the Palestinian scholar Taqiyy al-Din al-Nabahani, in 1952, in Jordan.[9] Al-Nabahani (1909–1989), though originally a member of Egypt's Muslim Brotherhood, later founded branches of his party in Jordan, Syria, Lebanon and Iraq.[10]

Salih Siriyya was born in 1933 in a village near Haifa in Palestine. He witnessed the Palestinian struggle, suffered the condition of occupation and then exile to Jordan where Jordanians attacked the emigrated Palestinians in Amman and Jarash in 1970.[11] He became a revolutionary activist, abandoning Jordan when his political activities were discovered. He tried to cooperate with various 'Arab regimes such as Iraq and Libya, but finally moved to Cairo in 1971.[12] At that time, he was an army officer in the Liberation Party led by al-Nabahani. He also gained a PhD in education before his arrival in Egypt. On his arrival, he secured a position in one of the specialized education agencies within the 'Arab League.[13] Siriyya's experience enabled him to form an Islamic group in Egypt. Most of the members of this group were from Alexandria and Cairo. Despite his awareness of Qutb's ideas and the fact that he had met Hasan al-Hudaybi, the Supreme guide of the Ikhwan before his death in 1973, Siriyya based his group on the ideas of the Liberation Party.[14] Their aim was simply to overthrow the government and establish the Islamic State in any Arab country. For them, the Qur'an's existance and the knowledge about Islam is everywhere in the society, but the various governments are obstacles to the establishment of the sovereignty of *shari'ah*. To Siriyya, the case was not against the Arab society, but rather against the rulers. To him, the society is Muslim, but the ruler is a *kafir* (unbeliever) and must therefore be removed by force.[15]

This was the first time an Islamic group had openly announced its aim to overthrow the government, an aim repeatedly rejected by the Muslim Brotherhood (Ikhwan), whose founding leader Hasan al-Banna (1906–1949) made it clear that 'we do not seek power for ourselves but we seek rule by *shari'ah*'.[16] This policy, however, was influenced by the treatment of the Ikhwan at the hands of the regime. As the time passed on, Qutb's experience led him to make inquiry of how the sovereignty of *shari'ah* could be implemented if the power remains in the hands of those who torture and execute anyone advocating the application of *shari'ah*. In addition, propaganda against Islamists was widespread in the state media. It was the only permissible media and the staff members also were appointed only by the government. On the other side, the Islamists had no journals, or newspapers, and no window or access to public debate. Mosques were full of political police and discussing political Islam, vocally or in writing, on buses or at train stations, in public places, or in a mosque, in a pamphlet or in any other form, meant one word, that is that one could be charged with sedition.[17]

The regime then intended to force, in one way or the other, the consumers to purchase the product of one *idea*. However, in the eyes of many, the most desirable of all products is the forbidden one. For example, confiscating a book will increase the desire of many people for reading it. In this way the waves of conflicts began between the regime and its opponents. The conflict then developed in step with the behaviour of both sides to violence and terror on the national and later on the international levels.

This behaviour shifted the thought of Islamists to seek power for themselves as a means to establish rule by *shari'ah*. Qutb attempts to answer the questions posed by al-Banna: how were the Muslims to find a voice? In his response, Qutb based his idea on two things – theory and practice or creed and method. For him, the two are one comprehensive and integrated concept. This means that there is no belief in the absolute sovereignty of Allah without practising His *shari'ah*.[18] Practising *shari'ah* in a system based on *jahili* laws is difficult, because *jahiliyyah* is the complete antithesis of Islam.[19] According to Qutb, 'the rulers do not facilitate the practise of *shari'ah* in the banks, in education or in other spheres of human life. It is as if Islam only involves praying in the mosque under the supervision of political police'.[20] This view was probably the basis for Qutb's perception of *jihad* as the only alternative to deal with such conditions. The concept of *jihad* will be discussed later under the Jihad group. Here, however, the *jihad* would remove the obstacles for implementation of *shari'ah*.[21] Either way, for Qutb, *jihad* required educational and ideological training and preparation, a step not considered by Salih Siriyya's group.[22] Qutb points out that in order to establish the *shari'ah*, 'Muslims must first undergo various stages of educational and ideological training. Muslims must take power, but the change should come from the people'.[23] This is the difference between Qutb and Siriyya al-Banna.

Siriyya was not one of Qutb's followers and his group did not seek to hold Qutb's ideas or his programme.[24] Siriyya's aim was political. His group suggests an Islamic State by force: Change from the top down in a conventional way.[25] For Siriyya, Qutb's programme which begins with preparation of the individual, and the society, and then ultimately establishes the Islamic State is good as long as the government is willing to establish the Islamic system. For Siriyya argued that this gradual approach of the Brotherhood, al-Banna, and later Qutb, had led to the latter's death, and they failed to establish the Islamic State. For Siriyya, the people already knew the teachings of Islam and were ready but nothing had been actually done by Sadat.[26] Therefore, the right course was to overthrow the regime and proceed to the task of applying the *shari'ah*. In April 1974 he expanded his group, obtained some weapons and made a failed attempt to take control of the Military Technical Academy in Cairo.[27] The Islamic State was thus the aim of both Qutb and Siriyya, but their means were different.

THE SOCIETY OF MUSLIMS

This organization set up by Shukri Mustafa, was 'the most public and least violent of all the groups'.[28] Shukri Mustafa was born in 1942 in Upper Egypt in Abu Kharus, a village close to Qutb's own village of Musha. At the University of Asyut, Shukri may have come across Islamic groups and began to distribute leaflets propagating Islam within the university. For this he was first arrested in 1965, faced a Military Court and was given six years hard labour.[29]

He went to the same prison where Qutb and various other Muslim Brothers were tortured and some of them were later executed. During his six years behind bars, the young student Shukri probably asked himself what exactly was so criminal in propagating Islam, the creed of the people. Harsh treatment in prison probably convinced Shukri and other youth there, that those torturing them were *jahili* people and that the political system and the law that allowed this were part of the world of *jahiliyyah*.[30] Shukri also observed that 'students propagating secular Socialism enjoy freedom'.[31] At that time, both in the press and at the mosques, the term *jihad* was repeatedly used to stir up Islamic sentiment amongst the people against the enemy symbolized by Israel. In later testimonies at court, the young prisoners regularly used the word *jihad* against those who had incriminated and tortured them.[32]

The influence of Qutb can be seen in all Islamic militant groups, including Shukri's group. All of them agreed that the Egyptian political system constituted *jahiliyyah*, although they differed from Qutb and from each other in their solutions. Some opted for a tactical discretion vis-à-vis the regime while they were still weak. Preparation was the key for the development of inner strength 'until we get to a stage where we can confront the *jahiliyyah* openly'.[33] Other groups preferred 'immediate' denunciation of a 'system of *jahiliyyah*', and they voted to 'separate' themselves unequivocally from it. Shukri Mustafa, who supported the denunciation of society, together with other youth established a group and called it 'The Society of Muslims'. They were later called by the press '*al-Takfir wa al-Higrah*',[34] a label indicating that the group is practising emigration and charging others with unbelief. What should be remembered here is that all these preparations were behind bars from 1965 to 1971.[35] In other words, the Society of Muslims was formed behind bars. This point was referred to by Muhammad 'Umarah, Ma'mun al-Hudaybi and Muhammad al-Ghazali to note the responsibility of the state in resorting the youth to *jihad*.[36] This group abducted and killed Shaykh Mahmud Husayn Dhahabi in July 1977. They were duly brought to trial by Military Court (despite being civilians) and Shukri was condemned to death and executed on 22 March 1978. While they were awaiting trial they were interviewed by various academics. From the American University in Cairo, Professor Saad Eddin Ibrahim (1980: 441),[37] noted his observation of the detainees' feelings:

> Thinking of the joy and rewards of martyrdom is said to make any physical torture by the enemies of Islam quite bearable. Several members reported that the stories they had heard about the torture of the members of the Muslim Brotherhood in 1966 had had a profound effect on them. The severe torture seems to have marked sharply the dividing line in their minds between a merciless *jahiliyyah* society and the Society of Muslims.[38]

Thus, the youth considered the regime, the law and the system as unquestionably *jahili*, since they had experienced its violence firsthand.

According to Hasan Hanafi (1988), the violence of the State was one of the significant factors why this group had resorted to violence.[39] After his first release from the prison in 1971, Shukri Mustafa had completed a Bachelor's Degree in Agricultural Sciences and expanded his following. At this point, after the seminal influence of Qutb inside the fact, Shukri was is favour of long-term educational and ideological training.[40] A transitional programme would involve training individuals to live in a society where the Islamic *shari'ah* was observed. This programme was similar to Qutb's programme of an Islamic order. This means that Qutb's ideas and programmes influenced Shukri Mustafa's group. In describing the goals and personal behaviour of these groups, Saad Eddin Ibrahim stated,

> The individual member was asked not only to adhere to the ideas and principles of the group but also to engage in a serious transformation of his own behavior, attitudes and relationships. In other words, the Society of Muslims represented the kind of movement aiming at fundamental, simultaneous transformation of both the individual and society. It was quite evident to us that typical members felt, and readily expressed, a moral superiority vis-à-vis people outside the movement. Their ability to impose self-discipline in accordance with the commandments and the prohibitions of Islam, while others cannot or will not, was the source of this feeling. But it was equally evident that, aside from the moral superiority, members felt deep joy in defying society and its physical means of coercions. Several who claimed to have been severely tortured reported having visions and dreams of prophets and saints welcoming them to the Garden of Eden or to the just Islamic society that would be established after their martyrdom.[41]

In the early stage, the expansion of The Society of Muslims was thus critical to its members, as this would reduce the scope and extent of *jahiliyyah*.[42] Changes to the current system might thus come about automatically by educational and ideological training of the people. The group was also able to recruit a member of al-Azhar to guide them on the religious matters.[43] Speaking of Islamic groups, in general, including Shukri's group, John Voll stated that

> The *Jama'at* (groups) hoped to create a truly Islamic society by first transforming university life, and they did prove useful in the overcrowded universities. They organized tutorials, assisted students in acquiring books, and claimed some facilities for women. They tried to purify the universities from showing unapproved films on the campuses. As the group gained strength and dominated all student organizations, it was a special target for the government.[44]

This success, for the Islamists, meant that the system of *jahiliyyah* lost to some extent some support in the universities. Success in reforming university life encouraged them to expand to the towns and villages around the University of Asyut.

Speaking of the involvement of the Islamists in Egyptian society, particularly, in the province of Asyut, the Egyptian Journal *Sabah el-Kheir* outlined how the 'extremist groups' work to increase their numbers, and disseminate their ideas of '*takfir*' and '*jihad*'. The Journal emphasized how the Islamists work to stimulate the mind of 'the young', win them over, and 'neutralize the older'. The Journal outlined their pattern of recruitment, and how they prepare the young to accept and digest the ideas of 'Sayyid Qutb's *Milestones* the constitutional book of the groups'. The Journal pointed out how and why 54 villages were willing to come under their control. So, the groups carried out some useful projects like those at the university. They organized clinics and pharmacies run by physicians and pharmacists who are members of the groups. They organized a programme that allowed patients to be visited by physicians in their homes, if the patients were unable to visit a clinic. The members who are engineers established what could be seen as a stadium and sports training supervized by specialists from the groups became a reality, as did food supply, facilities for women and traffic control. They established small businesses and industries, which created the opportunity of employment for a considerably large number of people. Members who were veterinarians practised their skill in this important sphere. The journal reported a significant large number of projects to indicate how the Islamists were challenging the capacity of the government in providing essential services. It was a warning that the rapid expansion of the Islamists in Upper Egypt where the inhabitants of these 54 village were Muslims and Christians were all happy with the Islamic groups and their leaders. This can be seen as a general pattern that the Islamic groups usually follow in order to increase their numbers.[45]

The involvement of the groups of *Takfir* in the society was helped by the fact that the province of Asyut is the birthplace of both Qutb and Shukri. It was there that Shukri was born, graduated from the University of Asyut in Agricultural Sciences, and worked for the government as an Agronomist, visiting farmers and communicating with the peasants. According to Kepel, Shukri's village was about 'thirty kilometers south of Asyut', and about a 'few hours away on foot' from Qutb's village. Kepel says that 'in this forgotten corner of Egypt, the villages of the region have generally been Islamicist breeding-grounds'.[46] Kepel pointed out that

> Shukri and his first disciples would roam the environs of Asyut, preaching in the hamlets and villages and gathering young men who would join the group. Success came rapidly, and by 1972 the police were keeping a watchful eye on his activities.[47]

Despite the media's attempts to draw the State's attention to the involvement of Shukri's group in the Egyptian society, as Kepel asserts, 'the State did not consider Shukri and his companions especially dangerous'.[48]

Hasan Hanafi, Professor of Philosophy at Cairo University, who currently leads a school of thought which calls itself 'the Islamic left' notes that in these villages and elsewhere, the Society of Muslims 'created Islamic environments in varying ways. They established educational and ideological training, interest-free loans, small industries, responsible interpretation and application of Islamic law within possibilities available to them'.[49] Amongst their religious activities of worshiping, studying, and proselytizing or exercising, were economic enterprises that launched 'small-scale businesses, like bakeries, bookshops, candy making and vegetable gardening. Gradually, the typical villager became quite dependent on the group to satisfy his spiritual, social and economic needs'.[50] This indicates that the members of this group were using their skill to promote their own group and were able to draw the attention of the wider Egyptian society.[51]

To this point, one of the implications of this is that the manner of the activity of 'The Society of Muslims' led by Shukri Mustafa in Egypt is parallel with Islamic societies living in free market countries like, Australia, London or North America where entrepreneurs are encouraged. The difference between Egypt and the liberal world is that Muslims there are 'free to expand their societies, publishing, distributing pamphlets, preaching and calling others to join them'. Fredrick (1994) continues,

> Whenever I attend Islamic conferences in North America, I find copies of Qutb's *Milestones* available for sale in abundant supply. Muslim college and university students, especially, herald its virtues as a blueprint for making what Qutb called *hijrah* (emigration) from the world of *jahiliyyah* to the society of authentic Muslim faith and order. However, the Muslim societies in the non-free market world experience persecution and restrictions.[52]

This means that the ideas of Qutb have influenced not only the Islamic organizations in Egypt but also Muslim societies outside it. Nevertheless, no Islamic society in North America has migrated with Qutb's *Milestones*. They remained in the cities of North America and created their Islamic environment there where they are free to do so. Similarly, the Society led by Shukri Mustafa in Egypt did not emigrate from Egyptian cities and villages. They were never, as claimed by Youssef (1985: 79), 'living in isolated camps in the desert'.[53] Members of the group often lived in cities and towns. Most of them were skilled and worked in government institutions. Most of the members were 'of rural or small-town background, from the middle or lower class, with high achievement and motivation, upwardly mobile, with science or engineering education, and from a normally cohesive family'.[54] Shukri Mustafa himself was employed by the Ministry of Agriculture and was thus able to expand his group through meeting farmers in the villages. In addition to their clinics, pharmacies, and other businesses, some members of The Society of Muslims were working in the Gulf countries.[55] They were financially able to establish interest-free loans. This also was one way to help people and to turn their attention to the group. The point is that the group was not isolated from the people. Expansion also occurred naturally through interaction.

The authorities were well aware of the movement and its activities. However, there was no violence until 1973 when the government arrested some members for distributing pamphlets written by Shukri Mustafa 'criticizing the system in Egypt as *jahiliyyah* and propagating his Society of Muslims'.[56] Their aims, thus so clearly enunciated, drew the attention of the security forces to them. The media chose to treat them as people who were ignorant and eccentric or as Sadat said, 'crazy'.[57] Sadat also described them and their goal as 'reactionary gang and religious fascism'.[58] This theme of criticism was also used by the Egyptian Marxists on a wider scale to criticize all the 'Islamic groups in general, the Muslim Brotherhood, al-Azhar and its institutions, its education, and its publications concerning social, political, economic, intellectual, and moral issues. Such activity was seen by Marxists as mere retardation, reactionary and religious fascism'.[59]

However, in the period following the war of 1973, the Islamic movement significantly increased in Egypt. In the universities, Islamic conferences began to be attended by prominent Muslim scholars and academics. Islamic journals began to be published. Within this environment, the expansion of the Society of Shukri Mustafa included government organizations, various Ministries, the army, the police force, al-Azhar, educational institutions and other community organizations and State bodies.[60]

The group was also able to demonstrate its public strength on religion occasions, including functions attended by President Sadat himself. In a dialogue on Egyptian Radio with President Sadat, Shukri's group pointed out the need for reform towards an Islamic State. Speaking of Shukri's group, Hanafi (1989), emphasized that

> the group was able to stand firmly in a direct dialogue with the President on Egyptian Radio, as the club of the Nasserist thought was doing in the universities in the past few years. The group also described the eminent staff of the President as a group misleading him. The President found himself in a defensive position and was unable to convince his opponent.[61]

Thereafter it was announced that there would be 'no religion in politics and no politics in religion'.[62] Here, Sadat returned to the theme implied by the previous regime and its ideological position, as outlined by 'Ashmawi and Shamir.

In 1974, the media intensified its propaganda against Shukri and his group, particularly after the attempted *coup d'état* organized by the previously discussed Siriyya's Military Academy Group. The media took advantage of the incident and published articles and cartons, criticizing the Islamist groups in general.

In May 1975, Musa Sabri of *al-Akhbar* newspaper published an article criticizing the Society of Muslims, describing them as 'homosexual, bearded and mentally-ill people like cavemen[63] who refused to cooperate with modern society or wear modern clothes instead of their garments and turbans'.[64]

In 1976, the media, or in Mahfuz's words 'another philosophized editor who copied his article literally from the report of the State's Security Apparatus, labelled the group in media style with the title *al-Takfir wa al-Hijrah*. The media explained the title by analogy with the emigration (*hijrah*) of the Prophet from Makkah to Madinah in 622'.[65] This phrase was rapidly circulated and a number of writers analysed the group by means of historical references to Islamic history, especially the reconquest of Makkah by the Prophet. One can imagine the difficulties of trying a way to express the exact views of this group and their lifestyle particularly when the analysis expressed itself as analogous with the emigration of the Prophet. Some authors claimed that these people 'fled away'[66]; others that the group was 'camping in the desert'.[67] Another writer defined the desert to be closer to the Valley of Hijaz as 'the mountains of Egypt'[68], even 'Arabia'[69], as if in preparation for a victorious return. They analysed these people as if they had no home, or children, or were unemployed, or as if they were an army division living and moving on as if in no Man's Land.

According to the Egyptian Minister of Interior, 'No Man's Land' does not exist in Egypt,[70] and there is not a report to justify that this group moved or was moving towards the Arabian Mountains. President Sadat himself said that the police had arrested them in 'Cairo and other Egyptian towns'.[71] Based on the connotation of the *hijrah*, some writers saw Shukri Mustafa the leader of this group as a prophet. They made up comments by Shukri such as 'there is a secret meaning in every word of the Qur'an, and Shukri Mustafa alone knows this secret meaning'.[72]

Among the basic principles of the Muslim faith is to believe that there is no prophet after Muhammad. If Shukri Mustafa's teachings were unorthodox, it is unlikely that his group would have expanded among thousands of Egyptians in varying professions. Had Shukri Mustafa claimed knowledge of everything in the Qur'an, it seems likely this claim would have emerged before the conflict between him and the authorities.

Such exaggeration is similar to the media's attempts to portray Qutb as a 'communist agent',[73] and sometimes a prophet 'like Yusuf knows the unknown'.[74] The same claimant mentioned some Qur'anic verses concerning the Prophet Yusuf (Qur'an, 12: 35–41) because verse 12: 40 speaks of the *'ubudiyyah* (servitude) and *hakimiyyah* (sovereignty). Regarding this claim, what should be remembered are the following:

1 The claimant, Hammudah (1990, 132–3) has not mentioned his source.
2 He claims that Qutb in prison was 'pondering ideas' to describe the system of 'Abd al-Nasser and to answer back in 'revenge against Nasser'.

3 Qutb's friend 'Muhammad Hawwash was living with Qutb in the treatment cell' and brought to Qutb the suitable answer. (Hawwash was executed with Qutb in 1966).
4 Hawwash said to Qutb 'The Prophet "Yusuf" has came to him in the dream and demanded him to tell (Qutb) that what he [Qutb] searches for is in the *surah* "Yusuf" ' verses (35–41).
5 Hammudah went on to show what these verses say: that 'these verses are saying that Yusuf went to prison with two youths of the servants of the King. One of them said to the other that he saw dream . . .' (to the end of the story, pp. 132–3). Hammuda then linked the story to verse 67 'The Judgement (*al-hukmu*) is Allah's alone', and stated that 'this is the result – a beam of light in the darkness of bewilderment and prison – *al-hakimiyyah* is Allah's alone'.
6 In these, Hummudah puts Qutb in parallel with the Prophet Yusuf. Yusuf's friend told him about the dream in prison and resulted in that '*hakimiyyah* is Allah's alone'. Similarly, Qutb's friend tolled him about the dream in prison and resulted in that '*hakimiyyah* is Allah's alone'. This similarity is Hammudah's claim.[75]

Such media coverage concerning Islamic groups provides little help to scholars or researchers. The expression '*al-Takfir wa al-Hijrah*' is misleading and as Mahfuz notes, 'used by the group's enemies to downplay the significance of the group inside Egypt and outside it'.[76] This may well have misled people who produced studies, theories, and interpretations concerning national security, policies and decisions about the future of Egypt. President Sadat, for instance, issued a new Family Law and passed it in the absence of the parliament, claiming it was based on *shari'ah*; a tactical move, perhaps. This law in 1985 was reissued by President Mubarak who claimed that the new law was also based on *shari'ah*.[77] According to Farag Fudah (1988: 15) the 'Family Law has changed three times in ten years . . .'[78] This implies that the problem was diagnosed as being only related to the Family Law, not to the educational system and its law, the civil law, the commercial law, the administrative law and other laws and codes against corruption, repression, oppression and humiliation. The education and socioeconomic conditions of the environment, which caused those people to recruit themselves in that way, perhaps, cannot be solved by the Family Code or by this way of the governmental sponsored media coverage. Most of these people came from the lower classes and lower middle classes in Egypt. The countrywide urban uprising, which is known as the food riot of 17 and 18 January 1977, illustrates the point which 'reflects the mounting frustrations of lower classes and lower middle classes in Egypt vis-à-vis the negative payoff of President Sadat's socioeconomic policies'.[79] Also,

> The militants perceive Egypt's present economic problems as the outcome of the mismanagement of resources, the application of imported policies, conspicuous consumerism, the corruption of top officials and low

> productivity. Over-population, scarcity of cultivable land and other natural resources, the burdens of defense, and the war efforts are not considered causes of or crucial factors in Egypt's present economic difficulties. The militants' blueprint for dealing with Egypt's problems is rather straightforward; it requires austerity, hard work, and self-reliance.[80]

The problem then is not only the Family law, but also socioeconomic and other problems, that are usually felt by those lower classes and lower middle classes in Egyptian society. How is Family Law related to violence of the Islamic groups? The nightspots of the Pyramids Road were considered by the Islamists as a sinful spot in Cairo. This area was seen be the Islamists as symptoms of moral and social corruption of the social system. According to Ayubi,

> In this sinful nightspot, the oil shaykhs, and the nouveaux riches scattered their money endlessly around the deprived fleshpots of this infamous highway on alcohol and immorality! In the food riots of January 1977, bearded youth (i.e. members of Islamic groups) were seen setting fire to the nightclubs and cabarets and smashing the wicked whiskey bottles. The belly dancing and other sinful activities around these nightspots were considered a particularly serious affront during Ramadan the Muslims' holy fasting month. The government's solution to this conflict between touristic considerations and religious sensibilities was typical of its masking techniques in 1979. It was decreed that the belly dancing could continue during the holy month, but each performance should include some religious songs in between the usual items! It is easy to appreciate how people who took their religion seriously were outraged by this sort of humbug.[81]

This 'sort of humbug' was the result of a misleading campaign of the mass media. The reason then behind the violence of this group was the violation by the State of the Egyptian constitution, which decreed Islam, as the religion of the State.

In the universities, according to Hasan Hanafi, students usually form societies of varying activities. Among these societies, 'the communists propagate communism'.[82] The 'society of the Satan, found in the American University, propagate their devil,[83] and the society of the pharaonic god, *Horus* propagate Horus's religion'.[84] The 'Nasserites propagate Nasserism, the democrats propagate their democracy, and the Society of Muslims propagates Islam'.[85] According to Public Prosecutor Ibrahim al-Qaliobi's report on 26 January 1977, 'the revolutionary current of the Egyptian Communist Labor Party was working in the universities. On 20 January 1977 Sayyid Husayn Fahmi, the Interior Minster, announced that the authorities had uncovered a plot trying to burn down Cairo. This information was repeated on 30 January by the Prime Minister, in the People's Assembly. He added that the Nationalist Progressive Unionist Party, one of the officially approved parties 'had involved itself shamefully in this abominable national crime'.[86]

Thus, on the one hand, there was evidence of aggression by the an approved party, while this Islamic group on the other, was not entitled to status as a political or even a religious party. Until their trial in 1977, their activity was to distribute pamphlets at the university. By then all doors were closed to them.

In late 1974, 14 students who also were members of Shukri's group were arrested for distributing pamphlets propagating Islam and calling upon people to join their Society of Muslims. It was this that triggered the violence. The group decided to respond to what they saw as the State's past aggression. Prior to this, and for eight months, Shukri had written to Egyptian radio, television and press, seeking to publish the facts and what was happening to his group. However, all his dispatched articles to the Egyptian media were simply ignored and went with no success, and criticism of the group continued to make the front pages of daily newspapers. In Kepel's words 'Shukri tried to issue communiqués correcting this caricature . . . but none of his communiqués was published . . .'[87] According to Muhammad Mahfuz, one of the journalists of the time covering the event,

> The attacks by the media irritated the Society of Muslims and caused them to write requesting a chance to explain themselves but their articles were rejected. I still remember a few of them entering our offices demanding a dialogue with us. But those who were in charge of these institutions prevented a response by us . . . These institutions deprived the Islamists of their right to publish their articles or to explain their view to the public. The media continued to mislead the public and to frustrate the Society of Muslims. The issue of the media became very important on the agenda of the Islamists. This was the cause of the war between the Islamists and the writers and editors, all are appointed by the State Security Apparatus.[88]

Eventually, the war between the Islamists and the media developed into a confrontation between Islamists and the government. The cause of the ensuing violence was not the influence of Qutb's ideas but of provocation by the State and exaggeration by its mass media. The media was a crucial factor, creating the gap between the President and the group. This can be clearly seen in Shukri's view of the daily relations with the Sadat regime, when he says: 'There is no doubt that the Sadat regime is a thousand times better than Nasser's. Nasser would never have allowed us to act as we are now acting, nor to carry out our *da'wa* openly.'[89] This also reflects the group's earlier saying to President Sadat that there are people misleading him.[90]

Until 1977, there was no violence reported in relation to Shukri's group. The Security Apparatus of the State knew the general leader, Shukri, and the regional leaders of the group. According to Kepel,

> General Intelligence was in contact with the Society of Muslim's second-in command, Mahir Bakri, who have advocated collaboration between the

> Society and the State intelligence services against the other tendencies of the Islamicist movement, in particular the putschist disciples and admirers of Siriyya.[91]

In the context of the cooperation, the arrest of 14 students, who were leaflet distributors and members of Shukri's group took the group by surprise. This, together with the media attack which marked the group '*Takfir wa Hijrah*, deviant cavemen, abnormal, heretic, *kharijites*',[92] and 'fanatical criminals on the front pages of the semi-officials Cairo daily al-Ahram',[93] led the group to reconsider its opinion about the cooperation with the State intelligence. In the context of this pressure, according to Kepel,

> Throughout the first six months of 1977, Shukri ceaselessly demanded that the fourteen 'martyrs' be released and that the press offer its readers an accurate picture of the Society of Muslims. He mobilized all the group's energies, explaining that they had now entered the 'stage of general proclamation'. They sent communiqués to the newspapers and tried to deliver statements to radio and television journalists. Shukri also wanted to publish a small book he had written, called *al-Khilafah* (The Caliphate). None of these initiatives worked.[94]

Here, the group's view that 'Sadat regime as a thousand times better than Nasser's' began to change and they began to regard the regime with suspicion. This is emphasized by one of Shukri's close associates, that 'whereas Nasser had struck at the Islamicist movement with a hammer, Sadat was strangling it with a silken cord'.[95] This marked the beginning of the cycle of violence of this group.

On 3 July 1977, when the group kidnapped al-Shaykh Mahmud Husayn al-Dhahabi the Minster of *Awqaf* (Islamic Endowments), they declared their responsibility and their conditions for his release.[96] These were as follows:

1. To free the *Jama'at* detainees of the group.
2. Announce a general amnesty for the members sentenced in absentia.
3. A ransom of LE 200,000 in unmarked bills.
4. An official, front-page apology from *al-Ahram*, *al-Akbar* and *al-Jumhuriyyah* newspapers and from *Uctober*, *Akhir Sa'ah* [magazines] and *al-Azhar* journal for their published allegations and misleading information against the Society of Muslims.
5. Permission to publish a book under the title *al-Khilafah*.
6. A committee to be established, composed of experts to investigate the violation and corruption in the Office of the General Prosecutor of the Court of the Security of State and the Judges on the bench; the General Intelligence Agency and the Office of the General Prosecutor of al-Mansurah province.
7. This announcement to be broadcast in its entirety on the evening news of 8.30 p.m. on 3 July 1977.

8 Details of this communiqués to be published in the three major Egyptian dailies newspapers on Monday 4 July; in the Syrian newspapers *al-Ba'ath*; in the Lebanese *al-Nahar*, and in the major newspapers of Saudi 'Arabia, Kuwait, Jordan, Sudan, Turkey, Iran; as well as *New York Times* (USA), *Le Monde* (France); *The Sunday Times* and *The Guardian* of Great Britain. Each paper with its language.[97]

At the end of this document, the warning was given of intent to kill their hostage if the conditions were not met. The declaration of conditions, which was never published, deserves systematic analysis to understand why the Islamic groups resorted to violence. It reflects the accumulated pain and pressures of oppressed and persecuted people who finally became convinced that they must do something for the East and the West to hear their voice. It also indicates how the media and other government institutions drove them to the desperate action of killing and thus themselves being killed.[98]

The declaration indicates that the Islamic group felt they were oppressed by the State and living under its pressure and surveillance. The police had previously arrested them for distributing pamphlets, and their whereabouts was known. The authorities chose not to deal with the problem immediately but allowed the situation to escalate, to use the case against Islamists. Islamist killing of a Muslim scholar and official was seen as a good case to be used to deflect the attention of al-Azhar and thus the people, to the central objective behind the activity of Islamists. A gap between al-Azhar and the Islamists was now established in a way that facilitated the State to crush the ideas behind the Islamists and their sympathizers from al-Azhar and the public. Consequently, the Minister died and when the police moved in to arrest the Islamists, it was too late to resolve the confrontation.[99]

However, why the Islamists kidnapped al-Shaykh al-Dhahabi, a distinguished al-Azhar scholar and pious Muslim is unclear. According to Mahfuz, the reason was that

> the authorities had asked Shaykh al-Dhahabi to explain the ideological position of the Islamic groups. In July 1975 [two years before the Islamists kidnapped him] the Shaykh wrote an official article, published under the name of his Ministry. He called the Islamists the new *Kharijites*,[100] condemned the Islamic groups in general, and 'warned' people about the 'danger' of affiliation with them. This article then was used by the media for the propaganda against the Islamists.[101]

It is significant that the article was not a personal opinion, but was ministerial policy on the specific issue of political Islam. This Ministry controls most of the mosques and Imams in Egypt and banned the Islamic groups from using these mosques for teaching. The article also misled the government, downplayed the significance of the Islamist cause, gave the authority the green light to crush the Islamic group, and did not help the government in understanding the concept of political Islam. The article thus violated the basic principles of the concept of governance in Islam. Shaykh al-Dhahabi knew the first speech of Abu Bakr (First Caliph) when Abu Bakr first came to power. The Shaykh also knew that 'Umar, 'Uthman and 'Ali repeated almost the same words of Abu Bakr after him when they first came to power. The first speeches of the Four Rightly Guided Caliphs are familiar grounds in the Arabic literature. Most of the ordinary Muslims are aware of these speeches.[102]

Another important aspect of the Rightly Guided Caliphs speeches, is their reference to government authority stemming not from a political party or the Muslim community but from the activity of facilitating the application of the *shari'ah*.[103] Before the Egyptian Revolution of 1952, al-Maraghi was a professor of Islamic law at al-Azhar in 1949. The Sorbonne graduate professor Abd al-Rahaman Tajj (1896–1975), was Shaykh al-Azhar in the year 1952 after the Revolution.[104] Both al-Maraghi, and Tajj supported Qutb's view that if Muslims accept the ruler but he then abandons the *shari'ah*, Islam calls him dictator (*taghut*) and ordered the Muslim community to strive against him.[105] These principles were not included in the article by Shaykh al-Dhahabi nor did he highlight the defects of the current sociopolitical system or bring to the authority's attention the concept of political Islam. Thus, the Islamists claimed, Dhahabi colluded with the current regime, effectively supporting laws that permitted 'nightclubs' and 'cabarets' to function during the holy month of Ramadan. He also authorized action against the Islamic groups and called them *Kharijites*. Dhahabi legitimized for the government to label 'members of these militant groups as deviants, abnormal, heretics, and khawarij . . . The State nevertheless continues to treat members of these groups as common criminals . . .'[106] According to Muhammad al-Khidr Husayn Shaykh al-Azhar (1930), Mustafa Sabri Shaykh al-Islam of Turkey in 1918 and Professor Muhammad Bikhit al-Muti'i (1856–1935) Shaykh al-Azhar in 1914, the article by Shaykh al-Dhahabi constitutes what can be seen as 'conspiracy against Islam'.[107] At the Islamic Conference for Science which was held at The University of al-Azhar in the period 24–29 October 1992, Professor Gad al-Haq 'Ali Gad al-Haq Shaykh al-Azhar noted that 'As I said earlier, Islam has come to rule (*yahkum*) all affairs of human life . . . .'[108] On the day of the Festival of Sacrifice, in 1979, the prominent Muslim Professor Shaykh Yusuf al-Qaradawi[109] gave a speech about this Muslim occasion in 'Abdin Squire which is located in front of the Presidential Palace in Cairo. Qaradawi stated that

> The youth of the Islamic groups are Egypt's representatives. They are not the representatives of the cabarets and casinos of the Pyramid Road or the dancers and cinema stars. Egypt is not of the unveiled women; Egypt is the university's veiled women who adhere to the *shari'ah* Egypt is the land of al-Azhar with its thousand years of Islam and its *shari'ah* . . .[110]

The government used the article of al-Dhahabi and moved against the Islamic groups who also decided to confront the government. They kidnapped the official they were able to identify as an obstacle on their path for the rule by *shari'ah*. He is the one who had authorized the activity of the government against them. His article which provided support of the regime also did not help to protect the *'ulama* or al-Azhar institutions from the State's criticism and accusation.

Subsequently, the Military Court criticized al-Azhar as a whole accusing its shaykhs of not observing their responsibilities properly. The officers or the generals of the Military Court believed that they understood Islam and its *shari'ah* better than al-Azhar and its academics and the *'ulama*. According to General Makhluf the head of the Military Court 'all the officers who participated in the interrogations had at least masters degree, if not doctorates, in law'.[111] This law, indeed, is not the Islamic law or the *shari'ah*. The Court declared: 'the movement of the Islamic groups is the result of the failure of the *'ulama* to teach the youth the reality of Islam'.[112] This comment, which made the front pages of all newspapers in the Arab world, may be seen as an attack on the Islamic institutions, the *'ulama* and Islamic groups themselves. It would seem that the military regime considered itself the only unbiased observers and protectors of Islam.[113] It should also be noted that the Military Court put the responsibility not on Qutb but on al-Azhar and the shaykhs.

Professor 'Abd al-Halim Mahmud, the Sorbonne graduate and the then Shaykh al-Azhar (1973–1978), was in London, from 3–7 July 1977, when al-Dhahabi was killed. On his return, he found his *'ulama* charged with failure, by General Makhluf the head of the Military Court, a serious threat to the credibility of all Islamic institutions. Mahfuz notes that the Shaykh al-Azhar 'dispatched an article at once to *al-Aharm* newspaper, but it was simply ignored'.[114] One cannot help but wonder why. To treat Shaykh al-Azhar like the Islamic activist Shukri Mustafa simply by silence, may mean both were extremists who could safely be dismissed. As for the Shaykh, he insisted on publishing his article. It appeared, ten days later in *al-Ahram*.[115] In it, he corrected the position of Shaykh al-Dhahabi, and discussed the concept of political Islam. He also explained reasons, which caused the people of any era to stand against their rulers. Among his saying was that 'violence may occur [when] the action of the regime in power constitute unacceptable Islamic behavior, and does not govern according to the *shari'ah*'.[116]

Here Shaykh al-Azhar is in agreement with Qutb's key ideas regarding the centrality of Islam and of *hakimiyyah* as in Qutb's *'Adalah*, *Zilal* and *Ma'alim* all of which were originally approved by al-Azhar. In particular, Shaykh al-Azhar supported Qutb's view that the current status quo in Egypt is not Islamic simply because the system is not based on the *shari'ah*.[117] The grand Shaykh accused the group for their committed crime, according to Kepel,

> he nevertheless, explained that the cause of the phenomenon lay in the fact that power in Egypt had long been held by people whose political philosophy was not rooted in the religious culture of the country. It was

> this that explained why disoriented youth perceived society as *jahiliyyah*. This was not the line of the military prosecutor, who said instead that the sect had cloaked itself in a religious garb in order to conceal its crimes.[118]

However, the Military Court which condemned Shukri and accused al-Azhar was acting beyond its own jurisdiction, not according to *shari'ah*. Nor was the judgement made according to Islamic law. Indeed, because Islamic law was not applied, this indicates the government is not a legitimate authority.[119] Consequently, striving against the regime was justifiable. Shaykh al-Azhar rejected the accusation of the failure of the religious institution and laid the entire responsibility at the feet of the political regime and its laws.

Another important issue raised by the Shukri case is the question of *ijtihad* (independent judgement) and its use in Muslim societies. In the Military Court, which was held in Cairo on the sixth, seventh, and eighth November (1977), 'Shukri called for *ijtihad*' based on the Qur'an and the Sunnah to expedite the application of *shari'ah* in Egypt. Shukri confronted the regime and its systems as a whole, in the following statement to the Court:

> The condition of Muslims has deteriorated since *ijtihad* has diminished. The claim that the 'door of *ijtihad*' should remain closed and opinions of the imams of *fiqh* (jurisprudence) should not be studied in the light of the problems of our time is unjustifiable. The imams have always done their utmost to facilitate the application of *shari'ah*. Al-Shafi'i developed his school when he came to Egypt... Why cannot we simply base our life on the Qur'an and the Sunnah, the source of all, if the explanation of the rules of *fiqh* needs further explanation and *fatwa* after *fatwa* (legal opinion). The *fatwa* of al-Shaykh Mahmud Shaltut[120] permitted bank interest to suit Nasser. Al-Shaykh Mutwalli al-Sha'rawi[121] permitted bills of security (*sanadat maliyyah*) which were issued by the State based on interest. Al-Shaykh Su'ad Jalal issued a *fatwa* that drinking beer is allowable because beer is not like wine (*khamr*)....
>
> Our society [Egypt] does not prohibit prostitution, but considers it the revenue of a tourist economy. Our society does not help the youth, males and females, to prepare an accommodation to establish a family. What are the consequences of this? It results in moral corruption. The society permits bank interest and allows it to be the basis of State finances. Liquor and prohibited intoxication perpetrated through factories owned by a State that called itself Muslim. The earthly law used in the courts of the State that calls itself Islamic opposes the establishment of divine law... Consequently, we are responsible for cleaning up this mess. I will do my responsibility and I will call upon others to do likewise....
>
> The Ministry of Endowment controls most of the mosques and is employs the imams, usually from al-Azhar, to teach according to orders of the government, not according to the order of Allah. The speech of Friday Prayer is written by the Ministry, and comes to the imam carrying the signature of the Minister and the stamp of the Ministry. This type of

mosques cannot justify its existence.... Friday Prayer in the government mosques is meaningless under a *jahili* system like this which governs our affairs. It will be lawful when the *shari'ah* rules the society. Mosques will then speak freely in the name of Allah not in the name of the government...

To achieve this change, there is must be power, but our group is still weak. We are expanding the group, training the individuals and preparing ourselves to bring Islam into our life... Power, like any phenomena, has stages and the first of these stages is to break the oppressive siege and then blast off. Victory depends on many things among which is quantity, therefore, we are trying to increase our numbers...

[Question from the Court]: 'Is your group so weak that it has not yet reached the autonomous stage to pray the Friday Prayer?' [Shukri answered] 'That is not true. Absolutely not. And the reason for this lies in the restriction and prosecutions. In the past five years – the age of our group – we have been prosecuted fifteen times, that is, three court-cases a year. We have suffered the pain of torture and imprisonment in each case. Where can we get our power? I [Shukri] consider that you [Judge] should be in my place behind the bars, and I should be in your place on the Bench of judgement...[122]

Is the cause of frustration, conveyed so well in Shukri's words, to be laid at Qutb's door or is it due to the failure of the sociopolitical system and the activity of the State vis à vis the Islamic group?[123] The man who made this speech had spent six years of hard labour in Nasser's prisons. He suffered torture while he was still only distributing leaflets. Shukri finally arrived at the point where he renounced any allegiance to the State. He rejected mosques controlled by the government, all government policies and functionaries including the police, the Military Court, the army and Egypt as a whole. He said:

I am not willing to go to war against Israel under the Egyptian flag. All types and forms of the Egyptian police do not differ from the Israelis and we will announce the war against both of them as soon as we are able...[124]

Violence was thus a reaction to what was perceived as social anarchy: sociopolitical, economic, moral and intellectual. The State responded by charging them with infidelity (*kufr*) or '*takfir wa hijrah*'.[125] Requests from the defense counsel to call 'Abd al-Halim Mahmud Shaykh al-Azhar as a witness were refused by the Military Court. According to Kepel,

The Court, refused the request of Shukri's lawyer, made in his opening statement on 23 October [1977], to summon 'Abd al-Halim Mahmud to testify at the trial; al-Azhar's line on the Society of Muslims was thus concealed. Nor was the State inclined to allow the military origins of the regime issued of the 1952 revolution to be placed on trial. Censure of Shukri's activities and ideology had to be expressed with a single voice.[126]

This voice was 'the military prosecutor, General Makhluf, who articulated the official view of Shukri and his group in the newspapers and at the hearings... In other words, the opinion of the group to which the victim belonged went unheard'.[127] This explains the claim that made Shukri a prophet who knows the secret meaning of every word in the Qur'an, as outlined earlier. Kepel's statements, here, suggest also that the Court did not see the issue as religious but rather as criminal, a matter of armed sedition.

Accused by the military court, Shaykh al-Azhar had no option other than to keep silent. However, the publication of the Court record on 12 March 1978 had broke the silence of the grand Shaykh. Again, the Court charged al-Azhar and the *'ulama* with having failed in their tasks of education and training. In reply, Shaykh al-Azhar dispatched another article to the Egyptian newspapers but all refused to publish it. This time, Shaykh al-Azhar sent the article out of Egypt to be published on the front pages in the Arab newspapers. The article received a wide coverage. Shaykh al-Azhar clearly saw the matter differently. According to Mahfuz, the Shaykh

> strongly disputed the skill and the capacity of the Military Court to try a religious case or to investigate religious opinions. He challenged the causal connection made by the Military Court between the killing of al-Dhahabi and Islamic notions held by the group. He also accused the State, despite its support for the rule of law and free speech, of breaking these rules itself.[128]

In his article, 'Abd al-Halim Mahmud, Shaykh al-Azhar had stated that

> the government desires the *'ulama* of al-Azhar to condemn the thought of people whom we have not had a chance to meet and are now refused access to. This is quite illegal and not justifiable in any creed or in any religion.[129]

To summarize, the Society of Muslims led by Shukri Mustafa was able to bring the Islamic Institution, the highest Islamic authority led by Shaykh al-Azhar Abd al-Halim Mahmud, face to face with the military regime for the first time since the Revolution of 23 July 1952. Shukri Mustafa and his group saw the successful publication of the articles by the Shaykh al-Azhar as a moral and intellectual victory. The violence cannot be laid at Qutb's door. Qutb supported the idea of the rule by *shari'ah* which was also supported by Al-Azhar. Generally, Qutb's ideas were orthodox. The violence was seen by supporters of the group as provoked by the State, which had violated its own laws of human rights, by refusal to respect the creed of the people and their Islamic traditions.[130]

THE SOCIETY OF JIHAD

Shukri Mustafa, the leader of the Society of Muslims labelled by the regime *takfir wa hijrah*, did not leave behind him any accounts explaining his views except those dialogues between him and 'the military prosecutor, General Makhluf, who articulated the official view of Shukri and his group in the newspapers and at the hearings . . . In other words, the opinion of the group to which the victim belonged went unheard'.[131] The group's objectives that focused upon Islamic teaching, ideological and organizational training of individuals for social reform failed to be realized. A total of 189 individuals were charged, 12 were sentenced to life imprisonment, 4 to death and the rest were freed. This led to the other Islamic groups which were already at work in Egypt to reshape their ideas, strategies and plans of action. Those of Shukri's group who had escaped arrest, joined other Islamic groups in Egypt. Among these groups was that led by Muhammad 'Abd al-Salam Faraj, al-Jihad.

Muhammad 'Abd al-Salam Faraj (1954–1982) graduated in Engineering at Cairo University and was working for the University. After the failure of Shukri's group to achieve their goals, 'Abd al-Salam Faraj reformed the thought, and the activity of his Islamic group. This group, now known as the Jihad Group, was later to assassinate President Sadat.[132] The objective of the group revolved around the theory and practice of *jihad*. For him *jihad* is the Missing Ordinance. In 1981 'Abd al-Salam Faraj published a text, *Al-Faridah al-Gha'ibah* (The Missing Ordinance). The book consisted of quotations from Muslim scholars and Imams, some *hadith* from the Prophet and some Qur'anic verses.[133] Although only a hundred pages long the manifesto was to have a substantial impact on Egypt and amongst the Islamists. Regardings Faraj's book, Jansen (1986) stated

> No one reading the text of '*The Neglected Duty*' can fail to be impressed by its coherence and the force of its logic. Even it its author had not been a member of the group that killed President Sadat, the pamphlet would have had great value on its own. Even if Sadat had not been killed by the group that is for all times associated with this pamphlet, the pamphlet would have had value, not as a historical document about the assassination of a Nobel Prize winner, but as the portrait of a mentality that exist and probably has existed for a long time . . .[134]

In his analysis of the condition of Egypt, Abd al-Salam Faraj differed from Qutb and Shukri. For Faraj, preparing individuals to bring about change was unnecessary. As have been shown, educational and preparation programmes, including those of al-Banna, Qutb and Shukri were ineffective.[135] For Faraj, Islam is there in the society, in the hearts of the people, in the homes, in the mosques and on the streets. It was simply the case that Islam had been excluded from power. This same power had stalled non-Islamic programmes for change, and attempts at reform. It had prosecuted the Muslims, imprisoned them and executed their leaders. It was the government that was the problem. Faraj concluded that power must be confronted by power. The basic rights require power for protection. It is the power exemplified in the notion of *jihad*, the missing ordinance.[136]

Faraj's view differed from Qutb but was in agreement with Nasser whose ideas on jihad as the struggle for basic rights had enlightened him. On 8 March 1965, when most of the Muslim Brothers, Qutb and the young Shukri Mustafa were in prisons, Nasser delivered a speech in Upper Egypt in the city of Asyut, the birthplace of both Qutb and Shukri where the *jihad* groups have strength. Nasser stated that

> the wishes and objectives are the rights of all human beings . . . but a right cannot be established just by thinking about it. The right is work and sacrifices. It is only the *jihad* in the way of the doctrine . . . It is a *jihad* against the other, and a *jihad* against the soul . . .[137]

These revolutionary words and their associations are among the basis of the theory and practise of Faraj's group of *jihad*. In the way of doctrine, Faraj emphasises that

> *jihad* for God's cause, in spite of its extreme importance and its great significance . . . , has been neglected by the *'ulama* of this age. They have feigned ignorance of it, but they know that it is the only way to the return and the establishment of the glory of Islam anew.[138]

He further stresses that people should believe that these great things cannot take place by only wishing and thinking about it: 'There is no reason to waste effort and time on dreams.'[139] Remarks like these indicate that the youth are usually influenced by the 'leaders, the press, Mosques, and television'.[140] Faraj reads for Qutb, Kishk, Ibn Taymiyyah, al-Skawkani and other leaders and Imams. But the experience of the Ikhwan and the later Islamic groups with the regime, led Faraj to keep distant from Qutb and the Ikhwan in general. According to Hanafi, members of the *jihad* group were reading very widely from the classic and modern Islamic sources. In pointing out these sources and their authors, Hanafi noted that Qutb's *Ma'alim* was not among the sources of the *jihad* group's interest. To Hanafi, 'the group of *jihad* was in a more advanced stage than that presented by Qutb in *Ma'alim*'.[141] This means that the idea is one thing, but how to implement it is another. In other words, to establish the rule by *shari'ah* is one thing, but how to bring about the establishment of the rule by *shari'ah* is another. The rule by *shari'ah* is the thing that Qutb and the Jihad group agreed upon, but they differed on the method of bringing the society to the fold of *shari'ah* rule. In this sense, Hanafi means that the Jihad group's method for transition was in a more advanced stage than the transitional programme planned by Qutb in *Ma'alim*. In other words, Qutb's transitional programme of educational and ideological training of the individual and the society, and then ultimately establishing the Islamic State, had already proved a failure in the eyes of the Jihad group. Thus, Hanafi saw that the Jihad group's programme which begins by overthrowing the government and then proceeding to the task of applying the *shari'ah*, was more advanced than Qutb's programme which begins by educational and ideological training on a wider scale, and then ultimately establishing the Islamic State.[142]

In fact, the idea of *jihad* is itself based on the concept of *hakimiyyah* a basic principle of Islamic belief.[143] Since Qutb had enunciated the concept of *hakimiyyah*, a number of intellectuals had sought out the *jihad* groups. They were attracted to the idea of *hakimiyyah*. And what were the practical implications of *hakimiyyah*, how was one to implement the concept of *hakimiyyah* in the state? The concept of *hakimiyyah* became the driving question for Qutb in 1965, Salih siriyya in 1974, Shukri Mustafa in 1977 and for Faraj in 1981. The link between Faraj and Qutb's ideas was to appear in Court records that analysed the development of Faraj's group, in particular the notion of *takfir* (charge with unbelief), *hakimiyyah* (sovereignty) and *jahiliyyah*. This emerged in cross-examination during the trial of Sayyid Qutb in 1965, as seen in the following excerpt from the transcript.

Question: What is the meaning of the expression *al-hakimiyyah*?

Qutb's answer: It means that the *shari'ah* of Allah is the foundation of Legislation. Allah Himself does not descend to govern, but descended His *shari'ah* to govern. The Qur'anic texts say that the *hakimiyyah* of Allah will be implemented by the implementation of His *shari'ah*.

Question: What is the way to achieve the final goal? And what is this goal in your view?

Answer: The final goal, upon which we agree, is to establish an Islamic system governed by the *shari'ah*, not by man-made law. The way to achieve that is Islamic education, teaching and wide scale Islamic cultivation of individuals and groups.

Question: Do you agree that the Muslim *ummah* has not existed for a long time and must be reconstructed?

Answer: The concept of the Muslim *ummah* needs to be explained. The Muslim *ummah* is the *ummah* which governs all aspects of life – political, social, economic, moral and so on as well as, the *shari'ah* of Allah and His program. In these terms, the Muslim *ummah* does not now exist in Egypt, nor in any place on the face of the earth. But this does not mean there are no Muslims. This is because, an individual is governed by his creed and his morals, but what governs the affairs of the *ummah* is the sociopolitical system.[144]

One might argue that, if the *ummah* does not exist, how and in what sense do individual Muslims exist when Qutb also says that Islam no longer exists.[145] Qutb means Islam no longer exists as a social, legal and economic system in society, since the Sovereignty of Allah has ceased to rule over the sovereignty of man.[146] This leads to consideration of what the *'ulama* now say concerning Sovereignty. This also is detailed earlier and in previous chapters (see Chapter 1). Here my source for this is the *Gamal Abd al-Nasser Encyclopedia of The Islamic Jurisprudence* published in 1961 when Qutb was in prison.[147] In this multivolume document there is not a specific contributor who was mentioned, but introduced by Hasan Ma'mun, Shaykh al-Azhar, who also referred to the Supreme Council of Islamic Affaire of the United Arab Republic (Egypt and Syria). In this document, the *'ulama* pointed out the ideological nature of *hakimiyyah* in the Islamic system. They stated

> There is no *hakim* (sovereign) other than Allah, there is no *hukm* (rule) except the *hukm* of Allah, and there is no *shari'ah* (law) except the *shari'ah* of Allah. This is what Muslims have agreed upon, even the Mu'tazilities, the people of justice. All Muslims agreed that the *hakim* is Allah alone, and the rule is His rule, that is, the *shari'ah*. The highest legal and governmental authority is Allah. Allah's wisdom did not empower anybody, nor even the prophet Muhammad, to legislate for the people as he wishes or govern them on the basis of his own authority.[148]

This concurs with what Qutb enunciated in *Adalah*, *Zilal* and *Ma'alim*, and shows him to be part of the Muslim consensus of the day. Qutb's answer to the Court and the opinion of the *'ulama* regarding *hakimiyyah* confirm that *hakimiyyah* is the basis of the Muslim creed of faith both as ideal and as *shari'ah* in state. Thus, the *jihad* is based on *hakimiyyah* as the fundamental principle of Islam. On this principle, there is no difference between Qutb and the *'ulama*.[149] Difference arises on how to explain the *jihad* and on what *hakimiyyah* is at practical level. As emerged in Court, Qutb will countenance nothing other than that 'practising *hakimiyyah* means practising the *shari'ah*'. But how is the *shari'ah* to be implemented? Here, Qutb's answer was 'Islamic education, teaching and wide-scale cultivation of individual and groups'.[150]

There would thus appear to be no need for *jihad* if *hakimiyyah* (governing by *shari'ah*) exists, or at least if there is a programme preparing individuals and society for it.[151] This position reflects the consensus view,[152] because '*jihad* is one of the pillars of Islam that every Muslim in general must believe'.[153] Therefore, all Islamic groups have *jihad* as the last option on their agenda. According to Hasan Hanafi, *jihad* was on the agenda of 'Ibn Hanbal (164–241/781–855), Ibn Taymiyyah (661–728/1263–1327), Ibn al-Qayyim (d. 751/1350), Ibn Abd al-Wahhab (1703–1792) and al-Shawkani (1250/1831)'.[154] Ibn Taymiyyah, for instance, considered *jihad* justified against the Mongols whom he condemned as unbelievers. In modern times the Muslim Brotherhood (civilians and army officers) used *jihad* against the British and their supporters as a way to rationalize the Revolution of 1952.[155]

From the period of 1952 onwards, until the death of Shukri Mustafa in 1978, no Islamic group adopted *jihad* as the only option to establish the Islamic State. It was the strategy of last resort. The term *jihad* had been used by the Egyptian regime before and after the War with Israel in 1967 until the peace process began after the War of 1973.[156] Islamic groups thus developed their ideas in conjunction with the development of events in the Middle East. This development also was marked and significantly reshaped through the disputes between Islamists and Egyptian regime before and after 1952. It was not until Muhammad 'Abd al-Salam Faraj that the idea of *jihad* was openly declaimed as central in the confrontation of the regime. That *jihad* which was seen as the only option available to establish the Islamic State ruled by *shari'ah* was the thesis of Faraj's book *The Missing Ordinance*.[157] Thus the reason, which moved Faraj to this stage, was the attitude and the activity of the regime that persecuted all educational attempts of other Islamic groups.[158] Muhammad Salim al-'Awwa, Professor of Islamic Law at Oxford and sometimes Cambridge and who is currently at Cairo University noted the historical progression of the term *jihad* combined with its relevance in the immediate environment. He writes,

> After 1967, the term *jihad* was repeatedly used on all levels. The *jihad* is an Islamic duty that has always attracted youth. How can one trace the source of Islamic thought on the subject of *jihad*? The youth did not turn their face seeking al-Azhar. In their view, al-Azhar is a government body. Instead they went in search of historical situation and conditions similar to today's that had faced earlier Muslims. They found this condition was during the time of the Mongols and the ideological position of Ibn Taymiyyah (1263–1327) at that time. The ideas of Ibn Taymiyyah have thus re-surfaced, though they are applied in rather different circumstances than those of Ibn Taymiyyah . . .[159]

The point here is that Faraj and his *jihad* group were influenced by the ideas of Ibn Taymiyyah rather than by the ideas of Qutb.[160] Faraj saw *jihad* both as an important creed and as the only way for actual change in Egypt. He criticized the *'ulama* because, he considered that they had neglected the duty of *jihad* completely.[161]

'Abd al-Hafiz, himself an army officer and one of the *'ulama* of al-Azhar published a book in 1972 entitled *Social Revolution in Islam*. In this book which was introduced by Shaykh al-Azhar Muhammad al-Fahham in 1972, 'Abd al-Hafiz criticized the *'ulama* openly and pointed out that *jihad* ought be the second pillar of Islam after the confession of faith. In his flamboyant style, 'Abd al-Hafiz asks,

> Where are they, the men of religion, the *'ulama* of *shari'ah*? Where are they, individually or collectively? Where are they to remove the veil that now lies over *jihad* and reveal its position in the *shari'ah*. We have not found one scholar who speaks openly or says what he believes. No, we have found no one to tell the truth since the day when our society submitted to the lash of oppression and occupation! This is why writers have ignored the position of *jihad* as a basic principle in Islam.

> The *'ulama*, or whom the oppressor stamped his slogans...based their miserly interpretation, their poor understanding, and their ignorant judgements on their own narrow-mindedness, their feeling of weakness and negativity. They transgressed with themselves the *hadith* of the Prophet: 'Islam is based on five pillars...' They ignored *jihad* completely...[162]

Belief in *jihad* is thus not beyond the auspice of consensus; nor is it a new phenomenon brought about by Faraj or Qutb, or Ibn Taymiyyah, or 'Abd al-Hafiz or even the Shaykh al-Azhar Muhammad al-Fahham. The point is that *jihad* is a belief, so why did Faraj and the *jihad* groups focus their growing interest in Ibn Taymiyyah and resort to *jihad* as the only option?

In answer to the question 'What is the difference between your views and that of Muhammad 'Abd al-Salam's group?' al-Dawalibi (leader of *jihad* group in El-Minya in Upper Egypt) answered that 'there was no difference. The ideas, programs and the aims had one goal, to establish the rule of *shari'ah* by overthrowing the government'.[163] He went to Cairo to see 'Abd al-Salam Faraj. On his return to El-Minya, al-Dawalibi said that 'I consider the thoughts of Muhammad 'Abd al-Salam useful in addressing Islam and its comprehensiveness. About a year ago, he reshaped his ideas into a practical ideology.'[164] Asked 'what is the purpose of establishing the Islamic State?' Karam Zuhdi another leader of *jihad* in Asyut's answer was 'to establish the rule of *shari'ah* in all aspects of human life'.[165] These examples illustrate the growing appetite of *jihad* groups for the rule of *shari'ah*.

In Court, 'Abd al-Salam Faraj asked 'Are we living in an Islamic State? This will be true only if the *shari'ah* is the highest legal and governmental authority.'[166] He found support for his view in Islamic history, particularly in the works of Ibn Taymiyyah and his views on the Mongols. For, according to al-'Awwa,

> The Tartars were seen by Faraj as Muslims like the Muslims are in Egypt, praying and performing ritual duties, while the regime prosecutes Muslim leaders, imprisons them, and executes them. Twentieth century Cairo is also like the thirteenth century Mar Dien for Faraj. Both Cairo and Mar Dien are governed by systems other than the *shari'ah* yet both peoples are Muslims. The constitution of Mar Dien which was called *al-Yasiq* [also called *al-Basiq*] was a mixture of Judaic, Christian, and pagan laws and some of Islamic rules similar to the constitution of modern Egypt.[167]

For the Islamists, 'Muzaffar Najm al-Din of Mar Dien became Muhammad Anwar al-Sadat of Cairo'.[168]

Ibn Taymiyyah issued a *fatwa* (legal opinion) condemning the infidelity of rulers of his time. He demanded that Muslims must fight the regime to restore the rule of *shari'ah*. 'Abd al-Salam Faraj learnt that Imam Ibn Taymiyyah himself led the *jihad* against the Mongols. Consequently, the *jihad* group became increasingly interested in the works of Ibn Taymiyyah whose name is usually linked with other Muslim Imams and scholars like Imam Ibn Hanbal, Ibn al-Qayyim, al-Shawkani and al-Alusi (d. 127/743) and other as sources eulogizing *jihad* and bewailing the deterioration of Muslims today.[169] *Jihad*, as asserted by Ibn Taymiyyah and Ibn Kathir, is established in the Qur'an, the Sunnah and the Muslim consensus. According to Ibn Kathir

> *jihad* should be waged firstly against the Muslims who, believing that, Allah is the Sovereign and there is no rule except the rule of Allah and that there is no *shari'ah* except His *shari'ah*, in fact govern by other than the *shari'ah* of Allah.[170]

'Abd al-Salam Faraj used such authorities to develop ideas on *jihad* and began to expand his group. He was able to recruit police and army officers, lieutenants and colonels, students, medical doctors, professors, engineers and other professionals. Among the members of this latter group, Dr. 'Abd al-Rahman, a professor in Islamic jurisprudence, became a source for the group on knowledge of legal issues.[171] Another member, Major 'Abbud al-Zumur, was educated at the Military Secondary College and then graduated from the Military Academy in Cairo. He became an officer in the General Intelligence Agency and one of the presidential guards of President Anwar al-Sadat. (He was 36 years of age when Sadat was assassinated in 1981. He will be free in 2005).[172] Lieutenant 'Abd al-Hamid another member, also graduated from the Military Academy, became an air force commander, and a sports champion. Ayman al-Zawahiri was a Doctor of surgery who published a number of books in his field, but also several on the subject of *jihad*. Among his books are: *Five Hundred Pages and the Bitter Harvest: Fifty Years of Experiments by the Muslim Brotherhood*; *The Mayor in Preparing the Inclination*.[173] Later, he published *Knights Under The Prophet's Banner*; *Meditation on the Jihad Movement; Allaying the Anger in the Believer's hearts; and Meditation Under the Roof of the World*. These writings discuss the Brotherhood's relationship with the Egyptian regimes, explaining the events of their Jihad in Egypt and outside, suggesting reasons why their groups resorted to *jihad* and further viewing how and why they differed in their views from both the Brotherhood and Qutb.[174]

Mamduh Muharram another member of *jihad* was a colonel and qualified engineer who stated that

> I started to read commentaries on the Qur'an during the 1970s. Also I used to go to the mosques where the imams merging Islam with politics in their teaching. I especially liked to go and hear al-Shaykh Kishk, Youssuf al-Badri, and al-Mahallawi. From these imams, I became convinced by of the importance of rule by *shari'ah*.[175]

Lieutenant Khalid al-Islambuli (born 1957), who was later to assassinate Sadat, also graduated from the Military Academy and became a commander of field artillery.

Members were generally recruited in the same way and there was strict observation of the rules. This indicated that the *jihad* group believed in the unification of religion and politics. One of their objectives was to 'force the elite either to conform to the precepts and edicts of Islam or to step down. In other words, a serious challenge to the status quo [of the under society] is built-in component to any militant Islamic ideology'.[176] Membership of the group 'ranged across the gamut of Egyptian society and the wide expanse of Egyptian geography, from Upper Egypt in the South to Alexandria in the North'.[177] Civilians and army officers, who affiliated themselves with the *jihad* group, no doubt reflected both the mood of the military and Egyptian community as a whole. For the *jihad* groups, a civil authority that does not facilitate the application of *shari'ah*, whilst it observes other duties like praying and believing that Allah is the highest authority is merely hypocritical. It was therefore, not difficult for 'Abd al-Salam Faraj to see in modern Cairo, the decadence of ancient Mar Dien. In September 1981, the various leaders of *jihad* met together with a professor from al-Azhar to convene what was effectively an Islamic Court to try the current regime. By then, they may have learned of the judgement of execution passed by the regime's Military Court. 'Abd al-Salam Faraj pointed out that difference was that 'the Jihad's court is Islamic, based on *shari'ah*. But, the regime's Military Court is based on fabricated laws similar to those of the Mongols'.[178]

Meanwhile, the tension was mounting in Cairo. The German Konard Muller and the Duch journalist Mark Blaisse were with Sadat in the 'last hundred days'. They stated that

> In mid-August, on our flight back from the United States to Cairo, a stopover at Salzburg had been planned. Chancellor Kreisky, however, warned Sadat that he could not guarantee his safety as a Syrian extremist organization was reported to be planning an attempt on his life.[179]

However, arrests began in Egypt and mounted rapidly. By September 1981

> about 1500 people – intellectuals, journalists, religious leaders and other opponents real and presumptive were arrested. A few newspapers were closed down. Apparently, the opposition had voiced its criticism too loudly. From outside Egypt, the steps taken by Sadat seemed, to say the least, undemocratic.[180]

The atmosphere grew worse, Egyptians were becoming angry.[181] Significantly, at this stage youth that assassinated President Sadat were not formally part of the *jihad* group. They were living a normal life, that is, not in a training camp, nor under any specific ideological influence. They did not even know each other until two weeks before the date of the assassination.[182] However, Lieutenant Khalid's brother (Muhammad al-Islambuli: born 1955) a member of *jihad* was arrested with other actives. His brother Khalid thereupon came forward and offered to kill President Sadat.

The *jihad* group led by Faraj had agreed that it was necessary to change the government in Egypt. However, some of them, particularly the military wing led by 'Abbud al-Zumur, emphasized the need to 'delay the political initiative for a few years, until their Islamic revolution could count on the popular support that would give it the same kind of success that Iranian Revolution had enjoyed'.[183] Others of them, the civilian wing, led by Faraj were keen to strike now that they had a volunteer able to participate in the Military Parade of 6 October 1981. Assassinating Sadat was thus a spontaneous action within a wider plan for an Islamic revolution to establish an Islamic State.[184] The whole case was triggered by the sweeping arrests made by the regime as noted earlier.

Later in Court, the *jihad* group repeatedly mentioned Ibn Taymiyyah and his *jihad* against the Mongols as if the decision of assassinating President Sadat had been made in the thirteenth century by Ibn Taymiyyah and carried out on 6 October 1981 by Lieutenant Khalid al-Islambuli. There was no mentioning of Qutb or the Ikhwan because they did not agree with either Qutb's programme or the methods of the Brotherhood – or indeed of any other Islamic group at that time. Muhammad 'Abd al-Salam Faraj's testimony in the Military Court indicates the thinking of the *jihad* group at the time:

Question: What are the programs of the Islamic groups other than your own?
Answer: There are many programs:

(i) al-Tabligh wa al-Da'wah (communication and outreach). Their program is to convey the Islamic massage to the people in their houses, coffee shops or public places, calling them to pray and perform ritual duties. They do not speak politics. This program cannot establish the Islamic condition because everything is under control of the government.
(ii) There is also the Ikhwan (Muslim Brotherhood). Their program is to prepare individuals and groups, avoiding any direct engagement with the government, and calling for an Islamic state. Their experiment failed along the way and their program resulted in prosecution and execution because everything is under government control. Now, they want to be a political party but this will never happen in this country and if it does happened, they will become part of the corrupt system.
(iii) There are Islamic groups in the universities believing that they will change the system from within. After graduation as doctors, engineers, teachers, judges, prosecutors, managers and other professional, the entire system then will be in their hands and they will be able to establish the Islamic State. This program, however, is also a kind of fantasy for their work in the State will strengthen its power not weaken it.
(iv) There are other groups like that of *Al-Samawi* who do not consider change by force and military participation. They believe that *jihad*

is nowadays confined to *da'awh* (communication and outreach) and that the people will know right from wrong.

(v) There are those who believe that religion is a personal matter. They do not help to establish an Islamic state. These do not value themselves or their religion. There are also groups to home the government gave farms in al-Khatatbah so as to close their eyes and keep them quite about corruption. This is bribery and conspiracy against Islam. Then there are the charity groups . . .

Question: In your book page 11, you speak of 'the law of the Mongols – *al-Yasiq* – which superimposed on the Islamic lands, and was, as you said, less offensive than laws imported from the West and enacted here in Egypt. What do you mean by this comparison?

Answer: The Mongol rulers did not implement the Islamic *shari'ah* in its complete form, and the rulers of today do not implement it at all.

Question: Do you know that the most corrupt people on the face of the earth were the Mongols? They collected all the Islamic books in Baghdad and threw them all into the river until the water was black with ink. They destroyed all the books of Islamic jurisprudence (*fiqh*) except those in Egypt. They burned Baghdad, Damascus, and Halab to the ground, and did not differentiate between soldiers and civilians, women, children and the elderly.

Answer: In history, the war of the rulers against Islam might take various types and forms depends on the era as the rulers of today fight Islam by various means . . .

Question: Who guided you to this example of Ibn Taymiyyah?

Answer: My reading of Ibn Taymiyyah.

Question: Don't you see the exaggeration of this comparison?

Answer: There is no exaggeration in this comparison.

Question: Explain how the 'legal guardian', who at your instigation and support was killed, Allah's mercy upon him, was fighting against Islam and the Muslims as the Mongols were?

Answer: Enough of war from him against Islam. He was preventing the *shari'ah* of Allah to be established in this Muslim country where every Muslim yearns to observe Islam. He was a war upon Islam, prosecuting Muslims and leaders, deriding the Law of Allah, and describing the dress of the Prophet's wives as tent to make his narrow-minded attendants laugh, making those listening to him in the People's Assembly mock the rules of Allah.

Question: Which of Allah's rules did the 'legal guardian' use as substance for mockery by the people as you say?

Answer: He called the dress the Prophet's wives used to wear tents. He called the limiting of a woman to her house, according to Qur'an 33: 33 backwardness. He called the Muslim youth who are observing the rules of Allah crazy and extremist . . . .[185]

Then, 'Abd al-Salam Faraj explained clearly why they had resorted to *jihad*. He said that the oppression and the violence of the State against *shari'ah* and against Muslims since 1952 were among the reason that resorted them to activism.

Question: You said in Court like the others, particularly the killers, that the reason for assassinating President Sadat was the burst of arrests that followed the last episode of sectarianism. What is your opinion of this, and to what extent did the last wave of arrests influence your plan?

Answer: The last episode brought enmity to the surface. There was no such plan to assassinate or to kill but we thought the Military Parade was an opportunity to do something so we did.

Question: Why did not you wait until the court had said its word about those who were arrested?

Answer: The case is not about individuals being arrested. It is the matter of the *shari'ah*.

Question: Why did not you wait until your were fully adult and your religious knowledge deepened?

Answer: Being young does not mean we are not able to shoulder responsibility. The Prophet himself said that he was victorious because of the youth and opposed by the elders.

Question: Why have you not been patient like the Prophet who waited for years in Makkah.?

Answer: Since the Revolution of July 1952 the Islamic movement has suffered the enmity and persecution of this Revolution. We are Muslims who wait. Our Revolution is not a victory for ourselves but for the rule of Allah.[186]

In Court, another member of *jihad*, Karam Zuhdi made two important points about *jihad*. The first is the obligation to fight the transgressor face to face; the second is strategy: to plan a *coup d'etat* supported by the people and the military. However, prior to these two options there is the possibility of *da'wah*, that is, to make the ruler aware of his theological option, and that by guidance and awareness of the truth, he may change. This pervasion can be face to face or by other means such as writing to him through the mass media. When the ruler comes to know his wrong position and persists in the wrong, our obligation is to confront him immediately to express the rights of the *shari'ah* regardless of our state of readiness. The opposition can be face to face, individual face individual, or by means of revolution by the people. Karam Zuhdi explains these in the following:

Question: What if the ruler refuses to govern by the rule of Allah?

Answer: In this case, as pointed out by Ibn Taymiyyah one is obliged to offer guidance, and if he forgot it, remind him of it repeatedly.

But if he persist in his deviation we will fight him to restore the rule of Allah.

Question: What methods are possible in fighting the ruler to restore the rule of Allah?

Answer: The method in *jihad* is firstly to say the word of truth openly to the ruler, and the second is *jihad* that is by using force. In this too there are two opinions. The first is that the Muslims of any number must fight the ruler even if all of them are killed. The second prefers to delay *jihad* until an Imam is found to lead the *jihad*. Then everything will be in order.

Question: Has this Imam been found in Egypt?

Answer: No. No Imam has come yet to restore the complete rule of Allah in Egypt.

Question: Who holds this view that one should delay the *jihad* until an Imam be found to lead the *jihad*?

Answer: This is the opinion of Imam Jalal al-Din al-Suyuti in his *al-Itqan fi 'Ulum al-Qur'an*.[187]

Question: Does this seem to be in agreement with the rules of *shari'ah*?

Answer: Yes, I see this now, and I do agree with this opinion.

Question: Is it lawful to kill the ruler whether his deeds are right or wrong?

Answer: It is unlawful to fight the ruler who facilitates the application of *shari'ah* even if he himself is corrupt. His corruption is his alone, and this is a personal matter. The Prophet says 'Do not fight the ruler as long as he is facilitating the application of *shari'ah*.' However, the ruler, who is at war with Islam, mocks Islamic rules, replaces them by other rules, stands in the way of establishing the *shari'ah*, and persecutes the *da'wah* is the ruler against whom Muslims must revolt.[188]

These divergences indicate that the *jihad* groups are not interested in Qutb's programme at all. The assassination of President Sadat on 6 October 1981 was clearly an attempt at Islamic revolution. Their preparation over the preceding weeks was not, however, enough for them to move in conjunction with public support. Their plans on 6 October did not reach the public, but the following day, on 7 October, some in Upper Egypt tried to take control of government places and failed in the end. The Islamists do hold some of Qutb's ideas, but then, many of these are basic principles of Islamic belief. Facilitating these basic principles needs a programme. Qutb's programme differs from those who seek immediate and direct action that work from the top down. It should be noted that there also is a tendency to downplay the significance of the Islamists in the media. The terms used to describe the Islamists did not help to deflect the attention of the youth from these groups.

Critics might argue that *jihad* groups became extremists because they considered the time had come for change. The same consideration can be applied to Nasser and others who considered the need for change in 1952.

Similarly, it is applicable to Field Marshal 'Amir, Minister of Defence and his group, who tried to overthrow Nasser's rule, but failed as the *jihad* group had failed.[189] It could also be applied to the Deputy President 'Ali Sabri and his group who sought to overthrow Sadat's rule, but failed. They were arrested on 15 May 1971 in an operation that Sadat called 'the corrective revolution' or 'May revolution'.[190] If any of 'Amir's group or 'Ali Sabri's group and-or 'Abd al-Salam Faraj's groups were fortuitous and had came to power, would the term extremism be applied to them? The answer to these and similar questions is that success makes revolutionaries heroes. As Sadat said, 'it is all about power'![191]

It could also be argued that the *jihad* groups were extremists simply because they assassinated Sadat and a number of officials. In 1906 the Egyptian authorities backed by the British prosecuted 'Abd al-'Aziz Jawish (d. 1929), condemned him and imprisoned him for three months.[192] His crime was an article he wrote on 25 August 1909 outlining the Dinishway incident of 1906 the year of Qutb's birth (9/10/1906).[193] This article was similar to articles by Qutb in that both were opinions.[194] Like the pamphlets distributed in the university by Shukri Mustafa they sought to persuade by the pen. In 1912, the Egyptian authorities backed by the British in Egypt prosecuted Muhammad Farid (d. 1919) the leader of the National Party after the death of Mustafa Kamil in 1908. They detained him for six months. All his crime was that he wrote an introduction to the poetry collection of Ali al-Ghayati, published in 1910 under the title *My Nationality*.[195] After his release, Muhammad Farid was imprisoned again for a year on charges that his ideas were critical and stirring the Egyptians against the highest legal and governmental authority of Egypt.[196]

Hasan al-Banna was assassinated in 1949 by an order from the highest legal and governmental authority of Egypt who may have been the Prime Minister and the Police Commissioner.[197] As Nasser himself pointed out before the Revolution of 1952, 'I was planning to assassinate a number of political leaders, officials and military commanders of the previous regime. However, when I read, in the morning newspapers, that the first attempt made on the life of one of the military commanders failed, I changed my mind'.[198] Egyptian authorities detained Sadat, calling him 'a terrorist'.[199] This was because of 'his involvement in the assassination of Finance Minister, Amin 'Uthman on 5 January 1946'.[200]

History certainly repeats itself in this part of the world. Those who have been prosecuted in the past tend to prosecute others. Qutb was detained for 15 years, 'tortured'[201] and was then executed and buried in an unmarked grave.[202] A photograph of Qutb hanging on the gallows was published on the front pages of the newspapers.[203] This also was because of his idea of the legitimate Sovereignty as opposed to sovereignty that lacks legitimacy. Qutb was not the only one who used the word *jahl* and its associates. In modern Egypt, Abduh, Shawqi, Wajdi, al-'Aqqad and other intellectuals[204] and scholars used the word *jahl* and its derivations, including *jahiliyyah*.[205] Here, however, the reference is Gamal ‘Abd al-Nasser. Nine months after the death of Qutb, the defeat in 1967 provided the opponents of Nasser's regime with substantial opportunity for criticism. The regime was charged with ignorance, corruption and moral deviation. In his report, Nasser blamed the *‘ulama* who, in his view, had not observed their responsibility towards what he called *‘al-jahl al-ijtima‘i’* (social ignorance).[206] On another occasion and in his speech of July 1967 (6 weeks after the defeat) marking the anniversary of the revolution, Nasser emphasized the sovereignty and total authority of God.

> He said, ‘Allah was trying to teach Egypt a lesson, to purify it in order to build the new society. The nation had to accept this testing as its destiny. It had known that the Israeli attack was coming but had been unable to prevent defeat.’ Nasser resorted to quoting a popular saying: ‘Precaution is pointless in face of fate.’[207]

History tells us that the Egyptians opposed the *Sovereignty* of the rulers in 1881, 1919 and in 1952. They later opposed the *Sovereignty* of Nasser in February 1968[208] and the *Sovereignty* of Sadat on 18 and 19 January 1977.[209] In each case, before and after the Revolution of 1952, those in power executed and imprisoned the opposition. So the reasons behind attempts to change the present should be studied in the light of reasons that had lead to change in the past. Attempted change in 1881 through 1952 is familiar ground.[210] Eighteen years after the change in 1952, the need for change and the reasons for the May Revolution of 1971 led by Sadat were explained by him as follows:

> In the previous eighteen years before my presidency, they tried to make Egypt a society of only malignancy and power, but the experiment failed 100% because it does not suit our character and disposition. We called for a *just dictatorship* or a *just taghut*.[211] When he came to us, he based the construction on sand, but the problem was not only this.... The most atrocious and shameful matters facing him was not the ailing economy, it was not the shameful condition of the army...but it was the generation of malignancy which resulted from the attempt of building the society of power.... In such societies, as I said, a non[e]-of human quality remained. This resulted in selfishness and individual desires. From malignancy and power came this condition of hardship and perplexity which youth is experiencing in Egypt today...They told them about a society that did not exist in reality nor in their inner soul...This created a conflict within the inner soul of youth...The acuteness of the conflict increased, hardship and perplexity became certain once the youth found the society of power collapsing before its eyes...[212]

Here, Sadat echoes Qutb's ideas in words and language and in agreement with it. Nasser's Socialism failed 100 per cent because it does not suit the character and disposition of the Egyptians. The system does not suit the human inclination in the Qur'an and in Qutb's words (*fitrah*). There was a conflict between the system and the inner soul of the people. This resulted in the condition of hardship, malignancy, perplexity, selfishness and individual desires, which distorted the quality of a human being. This is the condition, which Qutb labels *jahiliyyah*.[213] Also, Sadat was referring to Nasser's State, his failed Socialism, and the defeat of 1967 that were to become the reasons behind the violence of Islamists. None of these were part of Qutb's programme. The problem, as asserted by the Egyptian journal Rose El Youssef citing *American Times*, is that

> Egyptian government believes that the source of the violence of the Islamists is foreign, but reason lie in the political, social, economic, intellectual and moral problems in Egypt. The failure of Arab Nationalism, Arab Socialism, bureaucracy and corruption of political parties including the ruling Party, the need for an Islamic party working openly – these are among the reasons for Islamic activism in Egypt . . .[214]

The reasons according to *Newsweek* and cited in Rose El Youssef were 'the activity of the government against the Islamic activists, the prosecution and execution of their members are among the reasons of the violence of Islamists'.[215]

After Sadat, the administration of President Husni Mubarak has been marked by excess caution in policy-making and steady quiet leadership. A remarkable degree of stability was maintained during the 1980s, but the problems are still there. According to John Voll, Mubarak continues to suppress any forces that directly threaten the State, but his action tends to be focused and narrow.[216] His action is not in the style of Nasser – sweeping arrests of large numbers of people, nor that of the last months of Sadat's rule. Mubarak, however had arrested specific Islamists whilst also releasing a number of those detained by Sadat earlier in 1981 because he knew they were innocent.[217] Mubarak has also gradually injected more doses of religion into legislation, and increased the presence of religion in education, in the media and other spheres. However, according to Salame (1994: 213), 'these concessions were in areas that are sensitive from a broader moral and religious perspective, but involve applying tactics of delay at best and repression at worst in areas that are regarded as politically relevant in a stricter sense . . .'[218] Therefore, according to Ayubi,

> none of these proved effective because of the sociopolitical dimensions of the problem. It rather, inadvertently, added to the popularity of the persecuted movement. The government admitted that some of the Islamists who were arrested in 1987 were army officers. This has never been admitted before.[219]

This tactic of downplaying of reasons behind Islamist violence or of linking violence to Qutb's ideas or foreign influence will not help overcome the problem. This is simply because belief in the sovereignty of Allah over the universe, the heavens and the earth and what is in between them is fundamental to the consensus of the Muslim *ummah*. This is not a problem then. The problem is to consider there is a problem and how to deal with it. The violence of Islamic groups should be seriously studied, and the role of the Egyptian media in this conflict as a substantial factor should also be considered. In this regard, Charles Adams (1986) stated

> Despite its importance, however, and the attention that it attracts when some representative of the resurgence outlook carries out a particular dramatic action, such as the assassination of Anwar al-Sadat, Islamic resurgence is little understood by outsiders. In the press and other public communications media it is most often seen as religious fanaticism, simple anti-Westernism, reactionary longing for the past, or mindless terrorism. Most analysis evaluates it in harshly negative terms with little or no effort made to comprehend the deep discontents that have produced it or the internal logic of the stand that it upholds. However little one may like what happens, there must, after all, be compelling reasons for people to behave as they do even, and especially, when they react radically. To neglect the visions in people's minds or their motivations, as is most often the case with commentators on the resurgent movements, is to erect an inseperable barrier to understanding them. Admittedly, the opportunity to study resurgence groups at close range is rare and may require great dedication, but more and better information about these movements is a vital concern for scholars, government officials, diplomats and even the general public, if we are to respond intelligently to this important and potentially disruptive force of our time.[220]

Concluding remarks

There is no doubt that Qutb's ideas influenced not only Islamic militant groups in Egypt and the Egyptian regime, but it also had an impact on Islamic thought. Ideologically, all Islamic groups in Egypt agreed on total sovereignty (*hakimiyyah*) being to Allah alone. They call for the rule by *shari'ah*, but they have different approaches to achieve their goal. Their differences rest largely on their understanding of the concept of *jahiliyyah* and *hakimiyyah*. This also links to the intensity of feelings and its influence on the means the Islamists use to achieve their goals.

The Military Technical Academy Group is one of the *jihad* groups. This group considered *jihad* the only way to establish an alternative Islamic order in any Arab country. This group led by Salih Siriyya suggest an Islamic State by force: change from the top down in a conventional way. This is not Qutb's programme. Siriyya was not one of Qutb's followers and his group did not seek to hold Qutb's ideas or his programme. Siriyya was a member of The

Islamic Liberation Party established by Taqiyy Eddin al-Nabahani, in 1952, in Jordan. For Siriyya, Qutb's programme of preparation of the individual, and the society, and then ultimately establishing the Islamic State is good as long as the government is willing to establish the Islamic system. However, Siriyya used force and made a failed attempt to take control of the Military Technical Academy in Cairo in April 1974.

The Society of Muslims was formed by Shukri Mustafa when he was in prison during the period 1965–1970. After his release, Shukri led this group in the University of Asyut in Upper Egypt. At that time, the authorities knew Shukri Mustafa. His programme at that time was similar to Qutb's programme which is education on wider scale. The authorities confronted their programme as soon as it began to take its shape of wider scale. Shukri's group hoped to create an Islamic environment by first transforming university life, and they did prove useful in the universities. This success encouraged them to expand their plan. They went out of the university campus to work in wider society. It was a warning that the rapid expansion of the group in Upper Egypt where the inhabitants of some villages were Muslims and Christians were all happy with the Islamic group and its leaders. The authorities confronted this sort of expansion.

Consequently, the conflict between the group and the authorities began to take place. The group then was identified by the government authorities as *al-Takfir wa al-Hijrah* (excommunication and emigration). The role of the Egyptian press in the conflict between this group and the regime is significant. Shukri had written to Egyptian radio, television and to the press, seeking to publish the facts about his group but was simply ignored. This situation developed dramatically. This group abducted Shaykh al-Mahmud Husayn Dhahabi in July 1977. They declared their responsibility and their conditions for his release. The declaration of conditions, which was never published, reflects the accumulated pain and pressures of oppressed and persecuted people, and also indicates how the media and other government institutions drove them to the desperate action of killing Shaykh al-Dhahabi and thus getting killed themselves in the process.

They were duly brought to trial by Military Court and Shukri was condemned to death and executed on 22 March 1978. The Military Court also accused Al-Azhar and ignored its view in this case. Al-Azhar's view was published outside Egypt. Shukri Mustafa and his group considered al-Azhar's view an intellectual victory.

Consequently, Muhammad Abd al-Salam Faraj openly claimed *jihad* as central in the confrontation of the regime. That *jihad* which was seen as the only option available to establish the Islamic State ruled by *shari'ah* was the thesis of Faraj's book *The Missing Ordinance*. The group decided to respond to what they saw as the State's past aggression. Islamic groups thus developed their ideas in conjunction with the development of events inside Egypt and in the Middle East. He criticized the *'ulama* because, he considered that they had neglected the duty of *jihad* completely.

Faraj and his *jihad* group were influenced by the ideas of Ibn Taymiyyah, Ibn al-Qayyim, Ibn 'Abd al-Wahhab and al-Shawkani rather than by the ideas of Qutb. In their testimonies to the Military Court, *jihad* groups did not mention Qutb or the Ikhwan (Brotherhood) because they did not agree with either Qutb's programme or the methods of the Brotherhood – or indeed of any other Islamic group at that time. Their end, also like others, failed to establish the Islamic state by force.

Qutb's ideas as a factor in Islamic resurgence are quite significant, but they are one of many factors like the defeat in 1967, the Iranian revolution, corruption, oppression, repression, humiliations, the sponsored media and government style. Qutb's influence does not mean violence. His programme is educational.

Glossary

'abada	Verb perfect or past tense of to submit, to obey, to surrender
'abd and *insan*	Human being
'abid and *ibad*	Human beings
'alamiyyah	Universality
al-jahl al-ijtima'i	Social ignorance
'alim	(Plural *'ulama*) also used to refer to scientists, scholars and experts in any sphere of knowledge. *'Alim* derived from the same root of *'ilm* literally means 'those who know'
'aqidah	Creed
'aqlaniyyah	Rational
'ubudiyyah	Servitude: complete submission
'ulama	(Singular *'Alim*) scholars and experts in Islamic law and theology
'ushr/sadaqat	Charity
adab	Art or literature
afah	Contagion
ahkam	Wisest
akhtar	Most important
al-'Aql	Human intellect
al-'ulum al-bahtah	Mere sciences
al-din al-qayyim	Right religion
alhama	Inspired
al-hirfah al-barlamaniyyah	Parliamentarian craftsmen
al-hukmu	To govern, to rule, to judge
al-ishtrakiyyah al-'ilmiyyah	Scientific socialism
al-Ka'in al-insani	Human being
al-Ka'inat al-hayawaniyyah	Animal creatures, animal beings
al-Ka'inat al-maddiyyah	Material beings
al-Kawn	The universe, life and Man
al-khilafah	Caliphate
Allah	God the Creator

al-mal	Wealth
al-qawmiyyah al-'ulya	The higher nationalism
al-wahdah al-kubra	Great unity
al-wahy	Inspiration, revelation
ana fatartu al-shay'	I created the thing
ardu Allah	The Earth of God
aslama amruhu li-Allah	Surrendered his whole-self to God
awqaf	Endowments
ayah	Verse
ba'dyyah	Posteriority
badr	The place at which the first military confrontation between the Muslims and the *jahiliyyah* took place in (January 624) the second year of the *hijrah*
batil	Illegal
bayan	Explanation
bayat al-Qadi	The house of the Judge
da'awh	Callout, or lawsuit
dalal	Astray
damir	Conscience
dimuqratiyyh	Democracy
din tashri'i	Legislative religion
dustur	Constitution
fatara al-nasa 'alaiyha	The nature in which God has made mankind
fataw	Legal opinion, verdict
fatiri al-samawati wa al-ard'	The originator of the heavens and the earth
fa-uhkum	To govern, to Judge and to rule (imperative mood)
fiqh al-'ibadat	Jurisprudence of ritual laws
fiqh	Islamic jurisprudence; law
fitrah	The unchangeable constitution that Allah made innate to the universe, life and humankind
funun	Arts in general
futira 'ala shay'	Begin created with disposition to a thing
hadaynahu al-najdayn	We have shown him the two highways of life
hadith mawdu'	Hadith (saying of the Prophet); mawdu' (invented or not true)
hajj	Pilgrimage
hakama	To rule, to reign, to order, to command, to decide, to judge
hakim	Governor, arbitrator, ruler, justice, commander, judge, leader
hakimiyyah	The highest governmental and legal authority

'ibadah	Complete submission
'ibadat	Rituals (a branch of jurisprudence focusing on ritual laws)
'ilm	Science, or knowledge
'ilmaniyyah	Secularism
hakimun	Governors, arbitrators, rulers, commanders, judges, leaders
hal	Conditional or circumstantial expression, state of affair
hanif	True, orthodox
haqq	Right, true
hawa	Desires
hijrah	Emigration
hilm	Gentleness, patience, forbearing, calm
huda	Right guidance
hudan li al-muttaqin	Right guidance for those who fear God
hukm	To govern and to judge
hukman	Rule, government
idha al-sama'u infatarat	When the sky is cleft asunder
ijma'	Consensus of Islamic scholars on a point of Islamic law
ijtihad	Legal opinion through independent reasoning
ikhwan	Brethren or Muslim Brotherhood
iman	Belief
infitah	Openness
insaniyyah	Humanity, humankind
ishtrakyyah	Socialism
istakhlafa	To appoint as successor
istawa al-rajul	His manhood is firmly established
istawa	Firmly established
istibdad	Despotism, autocracy, absolutism, totalitarianism, dictatorship
ittihad ishtraki	Socialistic injustice, tyranny, persecution
jahalah	Ignorance
jahiliyyah	The condition of any place or society where Allah is not held to be the sovereign being or His law is the sole authority in human life and society
jahl	Ignorance
jama'at	Groups
jamid	Rigid, not flexible
jawhar	Essence, essential nature
jibillah	Natural or innate disposition
jihad	Struggle, holy war

jins	Demons
jinsiyyah	Nationality
jizyah	A compensation tax paid by non-Muslims citizens of an Islamic state in lieu of their service in the armed forces of the state
jubila	To have a natural deposition (tendency, inclination) for
ka'bah	The Sacred house
kafir	Disbeliever
kawniyyah	Universal
kaynunah	Being, entity
khaliqah	Natural or innate disposition
khalit/mazij	Mix
khamr	Wine
khilafah	Vicegerency
khudu'	Complete submission
khulafa'	Successors
khutima/khatama	Sealed
kufr	None-belief
ma'qul	Believable
madhahib	Schools of thought
majlis al-shura	Consultative council
mala'ikatu Allah	Angles of God
malik	King, possessor
manhaj hyatuh	Program of his life
manhaj	program
maqhur	Subdued, subjugated, conquered, compelled
masdar	Infinitive
mashi'ah	Will
mu'amalat	Interactions (a branch of jurisprudence focussing on laws other than ritual laws)
mubin	Clear, distinct, evident, obvious, unmistakable, intelligible, explicit
mujtahid	A person who is expert in *Shari'ah*
mulk	Kingdom, possessions
muqarrarat	Decisions, decrees
murakkab	Compound
mustahil	Impossible
mustakhlafah fihi	Solemnly appointed to take care of it
mutlaq	Absolute
muttaqi	Person fearing God
muttaqin	Persons fearing God
muttasilah	Connected
na'bud	to submit, to surrender (plural: first person mood or we)
naqatu Allah	She-camel of God

nass	Text
nizam al-hukm	System of government
nizam	System
nizamuna al-siyasi	Our political system
nuh	Noah
nur	Light
qablyyah	Anteriority
qada' wa qadar	Predestinations
qadar	Divine destiny, divine decree
qadiyya	Issue, case
qahir	Irresistibly supreme
qanuni	legally valid
qawm	Group of people, tribe
qayyim	Right authority above all
qiblah	Direction to which Muslims turn in praying
ra'smalyyah	Capitalism
riba	Usury, interest
rububiyyah	Lordship
ruhu Allah	Spirit of God
rusulu Allah	Messengers of God
sadaqah	Charity
sajiyyah	Natural or innate disposition
sama'u Allah	Heave of God, Sky of God
sawiyy	Upright
sawwa	Created and perfected
sawwaytahu	Created and perfected him
sha'a'ir	Religious duties
sha'b	People
shahru Allah	Month of God
shar'	Islamic law
shar'i	Islamically valid
shari'ah	Everything that Allah revealed to manage the affairs of human Life
shirk	Idolatry, polytheism, to associate partner with God
shurah	Consultation
shuyu'iyyah	Communism
sifah	Adjective, description
silm/salm/salam	Peace
siyadah	Sovereignty, sovereign authority, domination
sulalah	Linage, descent, stock, progeny, descendents
sultan	Authority
sunnah	Behaviour of the Prophet Muhammad: his sayings and deeds
surah	chapter
ta'ah	Obedience

taba'a 'ala qalbihi	Sealed on his heart
tabi'ah	Nature
tabi'atu al-insan	Nature of human being
tabi'atu al-kawn	Nature of the universe
tafahum	Mutual understanding
tafattarat al-ardu bi al-nabat	The seeds broke through the ground
tafattarat qudamahu	His feet are cleft
taghut	Tyranny, oppressor (ruler, law and system)
tahkum	To govern, to rule, to decide, to judge
takadu al-samawatu yatafattarna minhu	The heavens are about to burst
takaful ijtima'i	Social solidarity
takfir	Charging others with infidelity or atheism
taklif	Assignment, entrust, command, obligation
tasallut	To overpower, overcome, mastery, domination
tasawwur	Conception
taswiyah	Levelling, smoothing, equalization
tawhid	Oneness, unity
thabit	Constant, firm, stable, lasting, unshakable
thaqafah	Culture, literature, civilization
thawrah	Revolution
tubi'a	To have a natural disposition (propensity, tendency, inclination)
uluhiyyah	Divinity
ummah	Nation, the Muslim community
ummi	Singular of the plural *ummiyyin* and *ummiyyun*. It refers to the pre-Islamic Arabs and non-Arabs who have no Scriptures.
usuliyyah	Fundamentalism
wahy	Inspiration, revelation
waqi'iyyah	Realism, reality
watan	Homeland
wujud dawli	Internationally present; exist or being there
wujud qawmi	Nationally present; exist or being there
wujud siyasi	Political existence, political presence
ya'budun	obeying, worshipping, surrendering
yahkum	Governing, ruling, judging
yamlik	Possessing, owning, having, to appropriating
yathrib	The old name of Medina (Madinah) city in Saudi Arabia
zakah	Tax in Islam
zakat al-fitr	Tax given before the end of the fasting month of Ramadan
zakat	Tax of
zalam	Dark

Notes

Introduction

1 Smith, Cantwell (1977), *Islam in Modern History*, Princeton University Press, p. 157.
2 This group is also called 'Society of the Muslims'. See Ramadan, Abd al-'Azim, 'Fundamentalist Influence in Egypt: The Strategies of the Muslim Brotherhood and the Takfir Groups.', In Martin and Scott (eds), *Fundamentalisms and the State*, (1993), pp. 152–83, esp. 158.

1 Sovereignty (*al-Hakimiyyah*)

1 For further details, see my book *The Political Thought of Sayyid Qutb: The Theory of* Jahiliyyah, London: Routledge, chs 2, 4–7.
2 Qutb, Sayyid (1992), *Fi Zilal al-Qur'an*, Cairo: Dar al-Shuruq, vol. 3, pp. 1216–17; vol. 2, p. 1004.
3 The first edition of *Zilal* was completed in 1959, but some parts were revised in the second edition, published in 1961, see Boullata (2000), 'Sayyid Qutb's literary Appreciation of the Qur'an', in Boullata (ed.), *Literary Structures of Religious Meaning in the Qur'an*. Richmond: Surrey Curzon Press, pp. 354–71, esp. 361.
4 Qutb, *Zilal*, vol. 2, pp. 887–8; this quotation is from the revised part of *Zilal*.
5 Qutb, *Zilal*, vol. 2, pp. 888–9.
6 Kepel, Gilles (1985), *Muslim Extremism in Egypt: The Prophet and the Pharaoh*, Berkeley and Los Angeles: University of California Press, p. 47.
7 Abukhalil (1994), 'The Incoherence of Islamic Fundamentalism: Arab Islamic Thought at the End of the Twentieth Century', *Middle East Journal*, vol. 48. n. 4 (August), pp. 677–94, cf. p. 683.
8 Abukhalil, 'The Incoherence' *Middle East Journal*, vol. 48. n. 4, pp. 677–94, cf. p. 683.
9 Shepard, William (1996), 'Muhammad Sa'id al-'Ashmawi and the Application of the Shari'ah in Egypt'. *International Journal of Middle East Studies*, vol. 28, pp. 39–58, esp. p. 39.
10 Shepard, 'Muhammad Sa'id al-Ashmawi', *International Journal of Middle East Studies*, vol. 28, pp. 39–58, esp. p. 39; also see Ayubi, Nazih (1991), *Political Islam: Religion and Politics in the Arab World*, London: Routledge, p. 5.
11 Kepel, *Muslim Extremism*, pp. 61, 74, 103; Haddad, Yvonne Yazbeck (1983) 'Sayyid Qutb: Ideologue of Islamic Revival', in John Esposito (ed.), *Voice of Resurgent Islam*, Oxford University Press, pp. 67–98.

12 See Fahmi, 'Abd al-'Aziz (1963), *Hadhihi Hayati* (*This is my Life*), Cairo: Dar al-Hilal, pp. 153–8. Fahmi was born in 1870. He graduated in law in 1890, two years before his friend Ahmad Lutfi al-Sayyid (1872–1963). He then entered government service. He read European authors widely. He dabbled in politics as founder of the Constitutionalist Party. He was one of the delegation led by Sa'd Zaghlul (d. 1927) at the European conference in 1918 seeking Egyptian independence. He drafted the Egyptian Constitution of 1923, which declares Islam the religion of the State. He was the Minister of Justice who dealt with the issue of 'Ali 'Abd al-Raziq in 1925 and later wrote about it in his *This is my Life* published in 1963, Cairo: Dar al-Hilal.

13 Muhammad 'Umarah was born in 1931 in Egypt and was educated at al-Azhar. He took a Doctorate of philosophy (PhD) at Dar al-'Ulum in 1975. Currently he is professor of 'Islam and the philosophy of governance' at Cairo Universities and sometimes at Universities in Arab countries. His interests in this field can be seen through his works. He published 16 books. In addition, he published commentaries on medieval and contemporary works included all works of Rifa'ah al-Tahtawi (d. 1873), al-Afghani (d. 1897), 'Abduh (d. 1905), al-Kawakibi (d. 1902), 'Ali Mubarak (d. 1893) and Qasim Amin (d. 1908). He was awarded a few prizes among which is the first class of Literature Prize in Egypt.

14 'Umarah, Muhammad (1988), *Al-Islam wa 'Usul Al-Hukum li-'Ali 'Abd al-Raziq: Dirasah wa Watha'iq*, Beirut: al-Mu'assasah al-Arabiyyah li al-Dirasat wa al-Nashr, second edition, pp. 8–16.

15 al-Sawi, Muhammad Salah (1992), *Al-Muwajahah Bayna al-Islam wa al-'Ilmaniyyah*, Cairo: al-Afaq al-Dawliyyah li al-I'lam, pp. 32, 39.

16 For further details, see Fahmi, *Hadhihi Hayati*, pp. 153–8.

17 Kepel, *Muslim Extremism*, p. 62.

18 Haddad, 'Sayyid Qutb: Ideologue', in John Esposito, *Voice of Resurgent Islam*, pp. 67–98.

19 Abukhalil, 'The Incoherence', *Middle East Journal*, vol. 48, n. 4, pp. 677–94.

20 Mortimer, Edward (1982), *Faith and Power: The Politics of Islam*, London: Faber & Faber, p. 245.

21 'Abd al-Raziq, 'Ali, 'Islam wa Usul al-Hukm'. *al-Siasah*, 13 August 1925, cf. 'Umarah, *Al-Islam wa Usul Al-Hukum li-'Ali 'Abd al-Raziq*, pp. 62 and fn. 1, see p. 63.

22 'Abd al-Raziq, 'Ali, 'Islam wa Usul al-Hukm'. *al-Siasah*, n. 881, 1 September 1925, cf. 'Umarah, *Al-Islam wa Usul Al-Hukum li-'Ali 'Abd al-Raziq*, p. 74.

23 'Abd al-Raziq here refers to the report he has written in response to the Al-Azhar's seven comments against him. For further details and 'Ali's report, see 'Umarah, *Al-Islam wa Usul Al-Hukum li-'Ali 'Abd al-Raziq*, pp. 62–70.

24 'Umarah, *Al-Islam wa Usul Al-Hukum li-'Ali 'Abd al-Raziq*, pp. 71–2; 'Abd al-Raziq, 'Islam wa Usul al-Hukm', *al-Siasah*, n. 882, 2 September 1925; see his *Islam wa Usul al-Hukm*, pp. 35, 36, 84, 103.

25 Mustafa Abd al-Raziq was Shaykh al-Azhar in early 1920s and before 1927, see Ali, Kamal Hasan (1994), *Mashawir al-'Umr Asrar wa khafaya sab'ina 'aman min 'Umr Misr fi al-Harb wa al-Mukhabarat wa al-siyasah*, Cairo: Daral-Shuruq, first edition, p. 23; Lieutenant general Kamal Hasan Ali became Minister of defence in 1978–1980, and Prime Minister of Egypt in 1984–1985.

26 The word *khilafah* here means that there is no succession in the revelation that is that the Prophet is the chosen one, but his successor is not; the Prophet receives revelation from God, but the Prophet's successor does not receive revelation from God.

27 Fahmi, *Hadhihi Hayati*, pp. 153–4.

28 Allam, Fu'ad (1995), 'Akhtar Kutub Hasan al-Hudaybi min Ta'lif Mabahith Amn al-Dawlah'. *Rose el-Youssef*, no. 3507 (28 August), pp. 56–9.
29 Qutb was executed on 29 August 1966.
30 Takfir: branding others with *kufr* (unbelief).
31 After his release from prison, Shukri Mustafa led an Islamic group which was later labeled by the press *al-Takfir wa al-Hijrah* (practising emigration and charging others with unbelief).
32 He was one of the leading figures in the Supreme Council of the Ikhwan during al-Banna.
33 Allam, 'Akhtal Kutub Hasan'. *Rose el-Youssef*, 28 August 1995, pp. 57–8.
34 See al-Sawi, *al-Muwajaha*, p. 51.
35 Kepel, *Muslim Extremism*, p. 62.
36 Kepel, *Muslim Extremism*, p. 62.
37 See al-Hudaybi, Hasan (1987) *Du'ah la Qudah*, Cairo: Dar al-Tawzi' wa al-Nashr al-Islamiyyah, second edition, n.d., p. 43.
38 See al-Hudaybi, Hasan. *Du'ah la Qudah*, second edition, n.d., pp. 106–7.
39 Ibn Kathir, al-Hafiz Abi al-Fida' Isma'il (d. 774), *Tafsir al-Qur'an al-Azim*, Cairo: Dar al-Hadith, first edition (1988), vol. 1, p. 518; he uses words such as '*hukm*', '*tahakamu ila kitab Allah*', '*tahakamu ila hukkam al-jahiliyyah*', '*ytahakamuna ial al-taghut*', see *Tafsir*, vol. 1, pp. 518–19.
40 al-Jassas, Abu Bakr Ahmad b. 'Alial Razi (d. 980), *Ahkam al-Qur'an*, Beirut: al-Kitab al-Arabi, vol. 3, p. 181.
41 In January 1992 Shaykh al-Ghazali was one of the speakers in the debate held at the Cairo 'Book Fair', see al-Sawi, *al-Muwajahah*, pp. 49–50.
42 Al-Ghazali Muhammad (1991), 'Ihris 'Ala Qawl al-Haq walaw Kana Murra'. *Sabah el-Kheir*, no. 1828 (17 January), pp. 12–15.
43 al-Nawawi, Muhammad, 'Nizam al-Islam al-Siyasi', *al-Azhar*, December 1993, vol. 66, no. 6, pp. 878–84, esp. p. 879.
44 al-Zalabani, Rizq (1947), 'al-Siyasah al-Dusturiyyah al-Shar'iyyah: Shakl al-Hukumah wa 'Alaquatuha bi al-Ummah fi al-Islam", *al-Azhar*, vol. 18, n. 7, pp. 251–5, esp. 252; also see al-Maraghi, Abdul Aziz (1947), 'al-Tashri' al-Islami fi 'Asral-khulafa' al-Rashidin', *al-Azhar*, vol. 18, no. 7, pp. 27–31, 410–15.
45 Qur'an, 5: 44.
46 Qur'an, 5: 45.
47 Qur'an, 5: 47.
48 Qur'an, 5: 50.
49 The Imams here are the Leaders of (i) the Schools of Jurisprudence (*fiqh*), (ii) of the Hadith (sayings of the Prophet), (iii) of Tafsir (exegetes), (iv) and of Arabic Language, see Ibn Manzur, Abi al-Fadl Jamal al-Din Muhammad b-Makram al-Ifriqi al-Misri (d. 1310), *Lisan al-'Arab*, Beirut: Dar Sadr (1994), vol. 12, p. 26.
50 al-Qurtubi, Abi Abdullah Muhammad b. Ahamd al-Ansari (d. 1272), *al-Jami' Li Ahkam al-Qur'an*, Beirut: Dar Ihya' al-Turath (1985), vol. 6, p. 190.
51 al-Mawardi, Abi al-Hasan Ali Ibn Muhammad (d. 1057), *Al-Ahkam al-Sultaniyyah*, Beirut: Dar al-Fikr (1966), p. 5.
52 Al-Sawi, Muhammad Salah, *al-Muwajaha Bayna al-Islam wa al-'Ilmaniyyah*, Cairo: al-Afaq al-Dawliyyah Li al-I'lam, first edition, 1413 AH/1992 AD.
53 al-Sawi, *al-Muwajaha*, p. 36.
54 al-Sawi, *Fiqh al-Imamah al-'Uzma*, p. 25.
55 'Umarah, *Al-Islam wa Usul Al-Hukm li 'Ali 'Abd al-Raziq*, pp. 75–6.
56 'Abduh, Muhammad (d. 1905), *Tafsir Al-Manar*, Beirut: Dar al-Ma'arif, second edition, vol. 1, p. 11.

57 Muhammad al-Khidr Husayn was the Chief Editor of *Majallat al-Azhar* from the year 1930 when it was established, until 1933. He then became Shaykh al-Azhar in 1953. See Naguib, Muhammad (1955), *Egypt's Destiny*, London: Victor Collancz Ltd, p. 201; also see Husayn, Muhammad (1985), *al-Islam wa al-Hadarah al-Gharbiyyah*, Beirut: Mu'assat al-Risalah, seventh edition, p. 147.
58 al-Sawi, *Fiqh al-Imamah al-'Uzma*, p. 41.
59 *bid'ah* is commonly translated innovation. This can mislead us if we do not consider that any 'innovation' within the boundary of *shari'ah* is Islamically valid. Innovation not confirmed by the *shari'ah* is forbidden. Cf. Ibn Manzur, *Lisan*, vol. 8, p. 6. The shari'iah is not against innovation, as such, but there are rules to guide any development and renewal.
60 Mustafa Sabri, *Mawqif al-'Aql wa al-'Ilm wa al-'Alam Min Rab al-'Alamin* (the position of human intellect, knowledge and the world concerning Allah), cf. al-Sawi, *al-Muwajaha*, p. 36. Mustafa Sabri born in 1869, later became one of the committee (al-Mab'uthan) which discussed the constitution in Turkey from 1908 until 1918. He became Shaykh al-Islam in 1918. See Salamah Tawfiq (1995) 'Min Sirat Shaykh al-Islam Mustafa Sabri', *Majallat al-Azhar*, September, vol. 86, n. 4, pp. 539–43.
61 Khalid, Muhammad Khalid (1981), *al-Dawlah Fi al-Islam*, Cairo: Dar Thabit, p. 37, see pp. 39–104.
62 al-Bahiyy, Muhammad (1972), *al-Fikr al-Islami al-Hadith wa Silatihi bi al-Isti 'mar al-Gharbi*, Beirut: Dar al-Fikr (1972), sixth edition, p. 205.
63 Bakr, Abu Zayd, *Hukm al-Intima'*, pp. 72–3, cf. al-Sawi, *al-Muwajaha*, p. 35
64 *Akher Sa'a* [Cairo journal], 4 July 1990, n. 2663, pp. 12, 13, 60; also see Gad al-Haqq Ali Gad al-Haqq (1994), 'al-Uswah al-Hasanh'. *Al-Azhar*, August–September, vol. 67, Part III, pp. 280–2.
65 The United Arab Republic [Egypt and Syria], *Mawsu'at Gamal 'Abd al-Nasser al-Fiqhiyyah*, Cario: The Supreme Council of Islamic Affairs, vol. 1, p. 16, see pp. 17–19.
66 Ni'mah, Fu'ad, *Mulakhkhas Qawa'id al-Lughah al-'Arabiyyah (Summary of Arabic Grammar)*, Cairo: Nahdat Misr, fifteenth edition, n.d. vol. 1, p. 129; the first edition was in May (1973).
67 Sources of Arabic are saying: (a) The infinitive (*masdar*) of the trilateral verb '*hakama*' is '*hukm*', see Ni'mah, Fu'ad, *Mulakhkhas Qawa'id al-Lughah al-'Arabiyyah*, vol. 2, p. 142. (b) There is difference between verbal noun (*ism al-fi'l*) and infinitive (*masdar*) in Arabic. I have dealt with this grammatical matter, in relation to *jahiliyyah*, in my book *The Political Thought of Sayyid Qutb, The Theory of Jahiliyyah*, London: Routledge, see chapter 2. (c) The rhythm of the word *hakimiyyah* is the same rhythm of the word *jahiliyyah*. (d) As previously discussed for the word *jahiliyyah*, the word *hakimiyyah* can function as verbal noun and infinitive (*masdar*), but not a regular *masdar*. (e) The difference between the two words is that the Arabs derived from the word *jahiliyyah* the word *jahla'*, but there is no report of any derivation from the word *hakimiyyah*. (f) Translating the Arabic word '*masdar*' into English = both infinitive and verbal noun. (g) Translating the Arabic word '*ism fi'l*' into English = both infinitive and verbal noun. (h) The English translation, then, does not show the difference between the Arabic words '*masdar*' and '*ism al-fi'l*'. (i) The matter of considering *hakimiyyah* as a verbal noun (*Ism fi'l*) or infinitive (*masdar*) is a matter English, not Arabic grammar as such.
68 Wright W. L. L. D (1979), *A Grammar of the Arabic Language*, Cambridge: Cambridge University Press, third edition, p. 165.
69 Wright, *Grammar of Arabic*, pp. 165–6.

70 Ibn Durayd, Abi Bakr Muhammad b. al-Hasan (d. 933), *Kitab Jamharat al-Lughah*, Beirut: Dar al-'Ilm li al-Malayin, first edition (1978), vol. 1, p. 456; Ibn Manzur, *Lisan*, vol. 12, pp. 141–5; Rida Ahmad (1958), *Mu'jam Matn al-Lughah*, Beirut: Dar Maktabat al-Hayah, vol. 2, pp. 139–40; Al-Bustani, Abdullah (1927) *al-Bustan*, Beirut: al-Mataba 'ah al-Amrikiyyah, vol. 1, pp. 559–60.
71 Lane, Edward William (1955), *Arabic–English Lexicon*, Cambridge: Cambridge University Press, Book 1, part 2, p. 618.
72 Ibn Manzur, *Lisan*, pp. 140–5.
73 For further details see Wright, *Grammar of Arabic*, pp. 116, 140–1.
74 Ba'albaki, Rohi (1996), *al-Mawrid: Arabic–English Dictionary*, p. 447.
75 Martin Hinds and El-Said Badawi (1986), *A Dictionary of Egyptian Arabic (Arabic–English)*, Beirut: Librairie Du Liban, p. 218
76 Rida, Ahmad (1958), *Mu'jam Matn al-Lughah*, Beirut: Dar Maktabat al-Hayah, vol. 3, p. 140; also see Lane, *Arabic–English Lexicon*, Book 1, part 2, p. 618.
77 Wehr, Hans (1979), *A Dictionary of Modern Written Arabic*, Wiesbaden: Otto Harrassowitz, p. 230.
78 Qutb, *Zilal*, vol. 1, p. 295; vol. 3, p. 1219; cf. Ibn Taymiyah Taqiyy al-Din Ahmad, *al-'Ubudiyyah*, Beirut: Dar al-Kitab al-Arabi, first edition, pp. 20–4; see the Prophet's letter to Najran, in al-Ya'qubi Ahamd b. Isma'il (1980) *al-ya'qubi, Tarikh*, Beirut: Dar Beirut li al-Taba'ah wa al-Nashr, vol. 2, p. 81.
79 Qutb, *Zilal*, vol. 4, pp. 2019–20; Al *'Adalah al-Ijtima 'iyyah fi al-Islam*, Cairo: Dar al-Shuruq (1993), p. 79. 'Abd Rabbuh Sayyid Abd al-Hafiz (1980), *al-Thawrah al-Ijtima'iyyah fi al-Islam*, Cairo: Daral-Kitab al-Misry, p. 18; for critical analysis about Qutb's idea of Islam as a 'system', see Shepard, E. William, 'Islam as a System in the Later Writings of Sayyid Qutb', *Middle Eastern Studies*, 25/1 (January 1989): 31–50.
80 *Al-Mukhtar al-Sahah* (Arabic Dictionary), p. 265; al-Qurtubi, *al-Jami'*, vol. 16, pp. 10, 163; Muhammad Sallam, *Tarikh al-Tashri' al-Islami*, Beirut: Dar al-'llm, n.d., p. 11 'Abduh, Muhammad, *Tafsir*, vol. 2, p. 257; Awdah, Abd al-Qadir (1985), *Islam Bayna Jahl Abna'ih wa 'AJz 'Ulama'ih*. Beirut: Mu'assat al-Risalh, sixth edition, pp. 14–23.
81 Qutb, *'Adalah*, p. 197.
82 Weeramantry, Hidayatullah and Grand Shaykh of al-Azhar (1996), *Islamic Jurisprudence: An International Perspective*. United States: Macmillan Press, p. 1. As for the authors: Weeramantry is Professor of Law, Monash University – Australia. Currently, he is a Chief Judge at the International Court in Swaziland. He also was the chief Judge and Vice-President of the Republic of India. As to the Grand Shaykh, he is the Egyptian professor Sayyid Tantawi, who is currently Shaykh al-Azhar.
83 'Abd al-Baqi, Muhammad Fu'ad, (1992), *al-Mu'jam al-Mufahras li-Alfaz al-Qur'an al Karim*, Beirut: Dar al-Wafa', first edition. pp. 269–73.
84 al-Maraghi, al-Tashri' al-Islami, *Majallat al-Azhar*, vol. 18, n. 7, pp. 27–31, 410–15, esp. 410.
85 al-Qurtubi, *al-Jami'*, vol. 5, p. 376.
86 See Yusuf 'Ali, *The Holy Qur'an English Translation*, p. 1377, esp. verse (38: 26).
87 See Dawood, N. J. (1999), *The Koran*. England: Penguin Books, p. 319.
88 al-Qurtubi, *al-Jami'*, vol. 15, p. 189, see pp. 190–1 for further details of *hukm*.
89 Qur'an, 5: 44.
90 Qur'an, 5: 45.
91 Qur'an, 5: 47.
92 Qutb, *Zilal*, vol. 3, p. 1194.
93 Qutb, *Zilal*, vol. 5, p. 2807.

94 Qutb, *Zilal*, vol. 5, p. 2548.
95 Qutb, *Zilal*, vol. 2, p. 1110.
96 Qutb, *Zilal*, vol. 4, p. 2297; Qur'an, 18: 57; Qutb, *Zilal*, vol. 2, p. 1111.
97 Qutb, *Zilal*, vol. 2, pp. 695–6, see pp. 688, 690.
98 Translation was supervised by Muhammad Zayid and 'Umar Farrukh. Muhammad Zayid, professor at the American University of Beirut, revised the Penguin Classic translation of N. J. Dawood in 1980. Umar Farrukh, appointed professor of Islamic philosophy at the Islamic Maqasid School and member of the Islamic Research Association of Bombay. The first edition was published in 1980 with the permission of the Supreme Sunni and Sh'i Council of Lebanon, see, pp. 3–9 of this edition and see the translation of *surah* 67: 1, p. 423.
99 Qur'an, *Mushaf al-Madinah al-Nabawiyah*, Kingdom of Saudi Arabia (1410 AH) number 10278.
100 George, Sale (1825), *The Qur'an*, London: Thomas Tegg, esp. trans. of the title of *surah* 67
101 Pickthall, Marmaduke, *The Meaning of The Glorious Qur'an: Text and Explanatory Translation*, Delhi: Kutub Kkana, second edition, n.d., p. 642.
102 Ibn Manzur, *Lisan*, vol. 10, pp. 492–4.
103 Muhammad, Sulaymi al-Shakh (1998), *A Dictionary of Islamic Terms*, Beirut: Dar al-Fikr, p. 193; Qur'an, 114: 1–3.
104 Ibn Manzur, *Lisan*, vol. 10, pp. 491–7.
105 Qur'an, 3: 26.
106 Qutb, *Zilal*, vol. 2, p. 898.
107 See Kepel, *Muslim Extremism*, p. 62; Shepard (1996), *Sayyid Qutb and Islamic Activism: A Translation and Critical Analysis of Social Justice in Islam*, Leiden: E.J. Brill, p. xxv, p. 28, para. 13–14 ff.; Haddad, 'Sayyid Qutb: Ideologue', in John Esposito, *Voice of Resurgent Islam*, pp. 67–98; Abukhalil, 'The Incoherence', *Middle East Journal*, vol. 48, n. 4, pp. 677–94; Mortimer, Edward (1982), *Faith and Power: The Politics of Islam*, London: Faber & Faber, p. 245.
108 For the development of the development of Qutb's ideas see my book *The Political Thought of Sayyid Qutb, The Theory of Jahiliyyah*, London: Routledge, see chs 4, 5 and 7.
109 See Hardie's trans., p. 279; Shepard's trans., p. 351 para. 9; compare with chapter 'Shari'ah Kawniyyah' in Qutb's last book *Ma'alim*.
110 Qutb *'Adalah*, p. 24; Hardie's trans., p. 22; Shepard's trans., p. 31, para. 22.
111 Qutb, *'Adalah*, p. 25, Hardie's trans., p. 23, Shepard's trans., p. 32, para. 29.
112 See Qutb (1993), *al-Salam al-'Alami wa al-Islam*. Cairo: Dar al-Shuruq, pp. 13–14.
113 More details in Shepard, *Sayyid Qutb and Islamic Activism*, p. xxv, p. 28, para. 13–14 ff.
114 Qutb, *al-Shati' al-Majhul*, pp. 3–15, 19.
115 Sayyid Qutb (1981), *Kutub wa Shakhsiyat*, Cairo: Dar al-Shuruq, pp. 90–7; *Dirasat Islamiyyah*, Cairo: Dar al-Shuruq, pp. 149–50; *Fi al-Tarikh Fikrah wa Minhae*, Cairo: Dar al-Shuruq pp. 11–14, 17–19; *al-'Alam al-'Arabi* (Journal) vol. 1, n. 4, July (1947), p. 53.
116 In 1991, Egypt's newspapers announced the death of Yahya Haqqi, but they found him still living in Cairo. See *Sabah el-Kheir*: Thursday, 13 June 1991, n. 1849, pp. 48–50.
117 Qutb, *Mustaqbal al-Thaqafah*, pp. 11, 28, 134.
118 Sayyid Qutb (1995), *al-Taswir al-Fanni fi al-Qur'an*, Cairo: Dar al-Shuruq pp. 122–3, also see the first three lines, p. 124.
119 Sayyid Qutb (1993), *Mashahid, al-Qiyamah fi al-Qur'an*, Cairo: Dar al-Shuruq, eleventh edition, p. 114.

120 Qutb, *Mashahid*, p. 88, also pp. 51, 54, 91–2, 234–5, 237–9.
121 Qutb, *'Adalah*, p. 33, Hardie's trans., p. 32; Shepard's trans., p. 43, para. 14–16 ff.; also see *'Adalah*, pp. 23, 25, Hardie's trans., pp. 22–3; Shepard's trans., p. 25 para. 6, p. 26 para. 10, 28 para. 13 all with ff.
122 Qutb, *'Adalah*, p. 20; Hardie's trans., p. 18; Shepard's trans., p. 25, para. 6.
123 Qutb, *'Adalah*, p. 26; Hardie's trans., p. 23; Shepard's trans., p. 33, para. 34–5.
124 Qutb, *'Adalah*, p. 25, Hardie's trans., p. 23; Shepard's trans., p. 32, para. 28.
125 Qutb, *'Adalah*, p. 25; Hardie's trans., p. 22, Shepard's trans., p. 31, para. 24.
126 Qutb, *'Adalah*, p. 21; Hardie's trans., pp. 18–19, Shepard's trans., pp. 30–1 para. 19, 22–5.
127 Qutb, *Zilal*, vol. 4, p. 2373, see p. 2374.
128 Qutb, *Zilal*, vol. 1, p. 556; *'Adalah*, p. 23.
129 For further details, see Qutb (1995), *Khasa'is al-Tasawwur al-Islami wa Muqawwimatuh*, Cairo: Dar al-Shuruq, thirteenth edition, p. 75; see pp. 76, 79–80.
130 Qutb, *Zilal*, vol. 1, p. 556; *'Adalah*, p. 23.
131 Qutb, *Zilal*, vol. 1, p. 349; vol. 4, p. 1939; vol. 5, p. 3090; vol. 6, pp. 3360–7.
132 Qutb, *Zilal*, vol. 2, p. 888.
133 Qutb, *Zilal*, vol. 3, p. 1217.
134 Qutb, *'Adalah*, p. 197.
135 'Abduh, Muhammad, *Risalat al-Tawhid*. Cairo: Mataba'at 'Ali Subayh (1956), p. 41.
136 See Qur'an, 6: 61–2.
137 See Qur'an, 5: 17. For further texts that Qutb uses to elucidate sovereignty, see Qur'an, 6: 102; 25: 2; 6: 12; 25: 2; 35: 3; 29: 60; 11: 6; 35: 41; 30: 25; 36: 12; 6: 65; 646; 41: 11; 30: 25–6; 16: 49; 17: 44.
138 'Abduh, Muhammad, *Risalat al-Tawhid*, p. 62.
139 Qutb, *Khasa'is*, pp. 194–5.
140 Qutb, *Khasa'is*, p. 197.
141 Qutb, *Khasa'is*, p. 200.
142 For further details, see Qutb, *Zilal*, vol. 2, pp. 888–91.
143 Qutb', *'Adalah*, p. 26; Hardie's trans., p. 23; Shepard's trans., p. 33, para. 33.
144 Qutb, *'Adalah*, p. 33; Shepard, *Sayyid Qutb and Islamic Activism*, p. 43, para. 14.
145 Qutb, *'Adalah*, p. 35; Shepard, *Sayyid Qutb and Islamic Activism*, p. 45, para. 26 and ff.
146 Qutb, *'Adalah*, p. 25; Hardie's trans., p. 22; Shepard's trans., p. 31, para. 24; also for *'ubudiyyah, uluhiyyah, hakimiyyah*, see Shepard, p. xxv and fn. 21, p. xxvi.
147 Qutb, *'Adalah*, p. 33; Hardie's trans., p. 32; Shepard's trans., p. 43, para. 14.
148 Qutb, *'Adalah*, p. 182; Hardie's trans., p. 227; Shepard's trans., p. 320 para. 1.
149 See Qutb's introduction to al-Nadawi's (1984) book, *Madha Khasira al-'Alam, bi-Inhitat al-Muslimin*, Beirut: Dar al Kitab al-Arabi, pp. 12–16, esp. p. 13.
150 Qutb, *Rasmaliyyah*, p. 59.
151 'Abduh, Muhammad, *Risalat al-Tawhid*, p. 62.
152 Qutb, *Rasmaliyyah*, p. 57; also see 'Abduh, *Risalat al-Tawhid*, p. 62.
153 Qutb, *Nahwa Mujtama' Islami*, p. 142, see p. 143 and its fn.
154 Qutb *al-Salam al-'Alami*, pp. 15–17 the Qur'anic texts can be seen in Qutb's text.
155 Qutb, *'Adalah*, p. 80.
156 Qutb, *Zilal*, vol. 4, p. 2441.
157 Qutb, *Zilal*, vol. 4, p. 1852.
158 Qutb, *Zilal*, vol. 6, p. 3362.
159 Qutb, *Zilal*, vol. 5, p. 3093.

160 Qutb, *Zilal*, vol. 5, p. 3094.
161 Qutb, *Zilal*, vol. 6, pp. 3637–40.
162 Qutb, *Zilal*, vol. 6, p. 3643.
163 World Book Encyclopedia, Chicago, IL: A Scott Fetzer Company, vol. 18, p. 689, also *World Book Dictionary*, p. 2001.
164 Schacht, J. and Bosworth, C. E. (1974), *The Legacy of Islam*, second edition, Oxford: Oxford University Press, p. 159.
165 Martin, Seymour Lipset (1960), *Political Man: The Social Bases of Politics*, London: Heinemann, pp. 22–3.
166 George H. Sabine (1951), *A History of Political Theory*, New York: Holt, pp. 405–6.
167 George H. Sabine (1951), *A History of Political Theory*, pp. 408–11.
168 Rousseau (1968), *The Social Contract*, trans. Maurice Cranston, London: Penguin Books, p. 27.
169 George H. Sabine (1951), *A History of Political Theory*, pp. 468–70.
170 George H. Sabine (1951), *A History of Political Theory*, pp. 374–85.
171 Rousseau, *The Social Contract*, pp. 27–30.
172 Austin, J. (1873), *Lectures on Jurisprudence*, London: Murray, vol. 1, p. 227.
173 For further details, see Rousseau, *The Social Contract*, p. 84.
174 Qutb, *Zilal*, vol. 3, p. 1149; vol. 1, p. 210.
175 Qutb, *Zilal*, vol. 4, pp. 2477–8.
176 Qutb, *Zilal*, vol. 4, p. 2477.
177 Qutb, *Zilal*, vol. 4, p. 2477.
178 Qutb, *Zilal*, vol. 1, p. 384.
179 Qutb, *'Adalah*, p. 78; see Qur'an, 3: 19; 3: 83; 9: 33.
180 Qutb, *Zilal*, vol. 1, p. 132; vol. 2, pp. 888–91; *'Adalah*, pp. 32, 78; *Ra'smaliyyah*, pp. 122–3.
181 Qutb, *'Adalah*, p. 75; *Zilal*, vol. 3, p. 1434; vol. 4, p. 2019–20.
182 Qutb, *'Adalah*, pp. 76, 80; *Zilal*, vol. 1, p. 406; vol. 2, pp. 1004–15; vol. 3, pp. 1194, 1211, 1216–17, 1259, 1266.
183 Qutb, *Zilal*, vol. 1, p. 501; vol. 2, p. 3165.
184 Qutb, *al-Salam al-'Alami*, pp. 122–3; *Ra'smaliyyah*, p. 72.
185 Qutb, *Zilal*, vol. 5, p. 3165; al-Nawawi, 'Nizam al-Islam al-Siyasi', *al-Azhar*, 1993, vol. 66, n. 6, pp. 878–84.
186 The Companions called the Prophet 'president', see Ibn Kathir, *al-Bidayah*, vol. 2, p. 344.
187 Qutb, *Nahwa Mujtama' Islami*, p. 141; *'Adalah*, p. 83.
188 Qutb, *Zilal*, vol. 4, p. 2009; *al-Salam al-'Alami*, p. 122.
189 Qutb, *al-Salam*, p. 123.
190 Qutb, *Zilal*, vol. 2, p. 891; also see *Hadha al-Din*, p. 21.
191 Qutb, *Ma'alim*, pp. 10, 26; *Zilal*, vol. 2, p. 10823.
192 Qutb, *Zilal*, vol. 1, p. 211; vol. 2, pp. 891, 904–5, 1083; vol. 4, p. 1991; *'Adalah*, pp. 75–6, 82, 198; *al-Salam al-'Alami*, pp. 124–5; *Mujtama' Islami*, p. 63.
193 Dicey, A. Venn (1941), *Introduction to the Study of Law of The Constitution*, London: Macmillan, p. 23.
194 Strong, Charles Frederick (1963), *Modern Political Constitution: An Introduction to the Comparative Study of their History and Existing Form*. London: Sidgwick & Jackson, p. 10.
195 al-Mawardi, *al-Ahkam al-Sultaniyyah*, pp. 10–12; Qutb, *Zilal*, vol. 1, pp. 248–9; vol. 2, pp. 685–7; *'Adalah*, pp. 80–1.
196 Qutb, *Mujtama' Islami*, p. 151.
197 al-Zalabani, 'Siyasah Dusturiyyah' , *al-Azhar* ,1947, vol. 18, n. 7, pp. 130–6, cf. p. 130.

198 Khalifa, 'Abd al-Hakim (1961), *Islamic Ideology*. Lahore: Institute of Islamic Culture, p. 201.
199 Siddiqi, 'Abdul Hamid (1981), *Theocracy and Islamic System*. Lahore: Kazi Publications, p. 8.
200 Siddiqi, 'Abdul Hamid, *Theocracy and Islamic System*, p. 11.
201 Siddiqi, 'Abdul Hamid, *Theocracy and Islamic System*, p. 23.
202 Qutb, *'Adalah*, p. 82; Shepard, *Sayyid Qutb and Islamic Activism*, pp. 114–15.
203 'Abdul al-Hakim (1961), *Islamic Ideology*, p. 207.
204 The leader of the Islamic State can be called president. To refer to the Prophet, the leader of Islamic State, the companions used the term president. See, Ibn Kathir's, *al-Bidayah*, vol. 2, p. 344, account concerning Expedition of Ta'if.
205 Qutb, *al-Salam*, p. 122; *'Adalah*, p. 82; Shepard, *Sayyid Qutb and Islamic Activism*, pp. 114–15.
206 Qutb, *'Adalah*, pp. 14–15, 82; *al-Salam*, p. 123.
207 Qutb, *'Adalah*, p. 82.
208 Qutb, *Zilal*, vol. 2, pp. 690, 751–3; *Dirasat Islamiyyah*, pp. 187–212.
209 Qutb *'Adalah*, trans. by Hardie *'Social Justice in Islam'*, p. 93.
210 Qutb *'Adalah*, trans. by Hardie *'Social Justice in Islam'*, p. 94.
211 Qutb *'Adalah*, trans. by Hardie *'Social Justice in Islam'*, p. 95.
212 Qutb, *al-Salam al-'Alami*, p. 124, for further details, see pp. 122–6.
213 For the particulars of this study, Qutb's view on this matter as in the first edition of *Social Justice* (1949) is mentioned in the text and this also was based on Hardie's translation. For cross-reference, see Shepard's translation of the last edition of *Social Justice* (1964: two years before Qutb's death), Shepard, *Sayyid Qutb and Islamic Activism*, p. 112, para. 31, pp. 113–14, para. 36.
214 For these three items, see Qutb *'Adalah*, trans. by Hardie *'Social Justice in Islam'*, pp. 95–96.
215 Qutb, *'Adalah*, p. 81; Hardie's trans., pp. 94–5; see Shepard's trans., pp. 114–15.
216 'Awdah, 'Abd al-Qadir, *al-Islam bayna Jahl Abna'ih wa 'Ajz 'Ulama'ih*, n.d. p. 37, see 24–5.
217 Qutb *'Adalah*, trans. by Hardie *'Social Justice in Islam'*, p. 95.
218 al-Mawardi, *Al-Ahkam al-Sultaniyyah*, pp. 10, 30–1.
219 See Qutb's testimony to the Court on 19 December (1965), cf. Jawhar, Sami (1977), *al-Mawta Yatakallamun*, Cairo: al-Maktab at Misri al-Hadith, second edition, pp. 111–46, esp. p. 114.
220 Qutb *'Adalah*, trans. by Hardie *'Social Justice in Islam'*, p. 96.
221 Qutb, *al-Salam al-'Alami*, p. 124.
222 Qutb, *Zilal*, vol. 4, p. 1990.
223 Green V. H. H. (1956), *The Hanoverians 1714–1815*. London: Edward Arnold Publisher Ltd., p. 14, also see pp. 15–18. King James I was the first Stuart king of England. He became James VI of Scotland in 1567, and King James I of England in 1603, and ruled both England and Scotland until his death.
224 Qutb, *Zilal*, vol. 2, pp. 692, 696; vol. 4, p. 1990; *al-Salam*, p. 124.
225 Qutb, *Zilal*, vol. 2, pp. 693, 695; vol. 3, pp. 1195, 1217.
226 Qutb, *al-Islam wa al-Ra'smalyyah*, pp. 69–72; *Zilal*, vol. 2, p. 755.
227 Qutb, *al-Islam wa al-Ra'smalyyah*, p. 72; *'Adalah*, pp. 14–19, 82.
228 Qutb, *'Adalah*, p. 76; also see *Mujtama' Islami*, p. 88.
229 Qutb, *Zilal*, vol. 2, p. 1083–4; *'Adalah*, pp. 76–8, 198.
230 Qutb, *'Adalah*, p. 197, Shepard's trans., pp. 297–8, para. 140–1.
231 Qutb, *Zilal*, vol. 4, pp. 2008–11, for international relations, see vol. 3, pp. 1538–47, 1558.

232 For further details on how the Shari'ah protects the ruler and the ruled in the Islamic state, see, Weeramantry, H. and Grand Shaykh of al-Azhar (1996), *Islamic Jurisprudence: An International Perspective*. United States: Macmillan Press, that is chapter titled 'Islam and Human Rights'; 'Abd Rabbuh, *al-Thawrah*, pp. 72–116; 'Abdul al-Hakim (1961), *Islamic Ideology*. Lahore: Institute of Islamic Culture, pp. 205–8; Brohi, K. Allahbukhsh, 'Human Rights and Duties in Islam,' in *Islam an Contemporary Society*. London and New York: Longman (1982), pp. 231–52; David Pearl (1987), *A Textbook on Muslim Personal Law*. London: Croom Helm, second edition, pp. 41–57, 77–84, 100–20; Rahman, Fazlur (1966), 'The Status of the Individual in Islam', *Islamic Studies*, vol. 5, December (1966), n. 4, pp. 319–28; Rahman, Fazlur (1980), *Islam: Ideology and The Way of Life*. Malaysia: Noordeen, pp. 375–409.
233 Qutb, *al-Salam*, pp. 126–7.
234 Qutb, *al-Salam*, pp. 126, 130, 138, 142, 159.
235 Qutb, *al-Salam*, pp. 132–8 have further details and Qur'anic texts of this summary.
236 Qutb, *al-Salam*, p. 139, see pp. 140–59; see details in *'Adalah*, pp. 44–62, 94–5.
237 Qutb, *al-Salam*, p. 143, see pp. 144–60, details in *'Adalah*, pp. 83–6; *Zilal*, 6, pp. 3524–5.
238 Qutb, *'Adalah*, p. 83; Hardie's trans. p. 96; see Shepard's trans. p. 117, para. 46.
239 Qutb, *'Adalah*, p. 84; Hardie's trans. p. 97; see Shepard's trans. p. 118, para. 49.
240 'Abd Rabbuh, *al-Thawrah*, pp. 94–9.
241 Qutb, *Mujtama' Islami*, p. 65; also see this notion in *Zilal*, vol. 2, pp. 835–9.
242 Qutb, *Zilal*, vol. 2, pp. 840–1, 849; vol. 3, p. 1216; vol. 4, pp. 2006–10.
243 Qutb, *Mujtama' Islami*, p. 50.
244 Qutb, *Zilal*, vol. 2, p. 849; also see *Mujtama' Islami*, pp. 50–1.
245 Qutb, *Mujtama'*, pp. 51–2; *Zilal*, vol. 2, pp. 849, 988, 1010.
246 Qutb, *Zilal*, vol. 2, p. 849; vol. 4, pp. 2009–11; *Nahwa Mujtama' Islami*, pp. 50–1.
247 Qutb, *Mujtama'*, p. 52.
248 Qutb, *Mujtama'*, p. 56.
249 Qutb, *Mujtama'*, p. 57.
250 Qutb, *Mujtama'*, p. 5; *al-Salam*, pp. 163–5.
251 Qutb, *Zilal*, vol. 4, pp. 2009–10.
252 Qutb, *Zilal*, vol. 1, pp. 132, 211; vol. 2, pp. 89, 904.
253 Qutb, *Ra'smalyyah*, p. 67.
254 See Shepard, *Sayyid Qutb and Islamic Activism*, p. xxiv.
255 Qutb, *'Adalah*, p. 196, Hardie's trans. p. 248, Shepard's trans. p. 295, para. 102–3.
256 Qutb, *'Adalah*, p. 196, Shepard's trans. p. 296, para. 105, see this para. also on p. 328.
257 Qutb *Zilal*, vol. 2, p. 1011, for further details of this matter, see pp. 1009–13.
258 See Hardie's trans. '*Social Justice in Islam*', p. 227.
259 See Hardie's trans. '*Social Justice in Islam*', p. 228.
260 Qutb, *'Adalah*, p. 183; Shepard (1996), *Sayyid Qutb and Islamic Activism*, p. 278, para. 34.
261 For the earlier editions, see Shepard, *Sayyid Qutb and Islamic Activism*, p. 321, para. 3; for the last edition, see p. 320, para. 319.
262 Qutb, *Zilal*, vol. 2, pp. 685–6, 930, 1011, for further details of this matter, see pp. 1009–13.
263 Qutb, *Ma'alim*, p. 8.
264 See Court report on December 19, 1965, cf. Jawhar, *al-Mawta Yatakallamun* pp. 111–46.
265 Shepard, *Sayyid Qutb and Islamic Activism*, p. 277, para. 1, 31–2.

266 Shepard, *Sayyid Qutb and Islamic Activism*, p. xxviii; This passage of the early 'editions' is also found in the last edition. See Shepard, *Sayyid Qutb and Islamic Activism*, p. 8, para. 28; similar passage is also found in his last book *Ma'alim*, p. 8.
267 I should say individuals cannot practice complete Islam in a society based itself on non-Islamic code. But, in Qutb's view, there is only 'Islam', which is a complete system of life. Thus, phrases such as complete and incomplete Islam have no room in Qutb's thinking on the subject. For him there is only Islam or *jahiliyyah*. The word Islam then does not require the word complete, see Shepard's trans. of *Social Justice*, p. 320, para. 1; for the last edition, see Shepard, p. 277, para. 1.
268 Shepard, *Sayyid Qutb and Islamic Activism*, p. 321, para. 5.
269 Qutb, 'Hubal'. *Lahn al-Kifah*, pp. 13–14.
270 Shepard, *Sayyid Qutb and Islamic Activism*, p. xxviii; also see, p. 8, para. 28; for similar passage, see Qutb, *Ma'alim*, p. 8.
271 See *Zilal*, vol. 1, p. 291; vol. 6, pp. 3917–18.
272 Qutb, *Zilal*, vol. 6, pp. 3367, 3898–9; vol. 4, pp. 2144, 2300–2.
273 See Qutb, *Dirasat Islamiyyah*, p. 86.
274 See Qutb, *'Adalah*, p. 11; Hardie's trans., p. 8; Shepard's trans., pp. xxviii, 8, para. 28.
275 Shepard's trans., p. xxviii; also see, p. 8, para. 28; similar passage in *Ma'alim*, p. 8.
276 Sagiv, David (1995), *Fundamentalism and Intellectuals in Egypt*, London: Frank Cass, p. 24.
277 Qutb, *'Adalah*, p. 13; Shepard's trans., p. 21, para. 34; Hardie's trans., p. 9.
278 Qutb, *Salam 'Alami*, pp. 44–5.
279 Qutb, *'Adalah*, p. 31; Shepard's trans., p. 39, para. 1.
280 Qutb, *'Adalah*, p. 11; Shepard's trans., p. 8 , para. 28; Hardie's trans., p. 8.
281 Qur'an, 5: 44.
282 Shepard's trans., p. 321, para. 5 . He notes, 'edition 5 omits: "for we have institutions based on usury . . . and *Zakat* is not collected and of course not spent."' But he also noted that this passage is in editions 1–4 and 6; for this passage in the first edition see Hardie's trans., p. 227. Also, Qutb discussed usury and *Zakat* in all editions. For *zakat* in editions 1–5, see Shepard's trans. pp. 338–9, para. 273, 275–6, 280–1. In the last edition, see Shepard, p. 140, para. 60, p. 162.
283 Shepard, *Sayyid Qutb and Islamic Activism*, p. 320, para. 1.
284 Shepard, *Sayyid Qutb and Islamic Activism*, pp. 320–1, para. 2.
285 Shepard, *Sayyid Qutb and Islamic Activism*, p. 277, para. 1, 31–2.
286 Qur'an, 12: 40; 5: 49; 5: 45; 4: 65; 4: 59.
287 Qutb, *'Adalah*, pp. 182–3; Shepard's trans., pp. 277–9, para. 33–42 including the para. on Qur'anic texts which are not mentioned here.
288 Qutb, *Ma'alim*, p. 116.
289 Qutb, *Ma'alim*, p. 8; for similar point, see Qutb, *Zilal*, vol. 2, pp. 685–6.

2 Servitude (*al-'Ubudiyyah*)

1 Kepel, *Muslim Extremism*, pp. 48–9.
2 Ibn Manzur, *Lisan*, vol. 3, pp. 270–9; also see Ni'mah, Fu'ad, *Mulakhkhas Qawa'id al-Lughah al-'Arabiyyah*. Cairo: Nahdat Misr, fifteenth edition, n.d., part 2, p. 173 (the first edition was in 1973).
3 Ibn Manzur, *Lisan*, vol. 3, p. 270.
4 Ibn Manzur, *Lisan*, vol. 3, p. 270.
5 Ibn Taymiyyah (1987), *al-'ubudiyyah*, pp. 24–5.
6 Ibn Manzur, *Lisan*, vol. 3, p. 272.
7 Al-Razi, *Mukhtar al-Sahhah*, pp. 407–8.

8 Ibn Taymiyyah, *al-'ubudiyyah*, p. 9.
9 Qur'an, 4: 1; 20: 14.
10 al-Hudaybi, *Du'ah la Qudah*, second edition, n.d., p. 29; In the previous chapter, I argued on the authorship of this book.
11 Qutb, *Zilal*, vol. 4, p. 1991.
12 Ibn Kathir, *Tafsir*, vol. 2, p. 479; also see al-Qurtubi, *al-Jami'*, vol. 9, p. 192; vol. 13, p. 219.
13 Qur'an, 5: 56.
14 Al-Qurtubi, *al-Jami'*, vol. 17, p. 56; Ibn Taymiyyah, *al-'ubudiyyah*, p. 20; Ibn Kathir, *Tafsir*, vol. 4, p. 238; Al-'Asqalani, al-Hafiz b. Hajar, (1987), *Fath al-Bari li sharh sahih al-Bukhari*. Cairo: Dar al-Rayyan li al-Turath, vol. 8, pp. 465–6.
15 Qutb, *Zilal*, vol. 1, pp. 292–3.
16 Al-Qurtubi, *al-Jami'*, vol. 15, p. 243.
17 Al-Qurtubi, *al-Jami'*, vol. 15, pp. 242–4.
18 Al-Qurtubi, *al-Jami'*, vol. 20, pp. 225–8.
19 For these derivations see Wright, *Grammar of Arabic*, pp. 110–12.
20 Ibn Taymiyyah, *al-'ubudiyyah*, p. 74.
21 al-Qurtubi, *al-Jami'*, vol. 1, p. 145; also Ibn Manzur, *Lisan*, vol. 3, p. 272.
22 al-Qurtubi, *al-Jami'*, vol. 17, p. 55, see 56.
23 For a number of hadith on this matter, see Ibn Manzur, *Lisan*, vol. 3, pp. 271–8.
24 Safwat, Hasan Lutfi, Muhammad Abd Al-Azim Ali and Jalal Yahya Kamil (1994), 'Tatbiq al-Shari'ah al-Islamiyyah bayna al-Haqiqah wa Shi'arat al-Fitnah'. *Al-Azhar*, November, vol. 67, part 6, pp. 822–8, esp. pp. 823, 824; Lutfi, Muhammad and Galal, are the authors of a book of the same title of this article.
25 Safwat, Hasan Lutfi, Muhammad Abd Al-Azim Ali and Jalal Yahya Kamil (1994), 'Tatbiq al-Shari'ah'. *Al-Azhar*, November, vol. 67, part 6, pp. 822–8.
26 Abu Shuhbah, Muhammad (1969), *Fi Rihab al-Sunnah*. Cairo: al Majlis al-A'la li al-Shu'un al-Islamiyyah (The Academy of Islamic Research), p. 38.
27 'Abduh, Muhammad, *Tafsir*, vol. 3, p. 117.
28 al-Ghazali, Muhammad (1981), *Turathuna al-Fikri fi Mizan al-Shar' wa al-'Aql*, Cairo: Dar al-Shuruq, p. 151.
29 al-Ghazali, Muhammad, *Turathuna al-Fikri fi Mizan al-Shar' wa al-'Aql*, p. 184.
30 For further details about this matter, see Ibn Taymiyyah, *al-'ubudiyyah*, pp. 23–4.
31 See Wajdi, Muhammad Farid, *al-Islam fi 'Asr al-'Ilm*, Beirut: Dar al-Kitab al-Arabi, p. 618.
32 Ibn Taymiyyah, *al-'ubudiyyah*, pp. 74–9.
33 Qutb, *Khasa'is*, pp. 114–15, see p. 116; for further detail, see *Mujtama'*, pp. 50–2, 56–60, 65; *Zilal*, vol. 2, pp. 835–9, 1010; vol. 4, pp. 2009–11; also see discussion under the subtitle 'Shari'ah and Fiqh' in Chapter 1 in the present text.
34 See Shepard, *Sayyid Qutb and Islamic Activism*, p. 48, para. 39, p. 56, para. 63, see p. 371.
35 al-Sayyid, Ahmad Litfi (1963), *Mabadi' fi al-Siyasah wa al-Adab wa al-Ijtima'*. Cairo: Dar al-Hilal, Series of Kitab al-Hilal, n. 149, August (1963), pp. 60–2.
36 al-Hakim, Tawfiq (1970), *Tawfiq al-Hakim al-Mufakkir*. Cairo: Dar al-Kitab al-Jadid, n.d., pp. 87–8.
37 'Abduh, *Risalat al-Tawhid*, p. 156.
38 Qutb, *Zilal*, vol. 3, p. 1753.
39 Qutb, *Zilal*, vol. 6, p. 3387.
40 Qutb, *Zilal*, vol. 2, p. 709.
41 Qutb, *Zilal*, vol. 1, p. 207.
42 Qutb, *Zilal*, vol. 6, p. 3387; vol. 4, p. 1990.

43 Qutb, *Zilal*, vol. 1, p. 492.
44 Qutb, *Zilal*, vol. 2, pp. 1053–4, 1057.
45 Qutb, *Zilal*, vol. 2, pp. 888–9; also see vol. 3, pp. 1433–4.
46 Qutb, *Zilal*, vol. 3, p. 1256; see vol. 2, p. 1032; *'Adalah*, p. 198; Ibn Taymiyyah, *'Ubudiyyah*, pp. 46, 57, 70.
47 Qutb, *'Adalah*, p. 183.
48 Qutb, *Zilal*, vol. 1, p. 252; also see vol. 1, p. 438; vol. 2, pp. 1033, 1057, 1256–7; vol. 3, pp. 1255–7, 1397; vol. 4, pp. 1872–3, 2013, 2020.
49 Qutb, *Zilal*, vol. 3, pp. 1256–7; also see vol. 1, pp. 207, 346, 440, 492, 545; vol. 2, p. 709; vol. 3, p. 1434; vol. 4, p. 1990; vol. 6, p. 3525; *'Adalah*, pp. 201–2.

3 Universality of Islam

1 Ibn Manzur, *Lisan*, vol. 12, pp. 289–90.
2 Wehr, Hans (1971), *Dictionary of Modern Written Arabic*, Wiesbaden: Otto Harrassowitz, pp. 424–5.
3 Ibn Manzur, *Lisan*, vol. 12, p. 293.
4 Ibn Kathir, *al-Bidayah*, vol. 1, part 2, p. 225.
5 Ibn Manzur, *Lisan*, vol. 12, pp. 290–8.
6 Qutb, *al-Salam al-'Alami*, p.122.
7 Qutb, *Zilal*, vol. 2, p. 659; *'Adalah*, p. 26.
8 Qutb, *Zilal*, vol. 1, p. 573; *al-Salam*, p. 14; *'Adalah*, pp. 27–8.
9 Qutb, *Zilal*, vol. 1, pp. 576–8.
10 Qutb, *Zilal*, vol. 2, p. 1080; *al-Salam*, p.19; *al-Azhar*, May, 1996, vol. 68, part 12, pp. 1928–31.
11 Qutb, *Zilal*, vol. 5, p. 2764.
12 Qur'an, 30: 22.
13 Qutb, *Zilal*, vol. 1, p. 574.
14 Qutb, *Zilal*, vol. 5, p. 3147; Qur'an, 42: 13.
15 al-Qurtubi, *al-Jami'*, vol. 6, p. 30; Ibn Kathir, *Tafsir*, vol. 2, p. 2; Qur'an, 5: 3; 4: 79; 2: 107; 34: 28.
16 Qur'an, 11: 97; 3: 45–9; 37: 139–47; 11: 25; 71: 1; 11: 50; 26: 123–5; 11: 6; 26: 141–3; 11: 74–83; 26: 160–2; 11: 48; 26: 176–8.
17 Qutb, *Al-Salam*, p. 28; *Zilal*, vol. 5, p. 3090; vol. 6, pp. 3360–7; Qur'an, 3: 64; 5: 19; 5: 15–16; 5: 71.
18 Qutb Sayyid, *Islam the Religion of the Future*, p. 12.
19 Qutb, *Ma'alim*, pp. 108–49; *Islam the Religion*, p. 5; *'Adalah*, p. 20.
20 Qutb, *Zilal*, vol. 1, pp. 560–1; *'Adalah*, p. 79; *Al-Salm*, pp. 25, 36.
21 Qutb, *Zilal*, vol. 5, p. 3147.
22 Qutb, *Ma'alim*, p. 69; *'Adalah*, pp. 78–9; *Nahwa Mujtama' Islami*, pp. 102–4.
23 Qutb, *Ma'alim*, p. 108.
24 Qutb, *Khasa'is*, p. 190; also see *Zilal*, vol. 1, pp. 368–9.
25 Shepard, *Sayyid Qutb and Islamic Activism*, p. xxvi.
26 Qutb, *Khasa'is*, p. 197.
27 Qutb, *Mujtama' 'Islami*, p. 5, also pp. 11–13, 136; *Ma'alim*, pp. 21, 27, 29, 92; *Mushkilat Hadarah*, p. 186.
28 Qutb, *Zilal*, vol. 6, pp. 4002–5; *Ma'alim*, pp. 37, 54–7, 92, *Al-Salam*, pp. 15–17.
29 Qutb, *Zilal*, vol. 2, p. 709; vol. 4, pp. 1990, 2373, see p. 2374; vol. 6, p. 3387.
30 Qutb, *Adalah*, p. 22; see *Zilal*, vol. 2, p. 1379.
31 Qutb, *Zilal*, vol. 1, p. 511; vol. 2, pp. 1005–6; *Ma'alim*, pp. 28, 61, 132; *Mushkilat Hadarah*, p. 172.

32 Qutb, *Al-Salam*, pp. 22–4; *Zilal*, vol. 1, pp. 37–8, 39–41; *Islam the Religion*, pp. 18–19.
33 Qutb Sayyid, *Hadha al-Din*, pp. 29–30.
34 Qutb, *Hadha al-Din*, p. 34.
35 Qutb '*Adalah*, p. 154, Hardie's trans. pp. 177–8.
36 Qutb, '*Adalah*, p. 154, Shepard's trans. p. 224, para. 160.
37 Qutb, *Al-Salam*, p. 21.
38 Qur'an, 7: 11–12; 17: 61; 20: 16; 15: 33; see Qutb, *Zilal*, vol. 1. p. 58; vol. 3, pp. 1267–8; vol. 4, pp. 2137–41; Qurtubi, *Jami'*, vol. 1, p. 249.
39 Qutb, *Zilal*, vol. 1, pp. 573–4; vol. 2, p. 1379; *Mujtama' Islami*, p. 94; *Ma'alim*, pp. 129–32.
40 Qutb, *Mujtama'*, p. 92, see pp. 5–13, 92–102; *Ma'alim*, pp. 126,131; al-Nadawi, *al-'Alam bi-Inhitat al- Muslimin* (1984), *Madha Khasira*, Beirut: Dar al Kitab al-Arabi, pp. 92–194; Banna, *Rasa'il*, p. 347; Khumini, *Hukumah*, p. 5.
41 See Khatab, Sayed (2002), 'Citizenship Rights of Non-Muslims in the Islamic State of Hakimiyya Espoused by Sayyid Qutb', *Islam and Christian–Muslim Relations*, vol. 13, n. 2, pp. 163–87.
42 See Part II Ch. 2, subtitle 'Freedom and the role of human intellect (*al-'aql*)' in the present text.
43 Qutb, *Ma'alim*, p. 157; for further detail, see *Zilal*, vol. 2, pp. 659, 1080, vol. 5, p. 2764.
44 Qutb, *Zilal*, vol. 4, pp. 2514–15.
45 For further details on this matter, see *Zilal*, vol. 2, p. 807, 1039, 1112, 1121; vol. 3, pp. 1520, 1531; vol. 6, pp. 3350, 3684.
46 It is an annual tax paid by the non-Muslim citizens living in the Islamic state. Qutb, '*Adalah*, p. 79; *Mujtama'*, p. 114.
47 One of the pillars of Islam is *zakat*. It is payable only by Muslims from their cash savings, gold and silver property, trade merchandise, herds, of any type, agricultural crops, mining and treasure. If the amount of any of these categories is up to a known quorum, the Muslim must pay a particular percentage. The regulations for *zakat* are ordained by the Qur'an, explained in the Sunnah, and clearly known in the Islamic jurisprudence. Abu Yusuf, *al-Kharaj*, pp. 70, 103–4; Qurtubi, *Tafsir*, vol. 1, p. 343; vol. 17, p. 238; vol. 18, p. 16; al-Mawardi, al-*Ahkam al-Sultaniyyah*, pp. 113–25; Tubarah, Afif Abd al-Fattah (1993), *Ruh al-Din al-Islami: 'Ard wa Tahlil li Ilsul al-Islam wa Adabih wa Ahkamih Tahta Daw'u al-'Ilm wa al-Falsafah*, Beirut: Dar al-'ilm li al-malayin, pp. 346–51; Qutb, *Nahwa Mujtama' Islami*, pp. 114–18; '*Adalah*, pp. 88–100, 114–25.
48 Qutb, '*Adalah*, p. 79; see *Ma'alim*, pp. 69, 71; *Nahwa Mujtama' Islami*, pp. 102, 103; *Islam wa Ra'smaliyyah*, pp. 88–9; *Zilal*, vol. 2, p. 1378.
49 Qutb, '*Adalah*, pp. 79, 114–18; *Zilal*, vol. 5, p. 2772.
50 Qutb, '*Adalah*, pp. 79, 114–18; *Zilal*, vol. 5, p. 2772.
51 It is tax that to be paid on the produce of landed property of all Muslims at the rate of 10 per cent of the production if it is through natural rainfall, but at 20 per cent if through irrigation. Al-Mawardi, *al-Ahkam* al-Sulfaniyyah, p. 118; Qutb, '*Adalah*, p. 96; al-Bardisi Muhammad Zakariyya (1985), *Usul al-Fiqh*, Cairo: Dar al-Thaqafah lial-Nashr wa al-Tawzi, pp. 127–8; Zidan Abd al-Karim (1986), *Al-Madkhal li Dinasat al-Shari'ah al-Islamiyyah*. Beirut: Mu'assasat al-Risalah, ninth edition, p. 40.
52 Qutb, '*Adalah*, pp. 79, 114–18; *Nahwa Mujtama' Islami*, pp. 114–18, 124–5.
53 Qutb, *Islam the Religion of the Future*, p. 14.

54 Qutb, *Mujtama'*, pp. 92–8, see pp. 5–13, 98–102; *Ma'alim*, pp. 164–5; *Ra'smaliyyah*, pp. 59–62; see al-Nadawi, *Madha Khasira al-'Alam*, pp. 92–194; al-Banna, *Rasa'il*, p. 347; al-Khumayni (1979), *Hukumah*, p. 5. For further information concerning this issue see, Sabiq Sayyid (1985), *fiqh al-Sunnah*, Beirut: Dar al-Kitab al-Arabi, vol. 1, pp. 327–429.
55 See Qutb, *Islam the Religion*, pp. 61–2.
56 Russell Bertrand (1961), *History of Western Philosophy*, London: George Allen & Unwin, pp. 304–5; Qutb, *Khasa'is*, p. 70, see pp. 71–3; Qur'an, 2: 255; 3: 2–6; 21: 19–23.
57 Qutb, *Islam the Religion*, pp. 61–2.
58 'Magna Carta' in Latin means 'Great Charter'. King John, on 15 June 1215 AD, guaranteed much rights to the English aristocracy in this great document 'Magna Carta'. The ordinary people and the farmers gained little. They were hardly mentioned in the Charter, although they made up by far the biggest part of England's population. It is 'an error to say that Magna Carta guaranteed individual liberties to all people'. see Russell, *History of Western Philosophy*, p. 434.
59 Qutb, *Islam the Religion*, pp. 62–4; *al-Salam*, pp. 103–4.
60 Qutb, *Islam the Religion*, 61; *Mujtama' Islami*, pp. 12–13.

4 The innate character and moral constitution (*al-Fitrah*)

1 Qutb, *Ma'alim*, pp. 140, 141, 142; a*l-Salam al-'Alami*, pp. 8, 10; *'Adalah*, p. 21.
2 *Davies, Paul* (1992), *The Mind of God: Science and The Search For Ultimate Mining, London: Penguin*, p. 1; Qutb, Muhammad (1993), *al-Insan Bayna al-Maddiyyah wa al-Islam*, Beirut: Dar al-Shuruq, eleventh edition, pp. 22–3.
3 Russell, Bertrand, *History of Philosophy*, p. 13–14.
4 Qutb, *Khasa'is*, pp. 68–9.
5 Qutb, *Khasa'is*, pp. 56–8.
6 Asad, Muhammad (1969), *Islam at the Crossroads*, Lahore: Arafat Publication, pp. 7–8; Russell, *History of Philosophy*, pp. 136–9, 787; Qutb, *Islam the Religion*, pp. 34–7.
7 Qutb, *al-Islam wa Mushkilat al-Hadarah*, pp. 34–5.
8 Qutb, *Khasa'is*, p. 54.
9 Qutb, *Islam wa Mushkilat al-Hadarah*, p. 40; Qutb, Muhammad, *al-Insan*, p. 16.
10 Qutb, Muhammad, *al-Insan*, pp. 24–5; Aronowites, Stanley (1990), *The Crises in Historical Materialism: Class, Politics and Culture in Marxist Theory*, Minneapolis, MN: University of Minnesota Press, pp. 78–80.
11 Qutb, *'Adalah*, p. 24; *Islam the Religion*, pp. 37, 63–9; *Khasa'is*, pp. 64–5.
12 Qutb, *'Adalah*, p. 24; *Islam the Religion*, pp. 37, 63–9; *Khasa'is*, pp. 64–5.
13 Qutb, *Mushkilat al-Hadarah*, pp. 43–7, 111–15, 160, 184, 185; *Zilal*, vol. 2, pp. 629, 1104, 1109, *Khasa'is*, pp. 16, 25, 58–73, 77–86, 112, 148, 150, 172–5.
14 Qutb, *Mushkilat al-Hadarah*, pp. 62–3; *Zilal*, vol. 1, pp. 200, 441; vol. 2, p. 103; *'Adalah*, p. 24.
15 Ibn Manzur, *Lisan*, vol. 5, pp. 56, 58–9; Lane, *Arabic–English Lexicon*, p. 397.
16 Ibn Manzur, *Lisan*, vol. 5, pp. 56, 58–9; al-Qurtubi, *al-Jami'*, vol. 14, p. 27; al-Isfahani al-Raghib (1984), *Mu'jam Mufradat Alfaz al-Qur'an*, Nadim Mar'ashli (ed.), Beirut: Dar al-Kitab al-Arabi, p. 2415; Lane, *Arabic–English Lexicon*, p. 397.
17 Wright, *Grammar of Arabic*, pp. 110, 112.
18 Qur'an, 6: 79.
19 Qur'an, 82: 1.
20 Qur'an, 19: 90.

21 al-'Asqalani, *Fath al-Bari*, vol. 3, p. 18; Ibn Manzur, *Lisan*, vol. 5, p. 55.
22 al-Qurtubi, *al-Jami'*, vol. 14, pp. 24–31; vol. 18, p. 133; al-'Asqalani, *Fath al-Bari*, vol. 13, p. 520; Ibn Manzur, *Lisan*, vol. 5, pp. 56–8; al-Isfahani, *Mu'jam*, p. 310; Lane, *Arabic–English Lexicon*, p. 1823.
23 al-Qurtubi, *al-Jami'*, vol. 14, p. 25 on the views of Abu Hurayrah (d. 59/680) and al-Hasan Ibn Shihab (d. 428/ 1035).
24 Qur'an, 30: 30; also see Qur'an, 4: 10; 6: 14; 6: 79; 11: 51; 12: 101; 14: 10; 17: 51; 19: 90; 20: 72; 21: 56; 36: 22; 42: 5; 42: 27; 67: 2; 82: 1.
25 al-Qurtubi *al-Jami'*, vol. 14, pp. 25, 27–30; vol. 18, p. 133; al-'Asqalani, *Fath al-Bari*, vol. Introduction, p. 177; al-Ghazali-, Abi Hamid Muhammad b. Muhammad, *al-Iqtisad Fi al-I'tiqad*, Cairo: Maktabat al-Jindi, n.d., pp. 146–56; Ibn Kathir, *Tafsir*, vol. 2, pp. 125, 151.
26 For Moussalli, Qutb's view of '*fitrah* is but a complete submission to the dominion power which brought about the laws, which is in turn issued by God's will for the happiness of humanity', see Moussalli, Ahmad (1993), *Qira'ah Nazariyyah Ta'sisiyyah fi al-Khitab al-Islami al-Usuli*, Beirut: al-Nashir, first edition, p. 17.
27 Qutb, *Kasa'is*, pp. 63–73, 75, 78, 95, 119.
28 Qutb, *Ma'alim*, pp. 110–13; *Hadha al-Din*, pp. 51–65.
29 Qutb, *Kasa'is*, pp. 63–73, 75, 78, 95, 119; Wajdi, Farid, *al-Islam*, pp. 126–50.
30 Qutb, *Kasa'is*, pp. 63–73, 75, 78, 95, 119; *'Adalah*, pp. 75, 77–8, 81, 144–5, 147.
31 Qutb, *Zilal*, vol. 4, pp. 1938–40, 2390, 2391; *Mushkilat al-Hadarah*, pp. 13, 20, 33, 53, 57, 82.
32 Qutb, *Khasa'is*, pp. 11–12.
33 Muhammad, Yasien (1996), *Fitrah: The Islamic Concept of Human Nature*, London: Ta-Ha Publishers Ltd, p. 66, see pp. 56–8.
34 Muhammad, Yasien, *Fitrah*, pp. 65–6.
35 al-Qurtubi, *al-Jami'*, vol. 20, p. 15; Ibn Kathir, *Tafsir*, vol. 4, p. 500, al-Tabarsi AbiAli al-Fadl b. al-Hasan (1986), *Majama' al-Bayan* fi Tafsir al-Qur'an, Beirut: Dar al-Ma'rifah, vol. 1, p. 71; vol. 5, p. 498; Qutb, *Zilal*, vol. 6, p. 3883.
36 Muhammad, Yasien, *Fitrah*, pp. 65–6, esp. 65.
37 Muhammad, Yasien, *Fitrah*, p. 66.
38 Qutb, *Zila*l, vol. 4, p. 2138; vol. 5, p. 3027; Ibn Kathir, *Tafsir*, vol. 2, p. 550; al-Qurtubi, *al-Jami'*, vol. 1, p. 280; al-Tabarsi, *Majama' al-Bayan*, vol. 1, p. 71.
39 Qutb, *Zilal*, vol. 4, p. 2139, *al-Salam*, p. 9.
40 Qutb, *Zilal*, vol. 1, p. 53, see vol. 4, p. 2139; Wolfson Harry Austoyn (1976), *The Philosophy of Kalam*, Cambridge: Harvard University Press, pp. 602–3; for further details about these Arabic terms (*taswiyah, istiwa', fawdiyyah, tahtiyyah*) see Abduh Muhammad, *Tafsir al-Manar*, Beirut: Dar al-Ma'rifah, second edition, n.d., vol. 3, pp. 205–7.
41 Muhammad, Yasien, *Fitrah*, pp. 67–8.
42 Qutb, *al-Shati' al-Majhul*, pp.5–6.
43 Qutb, *al-Shati' al-Majhul*, p. 43.
44 Qutb, *Zilal*, vol. 6, p. 3639.
45 Qutb, *Khasa'is*, pp. 169–87.
46 Muhammad, Yasien, *Fitrah*, pp. 67–8.
47 Qutb, *Khasa'is*, p. 149; see also al-'Aqqad, *Allah*, p. 137.
48 Qutb, *Khasa'is*, pp. 72, 149.
49 Qutb, *Zilal*, vol. 4, pp. 1938–40, 2390, 2391; *Mushkilat al-Hadarah*, pp. 13, 20, 33, 53, 57, 82.
50 Muhammad,Yasien, *Fitrah*, p. 68.

51 See al-Qurtubi, *al-Jami'*, vol. 20, p. 124.
52 Qutb, *Khasa'is*, p. 190.
53 Qutb, *Khasa'is*, p. 178.
54 'Abduh, Muhammad, *Risalat al-Tawhid*, p. 41.
55 al-Qurtubi, *al-Jami'*, vol. 15, p. 24, see vol. 6, p. 22; Qutb, *Zilal*, vol. 4, p. 2139.
56 Muhammad, Yasien, *Fitrah*, pp. 65–6.
57 Muhammad, Yasien, *Fitrah*, pp. 65–6, esp. 65.
58 Muhammad, Yasien, *Fitrah*, p. 66.
59 Muhammad, Yasien, *Fitrah*, pp. 65–6.
60 Qutb, *Zilal*, vol. 6, pp. 3847, 3848, 3883; vol. 5, p. 3027; vol. 4, p. 2139; vol. 1, p. 53.
61 Ibn Manzur, *Lisan*, vol. 14, p. 414, esp. some earlier sources of Arabic grammarians including Anas b. Malik (d. 93/711), Sibawayh (d. 180/796), Ibn Faris (d. 395/1004), al-Farra' (d. 458/1065) and Abu Mansur (d. 460/1120).
62 Ibn Manzur, *Lisan*, vol. 14, pp. 414–15.
63 Ibn Kathir, *Tafsir*, vol. 4, p. 452.
64 Qutb, *Zilal*, vol. 6, p. 3883; Ibn Abbas Abdullah (1951), *Tanwir al-Miqyas min Tafsir Ibn 'Abbas*, p. 387; Qurtubi, *al-Jami'*, vol. 20, p.15; Ibn Kathir, *Tafsir*, vol. 4, p. 500; Tabarsi, *Majama'*, vol. 1, p. 71; vol. 5, p. 498.
65 In the case of Adam, Qur'an 15: 29; 38: 72 the word *sawwa* means 'created and perfected him' see, Qurtubi, *al-Jami'*, vol. 15, pp. 24, 227; Qutb, *Zilal*, vol. 4, p. 2139; vol. 5, p. 3027. For the creation processes of the descendants from Adam, see Qur'an 75: 38; 18: 37; 82: 7; 91: 7 the word '*sawwa*' means upright and perfected tendencies, see, Ibn Kathir, *Tafsir*, vol. 4, p. 480; al-Qurtubi, *al-Jami'*, vol. 10, p. 404; vol. 19, p. 246; Qutb, *Zilal*, vol. 6, pp. 3847, 3848. For the creation of heavens, Qur'an 79: 28 the word '*sawwa*' in this and similar verses means 'perfected it with no defects', see Qurtubi, *al-Jami*, vol. 19, p. 204; vol. 20, p. 75; Qutb, *Zilal*, vol. 6, p. 3816; Ibn Kathir, *Tafsir*, vol. 4, p. 515. For the creation of the earth, see Qur'an, 9: 14, the word '*sawwa*' in this and similar verses means leveled, see Ibn Kathir, *Tafsir*, vol. 4, p. 517; Qurtubi, *al-Jami'*, vol. 20, p. 79; Qutb, *Zilal*, vol. 6, p. 3919.
66 al-Qurtubi, *al-Jami'*, vol. 10, p. 24, vol. 15, p. 227.
67 Qutb, *Zilal*, vol. 1, p. 53; see vol. 4, p. 2139.
68 Qutb, *Khasa'is*, p. 16, see pp. 17–22.
69 Qur'an, 30: 30; 6: 79; 17: 51.
70 Qutb, *Zilal*, vol. 4, pp. 2136–7; *Mushkilat al-Hadarah*, p. 39, see, pp. 40–4, 47–9.
71 Qutb, *Mushkilat al-Hadarah*, p. 39, see pp. 40–6; see pp. 48–9; *Khasa'is*, pp. 42–4, 95–7.
72 Qutb, *Zilal*, vol. 1, p. 53, cf. vol. 6, pp. 3916–17.
73 Qutb, *Zilal*, vol. 1, pp. 53–4; vol. 3, pp. 1391–6; vol. 4, pp. 2137–45, vol. 6, pp. 3916–19.
74 Qutb, *Islam the Religion*, p. 5; *Zilal*, vol. 1, pp. 53–4; *Khasa'is*, pp. 96, 98.
75 Qutb, *Islam the Religion*, p. 15; *Mujtama'*, pp. 34–6.
76 Qutb, *Hadha al-Din*, pp. 17–18.
77 Qutb, *Hadha al-Din*, p. 25.
78 Qutb, *Hadha al-Din*, p. 6.
79 Qutb, *Hadha al-Din*, pp. 7–8.
80 Qutb, *Hadha al-Din*, p. 9.
81 Qutb, *Hadha al-Din*, p. 21.

82 Qutb, *Hadha al-Din*, p. 26.
83 Qutb, *Hadha al-Din*, pp. 27–8.
84 Qutb, *Zilal*, vol. 5, p. 2920.
85 Qutb, *Zilal*, vol. 5, p. 2922.
86 Qutb, *'Adalah*, p. 20; *Hadha al-Din*, pp. 23–24.
87 Qutb, *Ma'alim*, p. 109; *'Adalah*, p. 21; *Zilal*, vol. 6, pp. 3449–52.
88 Qutb, *Zilal*, vol. 1, p. 56; vol. 2, p. 659; vol. 6, pp. 3638–9.
89 Qutb, *'Adalah*, p. 22.
90 Qutb, *Khasa'is*, pp. 24–34; *Zilal*, vol. 1, pp. 150–1.
91 Qutb, *Khasa'is*, pp. 120, 122, 125; *Zilal*, vol. 1, pp. 150–1, 156.
92 Qutb, *'Adalah*, p. 22.
93 Qutb, *Zilal*, vol. 6, p. 3966.
94 Qutb, *Zilal*, vol. 3, pp. 1392–6, see vol. 6, p. 3966.
95 Qutb, *Zilal*, vol. 3, p. 1394; also see Ibn Kathir, *Tafsir*, vol. 2, pp. 261–4; al-Qurtubi, *al-Jami'*, vol. 7, pp. 314–19; vol. 2, p. 11; vol. 11, p. 120; vol. 14. p. 24; vol. 4, p. 69.
96 Qutb, *Zilal*, vol. 3, p. 1394.
97 Qutb, *Khasa'is*, p. 131; *Zilal*, vol. 1395, 1398; *'Adalah*, pp. 21–3; *Ma'alim*, pp. 110–13.
98 Qur'an, 75: 38, 18: 37, 83: 7, 32: 9, 91: 7, 15: 29, 38: 72.
99 For the word *sulalah* means stages, see Qutb *Zilal*, vol. 4, p. 2138; al-Qurtubi, *al-Jami'*, vol. 2, p. 203, vol. 6, p. 387, vol. 12, p. 109; Ibn Kathir, *Tafsir*, vol. 3, p. 240.
100 Qutb, *Zilal*, vol. 4, p. 2138; vol. 5, p. 3027; *al-Salam*, p. 19.
101 Qutb, *Zilal*, vol. 3, p. 1266.
102 Qutb, *Zilal*, vol. 3, p. 1266.
103 Qutb, *Zilal*, vol. 4, pp. 2139–40; see *'Adalah*, pp. 64, 85.
104 Qutb, *Zilal*, vol. 6, p. 3917, see vol. 3, pp. 1391–4, 1400.
105 Qutb, *Zilal*, vol. 6, p. 3917; *'Adalah*, pp. 33, 38, 44.
106 Qutb, *Zilal*, vol. 6, pp. 1917–18.
107 Qutb, *Khasa'is*, p. 76; *Zilal*, vol. 4, p. 2138; vol. 5, p. 3027; *al-Salam*, p. 19.
108 Qutb, *'Adalah*, pp. 32, 36, 38, 41.
109 Qutb, *Zilal*, vol. 6, p. 3917; vol. 3, p. 1394; Ibn kathir, *Tafsir*, vol. 2, pp. 261–4; al-Qurtubi, *al-Jami'*, vol. 7, pp. 314–19; vol. 2, p. 11; vol. 11, p. 120; vol. 14, p. 24; vol. 4, p. 69.
110 Qutb, *'Adalah*, pp. 24–5.
111 Qutb, *Zilal*, vol. 4, pp. 2139–40, see *'Adalah*, pp. 64, 85.
112 Qutb, *al-Salam*, pp. 10–11; *Zilal*, vol. 3, p. 1263; *Ma'alim*, p. 113.
113 Qutb, *Hadha al-Din*, pp. 55–6, 64; *Zilal*, vol. 3, p. 1394.
114 Qutb, *'Adalah*, pp. 11, 13, 80–1.
115 Qutb, *Zilal*, vol. 6, pp. 3351–2.
116 Qutb, *Zilal*, vol. 6, p. 3967.
117 Qutb, *Islam wa Mushkilat al-Hadarah*, pp. 108–11, 122–65.

5 Human intellect (*al-'Aql*)

1 Qutb, *Zilal*, vol. 2, pp. 764, 805–9, 1097–8.
2 Qutb, *Zilal*, vol. 2, p. 1098.
3 Moussalli, Ahmad (1993), *Qira'ah Nazariyyah Ta'sisiyyah fi al-Khitab al-Islami al-Usuli*, Beirut: al-Nashir Lial-Tiba'ah, first edition, p. 20.
4 Qutb, *Khasa'is al-Tasawwur al-Islami*, p. 87.

5 Qutb, *Zilal*, vol. 2, p. 806.
6 Qutb, *Zilal*, vol. 3, pp. 1187, 1218–19, 1255, 1753; vol. 2, pp. 1112–21.
7 Qutb, *Zilal*, vol. 2, p. 806.
8 Qutb, *Mushkilat al-Hadarah*, p. 33, see pp. 112, 130, 177.
9 Qutb, *Khasa'is*, p. 59.
10 Qutb, *Khasa'is*, p. 60; *Islam the Religion of the Future*, pp. 34–58.
11 Qutb, *Khasa'is*, p. 59, see, p. 55.
12 Qutb, *Khasa'is*, p. 61; also see *Mushkilat al-Hadarah*, pp. 33, 112, 130, 177.
13 Qutb, *Khasa'is*, pp. 61–2.
14 Qutb, *Khasa'is*, p. 62; see *'Adalah*, pp. 8–10; *Mushkilat Hadarah*, pp. 80–3; *Hadha al-Din*, pp. 74–7.
15 Hegel Georg William Friedrich (1956), *Philosophy of History*, New York: Dover Publications, pp. 395–8.
16 Qutb, *Khasa'is*, p. 62.
17 Qutb, *Khasa'is*, pp. 62–3; see Hegel, *Philosophy*, pp. 422–6.
18 Crane Brinton, 'Enlightenment', *The Encyclopedia of Philosophy* (1967), vol. 2, p. 521; see Qutb, *Khasa'is*, pp. 23–44, 61–74; al-Maydani, 'Abd al-Rahman Hasan (1985), *Kawashif Ziyuf al-Madhahib al-Fikriyyah al-Mu'asirah*, Damascus: Dar al-Qalam, pp. 65–72, 91–5, 159–60, 171–5, 762–30.
19 Qutb, *Khasa'is*, p. 63.
20 Qutb, *Khasa'is*, p. 61.
21 John, Passmore, 'Logical Positivism', *The Encyclopedia of Philosophy*, 1967, vol. 5, p. 53; also see Hume (1969), *Treaties of Human Nature*, pp. 516, 555–64 ff. about morality; see Russell, *History of Western Philosophy*, pp. 589, 592, 601, 757; also see al-Maydani, *Kawashif Ziyuf al-Madhahib al-Fikriyyah al-Mu'asirah*, pp. 71, 429–31, 442–9.
22 Qutb, *Khasa'is*, p. 72.
23 Qutb, *Zilal*, vol. 3, p. 1271; see vol. 2, pp. 1112–21; vol. 3, pp. 1226–7, 1766–7.
24 Qutb, *Zilal*, vol. 6, p. 3351, see vol. 6, pp. 3352, 3394; vol. 3, pp. 1263, 1271.
25 Robert Bauval and Graham Hancock (1997), *Keeper of Genesis: A Quest for the Hidden Legacy of Mankind*, London: Mandarin paperbacks, p. 139.
26 Will Durant (1953), *The Story of Civilization*, vol. 5, p. 572.
27 Qutb, *Zilal*, vol. 3, p. 1271.
28 Qutb, *Zilal*, vol. 3, p. 1271.
29 Jeans, James (1931), *The Mysterious Universe* – cited by Qutb, *Zilal*, vol. 3, p. 1271. Sir James's book is titled *The Universe Around Us*. It was first published in 1929, the second edition was in 1930, the third was in 1933, and the fourth edition was in 1944 and published by Cambridge University Press, London. The author prefaced all editions.
30 Schadwich, Owen (1975), *The Secularization of the European Mind in the Nineteenth Century*, Cambridge University Press, p. 173.
31 La Mattrie (1953), *Man a Machine*, p. 128; Cf. Durant, *The Story of Civilization*, vol. 9, p. 619.
32 Qutb, *Zilal*, vol. 3, p. 1271.
33 Russell (1918), *A Free Man's Worship: Mysticism and Logic*, New York: Simon & Schuster, p. 46.
34 The Book Company International (1996), *Mindpower*, Sydney: Orbis, p. 22, see 24, 84, 92.
35 Qutb, *Khasa'is*, p. 66.

36 Qutb, *Khasa'is*, p. 64, see pp. 65–72; Boucher, Douglas (1985), *The Biology of Mutualism: Ecology and Evolution*, New York: Oxford University Press, p. 9.
37 Boucher, *The Biology of Mutualism: Ecology and Evolution*, pp. 9–15.
38 Haberlandt, Karl (1997), *Cognitive Psychology*, Boston, MA: pp. 25, 199; see Qutb, *Zilal*, vol. 3, p. 1262.
39 al-Maydani, *Kawashif Ziyuf al-Madhahib al-Fikriyyah al-Mu'asirah*, pp. 310–15.
40 Qutb, Muhammad, *al-Insan*, pp. 19–24, 47–51, 55–9; Singer, Marcus, *Philosophy*, World Book Encyclopedia, Chicago, IL: A Scott Fetzer Company, vol. 15, p. 389; Qutb, *Khasa'is*, p. 66.
41 Qutb, *Zilal*, vol. 3, p. 1258.
42 Qutb, *Khasa'is*, p. 64.
43 Russell, Bertrand (1953), *The Impact of Science on Society*, New York: Simon & Schuster, p. 6.
44 Qutb, *Mushkilat al-Hadarah*, pp. 108, 130; *Khasa'is*, p. 56.
45 Qutb, *Hadha al-Din*, p. 47; see *Mushkilat al-Hadarah*, p. 113.
46 Qutb, *Mushkilat al-Hadarah*, pp. 78–79, 86–87, 108, 130; *Khasa'is*, p. 57.
47 Russell, *A Free Man's Worship: Mysticism and Logic*, p. 46.
48 Qutb, *Hadha al-Din*, p. 25.
49 Qutb, *Zilal*, vol. 2, p. 807.
50 Qutb, *Zilal*, vol. 2, p. 807.
51 Qutb, *Zilal*, vol. 2, p. 807.
52 Qutb, *Zilal*, vol. 2, p. 806, also see vol. 2, pp. 807, 1039, 1112, 1121; vol. 3, pp. 1520, 1531.
53 Qutb, *Zilal*, vol. 2, p. 807, also see vol. 2, pp. 1039, 1112, 1121; vol. 3, pp. 1520, 1531; vol. 6, pp. 3350, 3684.
54 Qutb, *Zilal*, vol. 1, p. 291.
55 Qutb, *Ma'alim*, p. 120.
56 Qutb's testimony to the Court 19 December 1965, cf. Jawhar, *al-Mawta Yatakallamun*, pp. 111–146, esp. 113.
57 Qutb, *'Adalah*, pp. 80, 82.
58 Qutb, *'Adalah*, p. 146.
59 Qutb, *Mujtama'*, pp. 121–2.
60 Qutb, *Zilal*, vol. 1, p. 291.
61 Qutb, *Zilal*, vol. 1, p. 291.
62 Qutb, *Zilal*, vol. 2, pp. 659, 1080; vol. 5, p. 2764; also al-Qurtubi, *al-Jami'*, vol. 6, p. 30; Ibn Kathir, *Tafsir*, vol. 2, p. 2; Qur'an, 5: 3; 4: 79; 2: 107; 34: 28.
63 Qutb, *Zilal*, vol. 6, pp. 3917–18; also see vol. 2, pp. 806–8; vol. 3, pp. 1391–4, 1400.
64 Qutb, *'Adalah*, p. 146.
65 Qutb, *Zilal*, vol. 2, pp. 808–9.
66 Qutb, *Zilal*, vol. 1, pp. 291–3; vol. 2, pp. 764, 805–9, 1097–8.
67 Qutb, *'Adalah*, pp. 32–43.
68 Qutb, *Zilal*, vol. 1, pp. 38–9.
69 Qutb, *Zilal*, vol. 6, pp. 3367, 3898–9; vol. 4, 2144, 2300–2.
70 Qutb, *'Adalah*, p. 52; also see, *Zilal*, vol. 6, pp. 3544–5; vol. 2, p. 732.
71 Qutb, *Zilal*, vol. 2, p. 732; see vol. 4, p. 2170; vol. 6, p. 3899.
72 Qutb, *Zilal*, vol. 2, p. 1169.
73 Qutb, *Zilal*, vol. 6, p. 3899.
74 Qutb, *Zilal*, vol. 2, p. 1169.
75 Qutb, *Zilal*, vol. 2, p. 1169.
76 Qutb, *Zilal*, vol. 2, p. 1168.

77 Qutb, *Zilal*, vol. 6, pp. 3917–18; see vol. 3, pp. 1391–4, 1400; also see *'Adalah*, pp. 33, 38, 44.
78 Qutb, *Zilal*, vol. 2, p. 1169.
79 Qutb, *'Adalah*, p. 79; similar statements in *Ma'alim*, pp. 69, 71; *Mujtama'*, pp. 102, 103; *Ra'smaliyyah*, pp. 88–9; *Zilal*, vol. 2, p. 1378; *Islam the Religion of the Future*, p. 14.
80 Qutb, *Zilal*, vol. 2, p. 1098; see vol. 2, pp. 805–9.

6 The universe (*al-Kawn*)

1 In the political sphere, see Qutb, *Zilal*, vol. 1, pp. 320, 326, 407–70; vol. 2, pp. 887–91; *'Adalah*, pp. 75–86. In economic: *Zilal*, vol. 3, pp. 1233–5; vol. 4, p. 1917; vol. 5, p. 2772; vol. 6, pp. 3856, 3906; *'Adalah*, pp. 87–125. About behaviour: *Zilal*, vol. 1, pp. 326–30, vol. 2, pp. 903–5, 990. About legislation, see *Zilal*, vol. 2, pp. 762, 895; vol. 3, pp. 1347–8. About philosophy, see *Zilal*, vol. 1, pp. 200, 280, 666, 811; vol. 2, p. 1070; vol. 3, p. 1273; vol. 5, p. 2809.
2 Webster's *New Compact Format Dictionary*, New York: ProSales, Inc. (1988), pp. 269–70.
3 al-Ba'labakki, Rohi, *al-Mawrid: A Modern Arabic–English Dictionary*, Beirut: Dar al-'ilm li al-Malayin, eighth edition, p. 722; also see Ibn Manzur, *Lisan*, vol. 8, p. 232.
4 Ibn Manzur, *Lisan*, vol. 8, p. 232.
5 Qutb, *Mushkilat al-Hadarah*, p. 19 ff. 1.
6 Qutb, *Mushkilat al-Hadarah*, p. 19.
7 Qutb, *'Adalah*, p. 22.
8 Qutb, *Khasa'is*, p. 71.
9 Qutb, *'Adalah*, pp. 201–2.
10 Qutb, *Khasa'is*, p. 67; *Mushkilat al-Hadarah*, pp. 92–3, 104; *Islam the Religion*, pp. 78, 87.
11 Qutb, *Mushkilat al-Hadarah*, pp. 34–44, 52–6, 104, 112; Wajdi, Farid, *al-Islam*, pp. 159–91
12 Qutb, *Khasa'is*, p. 67; *Mushkilat al-Hadarah*, pp. 92–3, 104; *'Adalah*, pp. 201–2; *Zilal*, vol. 1, pp. 200, 280, 666, 811; vol. 2, p. 1070; vol. 3, p. 1273; vol. 5, p. 2809.
13 Husayn, M. Muhammad (1985), *al-Islam wa al-Hadarah al-Gharbiyyah*, pp. 41, 55, 58, 128–32, 135.
14 Qutb, *Mushkilat Hadarah*, p. 19.
15 Qutb, *Mushkilat Hadarah*, p. 19 ff. 1.
16 Qutb, *Khasa'is*, pp. 56, 58, 65, 68, 72, 83, 148.
17 Qutb, *Zilal* vol. 2, pp. 1112–21
18 Qutb, *Zilal* vol. 1, p. 25.
19 Qutb, *Mushkilat Hadarah*, p. 20 ff.
20 Qutb, *Mushkilat Hadarah*, pp. 34–5, *'Adalah*, pp. 20, 75, *Zilal*, vol. 6, p. 3917.
21 For other subjects, see Qutb's dialogue on Haykal's statement that Islam is an Imperial power, in Qutb *Adalah*, p. 77, Hardie's trans., p. 90, Shepard's trans., p. 107.
22 Qutb, *Khasa'is*, p. 169 ff. 1.
23 Shepard, *Sayyid Qutb and Islamic Activism*, p. x.
24 Shepard, *Sayyid Qutb and Islamic Activism*, pp. x–xi.
25 Shepard referred to Mitchell, R. P. (1993), *The Society of the Muslim Brothers*, London: Oxford University Press, 1969, p. 249 and Binder, L. (1988), *Islamic*

Liberalism: A Critic of Development Ideologies, Chicago, IL: University of Chicago Press, p. 187, fn. 60, for these, see, Shepard, *Sayyid Qutb and Islamic Activism*, pp. x, ff. 3.

26 Hardie's trans., '*Social Justice In Islam*', p. 238.
27 Shepard, *Sayyid Qutb and Islamic Activism*, p. 285 line 15.
28 For '*nazariyyat al-hukm*', see Qutb, *Adalah*, p. 80; Shepard's trans., p. 111, paragraph 29.
29 Shepard, *Sayyid Qutb and Islamic Activism*, p. 104 ff. 1.
30 Shepard, *Sayyid Qutb and Islamic Activism*, p. 120, paragraph, 59.
31 Hardie's trans., '*Social Justice In Islam*', p. 99.
32 Qutb, Sayyid, *The Islamic Concept and its Characteristics*, trans. Muhammad Moinuddin siddiqui. American Trust Publications (1991), p. 105.
33 Qutb, *The Islamic Concept*, p. 105; For the ideological importance of the Qutb's phrase '*manhaj rabbani*', see Shepard, *Sayyid Qutb and Islamic Activism*, p. xlvii, p. 29 paragraph 16 and ff. 53, and Glossary p. 367.
34 Qutb, *The Islamic concept*, p. 106.
35 Qutb, *Islam the Religion*, p. 16, see *Zilal*, vol. 30, p. 184, trans. M. A. Salahi, and A. A. Shamis, Riyadh, Saudi Arabia.
36 World Book Encyclopaedia, vol. 4, p. 1078 esp. cosmos.
37 World Book Encyclopaedia, vol. 20, p. 159 esp. universe.
38 Qutb, *Khasa'is*, p. 5.
39 Qutb, *Khasa'is*, p. 16.
40 Qutb, *Mushkilat Hadarah*, pp. 108–9.
41 Qutb, '*Adalah*, pp. 24–5, see p. 22.
42 Qutb, *Zilal*, vol. 5, p. 3226.
43 Qutb, *Zilal*, vol. 4, pp. 2153.
44 Qutb, *Islam the Religion*, p. 34.
45 Qutb, *Ma'alim*, pp. 108–10.
46 Qutb, '*Adalah*, pp. 24–5, see p. 21.
47 Qutb, *Khasa'is*, p. 24.
48 Qutb, *Khasa'is*, p. 5.
49 Qutb, *Khasa'is*, pp. 45, 75, 95, 119, 151, 169, 189; *Mujtama'*, pp. 62, 92.
50 Qutb, *Islam the Religion*, pp. 15–17.
51 Qutb, *Islam the Religion*, pp. 15–17.
52 Qutb, *Ma'alim*, pp. 110–2.
53 Qutb, *Ma'alim*, p. 11.
54 Qutb, *Zilal*, pp. 3802, 3804–6, 3878, 3884.
55 Qutb, *Mujtama'*, pp. 63–7.
56 Qutb, '*Adalah*, p. 32.
57 Qutb, '*Adalah*, pp. 32–3.
58 Qutb, *Mujtama' Islami*, pp. 23, 49, 70–2; *Zilal*, vol. 2, pp. 1032–3; '*Adalah*, p. 26.
59 Kamenka Eugene (1983), *The Portable Karl Marx*, New York: Penguin, p. 136.
60 Kamenka, *The Portable Karl Marx*, p. 134.
61 Kamenka, *The Portable Karl Marx*, pp. 136–7, see pp. 135–9; for cross-examination, see Aronowitz, *The Crisis in Historical Materialism*, pp. 222–4; Qutb, *Ma'alim*, p. 11; *Zilal*, vol. 2, pp. 767, 1088, vol. 3, p. 1357; '*Adalah*, pp. 26–8; *Mushkilat Hadarah*, pp. 104–5.
62 Qutb, *Ma'alim*, p. 58.
63 Qutb, *Zilal*, vol. 4, p. 2144, see pp. 2143–5.
64 Kamenka, *The Portable Karl Marx*, pp. 133–4.
65 Qutb, *Khasa'is*, p. 41; *Zilal*, vol. 1, p. 343; vol. 4, p. 2144; *Universal Peace*, pp. 100–11.

66 Qutb, *Khasa'is*, p. 42.
67 Qutb, *Mujtama'*, p. 64.
68 Qutb, *Khasa'is*, p. 42.
69 Qutb, *Khasa'is*, p. 88, this is followed by a number of Qur'anic texts.
70 Qutb, *Islam the Religion*, p. 33.
71 Qutb, *Khasa'is*, p. 59.
72 Qutb, *Khasa'is*, p. 65.
73 Qutb, *Khasa'is*, p. 66.
74 Qutb, *Khasa'is*, p. 71.
75 Qutb, *Khasa'is*, p. 72.
76 Qutb, *Khasa'is*, p. 72; see, *Zilal*, vol. 2, p. 764.
77 Qutb, *Khasa'is*, p. 72.
78 Qutb, *Islam the Religion*, pp. 64, 67; see *Zilal*, vol. 2, pp. 764, 1097–8; *Khasa'is*, p. 73.
79 Qutb, *Ma'alim*, p. 140; *Islam the Religion*, p. 66.
80 Qutb, *Islam the Religion*, p. 46; *Khasa'is*, pp. 80–1.
81 Qutb, *Islam the Religion*, pp. 66, 73.
82 Qutb, *Ma'alim*, p. 140; *Islam the Religion*, p. 66; *Khasa'is*, pp. 66–7.
83 Qutb, *Ma'alim*, pp. 140, 142–3; *Mushkilat al-Hadarah*, pp. 108, 113–18.
84 Qutb, *Mushkilat Hadarah*, pp. 108, 112–17.
85 Qutb, *Ma'alim*, p. 142.
86 Qutb, *'Adalah*, p. 198.
87 Qutb, *'Adalah*, pp. 201–3; *Ma'alim*, pp. 140–1.
88 Qutb, *Mushkilat al-Hadarah*, pp. 124, 137, 145–8.
89 Qutb, *Khasa'is*, pp. 61–73, 82–6.
90 Qutb, *Khasa'is*, pp. 84, 128, 147–50.
91 Qutb, *'Adalah*, pp. 8–19, 26–30.
92 Qutb, *Khasa'is*, pp. 162, 165, 179; *Fi al-Tarikh*, pp. 38–40.
93 Qutb, *Khasa'is*, pp. 68–70.
94 Qutb, *Ma'alim*, p. 38; *Khasa'is*, pp. 50–7.
95 Qutb, *Ma'alim*, pp. 108–14.
96 Qutb, *Ma'alim*, pp. 110–11.
97 Qutb, *Ma'alim*, pp. 25–30.
98 Qutb, *Ma'alim*, p. 141, see pp. 116–19.
99 Qutb, *'Adalah*, pp. 201–2; see *Ma'alim*, pp. 116, 136–44.
100 Qutb, *Mushkilat al-Hadarah*, p. 177, see p. 178; *'Adalah*, p. 202.
101 Qutb, *'Adalah*, p. 204.
102 Qutb, *Zilal*, vol. 1, pp. 24, 811, 441, 200, 287; vol. 2, pp. 764, 815, 1034, 1035, 1039, 1098; vol. 3, pp. 1272, 1520, 1531, 1588; *Khasa'is*, pp. 64–6, 67–8, 70–1, 73–4, 83; *Ma'alim*, pp. 116, 119, 135–48; *'Adalah*, pp. 198–213; *Mushkilat Hadarah*, pp. 177–84; *Fi al-Tarkh*, pp. 23, 37, 58.
103 Qutb, *Khasa'is*, pp. 10–11; see *'Adalah*, pp. 42, 201–2.

7 Sovereignty and political establishments

1 Qutb, *'Adalah*, p. 75.
2 Haykal, Muhammad Husayn, *al-Imbraturiyyah al-Islamiyyah wa al-Amakin al-Muquddasah*, Cairo: Dar al-Hilal, n.d. pp. 39, 59, 73, 77, 82–3; compare with Qutb, *'Adalah*, pp. 75–80, 82–6.
3 'Abd al-Majeed (1967), *Arab Socialism In the Light of Islam and Arab Reality*, Cairo: The Supreme Council for Islamic Affairs, pp. 31–3, 58–62; Namiq, Salah al-Din, Abd Ellah Amin Mustafa and Lufti Abd al-Hamid (1966), *al-Ishtrakiyyah*

al-Arabiyyah, Cairo: Dar al-Ma'arif, pp. 229–43; Sulayyman, Adli (1964), *Ma'alim al-Hayah al-Ishtrakiyyah fi al-Jama'ah al-Arabiyyah*, first edition, pp. 12–29, 35, 47, 53, 102–28; Sulayman, Adli, *al-Suluk al-Ishtraki li-al-Muwatin al-Arabi*, Cairo, n.d. pp. 81–101; Mursi, Sayyid Abd al-Hammid Brigadier, *Insaniyyat al-Ishtrakiyyah al-Arabiyyah*, Cairo: Makatabat al-Qahirah al-Hadilhah, n.d. pp. 9–18, 29–46.

4 Rodinson, Maxim (1982), *Islam and Capitalism*, pp. 16–19, 31–42, 68, 77, esp. Marxism was considered as not only a revised version of Islam but also the only dynamic system that Muslims should follow, see pp. 202–4.

5 Haykal, *al-Imbraturiyyah*, pp. 16, 38, 63.

6 'Abduh, Muhammad, *Tafsir*, vol. 1, p. 12.

7 Qutb, *'Adalah*, p. 75.

8 Pennock J. Roland (1979), *Democratic Political theory*, Princeton, NJ: Princeton University Press, pp. 246–52; Dunn, John (1979), *Western Political Theory in the Face of the Future*, Cambridge: Cambridge University Press, p. 57, see pp. 55–80.

9 Al-Bazzaz, 'Abd al-Rahman (1962), Islam and Arab Nationalism, in Silvia G. Haim (ed.), *Arab Nationalism*, Berkeley, CA: University of California Press, pp. 172–176, 178–188.

10 Qutb, *Zilal*, vol. 6, pp. 3933, 3966; vol. 5, p. 3027; *Khasa'is*, p. 79.

11 al-Qurtubi, *al-Jami'*, vol. 14, pp. 24–31; vol. 18, p. 133.

12 Ibn Taymiyyah, *al-'ubudiyyah*, p. 70.

13 al-'Asqalani, *Fath al-Bari*, vol. 13, p. 520.

14 'Abduh, Muhammad, *Tafsir*, vol. 1, p. 218.

15 Ibn Manzur, *Lisan*, vol. 3, p. 270; see Ibn Kathir, *Tafsir*, vol. 2, p. 479; al-Qurtubi, *al-Jami'*, vol. 9, p. 129, vol. 13, p. 210; Qutb, *Hadha al-Din*, pp. 20–1.

16 Qutb, *Ma'alim*, pp. 110–13; *Mushkilat Hadarah*, pp. 24–6.

17 Qutb, *al-Islam wa Mushkilat Hadarah*, pp. 122–5; *Islam: The Religion*, pp. 34–58.

18 Qutb, *Ma'alim*, pp. 149, 151–7; *Zilal*, vol. 6, pp. 3933–66; vol. 5, pp. 3027–9; *Khasa'is*, p. 79–80.

19 Qutb, *Ma'alim*, pp. 152, 156–8.

20 Qutb, *Ma'alim*, pp. 149–61.

21 Qutb, *Khasa'is*, pp. 91–2; Qutb refers to Weiss's *Islam at the Crossroads*, translated into Arabic by 'Umar Farrukh, pp. 109–12; also See Weiss, Leopold (1955), *Islam at the Crossroads*. Lahore: Ashraf Publications, pp. 150–5.

22 World Book Dictionary, p. 1383, esp. nationalism.

23 Qutb, *Zilal*, vol. 1, p. 342.

24 Qutb, *Mujtama'*, pp. 96–7.

25 Qutb, *Ra'smaliyyah*, p. 59.

26 Qutb, *Ra'smaliyyah*, p. 61.

27 Translation of the word (*ummah*) by the word (nation) is accurate in dictionary terms, but the word nation does not reflect Qutb's thinking on the word *ummah*, unless the meaning of the word nation means 'a group of people bound together by Islamic belief', Qutb, *Zilal*, vol. 3, p. 1445 ff. 1.

28 Qutb, *Hadha al-Din*, p. 88.

29 Qutb, *Ma'alim*, p. 151.

30 Qutb, *Ma'alim*, p. 159; for further reading on Qutb's view of nationalism in connection to Islam, see *Zilal*, vol. 1, p. 512; vol. 4, p. 2115; *Nahwa Mujtama' Islami*, p. 92.

31 al-'Ashmawi, 'Thawrat Yulyu Ammamat al-Din' (The Revolution of July Nationalized the Religion), *Sabah al-Kheir*, Thursday, 19 April (1990), n. 1789, pp. 8–10, esp. 10.

32 Ibn Manzur, *Lisan*, vol. 12, pp. 499–504.
33 Shahrur, Muhammad (1990), *al-Kitab wa al-Qur'an*: Qira'ah Mu'asirah, Cairo: Sina' li al-Nashr, p. 575, see p. 578.
34 Qutb, *Ma'alim*, pp. 149–61, 165; *Zilal*, vol. 1, pp. 200, 414, 421, 512.
35 Qutb, *Zilal*, vol. 1, pp. 200, 414, 421, 510–12.
36 Qutb, *Zilal*, vol. 3, p. 1305; vol. 4, pp. 1891–2, 2370.
37 Qutb, *Zilal*, vol. 1, pp. 510–12; for a similar view, see *Ma'alim*, pp. 151, 156–61.
38 Huntington, Samuel (1996), *The Clash of Civilizations and the Remaking of World Order*, New York: Simon & Schuster, p. 174.
39 Huntington, *The Clash of Civilizations*, p. 175.
40 Huntington, *The Clash of Civilizations*, pp. 175, 177.
41 Qutb, *Zilal*, vol. 1, p. 126.
42 Pennock, *Democratic Political Theory*, pp. 57, 59, see pp. 55–78.
43 Farah, Caeser E. (1957), *The Impact of the West on the Conflict of Ideologies in the Arab Word*, pp. 310–34.
44 Qutb, *Zilal*, vol. 1, pp. 414–15; also see 'Abduh, Muhammad, *Tafsir al-Manar*, Cairo: Dar al-Ma'arif, second edition, n.d.
45 Qutb, *Zilal*, vol. 1, p. 511; *Ma'lim*, pp. 21, 162–3.
46 On eighth January (1992) Islamists and nationalists debated the issue publicly in Cairo: on the Islamist side were Muhammad 'Umarah, al-Ghazali and Ma'mun al-Hudaybi; the nationalists were represented by Farag Fudah and Muhammad Khalafallah. Speeches were then collected and published in al-Sawi, *al-Muwajahah*, see pp. 62–70, 142148; also see Fudah, Farag (1988), *al-Haqiqah al-Gha'ibah (The Missing Truth)*, Cairo: Dar al-Fikr li al-Dirasat wa al-Nashr Wa al-Tawzi', third edition, pp. 34–44, 76–8; 'Ashmawi, Muhammad Saeed (1987), *al-Islam al-Siyasi (Political Islam)*, Cairo: Sina, pp. 149–60; on the other side see 'Abduh, Muhammad, *Tafsir*, vol. 1, p. 11; Qutb, *Ma'alim*, pp. 108–15.
47 al-Dawalibi, Muhammad Ma'ruf (1994), 'Islam and Nationalistic and Secularistic Trends', in Kharofa, Ala'Eddin (ed.), *Nationalism, Secularism, Apostasy and Uuruy in Islam*, Kuala Lumpur: A. S. Noordeen, pp. 5–6.
48 Gaston, Maspero (1910), *The Dawn of Civilization*: London: London Society for promoting Christian Knowledge, fifth edition, pp. 36–50; also see Petrie W. M. Felinders (1895), *History of Egypt from the Earliest Times to the XVIth dynasty*, London: Methuen, vol. 1, pp. 12–14.
49 Qutb, *Zilal*, vol. 2, p. 673; see vol. 1, pp. 512–15; vol. 2, pp. 686, 1006; vol. 3, p. 1305; vol. 4, pp. 1891, 2459.
50 Qutb, *Zilal*, vol. 2, p. 673.
51 'Abduh, Muhammad, *Tafsir*, vol. 1, p. 25.
52 Qutb, *Zilal*, vol. 5, p. 2584 esp. verse (26: 2); also see vol. 4, p. 1851 esp. verse (11: 1); vol. 3, p. 1759 esp. verse (10: 1).
53 Qutb, *Zilal*, vol. 4, p. 2087.
54 'Abduh, Muhammad, *Tafsir*, vol. 1, p. 25.
55 Qutb, *Zilal*, vol. 2, pp. 685–6.
56 Qutb, *Zilal*, vol. 5, p. 2617, vol. 3, p. 1562 esp. open society for 'the Egyptian, the Persian . . . '.
57 See, Huntington, *The Clash of Civilizations*, pp. 59–60, 62, 269.
58 'Abduh, Muhammad, *Tafsir*, vol. 1, p. 24.
59 Qutb, *Zilal*, vol. 2, p. 673.
60 Ibn Khaldun, Abd al-Rahman b. Muhammad, *al-Muqaddimah*, Beirut: Mu'assasal-al-A 'lami li al-Matbu 'at, n.d., vol. 1, p. 543, see p. 544; also see 'Abduh, Muhammad, *Tafsir*, vol. 1, p. 24.

61 Ibn 'Asakir, *Kanz al-'Ummal*, Lahore: Kashmir Bazar, vol. 12, p. 47.
62 Qutb, *Zilal*, vol. 2, p. 673.
63 See Ibn Khaldun, *Muqaddimah*, pp. 543–55; Qutb wrote an article entitled '*The Arabic Language in the Muslim world*', *al-Risalah* (1951), n. 965, pp. 1469–71, but I have not had opportunity to see it.
64 'Abduh, Muhammad, *Tafsir*, vol. 1, p. 11.
65 al-Bayyumi, Muhammad Rajab (1994), 'al-Imam al-Akbar: 'Abd al-Rahman Tajj', *Majallat al-Azhar*, November, vol. 67, part 6, pp. 781–6, cf. p. 785.
66 Qutb, *Zilal*, vol. 4, p. 1891.
67 Qutb, *Ma'alim*, pp. 10, 151; also see Huntington, *The Clash of Civilizations*, p. 174.
68 The *qiblah* is the direction to which Muslims turn in prayer.
69 Qutb, *Zilal*, vol. 1, p. 134; see vol. 1, pp. 344, 412, 442; vol. 2, pp. 1005–6, 1126; Huntington, *The Clash of Civilizations*, p. 175.
70 Qutb, *Ma'alim*, pp. 27–8, 57–9.
71 See al-'Ashmawi (1987), *al-Islam al-Siyasi*, Chapter 'al-Qawmiyyah al-Islamiyyah', pp. 149–1701; Fudah, Farag, *al-Haqiqah al-Gha'ibah*, pp. 17–18, 119.
72 Ansari, Nasser (1987), *Mawsu'at Hukkam Misr* mina al-fara 'inah hatta al-Yawm, Cairo: Dar al-Shuruq, first edition, pp. 22–38.
73 Qutb, *Ma'alim*, pp. 151–2.
74 Ibn Kathir, *al-Bidayah*, vol. 2, part 1, pp. 47, 58, 64, 93, 173, 204, 211, 246, 255.
75 For the speech of the Prophet, see Ibn Hisham, Abd al-Malik (1995), *al-Sirah al-Natawiyyah*, Beirut: Dar Ihya al-Tulrath al-Arabi, first edition, vol. 1, p. 303, see, pp. 299–304.
76 al-Tabari Abi Ja'far Mahammad b. Janr, *Tarikh al-umam wa al-shu'ub*, Beirut: Dar al-Kutub al-'Ilmiyyah vol. 2, pp. 22–3.
77 al-Tabari, *Tarikh*, vol. 2, pp. 152–5.
78 Qutb, *Zilal*, vol. 2, pp. 1005–7; see also p. 1126; vol. 3, pp. 1562.
79 Qutb, *Zilal*, vol. 3, p. 1562; vol. 4, pp. 1885–8.
80 Rif'at, Mohammed (1947), *The Awakening of Modern Egypt*, London, New York: Longmans, Green, p. 12.
81 Ansari, *Hukkam Misr*, p. 24.
82 The capital city was called the 'White Castle', later called 'Memph' and then 'Memphis' and is still known by these names and is situated about 50 km from the modern capital city Cairo; for further details see Jacq, Christian (1996), *Ramses*, five volumes, see vol. 2, p. 6; Ansari, *Hukkam Misr*, p. 24.
83 Qutb, *Mashahid al-Qiyamah*, p. 15, see pp. 14–21.
84 Ansari, *Hukkam Misr*, pp. 22–38, for flags see p. 217, for the national anthem, see pp. 148–9, for the official stamp and sign, see pp. 183–96.
85 Jacq, Christian, *Ramses*, vol. 3, p. 8.
86 Tomlin, Eric W. Frederick (1959), *Great Philosophers of the East*, London: Arrow, pp. 44–5.
87 Husayn, Muhammad, *Islam wa al-Hadarah al-Gharbiyyah*, pp. 20–24.
88 Haykal, Muhammad Hasanayn (1994), 'Nahnu Nasiru bi-Sur'ah Mudhhilah Walakin la Na'rifu ila Ayn?', *Rose el-Youssef*, February 14, n. 3427, p. 42, Rifa'ah al-Tahtawi (d. 1873), Taha Husayn (d. 1973), Tawfiq al-Hakim (d. 1989), Husayn Haykal (d. 1953) and al-Aqqad (d. 1954) all were literary critics who had received Western education. Tahtawi was sent by Muhammad 'Ali (ruled Egypt from 1805 to 1848 and died in 1849) to study in France. Tahtawi lived in Paris for five years (1826–1831) and returned to lead westernization processes in Egypt; for further reading see Husayn, Muhammad, *Islam wa al-Hadarah al-Gharbiyyah*, pp. 18–30, 66.

89 Salt, Jeremy (1994), 'Strategies of Islamic Revivalism in Egypt', *Journal of Arab, Islamic and Middle East studies*, vol. 1, n. 2, p. 91.
90 Al-Liwa' [Jordanian Journal], 10 September (1986), n. 696 cited in al-Hilal [Egyptian Journal], September 1986 cf. Hanafi, Hasan (1990), 'al-Jama'at al-Islamiyyah la Tuwajih al-Aqabat', *Rose el-Youssef*, 16 April (1990), n. 3227, p. 32.
91 al-Khalidi Salah (1958), *Amrica Min al-Dakhil bi-Minzar Sayyid Qutb*, p. 299.
92 World Book Encyclopaedia, vol. 13, p. 614.
93 Hanafi, Hasan (1989), *al-Harakat al-Islamiyyah fi Misr*, Cairo: al-Mu'assasah al-Islamiyyah lial-Nashr, first edition, p. 45.
94 Qutb, *Dirasat Islamiyyah*, pp. 163–4.
95 al-Husari is a leading figure of Arab Nationalism, for further detail about his ideological position and his debate with Taha Husayn, see al-Kilani, Sami (1973), *Ma'a Taha Husayn*, Cairo: Dar al-Ma'arif, pp. 122–3. As for Sa'adah, he is the founder of the Syrian Nationalist Party. cf. Qutb, *Dirasat*, p. 166 ff. 1.
96 Asim, Muhammad, 'Mushkilatina fi Daw' al-Islam', in Qutb, *Dirasat Islamiyyah*, pp. 165–7.
97 Qutb, *Dirasat Islamiyyah*, p. 168.
98 Qutb, *Dirasat Islamiyyah*, p. 164.
99 For further details, see Mahmud Nasr, 'Fu'ad 'Allam Yftah Dhakiratahu 'ala al-Ikhwan al-Muslimun', *Uktuber*, 31 July (1996), n. 1030, pp. 44–5.
100 Qutb, *Zilal*, vol. 1, p. 126, see pp. 127–9; also see *Limadha A'damoni*, pp. 91–4.
101 Qutb, *Zilal*, vol. 1, p. 129.
102 Qutb, *Ma'alim*, pp. 149–50.
103 'Abduh, Muhammad, *Tafsir*, vol. 1, p. 11.
104 'Abduh, Muhammad, *Tafsir*, vol. 1, p. 6.
105 'Abduh, Muhammad, *Tafsir*, vol. 1, p. 25.
106 Al-Banna, *Rasa'il*, pp. 141–4.
107 Qur'an, 6: 38; 10: 19, 47; 11: 8; 12: 2; 13: 30; 16: 93, 120; 21: 92; 43: 22–3.
108 Asad, Muhammad (1980), *The Message of the Qur'an*, Gibraltar: Dar-al-Andalus, p. 177.
109 Ayubi, Nazih (1991), *Political Islam: Religion and Politics in the Arab World*, London: Routledge, p. 3.
110 Ibn Hisham, *al-Sirah*, vol. 2, pp. 115–8.
111 Qutb, *Zilal*, vol. 1, pp. 126, 129, 134, 344, 412, 442, 512; vol. 2, pp. 686, 1005–6, 1126; vol. 3, pp. 1305, 1562–3; vol. 4, pp. 1885–8, 1891–2, 2370; vol. 6, p. 3515; *Nahwa Mujtama' Islami*, pp. 18–23.
112 Qur'an, 43: 22–3.
113 Qutb, *Zilal*, vol. 4, pp. 1890–2.
114 Huntington, *The Clash of Civilizations*, p. 175.
115 Qutb, *Zilal*, vol. 1, p. 113.
116 Qutb, *Ma'alim*, p. 149.
117 Qutb, *Ma'alim*, p. 150.
118 Qutb, *Nahwa Mujtama' Islami*, p. 21; *Zilal*, vol. 4, p. 2101; vol. 6, p. 3515; *Ma'alim*, p. 149.
119 Qutb, *Zilal*, vol. 4, pp. 1885–8.
120 Qutb, *Ma'alim*, pp. 29–30; *Hadha al-Din*, pp. 85–7.
121 Qutb, *Hadha al-Din*, p. 87.
122 Qutb, *Ra'smaliyyah*, pp. 5–10; Rodinson (1960), *Islam and Capitalism* (English translation), p. 24; Weber, Max (1956), *The Protestant Ethic and the Spirit of Capitalism*, trans. Talcott Parsons, New York: Charles Scribener's Sons, p. I(e).

123 Qutb, *Mushkilat Hadarah*, p. 97.
124 Qutb, *Mujtama'*, p. 79, *Zilal*, vol. 2, pp. 924–5.
125 Qutb, *Mushkilat Hadarah*, pp. 97–100.
126 Qutb, *Mujtama'*, p. 81.
127 Aronowitz, *The Crisis in Historical Materialism*, pp. 72–5.
128 Weber, *The Protestant Ethic and the Spirit of Capitalism*, p. 36; Brinton Cran (1967), Enlightenment, *The Encylopedia of Philosophy*, vol. 2, p. 521.
129 E. A. Burtt (1955), *The Metaphysical Foundations of Modern Science*, Garden City, NY: Doubleday, p. 17.
130 Voltaire wrote in his *Treaties on Toleration*; He would have borne with absurdities of dogma had the clergy lived up to sermons and had tolerated differences but 'subtleties of which not a trace can be found in the gospels are the source of the bloody quarrels of Christian history'. Voltaire, *Selected Works*, p. 62, cf. Will Durant (1970), *The Story of Philosophy*, Washington: Washington Square Press, p. 237.
131 Will Durant (1953), *The Story of Civilization*, vol. 5, p. 572.
132 Rodinson, *Islam and Capitalism*, pp. 115–6.
133 Qutb, *Zilal*, vol. 1, p. 139.
134 Qutb, *'Adalah*, p. 90.
135 Qutb, *'Adalah*, pp. 88–102.
136 Qutb, *Mushkilat Hadarah*, p. 97.
137 Qutb, *Mujtama'*, p. 83.
138 Qutb, *Mujtama'*, p. 82.
139 Qutb, *Zilal*, vol. 1, p. 166; vol. 3, p. 1562; *Mujtama'*, pp. 136–7.
140 Qutb, *Hadha al-Din*, pp. 18, 51, 67; *'Adalah*, p. 100.
141 Qutb, *'Adalah*, p. 88; *Muskilat Hadarah*, pp. 89, 194; *Mujtama'*, pp. 138, 142, 144.
142 Qutb, *'Adalah*, p. 76.
143 Weber, Max (1956) *Max Weber on Capitalism, Bureaucracy and Religion: A Selection of Texts*, edited and in part newly trans. Stanislav Andreski, London: George Allen & Unwin (1983), p. 158 also see p. 111.
144 Qutb, *al-Salam*, p. 104.
145 Qutb, *'Adalah*, p. 87.
146 Qutb, *Zilal*, vol. 1, pp. 573–6.
147 Qutb, *'Adalah*, pp. 89–90; *Zilal*, vol. 1, pp. 326–30; vol. 2, p. 994; *al-Salam*, p. 135.
148 Qutb, *'Adalah*, pp. 89–90.
149 Qutb, *Zilal*, vol. 1, pp. 579–81.
150 Qutb, *Zilal*, vol. 5, pp. 2646–8.
151 Russell, *A Free Man's Worship: Mysticism and Logic*, p. 46; Burtt, *The Metaphysical*, p. 24.
152 Qutb, *'Adalah*, p. 90.
153 Qutb, *Mushkilat Hadarah*, pp. 89–90, 97–9; *Hadha al-Din*, pp. 19–26, 53, 76.
154 Qutb, *Zilal*, vol. 1, p. 422, for further details on the result of capitalism, see pp. 422–4; 472–6.
155 Qutb, *Mujtama'*, p. 83; *'Adalah*, p. 90.
156 Qutb, *'Adalah*, pp. 81, 90–4; *Zilal*, vol. 1, p. 341; vol. 2, pp. 751–3; vol. 4, p. 2144.
157 Qutb, *Mujtama'*, pp. 84–6.
158 al-Fangari, Muhammad Shawqi (1995), *al-Islam wa 'Adalat al-Tawzi'*, Cairo: al-Hay'ah al-Misriyyah al-'Ammah Lial-Kilab, p. 44.
159 Qutb, *'Adalah*, pp. 44–62; *Zilal*, vol. 1, pp. 319, 511.

160 Chapra, M. Umar, (1992/1413H), *Islam and the Economic Challenge*, Riyadh: International Islamic Publishing House, p. 18.
161 Qutb, *'Adalah*, p. 103.
162 Qutb, *Ra'smaliyyah*, pp. 44–8; *al-Salam*, pp. 72–7, 104, 136.
163 Qutb, *Ra'smaliyyah*, pp. 49–54; *al-Salam*, pp. 62–6, 130–7, 167–76.
164 Qutb, *'Adalah*, pp. 57, 90, 91, 103–5; *Ra'smaliyyah*, pp. 39–51.
165 Qutb, *Mujtama'*, pp. 83–4.
166 Qutb, *'Adalah*, p. 91.
167 Qutb, *Zilal*, vol. 5, p. 2772.
168 Qutb, *'Adalah*, p. 91.
169 Qutb, *'Adalah*, p. 92.
170 Qutb, *'Adalah*, p. 91.
171 Qutb, *'Adalah*, p. 92.
172 Qutb, *'Adalah*, p. 92.
173 Qutb, *'Adalah*, p. 99.
174 Qutb, *Mujtama'*, pp. 127–30.
175 Qutb, *'Adalah*, p. 93.
176 Qutb, *Ra'smaliyyah*, pp. 74–7, 80–2, 96, 99, 104.
177 Qutb, *'Adalah*, p. 96–8.
178 Qutb, *'Adalah*, p. 94.
179 Qutb, *'Adalah*, p. 95.
180 Qutb, *'Adalah*, p. 95.
181 Al-Qaradawi, Yusuf (1985), *The Lawful and the Prohibited in Islam*, Kuala Lumpur: Islamic Book Trust, p. 134.
182 Qutb, *Zilal*, vol. 1, p. 213, vol. 2, p. 663.
183 Qutb, *Zilal*, vol. 1, pp. 326–7; *Mushkilat Hadarah*, pp. 64, 70–7; *Zilal*, vol. 2, pp. 663, 667.
184 Qutb, *Mujtama'*, pp. 94–6.
185 Qutb, *'Adalah*, pp. 53–62, *Zilal*, vol. 1, p. 590.
186 Qutb, *Zilal*, vol. 1, pp. 307, 590, 591l; vol. 2, p. 994; *'Adalah*, pp. 67, 100, 119–125.
187 utb, *'Adalah*, p. 100.
188 Campion, H. (1939), *Public and Private Property in Great Britain*, London: Oxford University Press, pp. 14, 83.
189 Qutb, *Tifl mina al-Qaryah*, p. 21.
190 Qutb, *Tifl*, pp. 33, 37, 156, 182, 207.
191 Qutb, *'Adalah*, pp. 53–62; *Zilal*, vol. 1, p. 586.
192 Qur'an, 24: 33; 56: 63; 36: 71; 28: 77; 11: 87; 43: 32; 70: 34–5; 6: 142; 59: 7.
193 See Campion, H., *Public and Private Property in Great Britain*, pp. 14, 83.
194 Qutb, *Zilal*, vol. 1, p. 586.
195 Qutb, *Zilal*, vol. 1, p. 590, for further details about the difference between the rules of inheritance in Islam and other systems, see Qutb *Zilal*, vol. 1, pp. 586–97.
196 Qutb, *Zilal*, vol. 1, p. 586.
197 Qutb, *Zilal*, vol. 1, p. 586.
198 Qutb, *Zilal*, vol. 1, pp. 587–8.
199 Qutb, *Zilal*, vol. 1, p. 593.
200 Qutb, *Zilal*, vol. 1, p. 590, esp. the hadith which transmitted by al-'Ufi from Ibn Abbas.
201 Qutb, *Zilal*, vol. 1, p. 592.
202 Qutb, *Zilal*, vol. 1, p. 593.

203 Qutb, *Zilal*, vol. 1, p. 593.
204 See Qutb, *Zilal*, vol. 1, pp. 318–29.
205 Qutb, *'Adalah*, p. 101.
206 Qutb, *'Adalah*, p. 100; al-Qaradawi, *The Lawful and The Prohibited in Islam*, pp. 255–7.
207 Qutb, *Zilal*, vol. 2, 639, 893, *'Adalah*, p. 96.
208 Qutb, *'Adalah*, p. 100.
209 Qutb, *Zilal*, vol. 2, pp. 639–40, 893; *'Adalah*, pp. 102–5.
210 Qutb, *Ma'alim*, pp. 5, 10, 92, 96, 98, 108.
211 'Abd al-Majeed, *Arab Socialism*, 1967, p. 11.
212 Shahrastani (1986), *Milal wa Nihal*, vol. 1, p. 249; see al-Tabari, *Tarikh*, vol. 1, p. 419.
213 Bausani, Alessandrom (1971), *The Persians: From the Earliest Days to the Twentieth Century*, St. Matin, pp. 86–7.
214 Chapra, *Islam and the Economic Challenge*, p. 71, for more details see al-Maydani, *Kawashif Ziyuf al-Madhahib al-Fikriyyah al-Mu'asirah*, pp. 416–17.
215 al-Badri, Abol al-Aziz (1983), *Hukm al-Islam fi al-Ishtrakiyyah*, Al-Madinah: al-Matbáh al-'Ilmiyyah, fifth edition, pp. 65–7.
216 Griffith D. F. (1924), *What is Socialism? A Symposium on Distribution of Wealth in Islam*, London: Richards, cited by Wilczynski J. (1978), *The Economics of Socialism*, London: George Allen & Unwin, third edition, p. 21, for further details see Chapra, *Islam and the Economic Challenge*, p. 71, see p. 107 ff.
217 Qutb, *Zilal*, vol. 3, p. 1357, vol. 4, p. 2144.
218 al-Badri, *Hukm al-Islam fi al-Ishtrakiyyah*, p. 128.
219 Lichtheim, George (1978), *A Short History of Socialism*, Glasgow: Collins, pp. 308–9
220 Qutb, *Mujtama'*, pp. 86–8.
221 Qutb, *Zilal*, vol. 3, p. 1357, vol. 4, p. 2144.
222 Chapra, *Islam and the Economic Challenge*, p. 71.
223 Qutb, *Zilal*, vol. 2, pp. 1083–4, *Mujtama'*, pp. 86–8.
224 Qutb, *Zilal*, vol. 1, p. 323.
225 Qutb, *Mujtama'*, pp. 86–8; for a similar account, see *Zilal*, vol. 1, p. 326.
226 See Qutb, *Mujtama'*, pp. 86–7.
227 See Qutb, *'Adalah*, p. 75; see Shepard, *Sayyid Qutb and Islamic Activism*, p. 105, Para. 4.
228 Qutb, *Mujtama'*, pp. 86–7.
229 Qutb, *Khasa'is*, p. 17.
230 Qutb, *Zilal*, vol. 2, pp. 1083–4 (this part was revised and reflects Qutb's view in 1961); also see vol. 3, p. 1357 ff. 1, the revised *Zilal* is the second edition which was published in 1961.
231 Qutb, *Zilal*, vol. 4, p. 2131 (this part was not revised and reflects Qutb's view in the period 1952–1959); also see vol. 4, pp. 2144–5, 2195 (not revised).
232 Qutb, *Ma'alim*, pp. 116–17.
233 Qutb, *Zilal*, vol. 2, pp. 767, 1033, 1088; vol. 4, p. 2144; *'Adalah*, pp. 26–8, 48, 78.
234 Among these publications, Mursi, *Insaniyyat al-Ishtrakiyyah al-Arabiyyah*, pp. 9–18; Namiq *et al.*, *al-Ishtrakiyyah al-Arabiyyah*, pp. 229–43; Sulayman (1964), *Ma'alim al-Hayah al-Ishtrakiyyah fi al-Jama'ah al-Arabiyyah*, pp. 12–29, 35, 47, 53, 102–28; Sulayman, *al-Suluk al-Ishtiraki li-al-Muwatin al-Arabi*, pp. 81–101.

235 Robert, Stephens (1971), *Nasser: A Political Biography*, London: The Penguin Press, p. 344; Enayat, Hamid (1982) *Modren Islamic Political Thought*, Texas, The University of Texas Press, p. 140.
236 'Abd al-Majeed, *Arab Socialism*, p. 9.
237 Enayat, Hamid, *Modern Islamic Political Thought*, p. 140.
238 Enayat, Hamid, *Modern Islamic Political Thought*, p. 140.
239 Namiq *et al.*, *al-Ishtrakiyyah al-'Arabiyyah*, p. 299.
240 Enayat, Hamid, *Modern Islamic Political Thought*, p. 140.
241 Enayat, Hamid, *Modern Islamic Political Thought*, p. 141; see Mursi, *Insaniyyat al-Ishtrakiyyah al-Arabiyyah*, pp. 142–3.
242 Mursi, *Insaniyyat al-Ishtrakiyyah al-Arabiyyah*, pp. 142–3.
243 Mursi, *Insaniyyat al-Ishtrakiyyah al-Arabiyyah*, p. 131.
244 'Ashmawi, Muhammad Said (1990), 'Thawrat Yulyu Ammamat al-Din' (the Revolution of July nationalized the religion), *Sabah al-Kheir* (*Good morning*), Thursday, April (1990), n. 1789, pp. 8–10, esp. 10.
245 Mursi, *Insaniyyat al-Ishtrakiyyah al-Arabiyyah*, pp. 132–6.
Namiq *et al.*, *al-Ishtrakiyyah al-Arabiyyah*, pp. 229–43; Sulayman, *Ma'alim al-Hayah al-Ishtrakiyyah fi al-Jama'ah al-Arabiyyah*, pp. 12–29, 35, 47, 53, 102–28; Sulayman, *al-Suluk al-Ishtraki li-al-Muwatin al-Arabi*, pp. 81–101.
246 Umar, Hulayq, *Dawr al-Markisiyyah fi al-Ishtrakiyyah al-Arabiyyah*, Beirut: Dar al-Fikr al-Jadid, first edition, p. 104.
247 Group of Thinkers (1965), *al-Ishtirakiyyah fi al-Tajarib al-Arabiyyah*, Cairo, n.p., p. 217.
248 Umar, Hulayq, *Dawr al-Markisiyyah fi al-Ishtrakiyyah al-Arabiyyah*, p. 104.
249 Qutb, *Zilal*, vol. 2, pp. 1083–4; *'Adalah*, pp. 7–8, 11, 16–18, 78.
250 Robert, *Nasser: A political Biography*, p. 345.
251 Mursi, *Insaniyyat al-Ishtrakiyyah al-Arabiyyah*, pp. 8–9, 132–6.
252 Qutb, *'Adalah*, pp. 7, 76–8.
253 Qutb, *Zilal*, vol. 2, pp. 1083–4.
254 'Abd al-Nasser, Gamal (1955), *The Philosophy of Revolution*, Washington, DC: Public Affairs Press, p. 88.
255 See, Enayat, Hamid, *Modern Islamic Political Thought*, p. 142.
256 Isma'il, Sayful Dawlah (1965), *Usus Ishtrakiyyat al-Islam*, Cairo, n.p., p. 5.
257 Enayat, Hamid, *Modern Islamic Political Thought*, p. 142; also see al-Badri, *Hukm al-Islam fi al-Ishtrakiyyah*, pp. 62–3, 68.
258 Enayat, Hamid, *Modern Islamic Political Thought*, p. 142.
259 Enayat, Hamid, *Modern Islamic Political Thought*, pp. 142–3; for further details on Marxism in Arab Socialism see Umar, Hulayq, *Dawr al-Markisiyyah fi al-Ishtrakiyyah al-Arabiyyah*, pp. 51–5, 65–77, 85, 103–9.
260 Umar, Hulayq, *Dawr al-Markisiyyah fi al-Ishtirakiyyah al-Arabiyyah*, p. 103; also see pp. 217–28, 240, 246–52.
261 Qutb, *'Adalah*, 7, 76–8.
262 Shaltut, Muhammad, 'Socialism and Islam' in Kemal H. Karpat (ed.) *Political and Social Thought in the Middle East*. New York: Praeger (1968), pp. 126–32.
263 al-Bayyumi, Muhammad Rajab (1995) 'Min A'lam al-Azhar al-Duktur Muhammad al-Bahayy', *Majallat al-Azhar*, March, vol. 67, part 10, pp. 1373–7.
264 Enayat, Hamid, *Modern Islamic Political Thought*, p. 144.
265 Enayat, Hamid, *Modern Islamic Political Thought*, p. 144.
266 Qutb *Ma'alim*, pp. 5, 8, 9, 10, 12, 38, 58–60, 90, 98, 118–20, 122, 140.
267 Smith, *Islam in Modern History*, p. 157 .

268 Al-Bazzaz, 'Abd al-Rahman (1962), 'Islam and Arab Nationalism', in Silvia G. Haim (ed.), *Arab Nationalism*, Berkeley, CA: University of California Press, pp. 172–6, 178–88.
269 Al-Nadawi, Abu al-Hasan (1990), *Shakhsiyyat wa Kutub* (*Personalities and Books*), Damascus: Dar al-Qalam, pp. 101–11.
270 Qutb, *Ma'alim*, pp. 5, 8, 9, 10, 12, 38, 58–60, 90, 98, 118–20, 122, 140; *Mujtama' Islami*, pp. 86–8; *'Adalah*, pp. 7, 9, 11, 12, 76–8, 198–9; *Zilal*, vol. 2, pp. 1083–4.
271 Qutb, *'Adalah*, p. 7.
272 Plato (1951) *The Republic of Plato*, trans. Comford, Francis Macdonald, Oxford: Oxford University Press, pp. 142–4, 274–5.
273 Russell, *History of Western Philosophy*, p. 137; for Aristotle's criticism of Plato's view of Communism see Russell, *History of Western Philosophy*, pp. 199, 200.
274 Russell, *History of Western Philosophy*, p. 125.
275 Kamenka, *The Portable Karl Marx*, pp. 125–9.
276 Aronowitz, *The Crisis in Historical Materialism*, pp. 6–12.
277 Qutb, *Muskilat Hadarah*, pp. 21–3, 49, 50, 104.
278 Qutb, *Zilal*, vol. 4, p. 2144; vol. 2, pp. 1032, 1033.
279 Qutb, *Muskilat Hadarah*, p. 104.
280 Qutb, *Khasa'is*, p. 67; see *Ra'smalyyah*, pp. 19–20; see pp. 109, 110; *Zilal*, vol. 4, p. 2144; see Maclnnes, Neil (1967), 'Karl Marx', in *Encyclopaedia of Philosophy*, vol. 5, p. 172.
281 Qutb, *Khasa'is* p. 215; see John Plamenatz (1975), *Karl Marx's Philosophy of Man*, Oxford: Clarendon Press, pp. 11–13.
282 Qutb, *Khasa'is*, p. 84.
283 Qutb, *Khasa'is*, p. 84 and ff. 1.
284 Kamenka, *The Portable Karl Marx*, p. 126.
285 Qutb, *Khasa'is*, p. 67–8, see pp. 70, 71, 83; also see Russell, *History of Western Philosophy*, p. 737.
286 Kamenka, *The Portable Karl Marx*, p. 126; also see Qutb, *Khasa'is*, pp. 68, 70.
287 Qutb, *Khasa'is*, p. 70, see p. 68; *Zilal*, vol. 3, pp. 1356–7.
288 Qutb, *Khasa'is*, p. 70.
289 Kamenka, *The Portable Karl Marx*, p. 126.
290 Kamenka, *The Portable Karl Marx*, p. 127; for similar views see Qutb, *Khasa'is*, pp. 70–1; *Zilal*, vol. 2, p. 1088; al-Maydani (1985), *Kawashif Ziyuf al-Madhahib al-Fikriyyah*, pp. 440–1.
291 al-Maydani, *Kawashif Ziyuf al-Madhahib al-Fiikriyyah al-Mu'asirah*, pp. 439–40.
292 Kamenka, *The Portable Karl Marx*, p. 126.
293 Qutb, *Mushkilat Hadarah*, p. 104; *Mujtama'*, pp. 49, 50, 88–90; *Zilal*, vol. 4, p. 2144.
294 Qutb, *Zilal*, vol. 2, pp. 767, 1088, *'Adalah*, p. 28.
295 Qutb, *Ra'smalyyah*, pp. 25, 38, 45, 61, 109, 110; *Zilal*, vol. 4, p. 2144.
296 Qutb, *'Adalah*, pp. 10, 27; Aronowitz, *The Crisis in Historical Materialism*, pp. 81–3.
297 Qutb, *Muskilat Hadarah*, pp. 89–91; *Hadha al-Din*, pp. 21, 24.
298 Qutb, *Zilal*, vol. 2, pp. 1032–3, 1088; vol. 3, pp. 1356–7; vol. 4, p. 2144; Aronowitz, *The Crisis in Historical Materialism*, pp. 105–7.
299 Qutb, *'Adalah*, p. 26, see pp. 27–8; *Zilal*, vol. 2, pp. 767, 1088; vol. 3, p. 1357; vol. 4, p. 2144; *Mushkilat Hadarah*, pp. 104–5; *Hadha al-Din*, pp. 18–19, 27, 52–3, 67.

300 John Plamenatz, *Karl Marx's Philosophy of Man*, pp. 37–8.
301 Kamenka, *The Portable Karl Marx*, p. 127; Qutb, *Mujtama'*, pp. 49–50, 88–90; *Khasa'is*, pp. 85–6.
302 Kamenka, *The Portable Karl Marx*, p. 133; Qutb, *Mujtama' Islami*, pp. 88–9; *Khasa'is*, pp. 67–8, 85–6; al-Maydani, *Kawashif Ziyuf al-Madhahib al-Fikriyyah al-Mu'asirah*, pp. 440–1; Sakwa, Richard (1989), *Soviet Politics*, London: Routledge, pp. 8–11.
303 Qutb, *Mujtama'*, p. 90.
304 Qutb, *Muskilat Hadarah*, p. 89.
305 Qutb, *'Adalah*, p. 26 (this is from the last edition and reflects Qutb's view in the 1960s); similar is in *Zilal*, vol. 2, pp. 767, 1088; vol. 3, p. 1357; vol. 4, p. 2144 (this is form the last revised part).
306 Qutb, *'Adalah*, p. 27 (this is from the last edition and reflects Qutb's view in 1960s); also see *Mujtama'*, pp. 90–1 (this reflects Qutb's view in the 1950s).
307 Qutb, *Mujtama'*, p. 26.
308 Qutb, *Mujtama'*, p. 39.
309 Qutb, *Mujtama'*, p. 40.
310 Qutb, *Mujtama'*, p. 39.
311 Qutb, *Islam: the Religion*, pp. 65, 66; also see *Mushkilat Hadarah*, p. 91.
312 Aronowitz, *The Crisis in Historical Materialism*, p. 1.
313 Aronowitz, *The Crisis in Historical Materialism*, p. 8.
314 Qutb, *Zilal*, vol. 2, pp. 1032, 1033; *'Adalah*, pp. 10, 104, 105; *Hadha al-Din*, pp. 24, 26, 48.
315 Aronowitz, *The Crisis in Historical Materialism*, pp. 104–8.
316 Al-Salus Ali (1991), 'Islamic Economy', *Majallat al-Azhar*, n. 1411, pp. 80–104, cf. pp. 93–4.
317 Qutb, *Ma'alim*, p. 5.
318 Pennock, *Democratic Political Theory*, p. 3; Russell, *History of Western Philosophy*, pp. 78, 89, 91, 700, 737.
319 See al-Hakim, Tawfiq, *Tawfiq al-Hakim al-Mufakkir*, p. 95.
320 Marshall, Gordon, (1998), *A Dictionary of Sociology*, Oxford: Oxford University Press, second edition, p. 147.
321 Raymond, Boudon and Francois Bourricaud (1989), *A Critical Dictionary of Sociology*, Chicago, IL: The University of Chicago Press, p. 105.
322 See Marshall, Gordon, *Oxford Dictionary of Sociology*, p. 147.
323 Herald and Sun, (1954), *The New International Illustrated Encyclopaedia*, vol. 2, pp. 371–2.
324 Thomson, David (1957), *Europe Since Napoleon*, London: Longmans, p. 10.
325 Thomson, David, *Europe Since Napoleon*, p. 112.
326 Green V. H. H., *The Hanoverians 1714–1815*, p. 30.
327 Dunn, John (1979),*Western Political Theory*, p. 6; Russell, *History of Western Philosophy*, pp. 652, 665, 669, 700, 737.
328 Herald and Sun, *The New International Illustrated Encyclopedia*, vol. 2, p. 372.
329 Thomson, David, *Europe Since Napoleon*, p. 341.
330 Herald and Sun, *The New International Illustrated Encuclopedia*, vol. 2, p. 372.
331 Thomson, David, *Europe Since Napoleon*, pp. 341–2.
332 Herald and Sun, *The New International Illustrated Encyclopedia*, vol. 2, p. 372.
333 Thomson, David, *Europe Since Napoleon*, pp. 366, 367–8; al-Maydani, *Kawashif Ziyuf fi al-Madhahib al-Fikriyyah al-Mu'asirah*, p. 709.
334 Qutb, *Mujtama'*, pp. 86–7; *al-Salam*, pp. 130–42.
335 Groth, Alexander (1990), *Democracy in England*, World Book Encyclopedia vol. 5, p. 129.

336 Marshall, Gordon (1998), *Oxford Dictionary of Sociology*, p. 147.
337 Margolis, Michael (1979), *Viable Democracy*, p. 27.
338 Salih, Hafiz (1992), *al-Dimocratiyyah wa al-Hurriyyah*, Lahore: Dar al-Fath, pp. 9–10.
339 Salih, Hafiz, *al-Dimocratiyyah wa al-Hurriyyah*, p. 10.
340 See Herald and Sun, *The New International Illustrated Encyclopedia*, Melbourne, A Colorgravure Publication, vol. 2, pp. 373–4.
341 Graeme, Duncan (1983), *Democratic Theory and Practice*, Cambridge: Cambridge University Press, p. 3.
342 Qutb, *Khasa'is al-Tasawwur al-Islami*, pp. 89–92, 95–8.
343 Graeme, Duncan, *Democratic Theory and Practice*, p. 15.
344 Graeme, Duncan, *Democratic Theory and Practice*, p. 15.
345 Graeme, Duncan, *Democratic Theory and Practice*, p. 16, see p. 17.
346 Plato's critique is given in its most elaborate form in BKVIII of *The Republic*, ed. F. M. Cornford, Oxford (1949), esp. pp. 282–6 and 290–2. Aristotle's critique of Democracy is provided in *The Politics*, trans. by E. Barker, Oxford (1948), esp. in bk III, Ch. VII–XI, and bk IV, ch. IV, see pp. 207, 240, 241, 265, 275, 288, 302; Graeme, Duncan, *Democratic Theory and Practice*, pp. 16–17; Russell, *History of Western Philosophy*, pp. 196–205.
347 Dunn, John, *Western Political Theory in the Face of the Future*, p. 4, also see pp. 2–26.
348 Qutb, *Zilal*, vol. 2, p. 1083; Graeme, Duncan, *Democratic Theory and Practice*, p. 17.
349 Rousseau, *The Social Contract*, p. 112.
350 Kamenka, *The Portable Karl Marx*, p. 254; Russell, *History of Western Philosophy*, p. 735.
351 Kamenka, *The Portable Karl Marx*, p. 146, see pp. 53–62 for R. Lender's interview with Marx, on July the third of the year 1871; also see Aronowitz, *The Crisis in Historical Materialism*, pp. 259–66, Russell, *History of Western Philosophy*, p. 200.
352 Qutb, *Zilal*, vol. 2, p. 1083.
353 Qutb, '*Adalah*, trans. Shepard (1996), *Sayyid Qutb and Islamic Activism*, p. 324, para. 18.
354 Qutb, '*Adalah*, pp. 27–8; *Zilal*, vol. 2, p. 1083.
355 Russell, *History of Western Philosophy*, p. 670.
356 Rousseau, Jean-Jacques (1984), *A Discourse on Inequality*, trans. with an introduction and notes by Maurice Cranston, London: Penguin Books, p. 128.
357 Rousseau, *A Discourse on Inequality*, pp. 126–7; for further detail on all forms of government including Democracy, see pp. 130–7.
358 For the problems of Democracy, see Plato, *The Republic*, pp. 273–4, 276–7, 282–4, 291; Aristotle's critique of Democracy is provided in *The Politics*, trans. E. Barker, Oxford (1948), esp. in bk III, ch. VII–XI, and bk IV, ch. IV, see pp. 207, 240, 241, 265, 275, 288, 302; Russell, *History of Western Philosophy*, pp. 126–8, 150–3, 196–201; Dunn, John, *Western Political Theory in the Face of the Future*, ch. 1; Graeme Duncan, *Democratic Theory and Practice* pp. 13–24, 39–42; about sovereignty, see Austin, J., *Lecture on Jurisprudence*, London, vol. 1, p. 227; Rousseau, *The Social Contract*, pp. 136–50 esp. sovereignty.
359 Gasset, Jose Ortega (1961), *History as a System and Other Assays Towards a Philosophy of History*, New York: Norton, p. 21, see pp. 18–25, 38–42, 72–7; also see Berdyaev, Nicolai (1938), *The Fate of Man in the Modern World*, London: Student Christian Movement Press, second edition, p. 32, see pp. 31–3, 45–8, 57–62.

360 Rousseau, *The Social Contract*, p. 84, see 85.
361 Rousseau, *A Discourse on Inequality*, pp. 129–30.
362 Russell, *History of Western Philososphy*, p. 671, also see pp. 669–74; also see p. 671.
363 Graeme, Duncan, *Democratic Theory and Practice*, p. 23.
364 Graeme, Duncan, *Democratic Theory and Practice*, pp. 21–2; see Thuchdides, (1960) *The History of The Peloponnesian War*, trans. R. Livingstone, Oxford: Oxford Universiy Press, pp. 110–17.
365 Graeme, Duncan, *Democratic Theory and Practice*, p. 23, also see C.B. Macpherson (1966), *The Real World of Democracy*, Oxford: Oxford University Press, p. 26.
366 Graeme, Duncan, *Democratic Theory and Practice*, p. 24.
367 Dunn, John, *Western Political Theory in the Face of the Future*, pp. 26–7.
368 Graeme, Duncan, *Democratic Theory and Practice*, p. 24.
369 Qutb, *Ma'alim*, p. 5.
370 'Abd al-Hakim, Khalifa (1961), *Islamic ideology*, Pakistan: Institute of Islamic Culture, pp. 202–3; for Qutb's similar view on the point, see Shepard, *Sayyid Qutb and Islamic Activism*, p. 324, para., 18; al-Hakim, Tawfiq (1938), *Tahta Shams al-Fikr*, Cairo: Maktabat al-Adab wa Matba 'atiha, pp. 159–61; for more details about the vagueness of democracy, see Aronowitz, *The Crisis in Historical Materialism*, pp. 256–303; Marshall, Gordon, *Oxford Dictionary of Sociology*, p. 147.
371 Rousseau, *A Discourse on Inequality*, p. 133, see pp. 130–6.
372 Dunn, John, *Western Political Theory in the Face of the Future*, p. 27.
373 Qutb, *Hadha al-Din*, pp. 5, 11, 17, 29, 42, 51, 66, 79, 96.
374 Qutb, *Ma'alim*, pp. 108–10.
375 Qutb, *Hadha al-Din*, p. 5.
376 Qutb, *'Adalah*, p. 31; also see *Hadha al-Dine*, pp. 6, 18, 30, 41, 50, 65, 80, 95.
377 Graeme, Duncan, *Democratic Theory and Practice*, p. 24.
378 Rousseau, *A Discourse on Inequality*, p. 131.
379 Rousseau, *A Discourse on Inequality*, p. 126 ff., He referred to Cornelius Tacitus (d. 120), *History*, IV, xvii.
380 See Russell, *History of Western Philosophy*, p. 672, esp. Rousseau's doctrine of general will.
381 Dunn, John, *Western Political Theory in the Face of the Future*, p. 27; Graeme Duncan, *Democratic Theory and Practice*, p. 24. Margolis, Michael (1979), *Viable Democracy*, London: Macmillan, p. 125; see pp. 125–57.
382 Qutb, *Ma'alim*, p. 5.
383 Qutb, *'Adalah*, pp. 75–80.
384 Qutb, *'Adalah*, p. 76.
385 Qutb, *Hadha al-Din*, pp. 4249, *Zilal*, vol. 2, pp. 873–5.
386 Graeme, Duncan, *Democratic Theory and Practice*, p. 24.
387 Rousseau, *The Social Contract*, p. 179; Using the word 'Mahomet' in this form as it is, is reportedly insulting. As Qutb says, the use of the word 'Mahomed' in this form is meant to be similar to 'Mahound' in which 'Ma' is the first possessive pronoun and 'Hound', from the German 'Hund' meaning dog. Thus 'those insulters played with the forms of these words'. This was also brought to light by Leopold Weiss in his book *Islam at the Cross Roads* (cf. Qutb, *'Adalah*, p. 187); Shepard, *Sayyid Qutb and Islamic Activism*, p. 283, fn. 12. However, to insult was not Rousseau's intention at all, as appears here. He wrote the word in the same way that it was frequently written in Western languages at his time by those who have or have not any intention to insult.

388 Qutb, *Mujtama'*, pp. 71–8; *Zilal*, vol. 2, p. 994; vol. 4, p. 2144.
389 'Awdah, *Islam wa Awda'una al-Qanuniyyah*, pp. 18–19; Qutb, *Zilal*, vol. 1, p.343; vol. 2, p. 891.
390 Qutb, *'Adalah*, p. 81; *Dirasat Islamiyyah*, pp. 187–212.
391 'Awdah, *Islam wa Awda'una al-Qanuniyyah*, pp. 16–25.
392 Qutb, *Zilal*, vol. 4, p. 1937.
393 Qutb, *Zilal*, vol. 2, pp. 692–6, 751–5; vol. 3, pp. 1195,1217; vol. 4, p. 1990; *al-Salam*, p. 124; *'Adalah*, pp. 14–19, 82; *Dirasat Islamiyyah*, pp. 187–212.
394 Qutb, *Zilal*, vol. 2, pp. 970, 972, 977–8, 980, 984–1010; vol. 4, p. 1937; *'Adalah*, pp. 80–1.

8 Egypt's Islamic movement: influences and state responses

1 As to the period before Qutb's death in 1966, I have dealt with it in some details in an article 'Al-Hudaybi's Influence on the Development of Islamist Movements in Egypt', *The Muslim World*, 91(3 and 4), 2001, pp. 451–79.
2 The media labelled this group *'al-Takfir wa al-Hijrah'*, a phrase that can be translated into English only through approximations and paraphrases. The word *al-Takfir* means that the group is branding or charging others with infidelity or unbelief. The word *al-Hijrah* translates emigration. The phrase *'al-Takfir wa al-Hijrah'* then could read, 'branding others with infidelity and emigration'. But, the notion implied by this translation may lead to confusion. This is because the phrase meant that the group calls others infidels, but the group itself practices emigration. To avoid such confusion, Kepel translated the words of the phrase separately and sometimes through paraphrases. He translates the word *Takfir* as 'excommunication' (Kepel, *Muslim Extremism*, p. 72). Elsewhere, he uses paraphrases: 'They called the group *al-Takfir wa al-Hijrah* because it practised the excommunication (*Takfir*) and withdrew into the mountains (*Hijrah*)' (Kepel, *Muslim Extremism*, pp. 72, 77). However, 'excommunication' is a rather weak translation of *Takfir*. In translating *'al-Takfir wa al-Hijrah'*, 'Abd al-'Azim says: 'Literally: charging with atheism and emigration'. See Ramadan, 'Abd al-'Azim, 'Fundamentalist Influence in Egypt', in Martin Marty and Scott Appleby (eds), *Fundamentalisms and the State* (1993), pp. 152–64, esp. p. 158. This translation implies that the group charges others with both atheism and emigration which is not accurate. Sagiv's translation is this: 'the group for accusation of ignorance and for *Hijra*', see Sagiv, David (1995), *Fundamentalism and Intellectuals in Egypt*, p. 46. Here, the word *Hijrah* remained in Arabic in an attempt to avoid possible confusion. I prefer to translate the phrase *Takfir wa Hijrah* in this way: Practising emigration and charging others with unbelief.
3 'Ashmawi, 'Thawrat Yulyu Ammamat al-Din', *Sabah el-Kheir*, pp. 8–10, esp. p. 9.
4 Professor Shimon Shamir was the first appointed chairman of the Israeli Academic Centre in Cairo in 1987. In 1988, he was the Israeli Ambassador in Egypt, cf. *Uctober*, Sunday, 15 November (1992), n. 838, p. 32.
5 Shamir, Shimon, ed. (1967), *Egypt from Monarchy to Republic: A Reassesment of Revolution and Change*, Oxford: Westview Press, p. 52
6 'Ashmawi, 'Thawrat Yulyu Ammamat al-Din', *Sabah el-Kheir*, pp. 8–10, esp. p. 9.
7 Anis, Mona (2004), 'Thus Spoke Yehya Haqqi', *Al-Ahram Weekly*, n. 688 (29 April–5 May), in the books section.
8 Qur'an, 2: 248.
9 al-Kilani, Musa Zayd (1995), *al-Harakat al-Islamiyyah*, Fi al-Urdun wa Filistin, Beirut: Mu'assasat al-Risalah, second edition, p. 15.

10 al-Kilani, *Harakat Islamiyyah*, p. 15; Mahfuz, Muhammad (1988), *al-Ladhina Zulimu: al-Tanzimat al-Islamiyyah fi Misr*, London: Riad el-Rayyes Books, p. 120.
11 al-Kilani, *Harakat Islamiyyah*, p. 212; Mahfuz, Muhammad, *al-Ladhina Zulimu*, pp. 120–1.
12 Ibrahim, Saad Eddin (1980), 'Anatomy of Egypt's Militant Islamic Groups: Methodological Note and Preliminary Findings', *International Journal of Middle East Studies*, vol. 12, pp. 423–5, cf. p. 427.
13 Ibrahim, Saad Eddin, 'Anatomy', *International Journal of Middle East Studies*, vol. 12, pp. 423–5, cf. p. 435.
14 Mahfuz, Muhammad, *al-Ladhina Zulimu*, p. 121.
15 Ramadan, Abd al-'Azim (1993), 'Fundamentalist Influence in Egypt The Strategies of the Muslim Brotherhood and the Takfir groups', in Martin Marty and Scott Appleby (eds) *Fundamentalisms and the State*, The University of Chicago Press, pp. 152–64, cf. p. 157.
16 al-Banna, *Rasa'il*, p. 137.
17 Jawhar, *al-Mawta Yatakallamun*, pp. 111–46.
18 Qutb, *Ma'alim*, p. 108.
19 Qutb, *Ma'alim*, pp. 98–9.
20 Jawhar, *al-Mawta Yatakallamun*, pp. 93–4, see pp. 103–7.
21 Qutb, *Ma'alim*, pp. 45, 62–8, 167.
22 Qutb, *Ma'alim*, pp. 64–6.
23 Qutb, *Limadha A'damuni*, pp. 26–9, 42–5; esp. 28 also *Ma'alim*, pp. 167–8.
24 Ramadan, Abd al-'Azim, 'Fundamentalist Influence in Egypt', in Martin Marty and Scott Appleby (eds) *Fundamentalisms and the State*, pp. 152–64, cf. p. 154.
25 Ibrahim, Saad Eddin, 'Anatomy', *International Journal of Middle East Studies*, vol. 12, cf. p. 424.
26 Ibrahim, Saad Eddin, 'Anatomy ', *International Journal of Middle East Studies*, vol. 12, cf. p. 425
27 Ramadan, Abd al-'Azim, 'Fundamentalist Influence in Egypt', in Martin and Scott (eds) *Fundamentalisms and the State*, pp. 152–64, cf. p. 154.
28 Voll, John, (1991), 'Fundamentalism in the Sunni Arab World: Egypt and Sudan', in Martin and Scott (eds), *Fundamentalism Observed*, pp. 345–95, cf. p. 381.
29 Mahfuz, Muhammad, *al-Ladhina Zulimu*, pp. 120–21.
30 Ibrahim, Saad Eddin, 'Anatomy', *International Journal of Middle East Studies*, vol. 12, cf. p. 431.
31 Voll, John (1999), 'Fundamentalism in the Sunni Arab World: Egypt and Sudan', in Martin and Scott (eds), *Fundamentalism Observed*, pp. 345–95, cf. p.348, 381.
32 Ramadan, Abd al-'Azim, 'Fundamentalist Influence in Egypt', in Martin and Scott (eds), *Fundamentalisms and the State*, pp. 152–64, cf. p. 158.
33 Mahfuz, Muhammad, *al-Ladhina Zulimu*, p. 89; Ayubi, Nazih, *Political Islam*, p. 77.
34 Ibrahim, Saad Eddin, 'Anatomy', *International Journal of Middle East Studies*, vol. 12, p. 439.
35 Ibrahim, Saad Eddin, 'Anatomy', *International Journal of Middle East Studies*, vol. 12, p. 440.
36 Al-Sawi, *al-Muwajahah*, p. 139, esp. 'Umarah's view point, see pp. 223–5, 229, esp. Ma'mun's viewpoint, also see the introduction by Muhammad 'Umarah.
37 Saad Eddin is currently Professor of anthropology and sociology and the chairman of the Ibn Khaldun Institute for Sociological Studies at the American University in Cairo.

38 Ibrahim, Saad Eddin, 'Anatomy', *International Journal of Middle East Studies*, vol. 12, p. 441.
39 Hanafi, Hasan (1988), *al-Harakat al-Islamiyyah fi Misr*, Cairo: al-Mu'assasah al-Islamiyyah li al-Nashr, first edition, pp. 81–9.
40 Ibrahim, Saad Eddin, 'Anatomy', *International Journal of Middle East Studies*, vol. 12, p. 441.
41 Ibrahim, Saad Eddin, 'Anatomy', *International Journal of Middle East Studies*, vol. 12, p. 441.
42 Ramadan, Abd al-'Azim, 'Fundamentalist Influence', in Martin and Scott (eds), *Fundamentalisms and the State*, pp. 152–64, cf. p. 158.
43 Mahfuz, Muhammad, *al-Ladhina Zulimu*, p. 93.
44 Voll, J. 'Fundamentalism', in Martin and Scott (eds), *Fundamentalism Observed*, p. 381.
45 Sharaf al-Din, Nabil (1992), 'Kayfa Tawaghghala al-Irhab fi Qura al-Sa'id', *Sabah el-Kheir*, Thursday, 16 July, n. 1906, pp. 8–10, esp. p. 8.
46 For further details, see Kepel, *Muslim Extremism*, p. 37.
47 Kepel, *Muslim Extremism*, p. 76.
48 Kepel, *Muslim Extremism*, pp. 76–7.
49 Hanafi, Hasan, *al-Harakat al-Islamiyyah fi Misr*, p. 75.
50 Ibrahim, Saad Eddin, 'Anatomy', *International Journal of Middle East Studies*, vol. 12, p. 451 and fn. 20.
51 For further details on how their apparatus was working, see Ibrahim, Saad Eddin, 'Anatomy', *International Journal of Middle East Studies*, vol. 12, pp. 436–43.
52 Frederick, M. Denny, ed. (1994), *An Introduction to Islam*, Colorado: The University of Colorado Press, p. 350, see pp. 357, 362.
53 Youssef, Michael (1985), *Revolt Against Modernity: Muslim Zealots and the West*, Leiden: E. J. Brill, p. 79.
54 Ibrahim, Saad Eddin, 'Anatomy', *International Journal of Middle East Studies*, vol. 12, p. 440.
55 Ibrahim, Saad Eddin, 'Anatomy', *International Journal Middle East Studies*, vol. 12, p. 440.
56 Mahfuz, Muhammad, *al-Ladhina Zulimu*, p. 93; see Kepel, *Muslim Extremism*, pp. 76 and 77 top.
57 Mahfuz, Muhammad, *al-Ladhina Zulimu*, p. 183.
58 Sadat, Anwar (1965), *Qissat al-Thawrah Kamilatan* (*The Complete Account of the Revolution*), Cairo: al-Dar al-Qawmiyyah, p. 38, see pp. 39–41.
59 See *Rose el-Youssef*, 2 May (1994), n. 3438, p. 18.
60 Hanafi, Hasan, *al-Harakat al-Islamiyyah fi Misr*, p. 74.
61 Hanafi, Hasan, al-*Harakat Islamiyyah fi Misr*, p. 76.
62 Hanafi, Hasan (1989), *al-'Usuliyyah al-Islamiyyah*, Cairo: Maktabat Madbuli, p. 102.
63 According to the Qur'an, 18: 9–26, the people of the cave were youth having faith in Allah and found safety and refuge in the Cave. They were protected from the persecution and violence of the heathen, see Yusuf Ali's *Translation of the Meaning of the Qur'an* 18: 9–26. From the Christian viewpoint, the story told in Gibbon (1969), *The Decline and Fall of the Roman Empire*, London: The New English Library (end of chapter 33), see pp. 72, 78, 126, 132, 261–3, 335.
64 Mahfuz, Muhammad, *al-Ladhina Zulimu*, pp. 94–5; also see, Kepel, *Muslim Extremism*, p. 77.
65 Mahfuz, Muhammad, *al-Ladhina Zulimu*, p. 95; also see, Kepel, *Muslim Extremism*, p. 77.

66 No particular place mentioned. See, Voll, John, 'Fundamentalism', in Martin and Scott (eds), *Fundamentalism Observed*, p. 382.
67 Youssef, Michael, *Revolt against Modernism*, p. 79.
68 They mean by the mountains of Egypt, the chain of the mountains of Hijaz which separate Eastern Egypt from the Valley of both Makkah and Madinah (Hijaz).
69 Ayubi, Nazih *Political Islam*, p. 77.
70 See *Rose el-Youssef*, n. 3452, Monday, 8 August (1994), pp. 10–15.
71 Sadat's speech in Alexandria, *Al-Ahram*, 27 July (1974); 31 January (1977), pp. 1–2.
72 See Ahmad abu al-Wafa (1994), 'Irhabiyyun fi Ghurfat al-I 'dam', *Rose el-Youssef*, 15 August, n. 3453, pp. 26–8, esp. 28.
73 See *Rose el-Youssef* (1995), 28 August, n. 3507, p. 56. Also, when Qutb left Egypt to the United States in 1948 the communist media claimed that Qutb was an 'American agent'. See al-Khalidi, *Sayyid Qutb*, p. 192.
74 Hammudah, Adel, *Mina al-Qaryah ila al-Mishnaqh: Tahqiq Watha'iq*, *Sayyid Qutb*, Cairo: Sina li al-Nashr, third edition, pp. 132–3, he is the secretary in chief of the government sponsored Journal Rose el-Youssef in Egypt.
75 Hammudah, 'Adel, *Sayyid Qutb*, pp. 132–3.
76 Mahfuz, Muhammad, *al-ladhina Zulimu*, pp. 95–7.
77 *Al-Akhbar* [newspaper], 19 January (1999), p. 8 says 'President Mubarak is desirous for independent judicial authorities and justice: the men of Islamic and Christian religions discussed the new Family and Personal Status Law.'
78 Fudah, Farag, *al-Haqiqah al-Gha'ibah*, p. 15.
79 Ibrahim, Saad Eddin, 'Anatomy', *International Journal of Middle East Studies*, vol. 12, p. 424.
80 Ibrahim, Saad Eddin, 'Anatomy', *International Journal of Middle East Studies*, vol. 12, p. 432.
81 Ayubi, Nazih, *Political Islam*, p. 75, cites obvious *Al-Jumhuriyyah* [Egyptian newspaper], 15 July 1979; also see *Al-Akhbar*, 8 August (1979).
82 The Communists in Egypt were now under the leadership of Ibrahim Badrawi who in his open letter to President Mubarak emphasized that 'he prefers to work openly' and he referred also to few specific Marxist groups, see Ibrahim Badrawi (1993) 'al-Shuyu 'iyyun al-Misriyyun Yufaddilun al- 'Amal al- 'Alani', *Rose el-Youssef*, n. 3418, Monday, 13 December, p. 14.
83 The followers of the Satan call themselves 'Satanics. There are more than a hundred of them in Cairo says Misr al-Gadidah. Some others were found in other areas in Cairo. They have a nightclub in Zamalik in Cairo. They have a special sign and special ceremonies. Their preferred music is Rock and Roll and Depth Metal Music and its singer are stars such as the Israeli singer Star who tuned some of the Qur'anic *Surah* 59 (al-Hashr). With their sign they move freely, enter other clubs and attend general celebrations of social occasions. On 13 October 1994 they attended a concert in *Madinat Nasr* (Nasr City in Cairo) sponsored by Marlboro Company'. See al-Qamhawi, Hasn, 'Jama 'at al-Shaytan' (The Society of the Satan), '*Jaridat al-Sha'ab*' (al-Sha 'ab Journal), Friday, 3 November (1995), pp. 1, 3.
84 The Egyptian Journal *Sabah el-Kheir* detailed that 'The Islamists provide social affairs, but Horus groups provide the actions', *Sabah el-Kheir*, n. 2029, Thursday, 24 November (1994), pp. 8–10.
85 Hanafi, Hasan, *al-Harakat al-Islamiyyah fi Misr*, pp. 72–5.
86 *Al-Ahram*, 31 January (1977); Ibrahim, Saad Eddin, 'Anatomy', *International Journal of Middle East Studies*, vol. 1, p. 450.

87 Kepel, *Muslim Extremism*, pp. 77–8.
88 Mahfuz, Muhammad, *al-Ladhina Zulimu*, p. 95.
89 Kepel, *Muslim Extremism*, p. 95.
90 Hanafi, Hasan, *al-Harakat al-Islamiyyah fi Misr*, p. 76.
91 Kepel, *Muslim Extremism*, p. 95.
92 Ibrahim, Saad Eddin, 'Anatomy', *International Journal of Middle East Studies*, vol. 12, p. 426.
93 Kepel, *Muslim Extremism*, p. 95.
94 Kepel, *Muslim Extremism*, p. 96.
95 Kepel, *Muslim Extremism*, p. 95.
96 Ali, Hilal Desouqi (1982), *Islamic Resurgence in Arab World*, New York: Prager, p. 107.
97 Mahfuz, Muhammad, *al-Ladhina Zulimu*, p. 127; also see Kepel, *Muslim Extremism*, pp. 96–7.
98 Hanafi, Hasan, *al-Harakat al-Islamiyyah fi Misr*, pp. 77–84.
99 Mahfuz, Muhammad, *al-Ladhina Zulimu*, p. 129.
100 The *Kharijites* was a group of early Muslim dissidents who sought strict adherence to Islamic principles as they saw them. They disapproved of the behaviour and action of the fourth Guided Caliph Ali, as well as that of his challenger Mu'awiyah. The Khawarij fought them both at the same time and never consented to the central authority of the Umayyads in Damascus or the Abbasid in Baghdad. The mainstream Sunni establishment consider the *Khawarij* heretics.
101 Mahfuz, Muhammad, *al-Ladhina Zulimu*, pp. 132–3; also see Kepel, *Muslim Extremism*, p. 99.
102 See al-Tabari (1979), *Tarikh*, vol. 2, pp. 244–5, 257–9.
103 al-Alusi, 'Abi al-Fadl Shihab al-Din al-Sayyid Mahmud al-Baghdadi' (1987), *Ruh al-Ma'ani fi Tafsir al-Qur'an al 'Azim wa al-Sab' al-Mathani*, Beirut: Dar al-fikr li al-Tiba'ah wa al-Nashr, vol. 1, part 2, pp. 74–5; Ibn Kathir, *Tafsir*, vol. 2, p. 67, Ibn Taymiyyah, *al-'Ubudiyyah*, pp. 82–3; al-Mawardi, *al-Ahkam al-Sultaniyyah*, p. 5; Abduh, Muhammad, *Tafsir*, vol. 1, p. 11; see pp. 12–14; Qutb, *'Adalah*, pp. 76–8, 198.
104 al-Bayyumi, 'Fadilat al-Imam al-Akbar Abd al-Rahman Tajj', *al-Azhar*, vol. 67, part 6, pp. 781–6, for further detail see ch. 1.
105 al-Maraghi, 'al-Tashri' al-Islami', *Majallat al-Azhar*, vol. 18, no. 7, pp. 27–31, 410–5; also see *al-Azhar*, November (1994), vol. 67, part 4, pp. 781–6 see the footnotes of these pages for further sources; Qutb, *'Adalah*, pp. 76–8, 198.
106 See Ibrahim, Saad Eddin, 'Anatomy', *International Journal of Middle East Studies*, vol. 12, p. 440.
107 Mustafa Sabri, *Mawqif al-'Aql wa al-'Ilm wa al-'Alam min Rab al-'Alamin*, cited by al-Sawi, *al-Muwajaha*, p. 128, see pp. 118–54. Mustafa Sabri was born in 1869, later became one of the committee (*al-Mab'uthan*) which discussed the constitution in Turkey from 1908 until 1918. He became Shaykh al-Islam in 1918. See Salamah, Tawfiq (1995), 'Min Sirat Shaykh al-Islam Mustafa Sabri', *Majallat al-Azhar*, September, vol. 86, part 4, pp. 539–43; For al-Muti'i Shaykh al-Azhar, see al-Muti'i, Muhammad Bikhit (1926), *Haqa'iq al-Islam wa Usul al-Hukm*, Cairo: Maktabat al-Nahdah, pp. 127–8; al-Bayyumi, Muhammd Rajab (1996) 'Min A'lam al-Azhar: Muhammad Bikhit al-Miti'i', *Majallat al-Azhar*, January, vol. 68, part, 8, pp. 1175–80.
108 For further details about the papers, in particular, that of Professor Gad al-Haq see Basha, Ahmad Fu'ad (1992), 'Mu'tamar al-Tawjih al-Islami Li al-'Ulum: Jami'at al-Azhar', *Majallat al-Azhar*, December, vol. 65, part 6, pp. 888–912.

109 al-Qaradawi published more than twenty books and addressed himself to the many problems which confront Muslims. Currently, he is the Dean of the *shari'ah* College in Qatar.
110 Mahfuz, Muhammad, *al-Ladhina Zulimu*, p. 183.
111 Kepel, *Muslim Extremism*, p. 98.
112 Mahfuz, Muhammad, *al-Ladhina Zulimu*, p. 131; also see Kepel, *Muslim Extremism*, p. 99.
113 Mahfuz, Muhammad, *al-Ladhina Zulimu*, p. 131.
114 Mahfuz, Muhammad, *al-Ladhina Zulimu*, p. 136, notes: the editor in chief of *al-Ahram* was Hamdi al-Jammal.
115 The article published in al-Ahram newspaper on 16 July (1977).
116 Mahfuz, Muhammad, *al-Ladhina Zulimu*, p. 137.
117 Qutb, *'Adalah*, p. 82; from al-Azhar see Abd Rabbuh, *al-Thawrah*, pp. 350–1. This book was introduced on 25 February 1972 by Muhammad al-Fahham Shaykh al-Azhar.
118 Kepel, *Muslim Extremism*, p. 100.
119 Qutb, *'Adalah*, p. 14–19, 82, *Zilal*, vol. 2, pp. 692, 696, vol. 4, p. 1990, Abd Rabbuh, *al-Thawrah,* p. 85.
120 Mahmud Shaltut (1892–1963) was Shaykh al-Azhar (1958–1963) during the Nasser era.
121 The Minister of Endowments for the period 1976–1978 during the Sadat era.
122 Mahfuz, Muhammad, *al-Ladhina Zulimu*, pp. 98–128.
123 Hammudah, Adel (1990), *Sayyid Qutb*, pp. 159; al-Khalidi, *Sayyid Qutb*, pp. 544–8; Hanafi Hasan, *al-Harakat al-Islamiyyah fi Misr*, p. 47.
124 Ramadan, Abd al-'Azim, 'Fundamentalist Influence', in Martin and Scott (eds), *Fundamentalisms and the State*, pp. 152–64.
125 Ibrahim Saad, Eddin, 'Anatomy', *International Journal of Middle East Studies*, vol. 12, p. 424, see footnotes 9, p. 450.
126 Kepel, *Muslim Extremism*, p. 101.
127 Kepel, *Muslim Extremism*, p. 97.
128 Mahfuz, Muhammad, *al-Ladhina Zulimu*, p. 138; also see Kepel, *Muslim Extremism*, p. 101.
129 Mahfuz, Muhammad, *al-Ladhina Zulimu* p. 138; also see Kepel, *Muslim Extremism*, p. 101.
130 Hanafi, Hasan, *al-Harakat al-Islamiyyah fi Misr*, pp. 77–84.
131 Kepel, *Muslim Extremism*, p. 97.
132 Ramadan, Abd al-'Azim, 'Fundamentalist Influence', in Martin and Scott (eds), *Fundamentalisms and the State*, p. 158.
133 *Al-Ahram*, 8 December 1981; Abd al-Salam Faraj's book was translated into English by Johannes J. G. Jansen; See Jansen (1986), *The Neglected Duty*; New York: Macmillan Publishing Company.
134 Jansen, Johannes (1986), *The Neglected Duty*, New York: Macmillan, pp. xvii–xviii.
135 Voll, J. 'Fundamentalism', in Martin and Scott (eds), *Fundamentalism Observed*, p. 383.
136 Hanafi, Hasan, *al-Harakat al-Islamiyyah fi Misr*, pp. 101–2.
137 Munazzamat, al-Shabab al-Ishtraki (1972), *Abd al-Nasser: al-Fikr wa al-Tariq*, Cairo: Matba'at al-Ahram, p. 45.
138 See Faraj, 'al-Faridah al-Gha'ibah', In Johannes J. G. Jansen's book *The Neglected Duty*, New York: Macmillan Publishing Company (1986), pp. 160–1.

139 Faraj, 'al-Faridah al-Gha'ibah', In Jansen's book The Neglected Duty (1986), p. 164.
140 Hanafi, Hasan, *al-Harakat al-Islamiyyah*, p. 111.
141 Hanafi, Hasan, *al-Harakat al-Islamiyyah*, p. 109.
142 I have spelt out in some details Qutb's transitional programme, see Khatab, Sayed (2001), 'al-Hudaybi's Influence on the development of Islamist Movement in Egypt', *The Muslim World*, vol. 91/3 and 4 (Fall): 451–79, esp. pp. 466–8.
143 Abd Rabbuh, *al-Thawrah*, p. 245.
144 See Court report on 19 December 1965, cf. Jawhar, *al-Mawta Yatakallamun* pp. 111–46.
145 For Qutb's statements on this matter, see Shepard, *Sayyid Qutb and Islamic Activism*, p. 277, para. 1, 31–2.
146 Qutb, *Ma'alim*, p. 8.
147 This project was established by decree of President Nasser and produced by a committee made up of Egyptian and Damascus scholars and supervised by the Supreme Council of Islamic affairs of al-Azhar. The twenty volumes later were published on 23 July 1961 and dedicated to Gamal Abd al-Nasser to commemorate the Revolution of 1952 and its efforts towards Islam.
148 The United Arab Republic (1986), *Mawsu'at Gamal Abd al-Nasser al-Fiqhiyyah*, Cairo, vol. 1, part 2, pp. 16–20, cf. p. 16; also see pp. 44–5 esp. the viewpoint on the differences between *shari'ah* and the fabricated law.
149 Abd Rabbuh, *al-Thawrah*, pp. 242–51.
150 Jawhar, *al-Mawta Yatakallamun*, pp. 111–46; Qutb, *Ma'alim*, pp. 44–5, 56, 64–5.
151 Qutb, *Ma'alim*, pp. 64–5.
152 Barakat, Muhammad Tawfiq, *Sayyid Qutb: Khulasat Hayatih, Minhajuh fi al-Harakah wa al-Naqd al-Muwajjah ilaiyyh*, Makkah: Maktabat al-Manarah, n.d., p. 237.
153 Abd Rabbuh, *al-Thawrah*, pp. 242–51.
154 Hanafi, Hasan, *al-Harakat al-Islamiyyah*, p. 10; Yakan, Fathi (1987), *al-Islam: Fikrah, Harakah, Inqilab*, Beirut: Mu'assasat al-Risalah, eleventh edition, pp. 145–8.
155 Mitchell, *Society of Muslim Brothers*, pp. 154–5.
156 Al-'Awwa Muhammad Salim (1990), 'al-Mutatarrifun Taraku Fikr Ibn Taymiyyah wa Rawwaju afkarahu Dida al-Tatar', *Sabah el-Kheir*, 5 April, n. 1787, pp. 18–20.
157 Youssef, Michael, *Revolt Against Modernity*, p. 82, see Appendix I.
158 Mitchell, *Society of Muslim Brothers*, pp. 154–5; Mahfuz, Muhammad, *al-Ladhina Zulimu*, p. 200.
159 Al-'Awwa 'al-Mutatarrifun', *Sabah el-Kheir*, pp. 10–18.
160 Hanafi Hasan, *al-Harakat, al-Islamiyyah*, pp. 120–1, Mahfuz, Muhammad, *al-Ladhina Zulimu*, p. 238.
161 Mahfuz, Muhammad, *al-Ladhina Zulimu*, p. 230.
162 Abd Rabbuh, *al-Thawrah*, pp. 242–51, cf. pp. 243–4.
163 Hanafi, Hasan, *al-Harakat al-Islamiyyah*, p. 102.
164 Hanafi, Hasan, *al-Harakat al-Islamiyyah*, p. 102.
165 Hanafi, Hasan, *al-Harakat al-Islamiyyah*, p. 103.
166 Mahfuz, Muhammad, *al-Ladhina Zulimu*, p. 231.
167 Al-'Awwa, 'al-Mutatarrifun', *Sabah el-Kheir*, pp. 18–20.

168 Mahfuz, Muhammad, *al-Ladhina Zulimu*, p. 227; Hanafi, Hasan, *al-Harakat al-Islamiyyah*, p. 106.
169 Hanafi, Hasan, *al-Harakat al-Islamiyyah*, p. 22; Mahfuz, Muhammad, *al-Ladhina Zulimu*, pp. 233–5.
170 Ibn Kathir, *Tafsir*, vol. 2, p. 67 verse 5: 50; see pp. 65–7.
171 *Al-Mussawar* [Egyptian Journal], 16 April, (1993), n. 3567, pp. 6–7, 11.
172 Mahfuz, Muhammad, *al-Ladhina Zulimu*, p. 272; Al-Zumur will be free from prison in the year 2006.
173 Al-Zawahiri was aware of the Islamic history. The Arabic title of this book '*Al-'Umdah fi I'Dad Al-'Uddah*' is similar to the title of a book '*Al-'Umad*: The Mayor': written by Abd al-Jabbar Ibn Ahamad (320–415 AH) the Chief Judge of the Mu'tazilities during the Buwayh State (322–447 AH) in Iranian district. He packed the separation of his State from the Abbasied. Among his students was Abu al-Hasan al-Basri (d. 426 AH) the author of a book titled '*Sharh al-'Umad*'. For further reading see, al-'Asqalani (d. 852/1448), *Lisan al-Mizan* (first edition, Hyderabad, 1330 AH), vol. 5, p. 289; also see al-Basri Abu al-Hasan (1991), *Sharh al-'Umad*, vol. 1, pp. 13, 31.
174 Isam Zakariyyah, (1993), 'Washintun: Ihtimalat Saytarat al-Mutatarrifun 'ala Misr Kabus'. *Rose el-Youssef*, n. 3403, 30 August, p. 8; for further detail, see p. 9.
175 Hanafi, Hasan, *al-Harakat al-Islamiyyah*, pp. 103–4.
176 Ibrahim, Saad Eddin, 'Anatomy', *International Journal of Middle East Studies*, vol. 12, p. 430.
177 Ramadan, Abd al-'Azim, 'Fundamentalist Influence', in Martin and Scott (eds), *Fundamentalisms and the State*, pp. 152–64, cf. p. 161.
178 Hanafi, Hasan, *al-Harakat al-Islamiyyah*, p. 168.
179 Konard, Muller and Mark Blaisse (1981), *Anwar Sadat: The Last Hundred Days*, London: Thames and Hudson, p. 71.
180 Konard, Muller and Mark Blaisse, *Anwar Sadat: The Last Hundred Days*, p. 71.
181 Al-Marjah, *Muwaffaq* (1984), *Sahwat Al-Rajul al-Marid*, p. 491.
182 Mahfuz, Muhammad, *al-Ladhina Zulimu*, p. 275.
183 Ayubi, Nazih, *Political Islam*, p. 80.
184 Hanafi, Hasan, *al-Harakat al-Islamiyyah*, pp. 158–9.
185 Hanafi, Hasan, *al-Harakat al-Islamiyyah*, pp. 107–8.
186 Hanafi, Hasan, *al-Harakat al-Islamiyyah*, pp. 168–72.
187 al-Suyuti, Jalal al-Din Abi al-Fadl Abd al-Rahman Ibn Abi Bakr Ibn Muhammad Ibn Sabiq al-Din al-Khusayri al-Suyuti. Born in Asyut in Upper Egypt and died in Cairo in 911/1505. He is Imam in various fields of Arabic and Islamic culture. His works are about six hundred books, among them *Al-Itqan fi'Ulum al-Qur'an and Al-Ashbah wa al-Naza'ir fi Al-Arabiyyah*. See Atallah, Rashid Yusuf (1985), *Tarikh al-Adab al-'Arabiyyah*, Beirut: 'Izz al-Din, vol. 2, pp. 246–66.
188 Hanafi, Hasan, *al-Harakat al-Islamiyyah*, pp. 167–8.
189 Kishk, M. Jalal, Intikhabat Qadimah, '*Uktober*, n. 389, Sunday, 8 April (1984), pp. 14–15.
190 Konard Muller and Mark Blaisse (1981), *Anwar Sadat: The Last Hundred Days*, p. 75.
191 Al-Sadat, Muhammad Anwar, *al-Bahth 'an al-Zat*, Cairo: al-Maktab al-Misri al-Hadith, n.d., p. 113.
192 Jawish is also known as Shawish. He studied in the United Kingdom and taught Arabic in Oxford. He returned to Egypt to work in *Al-Liwa'* journal of

the National Party led by Mustafa Kamil. After the death of Kamil in 1908, Jawish became editor of the journal. Among his works, is *al-Islam Din al-Fitrah, and Asrar al-Qur'an*. cf. Al-Zayat, Ahmad Hasan, *Tarikh al-Adab al-Arabi*, Cairo, n.d., pp. 464–7.

193 Egyptian Ministry of Information (1985), *Muhammad Farid*, p. 13.

194 Qutb Sayyid (1945), 'Ayna Anta Ya Mustafa Kamil', *al-Risalah*, vol. 1, n. 624, pp. 632–3.

195 Al-Ghayati (1885–1956) studied at al-Azhar, but graduated at Geneva University. He established his journal in Geneva and Lausanne to advocate Egyptian independence. After 27 years he returned to work in Egyptian journals *Al-Basir* and *Al-Jawa'ib* with Khalil Mutran (b. 1871) and Mustafa Lutfi al-Manfaluti (d. 1925). Later, al-Ghayati moved to *Al-Liwa'* Journal of the Wafd Party. His poetry collection *Wataniyyati (My Nationality)*, which Qutb later came to memorize most of, was banned as soon as it was published in 1910, but republished in 1938. cf. Al-Ghayati, Huda (1994), 'Walidi (My Father)', *al-Azhar*, November, vol. 67, part 6, pp. 787–90.

196 Egyptian Ministry of Information (1985), *Muhammad Farid*, pp. 20–1.

197 Hammudah, Husayn Muhammad Ahmad (1989), *Safahat min Tarikh Misr: al-Fatrah mina 4 Fibrayir 1942 wa hatta Uktaber 1981: Asrar Harakat al-Dubbat al-Ahrar wa al-lkhwan al-Muslimun*, Cario: al Zahra' li al-I 'Iam al-Arabi, pp. 73–74.

198 Munazzamat al-Shabab al-Ishtraki (1972), *Abd al-Nasser: al-Fikr wa al-Tariq*, Cario: Matba'at al-Ahram, pp. 10–11.

199 Hanafi, Hasan, *al-Harakat al-Islamiyyah*, p. 67.

200 Al-Sadat, *al-Bahth 'an al-Zat*, pp. 97–102, 117–18, 147.

201 Habib, Tariq (1997), *Malaffat Thawrat Yulu Shihadat 122 min Sunna 'iha wa Mu'asiniha*, Cairo: al-Ahram li-altarjamah wa al-Nashr, p. 277, esp. the testimony of Amin Huwadi the Free Officer and then president of the General Intelligence Agency, and then Minister during Nasser regime.

202 Frederick, M. Denny, *An Introduction to Islam*, p. 350.

203 Mahfuz, Muhammad, *al-Ladhina Zulimu*, p. 275.

204 See 'Umarah, *al-Islam wa Usul al-Hukm li-'Ali 'Abd al-Raziq*, p. 11.

205 See my book *The Theory of Jahiliyyah*, Routledge (2005), chapter 5.

206 Munazzamat al-Shabab al-Ishtraki (1972), *Abd al-Nasser: al-Fikr wa al-Tariq*, Cario: Matba'at al-Ahram, p. 219.

207 Hopwood, Derek (1982), *Egypt: Politics and Society 1945–1984*, London: Allen & Unwin, p. 97.

208 'The good face of 23 July was disappeared . . . ' see Al-Sadat, *al-Bahth 'an al-Zat*, pp. 254–6, 289.

209 Hanafi, Hasan, *al-Harakat al-Islamiyyah*, p. 67.

210 Qutb, *Ra'smaliyyah*, pp. 5–40.

211 This is Qutb's expression used by his opponents. Adel Hammudah of the Egyptian magazine *Rose el-Youssef* notes that Qutb used this expression in an open letter to President Muhammad Naguib published in *al-Akhbar* [newspaper] on 8 August 1952. 'Egyptians suffered the dictatorship of the *taghut* for long time, and they also can handle a just dictatorship for six months until you change the situation.' For further details, see Hammudah, 'Adel, *Sayyid Qutb*, p. 112.

212 Al-Sadat, *al-Bahth 'an Al-Zat*, p. 113.

213 See Qutb, *Hadha al-Din*, p. 36.

214 'Isam Zakariyya, 'Washintun: Ihtimalat Saytarat al-Mutatarrifun 'ala Misr Kabus', *Rose el-Youssef*, n. 3403, 30, August (1993), p. 9; Kishk, Jalal (1989), Intikhabat Qadimah, *'Uktuber*, n. 389, Sunday, 8 April (1984), pp. 14–15.

215 'Isam Zakariyya, 'Washintun: Ihtimalat Saytarat al-Mutatarrifun 'ala Mist Kabus' *Rose el-Youssef*, n. 3403, 30, August (1993), p. 9; also see Kishk, Jalal, (1989), Intikhabat Qadimah, *Uktuber*, n. 389, Sunday, 8 April (1984), pp. 14–15.

216 Voll, J. 'Fundamentalism', in Martin and Scott (eds), *Fundamentalism Observed*, p. 384.

217 Voll, J. 'Fundamentalism', in Martin and Scott (eds), *Fundamentalism Observed*, pp. 384–5.

218 Salame, Ghassn, ed. (1994), *Democracy without Democrats: The Renewal of Politics in the Muslim World*, London: I. B. Tauris Publishers, p. 213.

219 Ayubi, Nazih, *Political Islam*, p. 86.

220 See Adams J. Charles (1986), 'Foreword', in Jansen's book *The Neglected Duty*, New York: Macmillan Publishing Company, pp. xiii–xiv.

Bibliography

Primary source collections

Published books

Qutb, Sayyid. *Muhimmat al-Sha'ir fi al-Hayah wa Shi'r al-Jil al-Hadir*. Cairo: al-Shuruq. n.d. (first published in Cairo by the Academic Publishing Committee in 1933).

Qutb, Sayyid. *Al-Shati' al-Majhul*. [Poetry collection]. El Minia: Matba 'at Sadiq. n.d. [A copy from the original at the University of London] (first published by Matba'at Sadiq El Minia Egypt in 1935).

Qutb, Sayyid. *Al-Taswir al-Fanni fi al-Qur'an*. Cairo: Dar al-Shuruq. (1995) (first published by Dar al-Ma'arif in Cairo in 1945).

Qutb, Sayyid. *Tifl Mina al-Qaryah*. Jaddah: al-Dar al-Sa'udiyyah. n.d. (first published by the Academic Publishing Committee in 1946).

Qutb, Sayyid. *Al-Madinah al-Mashurah*. Cairo: Dar al-Shuruq. n.d. (first published by Dar al-Ma'arif in Cairo 1946).

Qutb, Sayyid. *Kutub wa Shakhsiyyat*. Cairo: Dar al-Shuruq. (1981) (first published in Cairo by matba'at al-Risalah in 1946).

Qutb, Sayyid. *Ashwak*. Jaddah: al-Dar al-Sa'udiyyah li-al-Nashr. n.d. (First published in Cairo by Dar Sa'd in 1947).

Qutb, Sayyid. *Al-Naqd al-Adabi: 'Usuluhuh wa Manahijuhu*. Cairo: Dar al-Shuruq. Seventh edition. (1993) (first published in Cairo by Dar al-Fikr al-Arabi in 1948).

Qutb, Sayyid. *Dirasat Islamiyyah*. Cairo: Dar al-Shuruq. (1993) (first published in Cairo by the Committee of Muslim Youth in 1953).

Qutb, Sayyid. *Fi Zilal al-Qur'an*. Cairo: Dar al-Shuruq. (1992) (first published in series of 30 volumes begun in 1952 and completed in 1959, all volumes published in Cairo by Dar Ihya' al-Kutub al-Arabiyyah, 2nd edition published in Cairo in 1961; in the 7th edition the originally thirty volumes were collected in large eight volumes published in Beirut by Dar Ihya al-Turath al-Arabi in 1971; Then Dar al-Shuruq in Cairo and Beirut pushed the large eight volumes into even larger six volumes in 1973 and then continued to be published by al-Shuruq in six volumes; al-Shuruq's 17th edition in 1992 was also six volumes).

Qutb, Sayyid. *Limadha A'damuni*. Jaddah: al-Sharikah al-Sa'udiyyah li al-Abhath wa al-Taswiq. n.d. (This is his testimony which was written by Qutb himself in the Military Prison to the Military Court and dated 22 October 1965 and preserved at the State Security Court in the file of the lawsuit number 12 in the year 1965 classified as a higher state security of the Case number 484 Egypt/1965).

Qutb, Sayyid. *Al-Atyaf al-Arba'ah*. Second edition. (1967). n.p.

Qutb, Sayyid. *Nahwa Mujtama' Islami*. Cairo: Dar al-Shuruq. (1993) (constitutes a few of his articles which were published in the early fifties in *al-Muslimun* but after his death they were collected and published by Maktabat al-Aqsa in Jordan in 1969).

Qutb, Sayyid. *Naqd Kitab Mustaqbal al-Thaqafah fi Misr*. Jaddah: al-Dar al-Sa 'udiyyah. Second edition. (1969).

Qutb, Sayyid. *Ma'rakatuna ma'a al-Yahud*. Cairo: Dar al-Shuruq. (1993) (constitutes a few of his articles which were published in *al-Da'wah* in the early fifties and after his death they were collected and introduced by Zayn al-Abidin al-Rakabi and published in Jeddah by al-Dar al-Sa'udiyyah in 1970).

Qutb, Sayyid. *Tariq al-Da'wah fi Zilal al-Qur'an*. [Two volumes], vol. 1, Beirut: al-Dar al-'Arabiyyah li-al-Tiba'ah wa al-Nashr wa al-Tawzi'. (1971), vol. 2, Beirut: Mu'assasat al-Risalah. (1977).

Qutb, Sayyid. *Tafsir Surat al-Shura*. Cairo: Dar al-Shuruq. n.d. (This is a part has been extracted from his *Fi Zilal al-Qur'an* and published in Jeddah by al-Dar al-Sa'udiyyah without date; then published in Beirut by al-Dar al-'Arabiyyah without date; and published by Dar al-Shuruq in Cairo and Beirut also without date).

Qutb, Sayyid and Hashim al-Rifa'i. *Lahn al-Kifah*. n.p. and n.d. (Poetry collection).

Qutb, Sayyid, al-Banna and Mawdudi. *Al-Jihad fi Sabil Allah*. Cairo: Dar al-I 'tisam li al-Tiba 'ah wa al-Nashr wa al-Tawzi'. (1977).

Qutb, Sayyid. *Al-Yaum al-Akhir fi Zilal al-Qur'an*. Fourth edition. (1978).

Qutb, Sayyid. *Sina' Baiyna Atma' al-Isti'mariyyin wa al-Suhyuniyyiyn*. Cairo: Dar al-Islam. (1978).

Qutb, Sayyid. *Tafsir Ayat al-Riba*. Kuwait: Dar al-Buhuth al-'Ilmiyyah. n.d.

Qutb, Sayyid. *Al-Islam wa Mushkilat al-Hadarah*. Cairo: Dar al-Shuruq. (1983).

Qutb, Sayyid. *Al-Qasas al-Dini*. Cairo: Maktabat Misr. n.d.

Qutb, Sayyid. *Hadha al-Din*. Cairo: Dar al-Shuruq. (1990).

Qutb, Sayyid. *Fi al-Tarikh Fikrah wa Minhaje*. Cairo: Dar al-Shuruq. (1991).

Qutb, Sayyid. *Al-Mustaqbal li Hadha al-Din*. International Islamic Federation of Student Organization. Kuwait: Salimiah. n.d.

Qutb, Sayyid. *Islam the Religion*, trans. International Islamic Federation, Riyadh; Saudi Arabia, 4, n.d

Qutb, Sayyid. *Khasa'is al-Tasawwur al-Islami wa Muqawwimatuh*. Cairo: Dar al-Shuruq. Thirteenth edition. (1995). English Translation: Qutb, Sayyid, *The Islamic Concept and its Characteristics*, trans. Mohammad Moinuddin Siddiqui. USA: American Traust Publications. (1991).

Qutb, Sayyid. *Al-Adalah al-Ijtima'iyyah fi al-Islam*. Cairo: Dar al-Shuruq. (1993). English translation: Kotb, Sayed, *Social Justice in Islam*, trans. John B. Hardie. Washington: American Council of Learned Societies (1953). reprint: New York: Octagon Books (1970).

Qutb, Sayyid. *Al-Salam al-'Alami wa al-Islam*. Cairo: Dar al-Shuruq. (1993).

Qutb, Sayyid. *Ma'alim fi al-Tariq*. Cairo: Dar al-Shuruq. (1993).

Qutb, Sayyid. *Ma'rakat al-Islam wa al-Ra'smaliyyah*. Cairo: Dar al-Shuruq. Thirteenth edition. (1993).

Qutb, Sayyid. *Mashahid al-Qiyamah fi al-Qur'an*. Cairo: Dar al-Shuruq. Eleventh edition. (1993).

Qutb, Sayyid. *Ila al-Mutathaqilin 'an al-Jihad*. (1970). n.p.

Periodicals

Qutb, Sayyid, (1928). 'Ghazal al-Shiyukh Fi Ra'y al-'Aqqad'. *Al-Balagh al-Usbu'i*, 2 March, No. 67, pp. 32–3.
Qutb, Sayyid, (1928). 'Safhah min Safahat al-Isti'mar'. *Al-Balagh al-Usbu'i*, 2 August, No. 89, pp. 14–15.
Qutb, Sayyid, (1929). 'Al-Azmah al-Zawjiyyah'. *Al-Balagh al-Usbu'i*, No. 108, pp. 28–9.
Qutb, Sayyid, (1929). 'Al-Ikhtilat fi al-aryaf'. *Al-Balagh al-Usbu'i*, No. 112, pp. 29–30.
Qutb, Sayyid, (1929). 'Awdah ila Athar al-Ikhtilat'. *Al-Balagh al-Usbu'i*, No. 110, pp. 28–9.
Qutb, Sayyid, (1929). 'Idtirab Haniq'. *Al-Balagh al-Usbu'i*, 10 April, No. 108, p. 27.
Qutb, Sayyid, (1929). 'Ittirabun Haniq'. *Al-Balagh al-Usbu'i*, 10 April, No. 8, pp. 27–8.
Qutb, Sayyid, (1929). 'Uzlah Fi Thawrah'. *Al-Balagh al-Usbu'i*, 13 March, No. 104, pp. 26–7.
Qutb, Sayyid, (1933). 'Al-'Alam Yajri'. *Al-Risalah*, 15 September, No. 17, pp. 12–13.
Qutb, Sayyid, (1934). 'Al-Mar'ah Lughzun Basit'. *Al-Usbu'*, Wednesday, September, No. 45, pp. 9–10 [article 1].
Qutb, Sayyid, (1934). 'Al-Mar'ah Lughzun Basit'. *Al-Usbu'*, Wednesday, October, No. 51, pp. 9–10 [article 6].
Qutb, Sayyid, (1934). 'Al-Sahifah wa al-Madrasah: Ayyuhuma Tu'aththir wa-limadha?' *al-Balagh Al-Usbu'i*, 23 May, No. 26, pp. 14–15.
Qutb, Sayyid, (1934). 'Ila al-Shati' al-Majhul'. *Al-Ahram*, 28 February, p. 7 [a poem].
Qutb, Sayyid, (1934). 'Fi 'Alam al-Shi'r: Hadiyyat al-Karawan li al-'Aqqad'. *Al-Ahram*, February, p. 7.
Qutb, Sayyid, (1934). 'M 'rakat al-Naqd al-Adabi wa Dawafi 'aha al-Asilah'. *Al-Usbu'*, June, No. 31, pp. 16–18 [article number 1].
Qutb, Sayyid, (1934). 'Ma 'rakat al-Nad al-Adabi wa Dawafi 'aha al-Asilah'. *Al-Usbu'*, Wednesday, 25 July, No. 35, pp. 21–3 [article number 5].
Qutb, Sayyid, (1934). 'Mawakib al-'Ajazah aw Lawhat al-I'lanat'. *Al-'Usbu'*, September, vol. 1, No. 44, pp. 9–10.
Qutb, Sayyid, (1934). 'Qimat al-Fadilah Bayna al-Fard wa al-Jama'ah'. *Al-Usbu'*, June, No. 28, pp. 21–2.
Qutb, Sayyid, (1935). 'Al-Sirr (The Secret)'.*Dar al-'Ulum*, No. 3, pp. 82–6 [a poem].
Qutb, Sayyid, (1938). 'Bayna al-'Aqqad wa al-Rafi'i'. *Al-Risalah*, April, No. 251, pp. 692–4 [article 1].
Qutb, Sayyid, (1938). 'Bayna al-'Aqqad wa al-Rafi'i'. *Al-Risalah*, May, No. 255, pp. 854–7 [article 4].
Qutb, Sayyid, (1938). 'Bayna al-'Aqqad wa al-Rafi'i'. *Al-Risalah*, May, No. 256, pp. 903–7 [article 5].
Qutb, Sayyid, (1938). 'Ghazal al-'Aqqad'. *Al-Risalah*, August, No. 265, pp. 1263–6 [article 14].
Qutb, Sayyid, (1938). 'Ghazal al-'Aqqad'. *Al-Risalah*. October, No. 276, pp. 1703–5 [article 20].
Qutb, Sayyid, (1938). 'Sarah wa Ghazal al-'Aqqad'. *Al-Risalah*, July, No. 264, pp. 1224–7.

Qutb, Sayyid, (1938). 'Uslub al-'Aqqad'. *Al-Risalah*, October, No. 278, pp. 1777–80.
Qutb, Sayyid, (1939). 'Al-Taswir al-Fanni fi al-Qur'an'. *Al-Muqtataf*, 2 February, No. 94, part 2, pp. 206–22.
Qutb, Sayyid, (1939). 'Al-Ghina' al-Marid Ynkhur al-Khuluq wa al-Mujtama 'al-Misri'. *Al-Risalah*, September, No. 374, pp. 1382–4.
Qutb, Sayyid, (1939). 'Al-Taswir al-Fanni fi al-Qur'an'. *Al-Muqtataf*, 3 March, No. 94, part 3, pp. 313–18.
Qutb, Sayyid, (1939). 'Naqd Kitab Mustaqbal al-Thaqafah fi Misr li al-Ductur Tahah Husayn'. *Dar al-'Ulum*, 5 April, No. 4, pp. 28–79.
Qutb, Sayyid, (1940). 'Al-Mutribun wa al-Mutribat hum al-Tabur al-Khamis fi Misr'. *Dar al-'Ulum*, July, No. 1, pp. 52–6.
Qutb, Sayyid, (1940). 'Thaqafat al-Mar'ah al-Misriyyah'. *Al-Shu'un al-Ijtima'iyyah*, No. 4, pp. 34–8.
Qutb, Sayyid, (1941). 'Al-Sught Dalil al-Hurriha'. *Al-Shu'un al-Ijtima'iyyah*, No. 6, pp. 44–9.
Qutb, Sayyid, (1941). 'Al-Qahirah al-Khadda'ah'. *Al-Shu'un al-Ijtima'iyyah*, May, No. 5, pp. 30–3.
Qutb, Sayyid, (1941). 'Waylat al-Silm'. *Al-Risalah*, January, No. 395, pp. 68–9.
Qutb, Sayyid, (1942). ''Abqariyyat Muhammad li al-'Aqqad'. *Al-Risalah*, No. 469, pp. 665–7.
Qutb, Sayyid, (1942). ''Abqariyyat Muhammad li al-'Aqqad'. *Al-Risalah*, No. 470, pp. 683–5.
Qutb, Sayyid, (1942). 'Al-'Aqliyyah al-Ijtima'iyyah'. *Al-Shu'un al-Ijtima'iyyah*, No. 8, pp. 19–26.
Qutb, Sayyid, (1942). 'Al-Mujtama 'al-Salih wa al-Mujtama 'al-Mutawazin'. *Al-Shu'un al- Ijtima'iyyah*, No. 6, pp. 56–66.
Qutb, Sayyid, (1942). 'Al-Muqaddasat al-Insaniyyah wa al-Qawmiyyah'. *Al-Shu'un al-Ijtima'iyyah*, No. 11 pp. 32–6.
Qutb, Sayyid, (1942). 'Al-Wa'z al-Dini'. *Al-Shu'un al-Ijtima'iyyah*, No. 5, pp. 50–1.
Qutb, Sayyid, (1942). 'Kutub wa Shakhsiyyat'. *Al-Thaqafah*, No. 193, pp. 13–15.
Qutb, Sayyid, (1943). 'Al-Namazij al-Bashariyyah'. *Al-Risalah*, July, No. 522, pp. 529–31.
Qutb, Sayyid, (1943). 'Fi al-Tih'. *Al-Risalah*, December, No. 544, pp. 972–73.
Qutb, Sayyid, (1943). 'Fi Mafraq al-Tariq'. *Al-Shu'un al-Ijtima'iyyah*, No. 11, pp. 16–19.
Qutb, Sayyid, (1943). 'Fi Samim al-Rif'. *Al-Shu'un al- Ijtima'iyyah*, September, No. 9, pp. 19–23.
Qutb, Sayyid, (1943). 'Sulayman al-Hakim li Tawfiq al-Hakim'. *Al-Risalah*, April, No. 511, pp. 311–12.
Qutb, Sayyid, (1943). 'Sulayman al-Hakim li Tawfiq al-Hakim'. *Al-Risalah*, April, No. 512, pp. 332–4.
Qutb, Sayyid, (1943). 'Sulayman al-Hakim li Tawfiq al-Hakim'. *Al-Risalah*, May, No. 513, pp. 350–2.
Qutb, Sayyid, (1943). 'Wazifat al-Fan wa al-Sahafah'. *Al-Shu'un al-Ijtima'iyyah*, No. 12, pp. 24–8.
Qutb, Sayyid, (1944). 'Al-'Adalah al-Ijtima 'iyyah'. *Al-Shu'un al-Ijtima'iyyah*, No. 1, pp. 33–7.
Qutb, Sayyid, (1944). 'A'lam al-Islam'. *Al-Thaqafah*, June, No. 287, pp. 22–4.
Qutb, Sayyid, (1944). 'Al-Rabat al-Muqaddas li Tawfiq al-Hakim'. *Al-Risalah*, No. 598, pp. 2010–12.

Qutb, Sayyid, (1944). "Al-Siddiqah bint al-Siddiq'. *Al-Risalah*, January, No. 551, pp. 91–4.
Qutb, Sayyid, (1944). 'Hulm al-Fajr'. *Al-Risalah*, 7 October, No. 588, p. 917 [a poem].
Qutb, Sayyid, (1944). 'Min A'lam al-Islam: Muhammd Abduh'. *Al-Thaqafah*, October, No. 305, pp. 22–4.
Qutb, Sayyid, (1944). 'Misr wa al-Da 'ayah'. *Al-Shu'un al-Ijtima'iyyah*, No.1, pp. 39–42.
Qutb, Sayyid, (1945). "Addilu Baramijakum aw Insahibu Qabla Fawat al-Awan'. *Al-Risalah*, vol. 2, No. 627, pp.723–4.
Qutb, Sayyid, (1945). "Ala Hamish al-Naqd: Khan al-Khalili li Naguib Mahfuz'. *Al-Risalah*, December, vol. 2, No. 650, pp. 1364–6.
Qutb, Sayyid, (1945). 'Al-Jamal al-Fanni wa al-'Aqidah fi al-Qur'an'. *Al-Risalah*, June, No. 625, p. 677–9.
Qutb, Sayyid, (1945). 'Al-Jamal al-Fanni fi Taswir al-Qur'an'. *Al-Risalah*, July, No. 626, p. 711.
Qutb, Sayyid, (1945). 'Al-Mantiq al-Wijdani wa al-'Aqidah fi al-Qur'an'. *Al-Risalah*, vol. 2, No. 629, pp. 778–81.
Qutb, Sayyid, (1945). 'Al-Tanasuq al-Fanni fi Taswir al-Qur'an'. *Al-Risalah*, March, No. 610, pp. 278–81.
Qutb, Sayyid, (1945). 'Al-Taswir al-Fnni fi al-Qur'an'. *Al-Risalah*, January, No. 601, pp. 43–6.
Qutb, Sayyid, (1945). 'Al-Taswir al-Fanni fi al-Qur'an'. *Al-Risalah*, May, No. 621, pp. 569–70.
Qutb, Sayyid, (1945). 'Al-Taswir al-Fanni wa al-'Aqidah fi al-Qur'an'. *Al-Risalah*. November, No. 645, pp. 1225–7.
Qutb, Sayyid, (1945). 'Ayna Anta Ya Mustafa Kamil'. *Al-Risalah*, No. 648, pp. 1309–10.
Qutb, Sayyid, (1945). 'Hadhihi Faransa'. *Al-Risalah*, June, No. 624, pp. 632–3.
Qutb, Sayyid, (1945). 'Mabahith'an al-Taswir al-Fanni fi al-Qur'an'. *Al-Risalah*, May, No. 620, pp. 527–9.
Qutb, Sayyid, (1945). 'Siyasat Qatl al-Waqt'. *Al-Shu'un al-Ijtima'iyyah*, No. 12, pp. 23–7.
Qutb, Sayyid, (1945). 'Suwar Min al-Jil al-Jadid'. *Al-Risalah*, June 4, No. 622, pp. 579–81.
Qutb, Sayyid, (1945). 'Wazifat al-Sahafah fi al-Mujtama 'al-Hadith'. *Al-Shu'un al-Ijtima'iyyah*, No. 6, p. 56.
Qutb, Sayyid, (1946). 'Al-Damir al-Amrikani wa Qadiyyat Filistin'. *Al-Risalah*, No. 694, pp. 1155–7.
Qutb, Sayyid, (1946). 'Al-Qahirah al-Jadidah li Naguib Mahfuz'. *Al-Risalah*. December, No. 704, pp. 1440–3.
Qutb, Sayyid, (1946). 'Dars fi al-Tafsir 'ala Tariqat al-Taswir'. *Al-Risalah*, No. 653, pp. 14–17.
Qutb, Sayyid, (1946). 'Fadihah: Man Huwa al-Mas'ul?' *Al-Risalah*, vol. 1, No. 655, p. 88.
Qutb, Sayyid, (1946). 'Hamazat al-Shayatin li Abd al-Hamid al-Sahhar'. *Al-Risalah*. April, vol. 1, No. 668, pp. 433–5.
Qutb, Sayyid, (1946). 'Ila al-Iskandariyyah'. *Al-Risalah*, 22 July, No. 681, pp. 796–8.
Qutb, Sayyid, (1946). 'Laghw al-Sayf' *Al-Risalah*, 22 July, No. 681, pp. 5–6.
Qutb, Sayyid, (1946). 'Madaris li-al-Sukht'. *Al-Risalah*, 14 September, No. 691, pp. 1081–2.

Qutb, Sayyid, (1946). 'Qafilat al-Raqiq'. *Al-Kitab*, vol. 2, No. 8, pp. 290–1 [poem].
Qutb, Sayyid, (1946). 'Shi'r min al-Jazirah: Ahmad Abd al-Ghafur 'Attar'. *Al-Risalah*, November, No. 698, pp. 1278–80.
Qutb, Sayyid, (1946). ''Udu ila al-Sharq'. *Al-'Alam al-Arabi*, No. 2, pp. 3–4.
Qutb, Sayyid, (1947). 'Ahdafuna wa Baramijuna'. *Al-'Alam al-Arabi*, No. 1, p. 3.
Qutb, Sayyid, (1947). 'Al-Damir al-Adabi fi Misr: Shubban wa Shiyukh'. *Al-'Alam al-Arabi*, 4 July, vol. 1, No. 4, pp. 52–4.
Qutb, Sayyid, (1947). 'Lughat al-'Abid'. *Al-Risalah*, February, No. 709, pp. 134–6.
Qutb, Sayyid, (1947). 'Qiyadatuna al-Ruhiyyah'. *Al-Risalah*, January, No. 705, pp. 27–8.
Qutb, Sayyid, (1947). 'Wa al-Ana Ayyuha al-Arab: Ama Tazaluna Tantazirun?' *Al-Risalah*, No. 711, pp. 190–2.
Qutb, Sayyid, (1948). 'Mashru 'al-Qanun al-Islami Raqam 1'. *Al-Fikr al-Jadid*, January, No. 2 pp. 1–3.
Qutb, Sayyid, (1948). 'Mashru 'al-Qanun al-Islami Raqam 2'. *Al-Fikr al-Jadid*, January, No. 4, pp. 1–3.
Qutb, Sayyid, (1949). 'Hama'im fi New York'. Al-Katib al-Misri, December, No. 8, pp. 666–9.
Qutb, Sayyid, (1950). 'Akhi Abbas'. Al-Risalah, 3 July, No. 887, p. 756.
Qutb, Sayyid, (1951). 'Al-Kutlah al-Islamiyyah fi al-Mizan al-Dawli'. *Al-Risalah*, September, No. 949, pp. 1021–4.
Qutb, Sayyid, (1951). 'Al-Lughah al-Arabiyyah Fi al-'Alam al-Islami'. *Al-Risalah*, No. 965, pp. 1469–71.
Qutb, Sayyid, (1951). 'Amrica al-Lati Ra'ayt fi Mizan al-Qiyam al-Insaniyyah'. *Al-Risalah*, November, No. 957, pp. 1245–7 [article 1].
Qutb, Sayyid, (1951). 'Amrica al-Lati Ra'ayt fi Mizan al-Qiyam al-Insaniyyah'. *Al-Risalah*, November, No. 959, pp. 1301–6 [article 2].
Qutb, Sayyid, (1951). 'Amrica al-Lati Ra'ayt fi Mizan al-Qiyam al-Insaniyyah'. *Al-Risalah*, November, No. 961, pp. 1357–60 [article 3].
Qutb, Sayyid, (1951). 'Ayyuha al-Bashawat la Tatamassahu bi al-Islam'. *Al-Ishtrakiyyah*, 29 November, No. 32, pp. 15–19.
Qutb, Sayyid, (1951). 'Ila al-Ra'smaliyyin wa al-Musta 'mirin: Makanakum laTatamassahu bi al-Din'. *Al-Da'wah*, August, No. 29, pp. 32–6.
Qutb, Sayyid, (1951). 'Ila Ustadhina Doctor Ahmad Amin'. *Al-Thaqafah*, No. 663. pp. 7–8.
Qutb, Sayyid, (1951). 'Li al-Azhar Risalah wa-Lakinnahu La Yu'addiha'. *Al-Risalah*, No. 937, pp. 685–7.
Qutb, Sayyid, (1951). 'Madha Khasira al-'Alam bi-Inhitat al-Muslimin'. *Al-Risalah*, August, vol. 2, No. 947, pp. 965–7.
Qutb, Sayyid, (1952). 'Adab al-Inhilal'. *Al-Risalah*, No. 990, pp. 937–9. This article was republished in *Dirasat Islamiyyah* (1953) which was then reprinted a few times by Dar al-Shuruq in Cairo. In the ninth print (1993), this article is on pages (147–151).
Qutb, Sayyid, (1952). 'Fi Zilal al-Qur'an'. *Al-Muslimun*, No. 3, pp. 28–32.
Qutb, Sayyid, (1952). 'Fi Zilal al-Qur'an'. *Al-Muslimun*, No. 4, pp. 19–27.
Qutb, Sayyid, (1952). 'Fi Zilal al-Qur'an'. *Al-Muslimun*, No. 5, pp. 17–26.
Qutb, Sayyid, (1952). 'Fi Zilal al-Qur'an'. *Al-Muslimun*, No. 6, pp. 13–22.
Qutb, Sayyid, (1952). 'Fi Zilal al-Qur'an'. *Al-Muslimun*, No. 7, pp. 25–30.

Qutb, Sayyid, (1952). 'Fi Zilal al-Qur'an'. *Al-Muslimun*, No. 8, pp. 24–34.
Qutb, Sayyid, (1952). 'Fi Zilal al-Qur'an'. *Al-Muslimun*, No. 9, pp. 11–15.
Qutb, Sayyid, (1952). 'Idha lam takun Thawrah Fa-hakimu Muhammad Naguib'. *Rose el-Youssef*, No. 1262, p. 10.
Qutb, Sayyid, (1952). 'Ila al-Qa'id Muhammad Naguib'. *Al-Da'wah*, November, No. 93, pp. 4–6.
Qutb, Sayyid, (1952). 'Inna Ilahakum Lawahid'. *Al-Risalah*, No. 987, pp. 601–2.
Qutb, Sayyid, (1952). 'Mabadi' al-'Alam al-Hurr'. *Al-Risalah*, January, No. 1018, p. 15.
Qutb, Sayyid, (1952). 'Misr Awwalan: Na 'am wa-lakin'. *Rose el-Youssef*, No. 1275, pp. 10–11.
Qutb, Sayyid, (1952). 'Tabi 'at al-Fath al-Islami'. *Al-Azhar*, vol. 24, No. 1, pp. 21–5.
Qutb, Sayyid, (1952). 'Tariq Wahid'. *Al-Risalah*, No. 974, pp. 181–3.
Qutb, Sayyid, (1952). 'Ya Shabab'. *Al-Da'wah*, No. 98, republished in *Dirasat Islamiyyah* (1953) which was reprinted fiew times by Dar al-Shuruq in Cairo. In the ninth print (1993), this article is on pages (247–250).
Qutb, Sayyid, (1954). 'Fi Zilal al-Qur'an'. *Al-Muslimun*, No. 4, pp. 33–40.
Qutb, Sayyid, (1954). 'Fi Zilal al-Qur'an'. *Al-Muslimun*, No. 5, pp. 21–8.
Qutb, Sayyid, (1954). 'Qadiyyah wahidah wa Ummah wahidah'. *Al-Ikhwan al-Muslimun*, No. 8, pp. 3–5.
Qutb, Sayyid, (1957).'Bawakir al-Kifah'. *Al-Kifah al-Islami*, July 26, No. 29, pp. 3–10 [poem].
Qutb, Sayyid (1957). 'Hubal'. *Al-Kifah al-Islami*, July 26, No. 29, pp. 11–14 [poem].

Secondary source collections

Books

Al-'Utayfi, Gamal. *Min Minassat al-Ittiham*. Cairo: Dar al-Ma'arif. (1968).
Abd al-Baqi, Muhammad Fu'ad. *Al-Mu'jam al-Mufahras li-Alfaz al-Qur'an al-Karim*. Beirut: Dar al-Fikr li al-Tiba 'ah wa al-Nashr. (1992).
Abd al-Baqi, Muhammad Husayn. *Sayyid Qutb: Hayatuh wa Adabuh*. Egypt; al-Mansurah: Dar al-Wafa'. First edition. (1983).
Abd al-Majeed, Muhammad. *Arab Socialism In the Light of Islam and Arab Reality*, trans. Sha'ban Afifi. Cairo: The Supreme Council for Islamic Affairs. (1967).
Abd al-Nasser, Gamal. *Falsafat al-Thawrah*. Cairo: Maslahat al-Isti 'lamat. n.d.
Abd al-Ra'uf, Abd al-Mun 'im. *Arghamtu Faruq 'Ala al-Tanazul 'an al-'Arsh*. Cairo: al-Zahra' li al-I 'lam al 'Arabi. Second editon. (1989).
Abd al-Ra'uf, Muhammad. *A Muslim's Reflections on Democratic Capitalism*. Washington: American Interprise Institute for Public Policy Research. (1984).
Abd Rabbuh, Sayyid Abd al-Hafiz. *Al-Thawrah al-Ijtima'iyyah fi al-Islam*. Cairo: Dar al-Kitab al-Misry. (1980).
Abduh, Muhammad. *Risalat al-Tawhid*. Cairo: Matba 'at Muhammad Ali. (1956).
Abduh, Muhammad. *Tafsir al-Manar*. Beirut: Dar al-Ma 'rifah. Second edition (n.d.)
Abduh, Muhammad. *Tafsir al-Manar*. Cairo: al-Hay'ah al-Misriyyah al- 'Ammah li al-Kitab. (1972).
Abduh, Muhammad. *Tarikh al-'Ustadh al-'Imam Muhammad Abduh*. Cairo: Matba 'at al-Manar (1324/1903).
Abdulsalam, Ahmad Shehu. *Islam and Language*. Kuala Lumpur: Al-Hilal Publishing. (1999).

Abu al-Anwar, Muhammad. *Al-Ma'arik al-Adabiyyah fi Misr Hawla al-Shi'r*. A PhD Dissertation, Cairo: Dar al- 'Ulum. (1971).

Abu Bakr, Muhammad al-Awwal. *Sayyid Qutb wa al-Naqd al-Adabi*. Riyadh: Dar al-Rifa 'i li al-Nashr wa al-Tiba "ah wa al-Tawzi'. (1992).

Abu Rabi', M. Ibrahim. *Intellectual Origins of Islamic Resurgence in the Modern Arab World*. State University of New York Press. (1996).

Abu Shuhbah, Muhammad Muhammad. *Fi Rihab al-Sunnah*. Cairo: Majma' al-Buhuth al-Islamiyyah bi al-Azhar. (1969).

Abu Yusuf, Ya'qub b. Ibrahim b. Habib al-Ansari (d. 182/798). *Kitab al-Kharaj*. Cairo: Bulaq (1302 AH).

Adams, Charles. *Islam and Modernism in Egypt*. Oxford: Oxford University Press. (1933).

Al-Afghani and Abduh. *Al-'Urwah al-Wuthqa wa al-Thawrah al-Tahririyyah al-Kubra*. Cairo: Dar al-Arab li al-Bustani. (1957).

Afkhami, Mahnaz. *Faith and Freedom*. London: I.B. Tauris Publishers. (1995).

Ahmad, al-Jada' and Husni Jirar. *Shu'ara' al-Da'wah al-Islamiyyah*. Beirut: Mu'assasat al-Risalah. (1989).

Al-Ahsan, Abdullah. *Ummah or Nation? Identity Crisis in Contemporary Muslim Society*. United Kingdom: The Islamic Foundation (1992/1413 AH).

Ajami, Fou'ad. *The Arab Predicament: Arab Political Thought and Practice Since 1967*. Cambridge, MA: Cambridge University Press. (1992).

Al-'Ajuz, Ahmad Muhyi al-Din. *Manahij al-Shari'ah al-Islamiyyah*. Beirut: Mu'assasat al-Risalah. (1969).

Ali, A. Yusuf. *The Holy Qur'an: English translation of the meanings and commentary*. Lahore: Sh. Muhammad Ashraf. (1975).

Ali, Hilal Dessouqi. *Islamic Resurgence in Arab World*. New York: Prager. (1982).

Ali, Jawad. *Al-Mufassal Fi Tarikh al-Arab Qabla al-Islam*. Baghdad: Dar al-'ilm li al-Malayin. (1951).

Ali, Kamal Hasan. *Mashawir al-'Umr: Asrar wa Khafaya Sab'ina 'aman min 'Umr Misr fi al-Harb wa al-Mukhabarat wa al-Siyasah*. Cairo: Dar al-Shuruq. First edition. (1994).

Al-Alusi, Abi al-Fadl Shihab al-Din al-Sayyid Mahmud al-Baghdadi (d. 127/744). *Ruh al-Ma'ani Fi Tafsir al-Qur'an al-'Azim wa al-Sab' al-Mathani*. Beirut: Dar al-Fikr li al-Tiba'ah wa al-Nashr. (1987).

Amin, Ahmad. *Fajr al-Islam*. Cairo: Lajnat al-Ta'lif wa al-Tarjamah. (1928).

Amin, Mustafa. *Sanah Ula Sijn*. Cairo: Mu'assasat Akhbar al-Yawm. (1975).

Amir, Ali (Sir). *Short History of the Saracens*. London: Macmillan. (1951).

Ansari, Nasser. *Mawsu'at Hukkam Misr mina al-Fara'inah hatta al-Yawm*. Cairo: Dar al-Shuruq. First edition. (1987).

Al-'Aqqad, Abbas. *Diwan al-'Aqqad: Yaqazat Sabah*. Aswan: Matba'at Wihdat al-Siyanah wa al-Intaj. (1967).

Al-'Aqqad, Abbas. *Khamsat Dawawin li-al-Aqqad*. Cairo: al-Hayy'ah al-Misriyyah al-'Ammah li- al-Kitab. (1973).

Aristotle, *The Politics*, trans. E. Barker. Oxford (1948).

Arkun, Muhammad. *Al-Islam: al-Akhlaq wa al-Siyasah*, trans. Hashim Salih. Beirut: Markaz al-Inma' al-Qawmi. (1990).

Aronowitez, Stanley. *The Crisis in Historical Materialism: Class, Politics and Culture in Marxist Theory*. Minneapolis, MN: University of Minnesota Press. (1990).

Arsalan, Abu Abdullah Muhammad b. Sa'id. *Dhamm al-Jahl wa Bayan Atharah*. Cairo: Dar al-'Ulum al-Islamiyyah. n.d.

Asad, Muhammad. *Islam at the Crossroads*. Lahore: Arafat Publications. (1955).

Asad, Muhammad. *Islam at the Crossroads*. Lahore: Arafat Publications. (1969).

Asad, Muhammad. *The Message of the Qur'an*. Gibraltar: Dar al-Andalus. (1980).
Asad, Muhammad. *The Principles of State and Government in Islam*. Gibrattar: Dar al-Andalus. (1980).
Al-Asbahani, Abu al-Faraj Ali b. al-Husayn al-Umawi (d. 356/967). *Al-Aghani*. Beirut: Dar al-Kutub al-Islmiyyah. (1992).
Al-'Ashmawi, Muhammad Saeed. *Al-Islam al-Siyasi*. Cairo: Sina. (1992).
Al-Ashqar, 'Umar Sulayman Abdullah. *Mu'awwiqat Tatbiq al-Shari'ah al-Islamiyyah*. 'Uman: Dar al-Nafa'is. (1992).
Al-'Asqalani, al-Hafiz b. Hajar (d. 852/1448). *Fath al-Bari li Sharh Sahih al-Bukhari*. Cairo: Dar al-Rayyan li al-Turath. (1987).
Al-'Asqalani, al-Hafiz b.Hajar (d. 852/1448). *Lisan al-Mizan*. First edition. Hyderabad. (1330 AH).
Atallah, Rashid Yusuf. *Tarikh al-Adab al-'Arabiyyah*. Beirut: 'Izz al-Din. (1985).
'Attar, Ahmad Abd al-Ghafur.*Hadith fi al-Kutub*. Cairo: Matabat al-Nahdah al-Misriyyah. (1947).
Austin, J. *Lectures on Jurisprudence*. London: Murray. Volume 1. (1873).
'Awdah, Abd al-Qadir. *Al-Islam wa Awda'una al-Qanuniyyah*. Beirut: Mu'assasat al-Risalah. Sixth edition. (1985).
'Awdah, Abd al-Qadir. *Islam Bayna Jahl Abna'ih wa 'Ajz 'Ulama'ih*. Beirut: Mu'assasat al-Risalah. Sixth edition (1985).
Al-'Awwa, Muhammad Salim. *The Political System of the Islamic State*. Indiana: Indianapolis: American Trust Publication. (1980).
Ayubi, Nazih. *Political Islam: Religion and Politics in the Arab World*. London: Routledge. (1991).
Al-'Azm, Yusuf. *Ra'id al-Fikr al-Islami al-Mu'asir: al-Shahid Sayyid Qutb*. Damascus: Dar al-Qalam. First edition. (1980).
Al-'Azm, Yusuf. *Rihlat al-Daya' li al-I'lam al-Arabi al-Mu'asir*. Riyadh: al-Dar al Saudiyyah li al-Nashr. Third edition. (1980).
Al-Badri, Abd al-Aziz. *Hukm al-Islam fi al-Ishtrakiyyah*. Al-Madinah: al-Matba'h al-'Ilmiyyah. Fifth edition. (1983).
Al-Bahiyy, Muhammad. *Al-Fikr al-Islami al-Hadith wa Silatihi bi al-Isti'mar al-Gharbi*. Beirut: Dar al-Fikr. Sixth edition. (1972).
Al-Bahnasawi, Salim. *Adwa' 'Ala Ma'alim Fi al-Tariq*. Kuwait: Dar al-Buhuth al-'ilmiyyah. First edition. (1985).
Al-Ba'labaki, Rohi. *Al-Mawrid: A Modern Arabic-English Dictionary*. Beirut: Dar al-'ilm li al-Malayin. Eighth edition. (1996).
Balyuzi H. M. *Muhammad and The Course of Islam*. Oxford: George Roland. (1976).
Al-Banna, Hasan. *Majmu'at Rasa'il Hasan al-Banna*. Cairo: Dar al-Tawzi' wa al-Nashr al-Islamiyyah. (1992).
Bany al-Marjeh, Mouaffaq. *Sahwat al-Rajul al-Marid: al-Sultan Abd al-Hamid al-Thani wa al-Khilafah al-Islamiyyah*. Kuwait: Saqr al-Khalij. (1984).
Barakat, Muhammad Tawfiq. *Sayyid Qutb: Khulasat Hayatih, Minhajuh fi al-Harakah wa al-Naqd al-Muwajjah ilaiyyh*. Makkah: Maktabat al-Manarah. n.d.
Barber, Benjamin R. *Strong Democracy: Participatory Politics For a New Age*. California: The University of California Press. (1984).
Al-Bardisi, Muhammad Zakariyya. *Usul al-Fiqh*. Cairo: Dar al-Thaqafah li al-Nashr wa al-Tawzi'. (1985).
Barker, E. *The Politics*. Oxford: Oxford University Press. (1948).
Basset, R. *La Poesie Arabe*. Paris: Anteislamique. (1880).

Bausani, Alessandro. *The Persians: From the Earliest Days to the Twentieth Century*. New York: St. Martin's Press. (1971).

Berdyaev, Nicolai. *The Fate of Man in Modern World*. London: Student Christian Movement Press. Second edition. (1938).

Bibars, Diya' al-Din. *Al-Asrar al-Shakhsiyyah li Gamal Abd al-Nasser*. Cairo: Maktabat Madbuli. n.d.

Binder, Leonard. *Islamic Liberalism: A Critic of Development Ideologies*. Chicago, IL: The University of Chicago Press. (1988).

Binder, Leonard. *The Ideological Revolution in the Middle East*. New York: John Wiley. (1964).

Al-Bisri, Abu al-Husayn Muhammad b. Ali b. al-Taiyyb. *Sharh al-'Umad*. Al-Madinah: Maktabat al-'Ulum wa al-Hikam. First edition. (1990).

Blunt, Alfred *Al-Tarikh al-Sirri li Ihtilal Ingeltra Misr*, trans. Committee of Ikhtarna lak. Cairo: Matabi' Sharikat al-I'lanat al-Sharqiyyah. n.d.

Bobby, S. S. *A Fundamental Fear Eurocentrism and the Emergence of Islamism*. London: Z. Book Ltd. (1997).

Boucher, H. Douglas. *The Biology of Mutualism: Ecology and Evolution*. New York: Oxford University Press. (1985).

Brockelman, Karl. *Tarikh al-Shu'uh al-Islamiyyah*, trans. Amin Faris and Munir al-Ba'labakki. Beirut: Dar al-'Ilm Li al-Malayin. (1948–1949).

Bruce, B. Lawrance. *Defenders of God: The Fundamentalist Revolt Against the Modern Age*. San Francisco: Harper. (1989).

Al-Bulayyhi, Abd al-Rahman. *Sayyid Quth wa Turathihi al-Adabi wa al-Fikri*. Al-Riyadh: Matabi' al-Riyadh. (1991).

Burtt, Edwin A. *The Metaphysical Foundations of Modern Science*. Garden City, NY: Doubleday. (1955).

Al-Bustani, Abdullah. *Al-Bustan*. Beirut: al-Mataba'ah al-Amrikiyyah. Volume 1. (1927).

Cachia, Pierre B. A. *Taha Husayn*. London: Luzac and Campany. (1956).

Campion, H. *Public and Private Property in Great Britain*. London: Oxford University Press. (1939).

Chapra, M. 'Umar. *Islam and The Economic Challenge*. Riyadah: International Islamic Publishing House. (1995).

Choueiri, Youssef M. *Islamic Fundamentalism*. London: Pinter. (1990).

Clouston, W. A. (ed.). *Arabian Poetry*. London: Darf Publisher. (1986).

David Pearl. *A Textbook on Muslim Personal Law*. London: Croom Helm. Second edition. (1987).

Davies, Paul. *About Time: Einstein's Unfinished Revolution*. London: Benguin. (1995).

Davies, Paul. *The Mind of God: Science and the Search For Ultimate Mining*. London: Penguin. (1992).

Al-Dawalibi, Muhammad Ma'ruf. *Al-Dawlah wa al-Sultan*. Cairo: al-Sahwah. (1984).

Dawood, N. J. *The Koran*. England: Penguin Books. (1999).

Dayf, Shawqi. *Tarikh al-Adab al-'Arabi: al'Asr al-Jahili*. Cairo: Dar al-Ma'arif. (1981).

Diyab, M. Hafiz. *Sayyid Quth: al-Khitab wa al-Idiulujiyyah*. Beirut: Dar al-Tali'ah. (1988).

Doi, Abd al-Rahman. *Shari'ah: The Islamic Law*. Kuala Lumpur: A. S. Noordeen. (1984).

Donohue, J. J. and Esposito J. L. *Islam in Transition: Muslim Perspective*. Oxford: Oxford University Press. (1982).

Duncan, Graeme. *Democratic Theory and Practice*. Cambridge: Cambridge University Press. (1983).
Dunn, John. *Western Political Theory in the Face of the Future*. Cambridge: Cambridge University Press. (1979).
Durant, Will. *The Story of Civilization*. New York: Simon. (1953).
Durant, Will. *The Story of Philosophy*. Washington: Washington Square Press. (1970).
El-Zein, A. Samih. *The Factors of Muslims Weakness*. Cairo: Dar al-Kitab al-Misri. First edition. (1977).
Enayat, Hamid. *Modern Islamic Political Thought*. Texas: The University of Texas Press. (1982).
Eveland, Wilbur Crane. *Ropes of Sand: America's Failure in the Middle East*. London: W. W. Norton & Campany. (1980).
Fadlalah, Sayyid Muhammad Husayn. *al-Harakah al-Islamiyyah: Humum wa Qadaya*. Beirut: Dar al-Malak li al-Tiba'ah. Third edition. (1993).
Fahmi, Abd al-Aziz (Basha). *Hadhihi Hayati*. Cairo: Dar al-Hilal. Series of Kitab al-Hilal, n. 145, April (1963).
Faksh, Mahmud A. *The Future of Islam in the Middle East: Fundamentalism in Egypt, Algeria, and Saudi Arabia*. London: Praeger. (1997).
Al-Fangari, Muhammad Shawqi. *Al-Islam wa 'Adalat al-Tawzi'*. Cairo: al-Hay'ah al-Misriyyah al-'Ammah Li al-Kitab. (1995).
Al-Fangari, Muhammad Shawqi. *Al-Islam wa al-Mushkilah al-Iqtisadiyyah*. Cairo: Maktabat al-Salam al-'Alamiyyah. (1981).
Farah, Caeser E. *Problems of The Ottoman Administration in the Lebanon, 1840–1861*. Princeton: Princeton University. PhD dissertaion. (1957).
Farrukh, 'Umar. *Khamsat Shu'ara Jahiliyyun*. Beirut: Dar al-'Ilm li al-Malayin. n.d.
Farrukh, 'Umar. *Tarikh al-Adab al-'Arabi*. Beirut: Dar al-'Ilm li al-Malayin. (1985).
Al-Fawazan, Salih. *Kitab al-Tawhid*. Jaddah: Dar Ibn Rajab. n.d.
Faysal, Shukri. *Al-Mujtama'at al-Islamiyyah fi al-Qarn al-Awwal*. Beirut: Dar al-'ilm li al-Malayin. (1981).
Fernau, F. W. *Muslims on the March: People and Politics in the World of Islam*, trans. E. W. Diches. London: Robertt Hale Limitid. (1955).
Al-Fiqi, Ali. *Ibrahim Nagi*. Cairo: al-Hay'ah al-Misriyyah li al-Kitab. (1977).
Frederick, Mathewson Denny. *An Introduction To Islam*. Colorado: The University of Colorado press. (1994).
Fudah, Farag. *Al-Haqiqah al-Gha'ibah (The Missing Truth)*. Cairo: Dar al-Fikr li al-Dirasat wa al-Nashr wa al-Tawzi'. Third edition. (1988).
Gasset, Jose Ortega Y. *History as a System and Other Assays Towards a Philosophy of History*. New York: Norton. (1961).
Gaston, Maspero. *The Dawn of Civilisation*. London: London Society for Promoting Christian Knowledge. Fifth edition. (1910).
Geoege, Sale. *The Qur'an*. London: Thomas Tegg. (1825).
Al-Ghazali, Abi Hamid Muhammad b. Muhammad (d. 505/1111). *Al-Iqtisad Fi al-I'tiqad*. Cairo: Maktabat al-Jindi. n.d.
Al-Ghazali, Abi Hamid Muhammad b. Muhammad, *Ihya' 'Ulum al-Din*. Beirut: Dar al-Hadi, n.d.
Al-Ghazali, Abi Hamid Muhammad b. Muhammad. *Tahafut al-Falasifah*. trans. into English by Michael E. Marmura.
Al-Ghazali, Muhammad. *Turathuna al-Fikri fi Mizan al-Shar' wa al-'Aql*. Cairo: Dar al-Shuruq. (1981).
Al-Ghazali, Zaynab. *Ayam Min Hayati*. Cairo: Dar al-Shuruq. (1980).

Gibb, H. A. R. *Modern Trends In Islam*. Chicago: University of Chicago Press. (1947).

Gibb, H. A. R. *Studies on the Civilisation of Islam*. Princeton: Princeton University Press. (1982).

Gibbon, E. *The Decline and Fall of the Roman Empire*. London: The New English Library. (1969).

Goldziher, Ignaz. *Muslim Studies*. Albany, NY: University of New York Press. (1966).

Green, Stephen. *Taking Sides: America's Secret Relations With a Militant Israel*. New York: William Morrow and Campany. (1984).

Green, V. H. H. *The Hanoverians 1714–1815*. London: Edward Arnold (Publisher) Ltd. (1956).

Griffith, D. F. *What is Socialism? A Symposium on Distribution of Wealth in Islam*. London: Richards. (1924).

Group of Thinkers. *Al-Ishtrakiyyah fi al-Tajarib al-Arabiyyah*. Cairo. (1965). n.p.

Haberlandt, Karl. *Cognitive Psychology*. Boston Allyn. (1997).

Habib, Tariq. *Malaffat Thawrat Yulu: Shihadat 122 min Sunna'iha wa Mu'asiriha*. Cairo: al-Ahram li-altarjamah wa al-Nashr. (1997).

Haddad, Yavonne Yazbeck. *Contemporary Islam and the Challenge of History*. New York: State University of New York Press. (1982).

Al-Hakim, Tawfiq. *Qultu Dhata Yawm*. Cairo: Akhbar al-Yawm. Series Kitab al-yawm. First of August. (1970).

Al-Hakim, Tawfiq. *Tahta Shams al-Fikr*. Cairo: Maktabat al-Adab wa Matba'atiha. n.d.

Al-Hakim, Tawfiq. *Tawfiq al-Hakim al-Mufakkir*. Cairo: Dar al-Kitab al-Jadid. (1970).

Al-Hakim, Tawfiq. *Al-Rabat al-Muqaddas*. Cairo: Maktabat al-Adab. n.d. (first edition 1944).

Al-Hamawi, Ali Taqiyy al-Din Abi Bakr (d. 837/1434). *Khazanat al-Adab wa Ghayat al-Irab*. Beirut: Dar wa Matba'at al-Hilal. (1991).

Hammudah, Adel. *Sayyid Qutb Mina al-Qaryah ila al-Mishnaqah: Tahqiq Watha'iq*. Cairo: Sina li al-Nashr. Third edition. (1990).

Hammudah, Husayn Muhammad Ahmad. *Safahat min Tarikh Misr: al-Fatrah mina 4 Fibrayir 1942 wa hatta Uktuber 1981: Asrar Harakat al-Dubbat al-Ahrar wa al-Ikhwan al-Muslimun*. Cairo: al-Zahra' li al-I'lam al-'Arabi. (1989).

Hanafi, Hasan. *Al-Harakat al-Diniyyah al-Mu'asirah*. Cairo: Maktabat Madbuli. (1988).

Hanafi, Hasan. *Al-Harakat al-Islamiyyah fi Misr*. Cairo: al-Mu'assasah al-Islamiyyah li al-Nashr. First edition. (1986).

Hanafi, Hasan. *Al-Usuliyyah al-Islamiyyah*. Cairo: Maktabat Madbuli. (1989).

Hanafi, Hasan. *Al-Yasar al-Islami wa al-Wahdah al-Wataniyyah*. Cairo: Maktabat Madbuli. n.d.

Haqqi, Yahya. *Qandil Um Hashi*. Cairo: Dar al-Ma'arif. (1960).

Hardy, Thomas. *Tess of The D'urbervilles*. Introduction and notes by P.N. Furbank. London: Pan Books. (1995).

Hardy, Thomas. *The Mayor of Casterbridge*. Introduction by Ian Gregor, notes by Bryn Caless. London: Macmillan. (1974).

Hardy, Thomas. *The Trumpet Major*. Introduction by Barbara Hardy, notes by Laurel Brake and Ernest Hardy. London: Pan Books. (1995).

Hardy, Thomas. *Jude the Obscure*. London: Macmillan. (1974).

Haykal, Muhammad Husayn. *Al-Imbraturyyah al-Islamiyyah wa al-Amakin al-Muqaddasah*. Cairo: Dar al-Hilal. n.d.

Hegel, Georg William Friedrich. *The Philosophy of History*. New York: Dover Publications. (1956).

Herald and Sun. *The New International Illustrated Encyclopaedia*. Volume 2. Melbourne: Colorgravure Publication. (1954).

Hopwood, Derek. *Egypt: Politics and Society 1945–1984*. London: Allen and Unwin. (1985).

Al-Hudaybi, Hasan. *Du'ah la Qudah*. Cairo: Dar al-Tawzi' wa al-Nashr al-Islamiyyah, n.d. Intruduction of Muhammad Abdullah al-Khatib, 10 Jumada al-Ula, 1407 AH/ 10 January (1987).

Hufman, Murad. *Al-Islam Ka Badil*, trans. to Arabic by Muhammad Gharib. Mus'ssasat Bavaria. (1993).

Hume, David. *A Treatise of Human Nature*. New York: Penguin Group. Penguin Books. (1969).

Huntington, Samuel. *The Clash of Civilizations and the Remaking of World Order*. New York: Simon & Schuster. (1996).

Hurani, Albert. *Arabic Thought in The Liberal Age 1798–1939*. London: Cambridge University Press. (1983).

Husayn, Mirza Muhammad. *Islam and Socialism*. Lahore: Muhammad Ashraf. (1947).

Husayn, Muhammad. *Al-Islam wa al-Hadarah al-Gharbiyyah*. Beirut: Mu'assasat al-Risalah. Seventh edition. (1985).

Husayn, Taha. *Al-Adab al-Jahili*. Cairo: Dar al-Ma'arif. (1962).

Husayn, Taha. *Mustaqbal al-Thaqafah fi Misr*. Cairo. Dar al-Ma'arif. (1938).

Husayn, Taha. *Al-Wa'd al-Haqq*. Cairo: Dar al-Ma'arif. n.d.

Ibn 'Abbas, Abdullah (d. 68/687). *Tanwir al-Miqyas min Tafsir Ibn 'Abbas*. Prepared by Abi Tahir Muhammad b. Ya'qub al-Fayruzabadi (d. 817/1466). Revised by al-Azhar: Cairo (1951). Dar al-Jil: Beirut. n.d.

Ibn Abd Rabbuh, Abi 'Umar Ahmad b. Muhammad b. Abd Rabbuh al-Andalusi (d. 328/940). *Kitab al-'Iqd al-Farid*. Beirut: Dar al-Kitab al-Arabi. n.d.

Ibn al-Kalbi, Abi al-Mundhir Hisham b. Muhammad b. al-Sa'ib (d. 204/819). *Kitab al-Asnam*. Cairo: Dar al-Kutub al-Misriyyah. Third edition. (1995).

Ibn al-Qayyim, Shams al-Din Abi Abdullah Muhammad b. Abi Bakr (d. 751/1350). *Hidayat al-Hayara fi al-Rad 'ala al-Yahud Wa al-Nasara*. Beirut: Dar al-Kutub al-'Ilmiyyah. Second edition. (1994).

Ibn 'Aqil. *Sharh Ibn 'Aqil 'ala Alfiyyat Ibn Malik*. Beirut: Dar al-Kitab al-'Arabi. Second edition. Commentry of Hadi Hasan Hammudi. (1993).

Ibn 'Asakir, *Kanz al-'Ummal*. Lahore: Kashmiri Bazar. n.d.

Ibn Durayd, Abi Bakr Muuhammad b. al-Hasan (d. 321/933). *Kitab Jamharat al-Lughah*. Beirut: Dar al-'ilm li al-Malayin. First edition. Volume 1. (1978).

Ibn Hisham, Abd al-Malik (d. 218/ 833). *Al-Sirah al-Nabawiyyah*. Bierut: Dar Ihya al-Turath al-Arabi. First edition. Four volumes. (1995).

Ibn Hisham, Abi Muhammad Abdullah Jamal al-Din al-Ansari al-Misri (d. 761/1361). *Sharh Shudhur al-Dhahab fi Ma'rifat Kalam al-Arab*. Beirut: Dar al-Fikr. n.d.

Ibn Kathir, al-Hafiz Abi al-Fida'Isma'il (d. 774/1373). *Al-Bidayah wa al-Nihayah*. Cairo: Dar al-Rayyan li al-Turath. First edition. (1988).

Ibn Kathir, al-Hafiz Abi al-Fida'Isma'il (d. 774/1373). *Tafsir al-Qur'an al-'Azim*. Cairo: Dar al-Hadith. First Edition. (1988).

Ibn Khaldun, Abd al-Rahman b. Muhammad (d. 808/1405). *Al-Muqaddimah*. Beirut: Mu'assasat al-A'lami li al-Matbu'at. (1971).

Ibn Khaldun, Abd al-Rahman Muhammad. *Kitab al-'Ibar wa Diwan al-Mubtada' wa al-Khabar Fi Ayyam al-'Arab wa al-'Ajam wa al-Barbar*. Beirut: Mu'assasat al-A'lami li al-Matbu'at. (1971).

Ibn Manzur, Abi al-Fadl Jamal al-Din Muhammad b. Makram al-Ifriqi al-Misri (d. 711/1310). *Lisan al-'Arab*. Beirut: Dar Sadir. (1994).

Ibn Qutaybah, Abu Muhammad Abdullah b. Muslim (d. 276/ 889). *Al-Shi'r wa al-Shu'ara'*. Ahmad Shakir (ed.) Cairo: Dar al-Ma'arif. Volume 12. (1977).

Ibn Sa'd, Muhammad b. Mani' al-Hashimi (d. 230/843). *Al-Tabaqat al-Kubra* Beirut: Dar al-Fikr. First edition. Six volumes. (1994).

Ibn Sina, Abu Ali al-Husayn b. Abdullah (d. 429/1034). *Al-Ilayiyyat*. Commentary of Saeed Zidan and Sulayman Dunya. Revised by Muhammad Yussuf 'Isa. Cairo: al-Hay'ah al-'Ammah li-Shu'un al-Matabi' al-Amiriyyah. (1960).

Ibn Taymiyah, Taqiyy al-Din Ahmad (d. 728/1327). *Al-'Ubudiyyah*. Beirut: Dar al-Kitab al-Arabi. First edition. (1987).

Ibn Ya'qub, Majd al-Din Muhammad (al-Fayruzabadi). *Al-Qamus al-Muhit*. Cairo: Mustafa al-Halabi. Second edition. (1952).

Iqbal, Muhammad (Sir – 1875–1938). *The Reconstruction of Religious Thought in Islam*. London: Oxford University Press. (1934).

Isa, Salah. *Hawamish al-Maqrizi: Hikayat min Misr.* Cairo: Dar al-Qahirah li al-Tawzi' wa al-Nashr. (1983).

Al-Isfahani, al-Raghib. *Mu'jam Mufradat Alfaz al-Qur'an*. Nadim Mar'ashli (ed.). Beirut: Dar al-Kitab al-Arabi. (1984).

Ismael, Tareq and Rif'at el-Sa'id. *Communist Movement in Egypt 1920–1988*. Syracuse: Syracuse University Press. (1990).

Isma'il, Sayf al-Dawlah. *Usus Ishtirakiyyat al-Islam*. Cairo. (1965). n.p.

Izutsu. *God and Man in the Qur'an*. Tokyo. (1964). n.p.

Al-Jabarti, Abd al-Rahman Hasan (d. 1822). *Tarikh al-Jabarti: Tarikh 'Aja'ib al-Athar fi al-Tarajim wa al-Akhbar*. Ibrahim Shams al-Din (ed.). Beirut: Dar al-Kutub al-'Ilmiyyah. Three volumes. (1997).

Jacq, Christian. *Ramses*, trans. Mary Feeney. London: Simon & Schuster. (1998).

Jama'at Asdiqa' al-Shahid Sayyid Qutb. *Al-Shahid Sayyid Qutb*. n.d.

Al-Jassas, Abu Bakr Ahmad b. 'Ali al-Razi, (d. 370/980). *Ahkam al-Qur'an*. Beirut: Dar al-Kitab al-'Arabi. Volume 3 (1355 AH).

Jawhar, Sami. *Al-Mawta Yatakallamun*. Cairo: al-Maktab al-Misri al-Hadith. Second edition. (1977).

Jeans, James (Sir). *The Universe Around Us*. London: Cambridge University Press. Fourth edition. (1944). Reprint (1945).

Al-Jindi, Anwar. *'Alamiyyat al-Islam*. Cairo: Dar al-Ma'arif. Series Read: No. 426. (1977).

Al-Jindi, Anwar. *Adwa' 'Ala al-Fikr al-'Arabi al-Islami*. Cairo: al-Dar al-Misriyyah li al-Ta'lif wa al-Tarjamah. (1966).

Al-Jindi, Anwar. *Al-Hadarah fi Mafhum al-Islam*. Cairo: Dar al-Ansar. n.d.

Al-Jindi, Anwar. *Al-Musajalat wa al-Ma'arik al-Adabiyyah Fi Majal al-Fikr wa al-Tarikh wa al-Hadarah*. Cairo: Dar al-Ma'rifah. n.d.

Al-Jindi, Anwar. *Al-Qawmiyyah al-'Arabiyyah wa al-Wahdah al-Kubra*. Cairo: al-Dar al-Qawmiyyah li-al-Tiba'ah wa al-Nashr. (1962).

Al-Jindi, Anwar. *Al-Sahafah al-Siyasiyyah Fi Misr*. Cairo: Maktabat al-Anglu al-Misriyyah. (1962).

Al-Jindi, Anwar. *Shubuhat Fi al-Fikr al-'Arabi al-Islami*. Cairo: Dar al-I'tisam. (1977).

Joachim, Wach. *The Concept of the Classical in the Study of Religions: Types of Religious Experience: Christian and Non-Christian*. Chicago, IL: Chicago University Press. (1951).

Johannes, J. G. Jansen. *The Neglected Duty*. New York: Macmillan Publishing Company. (1986).

John, Esposito (ed.) *Voices of Resurgent Islam*. Oxford: Oxford University Press. (1983).

Juergensmeyer, Mark. *The New Cold War: Religious Nationalism Confrents the Secular State*. Berkeley, CA: University of California Press. (1993).
Al-Jumahi, Abdullah Muhammad Ibn Salam (d. 231/8450). *Tabaqat Fuhul al-Shu'ara'*. Cairo: Matba'at al-Madani. (1974).
Al-Kalbi, Abi al-Qasim Muhammad Ibn Ahmad. *Al-Tashil li-'Ulum al-Tanzil*. Muhammd Salim Hashim (ed.). Beirut: Dar al-Kutub al-'Ilmiyyah. First edition. (1995).
Khalid, Muhammd Khalid. *al-Dawlah Fi al-Islam*. Cairo: Dar Thabit. First edition. (1981).
Kalidi, Tarif. *Classical Arab Islam*. Princeton, NJ: The Darwin Press, Inc. (1985).
Kamenka, Eugne (ed). *The Portable Karl Marx*. New York: Penguin. (1983).
Kedourie, Elie. *Afghani and Abduh: An Assay on Religious Unbelief and Political Activism in Modern Islam*. London: Frank Cass. (1966).
Kepel, Gilles. *Muslim Extremism In Egypt: The Prophet and the Pharaoh*. Berkeley and Los Angeles, CA: University of California Press. (1985).
Al-Khabbas, Abdullah. *Sayyid Qutb, al-Adib al-Naqid*. Al-Zarqa': Maktabat al-Manar. First edition. (1983).
Khafaji, Abd al-Halim. *'Indama Ghabat al-Shams*. Kuwait: Maktabat al-Fallah. First edition. (1979).
Khalafallah, Muhammad. *Min al-Athar*. Cairo: Maktabat al-Anglu al-Misriyyah. n.d.
Al-Khalidi, Salah. *Amrica Min al-Dakhil bi-Minzar Sayyid Qutb*. Jaddah: Dar al-Manarah. First edition. (1985).
Al-Khalidi, Salah. *Madkhal ila Zilal al-Qur'an*. Jaddah: Dar al-Manarah. (1986).
Al-Khalidi, Salah. *Mafatih li al-Ta'amul ma'a Al-Qur'an*. Al Zarqa': Maktabat al-Manar. First edition. (1985).
Al-Khalidi, Salah. *Nazariyyat al-Taswir al-Fanni 'inda Sayyid Qutb*. Jaddah: Dar al-Manarah. Second edition. (1989).
Al-Khalidi, Salah. *Sayyid Qutb Min al-Milad ila al-Istishhad*. Damascus: Dar al-Qalam. Second edition. (1994).
Khalifa, Abd al-Hakim. *Islamic Ideology*. Lahore, Pakistan: Institute of Islamic Culture. (1961).
Khalid, Muhammad Khalid. *Muhammad wa al-Masih*. Beirut: Dar al-'Ilm li al-Malayin. Seventh edition. (1981).
Khalil, 'Imad al-Din. *Al-Manzur al-Tarikhi fi Fikr Sayyid Qutb*. Damascus. Dar al-Qalam. First edition. (1994).
Al-Kharbutli, Ali Husni. *Al-Islam wa al-Khilafah*. Beirut: Dar Beirut li al-Tiba'ah wa al-Nashr. (1969).
Kharofa, Ala' Eddin. *Nationalism, Secularism, Apostasy, and Usury in Islam*. Kuala Lumpur: A. S. Noordeen. First edition. (1994).
Kharofa, Ala'Eddin. *Islam: The Practical Religion*. Malaysia: A. S. Noordeen. (1992).
Al-Khayyam, 'Umar. *Ruba'iyyat al-Khayyam*. London: Bracken Books. (1995).
Al-Khumayni, Ruhallah Musawi. *Al-Hukumah al-Islamiyyah*. Hasan Hanafi (ed.). Cairo. (1979). n.p.
Al-Kilani, Musa Zayd. *Al-Harakat al-Islamiyyah Fi al-Urdun wa Filistin*. Beirut: Mu'assasat al-Risalah. Second edition. (1995).
Al-Kilani, Sami. *Ma'a Taha Husayn*. Cairo: Dar al-Ma'arif. November (1973).
Kishk, Muhammad Jalal. *Ala fi al-Fitnati Saqatu: Tahlil 'Ilmi bi al-Watha'iq li al-Fitnah al-Ta'ifiyyah*. Cairo: Maktabat al-Turath. First edition. (1412/1992).
Kishk, Muhammad Jalal. *Al-Nasiriyyun Qadimun*. Cairo: al-Zahra'. (1989).

Kishk, Muhammad Jalal. *Thawrat Yulu al-Amerikiyyah*. Cairo: al-Maktabah al-Thaqafiyyah. Third edition. (1994).

Lambton, Ann K. S. *State and Government in Medival Islam*. Oxford: Oxford University Press. (1981).

Lane, Edward William. *Arabic – English Lexicon*. Cambridge: Cambridge University Press. Third edition. (1972).

Langbaum, Robert. *Thomas Hardy in Our Time*. London: Macmillan. (1995).

Lesch, David W. *The Middle East and the United States: A Historical and Political Reassessment*. Colorado: Westview Press. (1996).

Levtzion, Nehemia and Voll, John Obert (eds). *Eighteenth-Century Renewal and Reform in Islam*. Syracuse: Syracuse University Press. (1984).

Lichtheim, George. *Marxism*. New York: Praeger. (1961).

Lichtheim, George. *A Short History of Socialism*. Glasgow: Collins. (1978).

Lings, Martin. *Muhammad: His life based on the Earlier Sources*. London: George Allen & Unwin. (1983).

Lyall, Charles James (Sir – 1845–1920). *Ancient Arabic Poetry: Chiefly Pre-Islamic*. New York: Hyperion Press. (1930).

Macpherson C. B. *The Real World of Democracy*. Oxford: Oxford University Press. (1966).

Mahdi, Fadl-Allah. *Ma'a Sayyid Qutb fi Fikrih al-Siyasi Wa al-Dini*. Beirut: Mu'assasat al-Risalah. (1978).

Mahfuz, Muhammad. *Al-Ladhina Zulimu: al-Tanzimat al-Islamiyyah fi Misr.* London: Riad el-Rayyes Books. (1988).

Mahfuz, Naguib. *Al-Shahhadh*. Cairo: Maktabat Misr. (1982).

Mahfuz, Naguib. *Thartharah Fawq al-Nil*. Cairo: Misr li al-Tiba'ah. (1967).

Mahfuz, Naguib. *Al-Harafish*, trans. Catherine Cobham. New York: Doubleday. (1977).

Mahmud, Mustafa. *Allah*. Beirut: Dar al-'Awdah. First edition. (1972).

Majid, Khadduri. *The Islamic Conception of Justice*. London: The Johns Hopkins University Press. (1984).

Al-Mallakh, Kamal. *Taha Husayn Qahir al-Zalam*. Cairo: Dar al-Kitab al-Jadid. n.d.

Mallet, Phillip. *The Achievement of Thomas Hardy*. London: Macmillan. (2000).

Mandur, Muhammd. *Al-Shi'r al-Misri Ba'da Shawqi*. Cairo: Jami'at al-Duwal al-Arabiyyah: Ma'had al-Dirasat al-Arabiyyah al-'Alamiyyah. (1958).

Mansur, Anis. *Man Qatal Man*. Cairo: Dar al-Katib al-'Arabi. (1969).

Al-Markaz al-'Arabi li al-Ma'lumat. *Khiyarat Sa'bah: Mudhakkirat Syruce Vance*. Beirut: al-Markaz al-'Arabi li al-Ma'lumat. (1983).

Margolis, Michael. *Viable Democracy*. London: Macmillan. (1979).

Marshall, Gordon (ed.) *A Dictionary of Sociology*. Oxford: Oxford University Press. Second edition. (1998).

Martin C. Richard. *Islamic Studies: A History of Religious Approach*. New Jersey: Prentic Holl. (1996).

Martin E. Marty and R. Scott Appleby (eds). *Fundamentalisms Project*. Chicago: The Univiersity of Chicago Press. (1991–1995).

Martin Hinds and El-Said Badawi. *A Dictionary of Egyptian Arabic: Arabic–English*. Beirut: Librairie Du Liban. (1986).

Al-Mawardi, Abi al-Hasan Ali Ibn Muhammad (d.450/1057). *Al-Ahkam al-Sultaniyyah*. Beirut: Dar al-Fikr. n.d.

Al-Mawardi, Abi al-Hasan Ali Ibn Muhammad. *Adab al-Dunia wa al-Din*. Beirut: Dar wa Maktabat al-Hilal. (1988).

Mawdudi, Sayyid Abu al-A'la (1903–1979). *First Principles of the Islamic State*. Lahore: Islamic Publications. (1983).
Mawdudi, Sayyid Abu al-A'la. *The Economic Problem of Man and its Islamic Solution*. Lahore: Islamic Publications. (1978).
Mawdudi, Sayyid Abu al-A'la. *Four Basic Qur'anic Terms*. Lahore: Islamic Publications. n.d.
Mawdudi, Sayyid Abu al-A'la. *Human Rights in Islam*. London: The Islamic Foundation. (1980).
Mawdudi, Sayyid Abu al-A'la. *Mabadi' al-Islam*. Beirut: al-Maktab al-Islami. n.d.
Mawdudi, Sayyid Abu al-A'la. *Nizam al-Hayat fi al-Islam*. International Islamic Federation of Student Organizations. Second edition. (1970).
Mawdudi, Sayyid Abu al-A'la. *Political Theory of Islam*. Lahore: Islamic Publications. n.d.
Mawdudi, Sayyid Abu al-A'la. *System of Government Under the Holy Prophet*. Lahore: Islamic Publications. (1989).
Mawdudi, Sayyid Abu al-A'la. *Theocracy and the Islamic State*. Lahore: KAZI Publications. (1981).
Mawdudi, Sayyid Abu al-A'la. *Towards Understanding Islam*. Lahore: Idara Tarjuman-ul Qur'an. Eighteenth edition. (1978).
Al-Maydani, Abd al-Rahman Hasan. *Kawashif Ziyuf fi al-Madhahib al-Fikriyyah al-Mu'asirah*. Damascus: Dar al-Qalam. (1985).
Michael Cook. *Commanding Rights and Forbidding Wrong in Islamic Thought*. Cambridge: Cambridge University Press. (2000).
Michael, A. Hoffman. *Egypt before the Pharaohs: The Prehistoric Foundations of Egyptian Civilization*. New York: Cambridge University Press. (1979).
Ministry of Justice. *Conferences of Riyad, Paris, Vatican City, Geneva, and Strasbourg on Muslim Doctrine and Human Rights in Islam. Between Saudi Canonists and Eminent European Jurists and Intellectuals*. Riyadh: Ministry of Justice. (1972).
Mitchell, Richard P. *The Society of the Muslim Brothers*. Oxford: Oxford Unversity Press. (1993).
Mortimer, Edward. *Faith and Power: The Politics of Islam*. London: Faber and Faber. (1982).
Moussalli, Ahmad. *Al-Usuliyyah al-Islamiyyah: Dirasah fi al-Khitab al-Aiydiyuluji wa al-Siyasi 'inda Sayyid Qutb: Bahth Muqaran li-Mabadi' al-Usuliyyin wa al Islahiyyin*. Beirut: al-Nashir li al-Tiba'ah. First edition. (1993).
Moussalli, Ahmad. *Qira'ah Nazariyyah Ta'sisiyyah fi al-Khitab al-Islami al-Usuli*. Beirut: al-Nashir Li al-Tiba'ah. First editiion. (1993).
Muhammad Sallam, *Tarikh al-Tashri' al-Islami*. Beirut: Dar al-'Ilm. n.d.
Muhammad, Yasien. *Fitrah: The Islamic Concept of Human Nature*. London: Ta-Ha Publishers Ltd. (1996).
Muhammad, Sulaymi al-Shaykh. *A Dictionary of Islamic Terms*. Beirut: Dar al-Fikr. (1998).
Muller, R. Konrad and Blaisse, W. Mark. *Anwar Sadat: The Last Hundred Days*. London: Thames and Hudson. (1981).
Munazzamat al-Shabab al-Ishtraki. *Abd al-Nasser: al-Fikr wa al-Tariq*. Cairo: Matba'at al-Ahram. (1972).
Munson, Henry. *Islam and Revolution in the Middle East*. London: Yale University Press. (1988).
Mursi, Sayyid Abd al-Hammid (Brigadier). *Insaniyyat al-Ishtrakiyyah al-Arabiyyah*. Cairo: Maktabat al-Qahirah al-Hadithah. n.d.

Musallam, Adnan Ayyub. *The formative Stages of Sayyid Qutb's Intellectual Career and His Emergence as an Islamic Da'iyah*. PhD Dissertation, University of Michigan. (1983).

Al-Muti'i, Muhammad Bikhit. *Haqa'iq al-Islam wa Usul al-Hukm*. Cairo: Maktabat al-Nahdah. (1926).

Al-Nabahani, Taqyy al-Din. *Al-Dawlah al-Islamiyyah*. Al-Quds. (1953). n.p.

Al-Nadawi, Abu al-Hasan. *Madha Khasira al-'Alam bi-Inhitat al-Muslimin*. Beirut: Dar al Kitab al-Arabi. (1984).

Al-Nadawi, Abu al-Hasan. *Mudhakkirat Sa'ih fi al-Sharq al-Arabi*. Beirut: Mu'assasat al-Risalah. Second edition. (1975).

Al-Nadawi, Abu al-Hasan. *Shakhsiyyat wa Kutub (Personalities and Books)*. Damascus: Dar al-Qalam. (1990).

Naguib, Muhammad. *Egypt's Destiny*. London: Victor Collancz Ltd. (1955).

Namiq, Salah al-Din, Abd Ellah Amin Mustafa, and Lutfi Abd al-Hamid. *Al Ishtrakiyyah al-Arabiyyah*. Cairo: Dar al-Ma'arif. (1966).

Nettler, L. Ronald. *Past Trials and Present Tribulations: A Muslim Fundamentalist's View of the Jews*. Jerusalem: The Hebrew University. (1987).

Ni'mah, Fu'ad. *Mulakhkhas Qawa'id al-Lughah al-'Arabiyyah*. Cairo: Nahdat Misr. Fifteenth edition. Volume 1 n.d., but numbered 3175. The first edition in May (1973).

Numayri, Ja'far Muhammad. *Al-Sadat: al-Mabadi' wa al-Mawaqif*. Cairo: al-Maktab al-Misri al-Hadith. (1981).

Pennock, J. Roland. *Democratic Political Theory*. Princeton NJ: Princeton University Press. (1979).

Peter, F. E. *Mecca: A Literary History of the Muslim Holy Land*. New Jersey: Princeton University Press. (1994).

Petrie W. M. Felinders (Sir). *History of Egypt From the Earliest Times to the XVIth dynasty*. London: Methuen. (1895).

Pickthall, Marmaduke. *The Meaning of The Glorious Qur'an: Text and Explainatory Translation*, Delhi: Kutubkhana, Ishayat-ul-Islam. Second edition. (1979).

Plamenatz, John. *Karl Marx's Philosophy of Man*. Oxford: Clarendon Press. (1975).

Plato. *The Republic of Plato*, trans. Cornford, Francis Macdonald. Oxford: Oxford University Press. (1949).

Al-Qaradawi Yusuf. *Al-Tarbiyah al-Islamiyyah wa Madrasat Hasan al-Banna*. Kuwait: al-Ittihad al-Islami al-Alami li al-Munazzamat al-Tullabiyyah. (1983).

Al-Qaradawi, Yusuf. *The Lawful and The Prohibited in Islam*. Kuala Lumpur: Islamic Book Trust. (1985).

Qumayhah, Mufid. *Sharh al-Mu'allaqat al-'Ashr*. Beirut: Matabat al-Hilal. (1994).

Qur'an. *Mushaf al-Madinah al-Nabawiyah*. Kingdom of Saudi Arabia (1410 AH) number 10278.

Al-Qurtubi, Abi Abdullah Muhammad b. Ahamd al-Ansari (d. 671/1272). *Al-Jami' li Ahkam al-Qur'an*. Beirut: Dar Ihya' al-Turath. Volume 6. (1985).

Qutb, Aminah. *Rasa'il Ila Shahid*. Amman: Dar al-Furqan. (1985).

Qutb, Aminah. *Fi al-Tariq*. Damascus: Dar al-Fikr. n.d.

Qutb, Aminah. *Fi Tayyar al-Hayah*. Second edition. (1967) n.p.

Qutb, Muhammad. *Al-Insan Bayna al-Maddiyyah wa al-Islam*. Beirut: Dar al-Shuruq. Eleventh edition. (1993).

Qutb, Muhammad. *Al-Tatawwur wa al-Thabat*. Cairo: Dar al-Shuruq. (1991).

Qutb, Muhammad. *Dirasat fi al-Nafs al-Insaniyyah*. Cairo: Dar al-Shuruq. Tenth edition. (1993).

Qutb, Muhammad. *Hal Nahnu Muslimun*. Cairo: Dar al-Shuruq. (1995).

Qutb, Muhammad. *Islam: The Misunderstood Religion*. Kuwait: Dar al-Bayan. n.d.
Qutb, Muhammad. *Jahiliyyat al-Qarn al-'Ishrin*. Cairo: Dar al- Shuruq. (1983).
Qutb, Muhammad. *Ma'rakat al-Taqalid*. Cairo: Dar al-Shuruq. (1993).
Qutb, Muhammad. *Manhaj al-Fann*. Cairo: Dar al-Shuruq. n.d.
Qutb, Muhammad. *Sayyid Qutb aw Thawrat al-Fikr al-Islami*. Beirut: Dar al-Hadith. Second edition. (1975).
Ra'ana, Irfan Muhammad. *Economic System Under 'Umar the Great*. Lahore: SH. Muhammad Ashraf. (1977).
Al-Rafi'i, Abd al-Rahman. *Al-Thawrah al-'Urabiyyah wa al-Ihtilal al-Inglizi*. Cairo: Matabat al-Nahdah al-Misriyyah. (1949).
Al-Rafi'i, Abd al-Rahman. *Tarikh al-Harakah al-Qawmiyyah wa Tatawwur Nizam al-Hukm fi Misr*. Cairo: Maktabat al-Nahdah. (1955).
Rahman, Fazlur. *Islam and Modernity: The Transformation of an Intellectual Tradition*. Chicago: University of Chicago Press. (1982).
Rahman, Fazlur. *Islam: Ideology and The Way of Life*. Malaysia: Noordeen. (1980).
Rahnema, Ali (ed.) *Pioneers of Islamic Revival*. Kuala Lumpur: S. Abd al-Majeed & Co. Publishing division. (1995).
Raymond, Boudon and Francois Bourricaud. *A Critical Dictionary of Sociology*, trans. Peter Hamilton. Chicago, IL: The University of Chicago Press. (1989).
Al-Razi, *Mukhtar al-Sahhah*. (Arabic Dictionary). Beirut: Dar al-'ilm. n.d.
Rida, Ahmad. *Mu'jam Matn al-Lughah*. Beirut: Dar Maktabat al-Hayah. Volume 2. (1958).
Rizq, Jabir. *Madhabih al-Ikhwan fi Sugun Nasser*. Cairo: Dar al-I'tisam. Two volumes. (1986).
Robert D. Lee. *Overcoming Tradition and Modernity*. Oxford: WestviewPress. (1997).
Robert, Bauval and Graham Hancock. *Keeper of Genesis: A Quest for the Hidden Legacy of Mankind*. London: Mandarin Paperbacks. (1997).
Robert, Stephens. *Nasser: A Political Biography*. London: The Penguin Press. (1971).
Rodinson, Maxim. *Al-Islam wa al-Ra'smaliyyah*, trans. Nazih al-Hakim. Beirut: Dar al-Tali'ah Li al-Tiba'ah. (1982).
Rousseau, Jean-Jacques. *The Social Contract*, trans. Maurice Cranston. London: Penguin Books. (1968).
Rousseau, Jean-Jacques. *A Discourse on Inequality*, trans. Maurice Cranston. London: Penguin Books. (1984).
Rousseau, Jean-Jacques. *The Confessions*, trans. J. M. Cohen. London: Penguin Books. (1953).
Rousseau, Jean-Jacques. *Revries of the Solitary Walker*, trans. Peter France. London: Penguin Books. (1979).
Russell, Bertrand. *A Free Man's Worship: Mysticism and Logic*. New York: Simon & Schuster. (1918).
Russell, Bertrand. *History of Western Philosophy*. London: George Allen & Unwin. (1961).
Russell, Bertrand. *The Impact of Science on Society*. New York: Simon & Schuster. (1953).
Sabiq, Sayyid. *Fiqh al-Sunnah*. Beirut: Dar al-Kitab al-Arabi. (1985).
Al-Sadat, Muhammad Anwar. *Al-Bahth 'an al-Zat*. Cairo: al-Maktab al-Misry al-Hadith. n.d.
Al-Sadat, Muhammad Anwar. *Qissat al-Thawrah Kamilatan*. Cairo: al-Dar al-Qawmiyyah li al-Tiba'ah wa al-Nashr. (1965).
Al-Sadat, Muhammad Anwar. *Waraqat Uktubar*. Cairo. (1974). n.p.
Saeed, Abdullah. *Islamic Banking and Interest*. Lieden: E.J. Brill. (1996).

Sagiv, David. *Fundamentalism and Intellectuals in Egypt*. London: Frank Cass. (1995).
Sakwa, Richard. *Soviet Politics*. London: Routledge. (1989).
Salame, Ghassn (ed.) *Democracy Without Democrats: The Renewal of Politics in the Muslim World*. London: I. B. Tauris Publishers. (1994).
Salih, Hafiz. *Al-Dimuqratiyyah wa al-Hurriyyah*. Lahore: Dar al-Fath. (1992).
Samarah, Ihsan. *Mafhum al-'Adalah al-Ijtima'iyyah fi al-Fikr al-Islami al-Mu'asir*. Beirut: Dar al-Nahda al-Islamiyyah. Second edition. (1991).
Al-Samurra'i, Ibrahim. *Fi al-Lahajat al-'Arabiyyah al-Qadimah*. Beirut: Dar al-Hadathah li al-tiba'ah. (1994).
Sartre, Jean-Paul (1905–1980). *Al-Wujudiyyah Madhhab Insani*, trans. Abd al-Mun'im al-Hifni. Cairo: Matba'at al-Dar al-Misriyyah li al-Tab' wa al-Nashr wa al-Tawzi'. (1964).
Al-Sawi, Muhammad Salah. *Al-Muwajahah Bayna al-Islam wa al-'Ilmaniyyah*. Cairo: al-Afaq al-Dawliyyah li al-I'lam. (1992).
Al-Sayyid, Ahamad Lutfi (1872–1963). *Mabadi' Fi al-Siyasah wa al-Adab wa al-Ijtima'*. Cairo: Dar al-Hilal. (1963).
Schadwich, Owen. *The Secularization of the European Mind in the Nineteenth Century*. Cambridge University Press. (1975).
Shadi, Salah. *Safahat min al-Tarikh*. Kuwait: Dar al-Shu'a'. (1981).
Al-Shafi'i, Abi Abd Allah Muhammad b. Idris (d. 204/ 819). *Diwan al-Imam al-Shafi'i*. Beirut: Dar al-Kitab al-Arabi. (1991).
Al-Shafi'i, Husayn. *Du'a'u al-Thawrah*. Cairo. n. d.
Al-Shahrastani, Abi al-Fath Muhammad b. Abd al-Karim b. Abi Bakr Ahmad (d. 548/1154). *Al-Milal Wa al-Nihal*. Beirut: Dar Sa'b. (1986).
Shahrur, Muhammad. *Al-Kitab wa al-Qur'an: Qira'ah Mu'asirah*. Cairo: Sina' li al-Nashr. (1990).
Al-Shak'ah, Mustafa Muhammad. *Islam bila Madhahib*. Cairo: al-Dar al-Misriyyah. (1991).
Shalabi, Ra'uf. *Jawahir al-'Irfan fi al-Da'wah wa 'Ulum al-Qur'an*. Cairo: Dar al-Tiba'ah al-Muhammadiyyah. First edition. (1986).
Shamir, Shimon (ed). *Egypt From Monarchy to Republic: A Reassessment of Revolution and Change*. Oxford: Westview Press. (1967).
Al-Sha'rawi, Muhammad Mitwalli. *Al-Muntakhab Min Tafsir al-Qur'an*. Beirut: Dar al-'Awdah. (1980).
Al-Sha'rawi, Muhammad Mitwalli. *Min Fayd al-Rahman Fi Tarbiyat al-Insan*. Cairo: Matabi' Mu'assasat Rose el-Youssef. (1981).
Shayegan, Daryush. *Cultural Schizophrenia: Islamic Societies Confronting the West*. London: Saqi Books. (1992).
Shepard, William. *Sayyid Qutb and Islamic Activism: A Translation and Critical Analysis of Social Justice in Islam*. Leiden: E. J. Brill. (1996).
Al-Shintimari, Yusuf b. Sulayman b, 'Isa al-Andalusi (al-A'lam – d. 476/1083). *Ash'ar al-Shu'ara' al-Sittah al-Jahiliyyin*. Beirut: Dar al-Fikr. (1982).
Siddiqi, 'Abdul Hamid. *Theocracy and Islamic System*. Lahore: Kazi Publications. (1981).
Silvia G. Haim (ed.). *Arab Nationalism*. Berkeley, CA: University of California Press. (1962).
Singh, N. K. and Agwan, A. R. (ed.). *Encyclopaedia of the Holy Qur'an*. Global Vision Publishing House. Tarun Offset Press. Maujpur, Delhi. First edition (2000), p. 808.
Smith, W. Cantwell. *Islam in Modern History*. Princeton, NJ: Princeton University Press. (1957).

Sulayman, Adli. *Al-Suluk al-Ishtiraki li al-Muwatin al-Arabi*. n.d.

Sulayman, Adli. *Ma'alim al-Hayah al-Ishtrakiyyah fi al-Jama'ah al-Arabiyyah*. First edition. (1964). n. p.

Sulayman, al-'Ashmawi Ahmad. *Al-'Alim al-Rabbani al-Shahid Sayyid Qutb*. (1969). n. p.

Surur, Muhammad Gamal al-Din. *Al-Dawlah al-Fatimiyyah Fi Misr.* Cairo: Dar al-Fikr al-'Arabi. (1970).

Al-Suyuti, Jalal al-Din Abu al-Fadl Abd al-Rahman b. al-Kamal Abi Bakr (d. 849/911). *Al-Muzahhar fi 'Ulum al-Lughah wa Anwa'iha*. Cairo: Gad al-Mawla wa Rifaqih. Two volumes. n.d.

Al-Tabari, Abi Ja'far Muhammad b. Jarir (d. 893/922). *Jami' al-Bayan fi Tafsir al-Qur'an*. Beirut: Dar al-Ma'arif. (1986).

Al-Tabari, Abi Ja'far Muhammad b. Jarir. *Tarikh al-Umam wa al-Shu'ub*. Beirut: Dar al-Kutub al-'Ilmiyyah. Six volumes. (1997).

Al-Tabarsi, Abi Ali al-Fadl b. al-Hasan. *Majma' al-Bayan fi Tafsir al-Qur'an*. Beirut: Dar al-Ma 'rifah. Five volumes. n.d.

Ta'ifah Min al-Mufakkirin. *Al-Ishtrakiyyah fi al-Tajarib al-'Arabiyyah*. Beirut: Dar al-Kitab al-'Arabi. (1965).

The Arab Republic of Egypt. *Mawsu'at Gamal Abd al-Nasser al-Fiqhiyyah*. Cairo: The Supreme Council of Islamic Affairs. Volume 1 (1986).

The Book Company International. *Mindpower*. Sydney: Orbis. (1996).

The Encyclopaedia of Philosophy. Paul Edwards (ed.) New York: Macmillan company and free press. (1967).

The Holy Bible. London and New York. Eyre and SpottisWoode. n.d.

Thomson, David. *Europe Since Napoleon*. London: Longmans. (1957).

Thuchdides. *The History of the Peloponnesian War*, trans. R. Livingstone. Oxford: Oxford University Press. (1960).

Tomlin, Eric Wlter Frederick. *Great Philosophers of the East*. London: Arrow. (1959).

Tubarah, Afif Abd al-Fattah. *Ruh al-Din al-Islami: 'Ard wa Tahlil li Usul al-Islam wa Adabih wa Ahkamih Tahta Daw'u al-'Ilm wa al-Falsafah*. Beirut: Dar al-'ilm li al-malayin. (1993).

'Umar, Hulayq. *Dawr al-Markisiyyah Fi al-Ishtrakiyyah al-'Arabiyyah*. Beirut: Dar al-Fikr al-Jadid. First edition. (1965).

'Umarah, Muhammad. *Al-Islam wa 'Usul al-Hukum li 'Ali 'Abd al-Raziq: Dirasah wa Watha'iq*. Beirut: al-Mu'assasah al-'Arabiyyah li al-Dirasat wa al-Nashr. Second edition. (1988).

Ushama, Thameem. *Hasan al-Banna: Vision & Mission*. Kuala Lumpur: A. S. Noordeen. First edition. (1995).

Van, Gelder. *The Bad and the Ugly*. Leiden: E.J. Brill. (1988).

Versteegh, C. H. M. and Hospers, J. H. *Arabic Grammar and Qur'anic Exegesis in Early Islam*. Leiden: E. J. Brill. (1993).

Voll, John Obert. *Islam: Continuity and Change in the Modern World*. Colorado: Westview. (1982).

Voltaire, Francois-Marie Arouet. *Candide*, trans. John Butt. England: Penguin Group. (1947).

Voltaire, Francois-Marie Arouet. *The complete Works of Voltaire*. Theodore Besterman (ed.) Toronto: University of Torinto Press; Oxford: Voltaire Foundation at the Taylor Institution (1968–1974), vol. 4, 5.

Voltaire, Francois-Marie Arouet. *Philosophical Dictionary*, trans. Theodore Besterman. London: Penguin Books. (1972).

Al-Wahidi, Abu al-Hasan Ali b. Ahmad (d. 468/1075). *Asbab al-Nuzul*. Beirut: Dar al-Kitab al-Arabi. Second edition. (1986).

Wajdi, Muhammad Farid. *Al-Islam Fi'Asr al-'Ilm*. Beirut: Dar al-Kitab al-Arabi. Third edition. n.d.

Wazarat al-I'lam. *Al-Thawrah al-'Urabiyyah*. Cairo: al-Hay'ah al-'Ammah li al-Isti'lamat. n.d.

Wazarat al-I'lam. *Muhammad Farid*. Cairo: al-Hay'ah al-'Ammah li al-Isti'lamat. n.d.

Weber, Max. *The Protestant Ethic and the Spirit of Capitalism*, trans. Talcott Parsons, with a Foreword by R. H. Tawney. New York: Charles Scribener's Sons. (1956).

Weber, Max. *Max Weber on Capitalism, Buearucreacy and Religion: A Sellection of Texts*.Edited and in part newly translated by Stanislave Andreski. London: George Allen & Unwin. (1983).

Weeramantry, Hidayatullah and Grand Shaykh of al-Azhar. *Islamic Jurisprudence: An International Perspective*. United States: Macmillan Press. (1996).

Wehr, Hans. *Dictionary of Modern Written Arabic*. Wiesbaden: Otto Harrassowitz. (1971).

Wendell, Charles. *Five Tracts of Hasan al-Banna*. Berkeley, CA: University of California Press. (1978).

Wilczynski, J. *The Economics of Socialism*. London: George Allen & Unwin. Third edition. (1978).

Wolfson, Harry Austryn. *The Philosophy of the Kalam*. Cambridge: Harvard University Press. (1976).

World Book Encyclopedia. Chicago: A Scott Fetzer Company. (1990).

Wright, W. L. L. D. *A Grammar of the Arabic Language*. Cambridge: Cambridge University Press. Third edition. (1979).

Yakan, Fathi. *Al-Islam: Fikrah, Harakah, Inqilab*. Beirut: Mu'assasat al-Risalah. Eleventh edition. (1987).

Al-Ya'qubi, Ahmad b. Isma'il. *Tarikh al-Ya'qubi*. Beirut: Dar Beirut li al-Tiba'ah wa al-Nashr. Volume 2. (1980).

Al-Yassini, Ayman. *Religion and State in the Kingdom of Saudi Arabia*. Boulder, CO: Westview Press. (1985).

Youssef, Michael. *Revolt Against Modernity: Muslim Zealots and the West*. Leiden: E. J. Brill. (1985).

Al-Zamakhshari, Abu al-Qasim Jar Allah Muhammad. *Al-Kashshaf 'an Haqa'iq al-Tanzil*. Calcutta: Matba'at al-Laysi. (1856).

Al-Zayn, Muhammad Khalil. *Tarikh al-Firaq al-Islamiyyah*. Beirut: Mu'assasat al-A'lami li al-Matbu'at. (1985).

Al-Zayyat, Ahmad Hasan. *Tarikh al-Adab al-'Arabi*. Lahore, Pakistan: Dar Mashr al-Kutb al-Islamiyyah, n.d.

Zidan, Abd al-Karim. *Al-Madkhal li Dirasat al-Shari'ah al-Islamiyyah*. Beirut: Mu'assasat al-Risalah. Ninth edition. (1986).

Zuhayri, Kamil. *Al-Ghadibun*. Cairo: Mu'assasat Akhbar al-Yawm. n.d.

Articles in books and periodicals (English)

Al-Abdin, A. Z., (1989). 'The Political Thought of Hasan al-Banna'. *Islamic Studies*, No. 28: 3, pp. 219–33.

Abed-Kotob, Sana', (1995). 'The Accommodationists Speak: Goals and Strategies for the Muslim Brotherhood of Egypt'. *Journal of Middle East Studies*, No. 27, pp. 321–39.

Abukhalil, As'ad, (1994). 'The Incoherence of Islamic Fundamentalism: Arab Islamic Thought at the End of the Twentieth Century'. *Middle East Journal*, No. 48: 4 (Autumn), pp. 677–94.

Ade, Shttu-Agbetola, (1989). 'The Equality of Man and Woman in Islam: Sayyid Qutb's Views Examined'. *Islamic Studies*, No. 28: 3, pp. 131–7.

Ali, Ameer, (1972). 'The Modernity of Islam'. *Journal of Islamic Culture*, pp. 1–8.

Ali Hilal, Dessouki, (1973). 'Arab Intellictuals and al-Nakbah: The Search For Fundamentalism'. *Journal of Middle Eastern Studies*, No. 9: 2 (May), pp. 186–95.

Anis, Mona, (2004). 'Thus Spoke Yehia Haqqi'. *Al-Ahram Weekly*, No. 688 (29 April–5May).

Ansari, Hamied, (1984). 'Sectarianism Conflict in Egypt and the Political Expediency of Religion'. *Middle East Journal*, No. 38: 3 (Summer), pp. 397–418.

Ansari, Hamied, (1984). 'The Islamic Militant in Egyptian Politics'. *International Journal of Middle Eastern Studies*, No. 16, pp. 123–44.

As'ad, Abukh, (1994). 'The Incoherence of Islamic Fundamentalism: Arab Islamic Thought at the End of the Twentieth Century'. *Middle East Journal*, No. 48: 4 (Autumn), pp. 677–94.

Ayubi, Nazih N., (1980). 'The Political Revival of Islam: The Case of Egypt'. *International Journal of Middle Eastern Studies*, No. 12, pp. 481–99.

Al-'Azmeh, Aziz. 'Populism Contra Democracy: Recent Democratist Discourse in the Arab World'. In Salame, Ghassn, (ed.) *Democracy Without Democrats: The Renewal of Politics in the Muslim World*. London: I. B. Tauris Publishers (1994), pp. 112–30.

Al-Baghdadi, A., (1984). 'Al-Mawardi's Contribution to Islamic Political Thought'. *Islamic Culture*. (October), pp. 327–31.

Al-Banna, Hasan. 'The New Renaissance'. In John Donohue and John Esposito (eds) *Islam in Transition: Muslim Perspectives*. Oxford: Oxford University Press (1982), pp. 78–83.

Al-Bazzaz, Abd al-Rahman. 'Islam and Arab Nationalism'. In Silvia G. Haim (ed.) *Arab Nationalism*. Berkeley, CA: University of California Press (1962), pp. 172–6, 178–88.

Al-Bazzaz, Abd al-Rahman. 'Islam and Arab Nationalism'. In John Donohue and John Esposito, (eds.) *Islam in Transition: Muslim Perspectives*. Oxford: Oxford University Press (1982), pp. 84–90.

Blau, Joshua, (1986). 'The Jahiliyyah and the Emergence of the New-Arabic Lingual Type'. *Journal of Jerusalem Studies in Arabic and Islam*, No. 7, pp. 35–43.

Boullata, J. 'Isa. 'Sayyid Qutb's literary Appreciation of the Qur'an'. In Boullata (ed.) *Literary Structures of Religious Meaning in the Qur'an*. Richmond: Surrey Curzon Press (2000), pp. 354–71.

Brinton, Cran. 'Enlightenment'. In *The Encyclopaedia of Philosophy*. Vol. 2. New York: The Macmillan Company and the Free Press (1967), p. 521.

Brohi, K. Allahbukhsh. 'Human Rights and Duties in Islam'. In *Islam an Contemporary Society*. London and New York: Longman (1982), pp. 231–52.

Calvert, John. '"The World is an Undutiful Boy": Sayyid Qutb's American Experience'. *Islam and Christian Muslim Relations*. Abngdon. Carfax Publishing Company. 11: 1 (March 2000), pp. 87–103.

Coury, Ralph M., (1995). 'The Arab Nationalism of Makram 'Ubayd'. *Journal of Islamic Studies*, No. 6: 1, pp. 76–90.

Crone, Patricia, (1984). 'Jahili and Jewish Law: The Qasamah'. *Journal of Jerusalim Studies in Arabic and Islam*, No. 4, pp. 153–201.

Al-Dawalibi, Muhammad Ma'ruf. 'Islam and Nationalistic and Secularistic Trends'. In Kharofa Ala'Eddin (ed.) *Nationalism, Secularism, Apostasy and Usury in Islam.* Kuala Lumpur: A. S. Noordeen (1994), pp. 1–17.

Dekmejian, Hrair, (1980). 'The Islamic Revivalism in the Middle East and North Africa'. *Current History Journal*, No. 456 (April), pp. 169–74.

Dekmejian, Hrair, (1980). 'The Search for Islamic Alternatives'. *Middle East Journal*, No. 34: 1 (Winter), pp. 1–12.

Dennis, Walker, (1993). 'The Collapse of Neo-Pharaonic Nationalism in Egyptian High Culture After 1930'. *Journal of Arabic, Islamic and Middle Eastern Studies*, No. 1, pp. 45–58.

Dicey, Albert Venn. *Introduction to the Study of Law of The Constitution*, London: Macmillan (1941).

Dunn, Mc, (1993). 'Fundamentalism in Egypt'. *Journal of Middle East Policy*, No. 2, pp. 68–77.

Ebert, Roger. 'Karl Marx'. In *World Book Encyclopeadia*. Vol. 13. Chicago: A Scott Fetzer Comp. (1990), pp. 236–8.

Elmesseri, Abd al-Wahhab, (1995). '1995 Special Issue: Secularism'. *The American Journal of Islamic Social Sciences*, No. 11: 4, pp. 587–94.

Fandy, Mamoun, (1994). 'Egypt's Islamic Group: Regional Revenges'. *Middle East Journal*, No. 48: 4 (Autumn), pp. 607–26.

Gad al-Haqq, Ali Gad al-Haqq, (1996). 'Islam as a Source of Balance'. *Al-Azhar*, No. 68: 12 (May), pp. 1927–31 [English].

George H. Sabine. *A History of Political Theory*, New York: Holt (1951).

Gerges, Fawaz, (1995). 'The Kennedy Administration and The Egyptian-Saudi Conflict in Yemen: co-opting Arab Nationalism'. *Middle East Journal*, No. 49: 2 (Spring), pp. 292–311.

Gorman, Anthony, (1996). 'In the Shadow of the Nation: the Politics of Egyptian Historiography in the Twentieth Century'. *Journal of Arabic, Islamic and Middle Eastern Studies*, No. 3: 1, pp. 117–26.

Groth, Alexander. 'Democracy in England'. *World Book Encyclopedia*. Vol. 5 (1990), pp. 126–30.

Haddad, Yvonne Yazbeck. 'Sayyid Qutb: Ideologue of Islamic Revival'. In John Esposito (ed.) *Voices of Resurgent Islam*. Oxford University Press (1983), pp. 67–89.

Haddad, Yvonne Yazbeck, (1983). 'The Qur'anic justification for an Islamic Revolution: The View of Sayyid Qutb'. *Middle East Journal*, No. 37 (Winter), pp. 14–29.

Hasan, Ahmad, (1996). 'Al-Shafi'i's Role in the Development of Islamic Jurisprudence'. *Islamic Studies* (September), No. 3, pp. 238–72.

Hathaway, Jane, (1995). 'The Military Household in Ottoman Egypt'. *International Journal Middle Eastern Studies*, No. 27, pp. 39–52.

Huff, Toby E., (1995). 'Islam, Science, and Fundamentalism'. *Journal of Arabic, Islamic and Middle Eastern Studies*, No. 2: 2, pp. 1–27.

Husayn, Taha. 'The Future of Culture in Egypt'. In John Donohue and John Esposito (eds) *Islam in Transition: Muslim Perspectives.* Oxford: Oxford University Press (1982), pp. 73–7.

Ibrahim, Saad Eddin, (1980). 'Anatomy of Egypt's Militant Islamic Groups: Methodological Note and Preliminary Findings'. *International Journal of Middle East Studies*, No. 12, pp. 423–53.

Ingram, Edward, (1995). 'The Geopolitics of the First British Expedition to Egypt – IV: Occupation and Withdrawal, 1801–3'. *International Journal of Middle Eastern Studies*, No. 31: 2 (April), pp. 317–46.

Iqbal, Javid. 'Democracy and the Modern Islamic State'. In John Esposito (ed.) *Voices of Resurgent Islam.* Oxford: Oxford University Press (1983), pp. 252–60.

Kamali, Muhammad Hashim, (1989). 'The Limits of Power in an Islamic State'. *Journal of Islamic Studies*, No. 28: 4, pp. 323–52.

Keynes, John Maynard. 'The Royal Societies: Newton Tercentenary Celebration 1949'. In Robert Bauval and Graham Hancock (eds) *Keeper Of Genesis: A Quest For The Hidden Legacy Of Mankind.* London: Mandarin Books (1969), chapter 8.

Khalid Bin Sayeed, (1986). 'Islamic Resurgance and Social Change'. *Islamic Culture*, LX, No. 1 (January), pp. 45–59.

Khalifa, Abd al-Hakim. 'Islamic Socialism'. In Daryush Shayegan (ed.) *Cultural Schizophrenia: Islamic Societies Confronting the West.* London: Saqi Books (1992), pp. 131–6.

Khatab, Sayed, (2001). 'Al-Hudaybi's Influence on the Development of Islamist Movements in Egypt'. *The Muslim World*, No. 91: 3 and 4 (fall), pp. 451–79.

Khatab, Sayed, (2002). 'Citizenship Rights of Non-Muslims in the Islamic State of Hakimiyyah Espoused by Sayyid Qutb'. *Islam and Christian-Muslim Relations*, No. 13: 2 (April), pp. 151–61.

Kienle, Eberhard, (1995). 'Arab Unity Schemes Revisited: Interest, Identity, and Policy in Syria and Egypt'. *International Journal Middle Eastern Studies*, No. 27, pp. 53–71.

Kister, M. J., (1980). 'Labbayka, Allahumma, Labbayka: On a Monotheistic aspect of a Jahiliyya Practice'. *Journal of Jerusalem Studies in Arabic and Islam*, No. 2, pp. 33–57.

Larbi, Sadiki, (1993). 'Progress and Retrogression of Arab Democratization'. *Journal of Arabic, Islamic and Middle Eastern Studies*, No. 1, pp. 80–102.

Lyon, Bryce. 'Magna Carta'. *World Book Encyclopeadia*. Vol. 13. Chicago: A Scott Fetzer Company. (1990), pp. 53–4.

Mclnnes, Neil. 'Karl Marx'. *Encyclopaedia of Philosophy*. Vol. 5. New York: The Macmillan Company and the Free Press (1967), p. 172.

Mckale, M. Donald, (1997). 'Influence Without Power: The Last Khedive of Egypt and the Great Powers, 1914–1918'. *Middle Eastern Studies*, No. 33: 1 (January), pp. 20–39.

MacNeal, Ropert H. 'Lenin'. *World Book Encyclopeadia*. Vol. 12. Chicago: A Scott Fetzer Company (1990), pp. 191–5.

Mahmud, (1966). 'Islam and Arab Nationalism: Complementary or Competitive'. *Middle East Journal*, No. 11: 2, pp. 11–15.

Marsot, Afaf Lutfi al-Sayyid, (1984). 'Religion or Opposition? Urban Protest Movements in Egypt'. *International Journal of Middle Eastern Studies*, No. 16, pp. 541–52.

Martin, Seymour Lipset. *Political Man: The Social Bases of Politics*, London: Heinemann (1960), pp. 22–3.

Mawdudi, Abu al-A'la. 'Nationalism and Islam'. In John Donohue and John Esposito (eds) *Islam in Transition: Muslim Perspectives*. Oxford: Oxford University Press (1982), pp. 94–7.

Morsy, M. Laila, (1995). 'American Support for the1952 Egyptian Coup'. *Journal of Middle Eastern Studies*, No. 31: 2 (April), pp. 307–16.

Al-Na'im, Abdullahi. 'The Dichotomy between Religious and Secular Discourse in Islamic Secieties'. In Mahnaz Afkhami (ed.) *Faith and Freedom*. London: I. B. Tauris Publishers (1995), pp. 51–60.

Nasim Hasan Shah, (1987). 'Islamic Concept of State'. *Islamic Studies*, No. 26: 1, pp. 97–115.

Nelson, Cynthia, (1973). 'The Virgin of Zeitun'. *Worldview*, No. 16: 9, pp. 8–22.

Podeh, Elie, (1996). 'The Drift Towards Neutrality: Egyptian Foreign Policy during the Early Nasserist Era, 1952–1955'. *Middle Eastern Studies*, No. 32: 1 (January), pp. 159–78.

Pollock, H. George. 'Sigmund, Freud'. *World Book Encyclopedia*. Vol. 7 (1990), pp. 530–1.

Qurayshi, Zaheer Mas'ud, (1966). 'Heritage of Egyptian Nationalism, 1798–1914'. *Islamic Culture*, (April), pp. 57–77.

Rabbat, Nasser, (1995). 'The Ideological Significance of the Dar al-Adl in the Medieval Islamic Orient'. *International Journal of Middle Eastern Studies*, No. 27, pp. 3–28.

Rahman, Fazlur, (1964). 'Riba and Interst'. *Islamic Studies* (March), pp. 1–43.

Rahman, Fazlur, (1966). 'The Status of the Individual in Islam'. *Islamic Studies*, No. 5: 4 (December), pp. 319–28.

Rahman, Syed Abdul, (1986). 'Iqbal's Concept of Sovereignty and Legislation in Islam'. *Islamic Studies*, No. XXV: 1, pp. 45–58.

Ramadan, Abd al-'Azim. 'Fundamentalist Influence in Egypt: The Strategies of the Muslim Brotherhood and the Takfir Groups'. In Martin E. Marty and R. Scott Appleby (eds) *Fundamentalisms and the State*. The University of Chicago Press (1993), pp. 152–83.

Rif'at, Mohammed. *The Awakening of Modern Egypt*, London and New York: Longmans, Green (1947).

Roberson B. A., (1994). 'Islam and Europe: An Enigma Or A Myth?' *Middle East Journal*, No. 48: 2 (Spring), pp. 288–308.

Salt, Jeremy, (1994). 'Strategies of Islamic Revivalism in Egypt'. *Journal of Arab, Islamic and Middle East studies*, No. 1: 2, pp. 90–100.

Al-Sayyid, Ahmad Lutfi. 'Egyptianness'. In John Donohue and John Esposito (eds) *Islam in Transition: Muslim Perspectives*. Oxford: Oxford University Press (1982), pp. 70–2.

Al-Sayyid, Marsot and Afaf Lutfi, (1984). 'Religion or Opposition? Urban protest in Movement Egypt'. *Internatunal Journal of Middle East Studies*, No. 16, pp. 541–52.

Schacht, J. and Bosworth, C. E. *The Legacy of Islam*, second edition, Oxford: Oxford University Press (1974), p. 159.

Shaltut, Muhammad. 'Socialism and Islam'. In Kemal H. Karpat (ed.) *Political and Social Thought in the Middle East*. New York: Praeger (1968), pp. 126–32.

Shepard, William, (1989). 'Islam as a System in the Later Writings of Sayyid Qutb'. *Middle Eastern Studies*, No. 25: 1 (January), pp. 31–50.

Shepard, William, (1996). 'Muhammad Sa'id al-'Ashmawi and the Application of the Shari'ah in Egypt'. *Middle East Studies*, No: 28, pp. 39–50.

Shepard, William, (2003). 'Sayyid Qutb's Doctrine of Jahiliyyah'. *International Journal of Middle Eastern Studies*, No. 35, pp. 521–45.

Al-Siba'i, Mustafa. 'Islamic Socialism'. In Daryush Shayegan (ed.) *Cultural Schizophrenia: Islamic Societies Confronting the West*. London: Saqi Books (1992), pp. 120–2.

Singer, Marcus G. 'Philosophy'. *World Book Encyclopeadia*. Vol. 15. Chicago, PL: A Scott Fetzer Company (1990), pp. 383–9.

Strong, Charles Frederick. *Modern Political Constitution: An Introduction to the Comparative Study of their History and Existing Form*. London: Sidgwick & Jackson (1963), p. 10.

Tolmacheva, Marina, (1995). 'The Medieval Arabic Geographers and the Beginning of Modern Orientalism'. *International Journal of Middle Eastern Studies*, No. 27, pp. 141–56.

Vatikiotis, P. J., (1957). 'Muhammad 'Abduh and the Quest for a Muslim Humanism'. *Islamic Culture*, (April), pp. 255–81.

Veitch, James, (1994). 'A Case of Mistaken Identity: Muslim and Fundamentalism'. *Arab, Islamic and Middle Eastern Studies*, No. 1, pp. 1–6.
Voll, John. 'Fundamentalism in the Sunni Arab World: Egypt and Sudan'. In Martin E. Marty and R. Scott Appleby (eds) *Fundamentalism Observed*. Chicago: University of Chicago Press, (1991), pp. 345–95.
Voll, John Obert, (1979). 'The Sudanese Mahdi: Frontier Fundamentalist'. *International Journal of Middle Eastern Studies*, No. 10, pp. 145–66.
Wadsworth Frank W. 'Hardy, Thomas'. *World Book Encyclopedia*. Vol. 9. Chicago, PL: A Scott Fetzer Company (1990), pp. 63–4.
Weiss, Dieter, (1995). 'Ibn Khaldun on Economic Transformation'. *International Journal of Middle Eastern Studies*, No. 27, pp. 29–37.
Weiss, Leopold. *Islam at the Crossroads*, Lahore: Ashraf Publications (1955).
Wilson, Margaret, D. 'Rationalism'. *World Book Encyclopedia*. Vol. 16 (1990), p. 150.
Youssef, Samir M., (1994). 'The Egyptian Private Sector and the Bureaucracy'. *Middle Eastern Studies*, No. 30: 2 (April), pp. 369–76.

Articles in books and periodicals (Arabic)

Abd al-Raziq, Ali, (1925). 'al-Islam wa 'Usul al-Hukm'. *Al-Siyasah*, No. 882, (2 September), pp. 18–21.
Ahmad Abu al-Wafa, (1994). 'Irhabiyyun fi Ghurfat al-I'dam'. *Rose el-Youssef*, No. 3453 (Monday, 15 August), pp. 26–8.
Ahmad, Makram Ahmad, (1993). 'Misr Laysat Iran walan Takun'. *Al-Mussawwar*, No. 3567 (16 April), pp. 6–7.
Al-Alfi, Hasan, (1994). 'Ikhtaraqna Sufuf al-Irhabiyyin bi-al-Kamil'. *Rose el-Youssef*, No. 3452 (Monday, 8 August), pp. 10–15.
Allam, Fu'ad, (1995). 'Akhtar Kutub Hasan al-Hudaybi min Ta'lif Mabahith Amn al-Dawlah'. *Rose el-Youssef*, No. 3507 (28 August), pp. 56–9.
'Amir 'Ali Ahmad, (1934). 'Tahta al-Misbah'. *Al-Usbu'*, No. 35 (Wednesday 25 July), p. 8.
'Amir, Hasan, (1994). 'Abd al-Nasser Kan Za'im Sufi'. *Rose el-Youssef*, No. 3427 (14 February), pp. 49–51.
'Ashmawi, Muhammad Sa'id, (1990). 'Thawrat Yulyu Ammamat al-Din'. *Sabah el-Kheir*. Cairo, Thursday 19 April (1990), n. 1789, pp. 8–10.
'Asim, Muhammad. 'Mushkilatina fi Daw' al-Islam'. In Syyid Qutb, *Dirasat Islamiyyah*. Cairo: Dar al-Shuruq, 9th print (1993), pp. 165–168.
Basha, Ahmad Fu'ad, (1992). 'Mu'tamar al-Tawjih al-Islami li al-'Ulum bi Jami'at al-Azhar'. *Al-Azhar*, No. 65: 6 (December), pp. 888–912.
Al-'Awwa, Muhammad Salim, (1990). 'al-Mutatarrifun Taraku Fikr Ibn Taymiyyah al-Mustanir wa Rawwaju Afkarahu Didda al-Tatar'. *Sabah el-Kheir*, No. 1787, (Thursday, 5 April), pp. 8–10.
Al-A'zami, Walid, (1957). 'Sada al-Kifah'. *Al-Kifah al-Islami*, No. 39 (4 October), p. 5 [poem].
Al-'Azm, Yusuf, (1957). 'Al-Risalah al-Ula'. *Al-Kifah al-Islami*, No. 30 (3 August), p. 9 [poem].
Al-Bayyumi, Muhammad Rajab, (1994). 'al-Imam al-Akbar: 'Abd al-Rahman Tajj'. *Majallat al-Azhar*, No. 67: 6 (November), pp. 781–6.
Al-Bayyumi, Muhammad Rajab, (1995). 'Min A'lam al-Azhar al-Duktur Muhammad al-Bahayy'. *Al-Azhar*, No. 67: 10 (March), pp. 1373–7.
Al-Bayyumi, Muhammad Rajab, (1996). 'Min A'lam al-Azhar: Muhammad Bikhit al-Muti'i'. *Al-Zhar*, No. 68: 8 (January), pp. 1175–80.

Al-Bayyumi, Muhammad Rajab, (1978). 'Sayyid Qutb Bayna al-'Aqqad wa al-Khuli'. *Al-Thaqafah*, No. 53 (February), p. 89.

Al-Disuqi, Muhammad, (1991). 'Wasa'il al-Ijtihad fi al-Fiqh al-Islami'. *Al-Azhar*, No. 63: 10 (April–May), pp. 1106–13.

Gad al-Haqq, Ali Gad al-Haqq, (1994). 'al-'Uswah al-Hasanah'. *Majallat al-Azhar*, No. 67: 3 (August–September), pp. 280–2.

Al-Ghayati, Huda, (1994). 'Walidi 'Ali al-Ghayati'. *Al-Azhar*, No. 67: 6 (November), pp. 787–90.

Al-Ghazali, Muhammad, (1991). 'Ihris 'Ala Qawl al-Haq walaw Kana Murra'. *Sabah el-Kheir*, No. 1828 (17 January), pp. 12–15.

Hafiz, Ahmad Hasan (1994). 'Al-Marsafi Ra'id al-Nahdah al-Mu'asirah'. *Al-Azhar*, No. 67: 4 (September), pp. 488–92.

Al-Hakim, Tawfiq, (1938). 'al-Shahhadhun'. *Akhir Sa'ah* (4 December), pp. 11–12.

Al-Hakim, Tawfiq, 'al-Shahhadhun'. In Tawfiw al-Hakim (ed.) *Qultu Dhata Yawm*. No. 23 Cairo: Mu'assasat Akhbar al-Yawm. Series of Kitab al-Yawm. 1 August (1970), pp. 115–17.

Al-Hakim, Tawfiq, (1945), 'Shajarat al-Hukm': In *Tawfiq al-Hakim al-Mufakkir*. Cairo: Dar al-Kitab al-Jadid (1970), pp. 83–102.

Al-Hakim, Tawfiq, (1941). 'Sultan al-Zalam'. In *Tawfiq al-Hakim al-Mufakkir*. Cairo: Dar al-Kitab al-Jadid (1970), pp. 27–69.

Hamrush, Ahmad, (1994). 'Alaqat al-Thawrah bi al-Amrikan'. *Rose el-Youssef*, No. 3451 (1 August), pp. 24–5.

Hanafi, Hasan, (1990). 'al-Jama'at al-Islamiyyah la Tuwajih al-'Aqbat'. *Rose el-Youssef*, No. 3227 (16 April), pp. 30–1.

Haqqi, Yahya, (1991). 'I'tirafat Yahya Haqqi'. *Sabah el-Kheir*, No. 1849 (Thursday, 13 June), pp. 48–50.

Haykal, Muhammad Hasanayn, (1994). 'Nahnu Nasiru bi-sur'ah Mudhhilah Walakin la Na'rifu ila Ayn?' *Rose el-Youssef*, No. 3427 (14 February), pp. 41–8.

Husayn, Taha, (1999). 'al-Shi'r al-Jahili'. *Al-Azhar*, No. 72: 4 (August), pp. 558–63.

Ibrahim Badrawi, (1993). 'al-Shuyu'iyyun al-Misriyyun Yufaddilun al-'Amal al-'Alani'. *Rose el-Youssef*, No: 3418 (Monday, 13 December), p.14.

'Isam Zakariyya, (1993). 'Washintun: Ihtimalat Saytarat al-Mutatarrifun 'ala Misr Kabus'. *Rose el-Youssef*, No. 3403 (Monday, 30 August), pp. 7–9.

Al-Khayyat, Abd al-'Aziz, (1994). 'al-Takaful al-Ijtima'i al-Islami'. *Al-Azhar*, No. 67: 3 (August–September), pp. 317–22.

Kishk, Muhammad Jalal, (1984). 'Intikhabat Qadimah'. *Uktuber*, No. 389 (Sunday, 8 April), pp. 14–15.

Makki, al-Tahir, (1986). 'Qutb wa Thalath Rasa'l lam Tunshar'. *Al-Hilal* (October), pp. 121–8.

Al-Maraghi, Abdul Aziz, (1947). 'al-Tashri' al-Islami fi 'Asr al-Khulafa' al-Rashidin'. *Al-Azhar*, No. 18: 7, pp. 27–31, 410–15.

Muhammad, Nasr, (1996). 'Fu'ad 'Allam Yftah Dhakiratahu 'ala al-Ikhwan al-Muslimun'. *Uktuber*, No. 1030 (31 July), pp. 44–5.

Muhammad, Sayyid Muhammd, (1994). 'Al-Ghazw al-Thaqafi wa al-Mujtama' al-'Arabi al-Mu'asir'. *Al-Azhar*, No. 67: 4 (September), pp. 533–40.

Mu'nis, Husayn, (1984). 'Ahmad Ibn Hanbal wa Sira' al-Din wa al-Dawlah'. *Uctuber*, No. 389 (Sunday, 8 April), pp. 20–2.

Al-Nawawi, Mahmud, (1993). 'Nizam al-Islam al-Siyasi'. *Al-Azhar*, No. 66: 6 (December), pp. 878–84.

Al-Qamhawi, Hasan, (1995). 'Jama'at al-Shaytan'. *Jaridat Al-Sha'b*, (Friday, 3 November), pp. 1 and 3.

Qinawi, Muhammad, (1991). 'Al-Islam al-Siyasi wa al-Sidam ma'a al-Sultah'. *Sabah el-Kheir*, No. 1849 (Thursday, 13 June), pp. 14–15.

Ramadan, Abd al-'Azim, (1977). 'Al-Din fi al-Sira' al-Siyasi'. *Sabah el-Kheir*, No. 1108 (31 March) pp. 19–23.

Sadat, Muhammad Anwar, (1974). 'Khitab al-Ra'is fi al-Iskandariyyah'. *Al-Ahram* (27 July), pp. 1–2.

Sadat, Muhammad Anwar, (1977) 'The Speech of Sadat in Alexandria [1974]'. *Al-Ahram*, (31 January), pp. 1–2.

Safwat Hasan Lutfi, Muhammad Abd Al-Azim Ali and Jalal Yahya Kamil, (1994). 'Tatbiq al-Shari'ah al-Islamiyyah bayna al-Haqiqah wa Shi'arat al-Fitnah'. *Al-Azhar*, No. 67: 6 (November), pp. 822–8.

Salamah Tawfiq, (1995). 'Min Sirat Shaykh al-Islam Mustafa Sabri'. *Al-Azhar*, No. 86: 4 (September), pp. 539–43.

Salamah, Usamah, (1993). 'Al-Ikhwan al-Muslimun Yumawwiluna al-Tatarruf'. *Rose el-Youssef*, No. 3418 (Monday, 13 December) pp. 8–11, 14.

Al-Salus Ali, (1991). 'Islamic Economy'. *Al-Azhar*, No. 1411, pp. 80–104.

Al-Sayyid, Ahmad Lutfi. (1907). 'Al-Farqu Baynana wa Bayna al-Gharib'. *Al-Jaridah*, No. 23 (3 April), pp. 2–3.

Al-Sayyid, Ahmad Lutfi, (1912). 'Al-Qalaq al-Fikri'. *Al-Jaridah*, No. 1665 (31 August), pp. 1–2.

Al-Sayyid, Ahmad Lutfi, 'Rawwidu Anfusakum 'Ala al-Istiqlal'. *Al-Jaridah*, No. 454 (2 September). In Ahmad Lutfi al-Sayyid (ed.) *Mabadi' fi al-Siyasah wa al-Adab wa al-Ijtima'*. Cairo: Dar al-Hilal. *Kitab al-Hilal Monthly Series*, August (1963), n. 149, pp. 60–62.

Shahin, Muhammad, (1991). 'Al-Lughah wa al-Adab wa al-Naqd: Nazariyyat Lughawiyyah: al-Zamakhshari wa Sufyan Ibn 'Uyayynah'. *Al-Azhar*, No. 63: 10 (April–May), pp. 1171–85.

Sharaf al-Din, Nabil, (1992). 'Kayfa Tawaghghala al-Irhab fi Qura wa Mudun al-Sa'id'. *Sabah el-Kheir*, No. 1906, (Thursday, 16 July), pp. 8–10.

Shihab, Mufid, (1994). 'Ma al-Ladhi Yajma' fi Muzaharatin Wahidah bayna al-Ikhwan wa al-Nasiriyyun: al-Islamiyyun Yuqaddimun al-Khadamat wa Huras Tuqaddimu al-Nashat'. *Sabah el-Kheir*, No. 2029 (Thursday, 24 November), pp. 8–10.

Al-Tawilah, Abd al-Sattar, (1994). 'Istifta' Didda al-Hukumah al-Diniyyah'. *Rose el-Youssef*, No. 3438 (2 May), pp. 18–19.

Al-Tuhami, Muhammad, (1945). 'Al-Huda wa al-Dalal'. *Al-Azhar*, No. 86: 4 (September), p. 566 [poem].

Wajdi, Muhammad Farid, (1934–1935). 'Muhimmat al-Din al-Islami fi al-'Alam: Da'watuhu li Mahw Athar al-Jahiliyyah'. *Nur al-Islam*, No. 5, pp. 71–161 [article 1].

Wajdi, Muhammad Farid, (1934–1935). 'Muhimmat al-Din al-Islami fi al-'Alam: Da'watuhu ila Ta'sis Dawlat al-Haqq'. *Nur al Islam*, No. 5, pp. 287–92 [article 2].

Yahya Haqqi, (1991). 'Isht wa Shuft wa Qara't Khabar Wafati'. *Sabah el-Kheir*, No. 1849 (Thursday, 13 June), pp. 48–50.

Al-Zalabani, Rizq, (1947). 'Al-Siyasah al-Dusturiyyah al-Shar'iyyah: Shakl al-Hukumah wa 'Alaqatuha bi al-Ummah fi al-Islam'. *Al-Azhar*, No. 18: 7, pp. 130–6, 251–55.

Index

Lightning Source UK Ltd.
Milton Keynes UK
09 January 2010

148343UK00003B/84/P